The Bedside,
Bathtub & Armchair
Companion to
Agatha Christie

Also by Dick Riley and Pam McAllister

The Bedside, Bathtub & Armchair Companion to Shakespeare

The Bedside, Bathtub & Armchair Companion to Sherlock Holmes

The Bedside, Bathtub & Armchair Companion to Agatha Christie

EDITED BY

Dick Riley & Pam McAllister

FOREWORD BY JULIAN SYMONS

SECOND EDITION

Additional Material Edited by Pam McAllister and Bruce Cassiday

CONTINUUM • NEW YORK • LONDON

2001
The Continuum International Publishing Group Inc
370 Lexington Avenue, New York, NY 10017

The Continuum International Publishing Group Ltd
The Tower Building, 11 York Road, London SE1 7NX

Printed in the United States of America
Library of Congress Cataloging-in-Publication Data

The new bedside, bathtub & armchair companion to Agatha Christie

Rev. ed. of: The bedside, bathtub & armchair companion to Agatha Christie, © 1979.
Bibliography: p.
1. Christie, Agatha, 1890-1976—Miscellanea.
2. Christie, Agatha, 1890-1976—Plot. 3. Detective and mystery stories, English—Stories, plots, etc.
I. Riley, Dick. II. McAllister, Pam. III. Cassiday, Bruce. IV. Bedside, bathtub & armchair companion to Agatha Christie.
PR6005.H66Z557   1986   823'.912   86-6960
ISBN 0-8264-1375-7

Quotes from books by Agatha Christie reprinted by permission of Harold Ober Associates Incorporated

"A Little Diversion: A Christie Crossword"; "The 'What's in a Name' Word Find"; "The Mousetrap Double-Crostic"; "The Agatha Christie Title Crossword"; "The Miss Marple Double-Crostic"; and "The Hercule Poirot Double-Crostic"—Copyright © 1979 by Dale G. Copps; "A Publishing Phenomenon" and "The Romantic Englishwoman"—Copyright © 1979 by Patricia Maida and Nick Spornick; "A Portrait of Agatha Christie" Copyright © 1979 by Julian Symons; "Jessica Fletcher: A Liberated Miss Marple?" By Emma Lathem, Originally Titled "Everybody's Aunt Comes on Like a Mike Wallace," reprinted with permission from TV GUIDE® Magazine. Copyright © 1985 by Triangle Publications, Inc., Radnor, Pennsylvania.

v

CONTENTS

CONTENTS

CONTENTS

x

CONTENTS

ACKNOWLEDGMENTS

This book would not have been possible without the contributions of many people. While no list could include them all, we would like to acknowledge some of them.

For their help in obtaining visual material, we would like to thank Seth Willenson of Films, Inc., Michael Klastorin, Marvin Siporin, the staff of the Performing Arts Research Center of the New York Public Library at Lincoln Center, and especially Elizabeth Leese, our British connection. For general assistance, and for suggesting

people to interview, our thanks go to Carol Brener and Bill Palmer of the bookstore Murder Ink.

For helping pull it all together, thanks to production manager Gary Zelko; and for contributions far above and beyond the call of duty, our gratitude to Pat Vitacco, art director of the volume. For long hours of work, for attention to detail, and for incredible dedication, special thanks are due Ungar staff member Olivia Kelly Datené.

D.R. and P. McA.

FOREWORD
A Portrait of Agatha Christie
by Julian Symons

When Agatha Christie died in January 1976, she was undoubtedly the most famous detective story writer in the world. In Britain alone all of her most popular titles sold in millions; in the United States they were almost equally successful; and in every European country her name was a household word. Her fame even extended to the heart of the Soviet bloc: an edition of some books published in Moscow sold out immediately.

The personality behind the creation of Hercule Poirot and Miss Marple was that of a shy and in most ways very conventional middle-class English lady. Agatha Mary Clarissa Miller was born in the Devonshire seaside resort of Torquay in 1890, the third child of a well-to-do American father and a mother who was markedly sensitive and aesthetically perceptive. In her charming autobiography Agatha gives very clear sketches of them both, her father an idle but agreeable man, her mother almost clairvoyant at times, and a person who saw life and people in colors that "were always slightly at variance with reality." Perhaps this is the quality she passed on most directly to Agatha, the romantic tendency to see everything a little bigger than life-size, to be fascinated by the mysterious and strange, and to weave stories that explained the strangeness.

There was nothing unusual about Agatha Miller's childhood, except that she never went to school. She was taught at home by her mother, and at times by governesses, and evolved elaborate games that she played by herself, games in which one can perhaps see the germ of the intricate plots she evolved in later years. In adolescence, like other young girls of her class and time, she went to dances (never unaccompanied, be-

cause "you did not go to a dance alone with a young man") where she found difficulty in managing her programme so that she danced with the right young man. She flirted, had proposals, and in 1914 married dashing Archie Christie, who became one of the first pilots in the Royal Flying Corps during World War I.

Agatha worked in a hospital and eventually found herself an assistant in the dispensary. There she conceived the idea of writing a detective story, something she had been challenged to do a year or two earlier by her elder sister Madge. Since she was surrounded by poisons, what more natural than that this should be a poisoning case. What kind of plot should it be? "The whole point of a *good* detective story was that it must be somebody obvious but at the same time, for some reason, you would then find that it was *not* obvious, that he could not possibly have done it." Readers of her first detective story, *The Mysterious Affair at Styles,* will remember that this is just what happens in the book.

Then there must be a detective. What should he be like? She was devoted to Sherlock Holmes, but recognised that she must produce a character outside the Holmes pattern. What kind of person? There were a variety of detectives flourishing in English fiction at the time, including the blind Max Carrados, whose sense of smell was so strongly developed that he could discern the spirit gum in a false moustache across a room, and the super-scientific Doctor Thorndyke, but Agatha Christie rightly thought that these were not her kind of detectives. Then she remembered a colony of Belgian refugees who had come to her part of Devon at the beginning of the war. Why not make her man a retired Belgian police officer? He would be meticulous, a tidy little man, always neat and orderly, with a slight flavour of absurdity about him. Since he was to be small, why not call him Hercules? And then the surname. She did not remember how she found the name Poirot, but it appeared. "It went well not with Hercules but Hercule—Hercule Poirot. That was all right—settled, thank goodness."

Such was the birth of Hercule Poirot. The book was completed in 1915, but had to wait five years for publication. It duly appeared, and although she made little money from it because of the outrageous agreement that she had signed as a raw and innocent author, she felt sufficiently encouraged to start another story.

One of the decisive events in her life was the publication of that first detective story. Another, six years later, was her disappearance for several days. Her car had been abandoned, and the police treated the case as one in which her violent death could not be ruled out. After a nationwide police hunt she was found in a hotel at the spa of Harrogate, in the north of England. It was immediately suggested that her explanation of loss of memory was not correct, and that the disappearance had been a publicity stunt.

What is the truth? Those who read her autobiography in the hope of finding an answer will be disappointed, for she makes no reference to the disappearance. But she does tell us the background of her life immediately before it, and this helps to explain what happened. Her much-loved mother had recently died, and the duty of clearing up everything in the house to which she was deeply attached fell upon Agatha. Her husband had told her that he could not bear illness, death, or indeed any kind of trouble, and there was no question of his staying in Devon with her. Under the stress of living again — and alone — in the house where she had spent an idyllically happy childhood, she broke down. She wept uncontrollably when she could not start the car, and was unable to remember her own name when writing a cheque. Then her husband told her that he was in love with another woman and wanted a divorce. This was the situation at the time of her disappearance. If one wanted a further indication that her story of amnesia was true, it would lie in the fact that during her stay in Harrogate she used the name of her husband's mistress.

For two or three years she was deeply unhappy, and although she went on writing, the books she produced are markedly inferior to her best work. Then she met somebody at a dinner party who talked to her about the entrancing quality of Baghdad, and said that she should also look at the archaeological finds recently made at Ur in Mesopotamia. She hurriedly canceled a projected trip to the West Indies and instead took the Orient Express, which went at that time all the way from England. She had a lifelong love of trains, feeling that some steam engines were personal friends, and as she says herself, trains and houses were always more real to her than most people.

The trip was eventful. It provided the basis for *Murder on the Orient Express* and for some other books, but something more important than that happened. She was delighted by the beauty of Ur, and on a second trip met a thin, dark young man named Max Mallowan, assistant to Leonard Woolley, who was in charge of the expedition. She went with Max Mallowan to see the desert city of Ukhaidir, and—as he afterward told her—it was when they were stranded in the desert for hours and she made no fuss about it that he decided to propose marriage. They were married in 1930, and it does not seem an exaggeration to say that, in spite of the fact that he was fourteen years her junior, they lived happily ever after. She accompanied him on archaeological digs, and these too provided the background for stories. Max Mallowan became one of the most distinguished

FOREWORD

figures in his field. In 1968 he was knighted, and three years later Agatha achieved the prime honour possible to a woman in Britain, when she was made a D.B.E., a Dame of the British Empire.

By the time of her death she had produced more than eighty crime stories, along with half a dozen romantic novels under the name of Mary Westmacott, several plays, some of which she had written herself and some adapted from books and stories by other hands, and two volumes of autobiography.

That is the account of a life, but what was she like as a person? There can be no doubt that the shock of discovering Archie Christie's unfaithfulness and the furor caused by the disappearance changed her. In her autobiographical pages one glimpses a different personality, more casual, reckless, and gay than the Agatha Christie of the 1940s and 1950s. No doubt she had always been different but now she was painfully shy with strangers, and, as she said herself, conversation with her was not easy. She absolutely refused to make speeches now that she was famous, and carried this so far that when she succeeded Dorothy L. Sayers as president of Britain's famous Detection Club, a deputy had to propose toasts and introduce guests.

She particularly disliked being interviewed, especially after one dinner when she chatted in the cloakroom with what seemed a pleasant young woman and found their conversation splashed across a newspaper's gossip page the next day in the form of an interview. She acceded most reluctantly to any request for an interview, and always made a stipulation that no question should be asked about the disappearance. "I cannot say that I look forward to it, but I suppose that as it is you it will be all right," she wrote to me when I suggested that we should have a conversation about crime stories for publication in an English paper. I took a tape recorder with me, but at first it

was far from all right. She answered in monosyllables, and I began to despair of her saying anything interesting. It was not until she realised that I was uneasy about whether the machine was recording and too ignorant of its operation to play it back that she relaxed and our conversation began to flow.

Even then she talked little about anything personal, although she spoke freely enough about her writing. Her view of the reasons for the success of *The Mousetrap* (which has run far longer than any other play in the history of the English theatre) were typically practical. It was a small play in a small theatre, which meant that the running costs were low, and you could take anybody to it, including children and old ladies. "It is not really frightening, it is not really horrible, it is not really a farce, but it has got a bit of all those things and perhaps that satisfies a lot of different people."

What about Poirot, what did she feel about him? Well, she had lots of letters from people, saying that she must love him. "Little they know. I can't bear him now." Because of her readers' reactions it was impossible to get rid of him, but she much preferred Miss Marple. Had she always wanted to write detective stories? Not particularly, she would have liked to try several different sorts of book. "But of course detective stories supported me and my daughter for years, and they had to be written." And if she had not been a writer? "I might have had a shot at sculpture, but I wouldn't have been any good at it. And, oh yes, I would quite have liked to be a hospital nurse."

So the interview went well, but at the end of it I knew little more about the woman who sat opposite me. At this time she was seventy years old, plump and well preserved, the model of that peculiarly English kind of country lady whom one sees serving tea on a green lawn, attending fêtes to raise funds for the local Conservative party, expressing entirely conventional opinions on almost every subject. And that picture is true enough, for part of her was that English country lady. The problem remains then: how did this perfectly nice conventional Englishwoman, with her fur coat and tweeds, her twin set and pearls, come to write so much about murder?

The answer, I think, is that there existed another and more interesting Agatha Christie. Yes, she was a conventional English woman; but she was also the woman who faced discomfort and danger intrepidly on expeditions with her husband, who thought that a few bites from bedbugs were of no account compared with the pleasures of travel and in particular of long train journeys, and who said that the best breakfast in the world was not a meal served off silverplate in a grand hotel but sausages cooked on a primus stove in the desert. Yes, her conversation was mostly commonplace, but behind it rioted an immensely ingenious, subtle, and one must say, potentially criminal imagination. In at least one real-life murder case the murderer had been influenced by an Agatha Christie story.

As a detective story writer her works belonged firmly to the world in which she had been brought up. No unpleasant physical details were allowed to enter her books, and we are not meant to feel any emotional involvement in relation to the body in the library or on the links. Her supreme skill was in the construction of plot, and she has never been excelled as a creator of deceptive puzzles, the kind in which through something said or something seen we are given a clue. If this clue is interpreted correctly it will tell us a murderer's identity, but if we make one of half a dozen other more obvious interpretations it will mislead us. A witness says what she has seen, and she is a witness of truth, but is it physically possible for her to have seen it? A remark is made that seems damning evidence against one character, but look at the remark again and it may point to another. We are told that a list of articles belong-

ing to passengers on a plane will help us to solve a crime and so it may, but we are likely to look for the wrong article,

It would seem that Agatha Christie had this kind of skill right from that splendid beginning with *The Mysterious Affair at Styles,* which is not to say that her books are even in merit. There is general agreement, although she would not have shared it, that the forty-odd Poirot books are better than the much smaller number featuring Miss Marple, and that the thrillers in which Tommy and Tuppence appear are inferior tales of a kind not suited to the Christie talent. It is accepted also that her work showed a decline from the middle fifties onwards that became steep towards the end of her life. When this has been said, however, there remain thirty or more books that are brilliant exercises in deception. Which are the best of these?

A list of my own dozen favorite Christies would certainly be headed by *The Murder of Roger Ackroyd*, which remains the best shock ending of all time and shows that as early as 1926 her mastery of her chosen form was complete. From the same decade I should choose also *The Mysterious Affair at Styles* and *The Man in the Brown Suit*, in which the Ackroyd trick was given a preliminary airing. The thirties was not only her most prolific but also her finest decade, including a whole series of marvellously-plotted books: *Peril at End House, Thirteen at Dinner, The A.B.C. Murders, Death in the Air, Death on the Nile*, and in 1939 the book that I would place second only to Roger Ackroyd, *Ten Little Indians*.

And the Christie level is almost as high in the forties. There is a poison story, *Sad Cypress* (she made considerable and varied use of her veneniferous knowledge), the unusually sinister *Towards Zero*, and *Death Comes As the End*, a *tour de force* set in ancient Egypt.

There is my dozen, but I must make room for a couple more, one from the fifties and one from

FOREWORD

the sixties. *What Mrs. McGillicuddy Saw!* is, for me, the most cunning of the Miss Marple stories, and *The Pale Horse* of 1961 is notable as the book in which the murder method—poisoning again—was actually used in real life.

What is the basis of her lasting attraction? In the years before her death she was rightly acknowledged as the queen of the Golden Age detective story, the puzzle pure and complex. She never thought of herself as a great or even a good writer, but she was the master conjurer of our time. That conjurer's sleight of hand, the infinitely various tricks of this Cleopatra of old Thames, will keep her best work fresh and fascinating to each new generation of readers as long as detective stories are read.

The following symbols identify each synopsis as to literary form and detective featured:

 Novel

 Short story collection

 Play

 Hercule Poirot

 Jane Marple

 Tommy and Tuppence Beresford

 Ariadne Oliver

THE BEDSIDE, BATHTUB & ARMCHAIR COMPANION TO AGATHA CHRISTIE

PREFACE

To Agatha Christie fans it seems like a long time since we were able to hover together in mutual suspense over a new Christie mystery. And though Dame Agatha cannot give us a new story, this book is offered as a kind of family reunion, a renewal of old friendships, a celebration of our favorite sleuths. Here they are again: the esteemed Hercule Poirot and the beloved Jane Marple, Tommy and Tuppence Beresford, Ariadne Oliver, Parker Pyne, and Harley Quin.

This book is a salute to the creations of one of the greatest storytellers of all time, Agatha Christie. Devoted readers all over the world have spent countless hours totally engrossed in the unfolding of her plots — plots that represent genteel mayhem at its best. In these Christie diversions, the violence is over in a paragraph or two and then it's on to the adventure, the pure puzzle, the red herrings . . . the fun.

Putting together this book, this tribute to one of the world's most popular writers, has been a little like trying to solve a Christie mystery. How could we best cover the vast amount of material produced by Dame Agatha? To help us we called upon over fifty writers from varied backgrounds who are united in their affinity to mysteries. Julian Symons, the well-known British mystery writer, contributes the only personal portrait of Christie to be found here: the rest of the articles in this *Companion* highlight and celebrate her work.

This volume is divided into synopses and features. We have provided a short, entertaining plot summary — written specially for this *Companion* — of every Christie novel and original play and many of the short stories. Here the reader will find the place and time of the stories,

words about the victims, suspects, and motives, and some idea of the action. But, you may rest assured, *no one gives away the final solutions*. The suspense is left intact.

In this book, therefore, you will *not* discover whodunit. You can, however, find reminders of the Christie books you have read and a taste of those Christie books you have not — a taste, we hope, that will whet your appetite for the books themselves.

Scattered throughout the synopses are Agatha Christie's own comments on the stories and how they came to be written. These quotes are taken from her autobiography.

The synopses of the novels, plays, and short story collections are arranged chronologically according to publication date. Several of the collections contain many of the same stories and do not, therefore, require separate treatment. For example, *The Listerdale Mystery* has been omitted because it duplicates most of the selections included in *The Golden Ball and Other Stories*.

The dramas summarized here are those originally written in play form and not the dramas that Dame Agatha first wrote as novels or short stories. *Alibi*, for example, is a play based on the novel *The Murder of Roger Ackroyd* and therefore is not synopsized. *Black Coffee*, on the other hand, is included because it was originally written for the stage. One exception to this is *Witness for the Prosecution*, originally a short story but much more familiar in its dramatized form, which is treated here as a play.

We have summarized a number of Dame Agatha's short stories, though limitations of space have precluded our synopsizing all of them. None

PREFACE

of the omnibus collections has been reviewed though several of these are included at the back of the book in the list of Christie publications currently in print.

Throughout this companion volume we have referred to the Christie books by the titles most familiar to Americans. We have chosen to use *Ten Little Indians*, for example, an American title, rather than the original *Ten Little Niggers* or the less familiar American title *And Then There Were None*. On the other hand, the original British title *Murder on the Orient Express* is much more identifiable to readers on both sides of the Atlantic than the alternate American title of the same novel, *Murder in the Calais Coach*. If you know a book by a title different from the one consistently used here, you can turn to the title index for reference to the preferred version used throughout the text.

While the synopses form an important part of this book, we also devote feature articles to particular themes in Christie's work. All articles were prepared especially for this volume. Some are pure fantasies, as is one in which Miss Marple, Harley Quin, and M. Poirot find themselves having tea with Alice in Wonderland, or another in which Miss Marple visits a shrink to confess her ... well, you'll have to read about her guilty secret.

There are also articles that can enlighten those unfamiliar with certain English customs found in Christie's writings. "A Nice Cuppa" traces the course of the English tea ceremony, while "The Condemned Ate a Hearty Meal" gives recipes for dishes enjoyed by her characters. "Out of the Top Drawer — Or, How They Dressed" details some of the English wardrobe customs as shown in Christie's books, and after reading it anyone will know better than to appear at an inquest in furs or Ascot in jeans.

Did you know that items as various as a ukulele string and the knob of a fireplace fender have been used by Christie's murderers to dispatch their victims? You can read the gory details in "The Cruder Methods: Knives, Guns, and a Concerto for Blunt Instruments."

We also have pieces on the movies made from Christie's books, including the phenomenally successful *Murder on the Orient Express* and *Death on the Nile*, along with the earlier films starring Margaret Rutherford. There's a Christie Mystery Map showing the locations of a number of stories; profiles of Poirot, Marple, and Ariadne Oliver; "Famous Last Words" — the dying declarations of a number of Christie victims; puzzles; poems; and just about anything a Christie fan would want.

We've called this *The Bedside, Bathtub & Armchair Companion to Agatha Christie* because that's exactly what it is — a volume that can be sampled at your leisure, one you can pick up and leaf through, stopping to read the synopsis of a favorite book, or to marvel at the range of Dame Agatha's knowledge of poisons, stopping again to fill out a crossword puzzle. The *Companion*, we hope, will be a source of hours of pleasure, a Christie treasury into which you can dip time and again, something that will enhance the continuing enjoyment of the work of one of the most popular and prolific writers in the history of publishing.

D.R. and P. McA.

A PUBLISHING PHENOMENON

Agatha Christie's status as a widely read author is more than secure. Her works show up in the bush of Nigeria, the alleys of Hong Kong, the beaches of Acapulco, as well as on the coffee tables of Mayfair and Fifth Avenue. Unlike Shakespeare, Christie appeals to such diverse lots as statesmen, financiers, teachers, bus drivers, clerics, girl scouts, and prisoners—among others. And unlike Shakespeare, Christie lived to see the astronomical sales of her books (though her publishers claim to have lost count of the exact figures) and enjoyed financial success (though the tax collectors have yet to discover where all the money went).

A 1962 UNESCO report attests to Christie's worldwide popularity, showing that translations of her works appear in more than one hundred languages. This astonishing distribution is matched only by the enormous quantity of "Christies" appearing in both hardback and paperback. Editors at Collins, her British publisher, estimate that from 10,000 hardback Christie editions published yearly in the 1930s, the figure rose to 50,000 by the 1950s. With the development of the paperback market, Christie editions published by Penguin, Pan, Fontana, Dell, and Pocket Books flooded bookstalls all over the world. *The Murder of Roger Ackroyd* alone has sold more than one million copies. And Christie has distinguished herself among the few authors who have had a million copies of their books published on the same day. American paperback editions alone have gone beyond the fifteenth printing and into the 500 millions of copies. And the copies continue to roll off the presses . . . by the millions.

PATRICIA MAIDA AND NICK SPORNICK

A CHRISTIE FAN CONFESSES
"I Get That Familiar Tingle When I See Her Books"
An interview with Ms. Jean R. Denton, editor of Fleming Gazette, *Flemingsburg, Kentucky*

EDITOR

You call yourself an Agatha Christie fan. How do you know you're a fan?

DENTON

I know because I get that familiar tingle when I see a book by Agatha Christie. The feeling comes over me that I'm in for a wrangling good time. There's an aura that emanates from the pages of her books: the country homes, the chintz-covered furniture, the servants. It's the feeling that I'm reading one of the great storytellers of all time. Whatever faults she had, she was a master story-teller. And she understood human nature better than any writer, I think, since Shakespeare. The characters she created were unique. No matter how briefly they were introduced they're all memorable. And they're all mint quality. Of course I have read everything she wrote.

EDITOR

I understand you like Miss Marple best. Why?

DENTON

Well, because she's typical of so many older women in a small town. She could be in a south-ern small town. Some of those old gals are very sharp. They've been around a long time, and seen and done a lot. They know!

Miss Marple's favorite lines are "Nothing is ever as it seems" and "Beware of your first impres-sions." Those things are wise. Agatha Christie was a very nice wise woman.

EDITOR

What do you like best about Miss Marple?

DENTON

Her doggedness and her determination. She races forward, and then she seemingly pulls back or she changes her tactics. If she's led up a blind alley she doesn't get discouraged, she simply goes another way. She'll always go into a store where there's an older salesperson who's seen a lot of the town come and go. Sometimes those older salesladies are gold mines of information.

EDITOR

What about her other characters?

DENTON

Well, Poirot seems to be more of a caricature than a character. And I always thought all of his eccen-tricities were more boring than interesting.

EDITOR

How about Tommy and Tuppence?

DENTON

It all was a bit much. They were never as fully de-veloped. The name Tuppence — Oh! Tommy and Tuppence! It just all seemed a little contrived.

EDITOR

Do you have a favorite Agatha Christie mystery?

DENTON

Well, I guess it would be *Sleeping Murder*. I don't think I ever laughed harder in my life. It wasn't really a funny book, but there was just something appealing. For example, one character in the book said the reason that young people didn't have the stamina in this day and age was because they

Jean R. Denton

didn't eat their breadcrusts when they were children. [laugh]

I thought to myself when I read it that she really did save the best for the last. It came out after she died because it was the last Miss Marple.

EDITOR
Do you reread her books? What is it like?

DENTON
It's just like reading it the first time, because her characters are so well developed that you can't catch it all on the first reading. You find all these goodies that you never knew were in the book.

EDITOR
Do you collect her books?

DENTON
Oh yes. I have nearly all of them, either in hard cover or in paperback. I live in a small town where there are no bookstores. I have to go to Lexington or Cincinnati to get books, and I just grab whatever I can find.

EDITOR
Did you used to anticipate the Agatha Christie for Christmas?

DENTON
You know I never realized the books came out then. Where I live, probably if it came out in a city like New York for Christmas, we wouldn't get it until April or May, so I never knew about this until I read a biography of Christie.

EDITOR
What other mysteries do you like to read?

DENTON
Well, next, I would say, although her characters, with the exception of one, do not grip you like Christie, is P. D. James. I've read all of hers. I really prefer British writers to American.

The Hammett and Chandler thing strikes me as being flakey. Now, I'm sure in the thirties and forties when they came out they were the nun's knickers, as someone said on television, but they wear me out. All those people swaggering and drinking and puffing away on cigarettes, it wears me out just thinking about it.

EDITOR
Do you read things besides mysteries?

DENTON
I have a lot of reading to do at work, reading proofs or preparing feature articles, and I try to keep up with the news. For pleasure I read mysteries. I have to read fast because after work I'll take a nap and eat a little supper and take a walk. Then, what reading I do has to be crammed in because I know I have to get to bed and get so much sleep before I get to work the next day.

The older I grow the less apologetic I am about reading. I just bought one hundred fifty-seven dollars worth of paperbacks, and that's what I'm going to do this winter for fun.

EDITOR
Can you give me a profile of a typical Agatha Christie fan? Do you know other fans?

A CHRISTIE FAN CONFESSES

DENTON

Not very many. I live in a very small town and so many people in our town are running around copying down writing on gravestones to trace their family tree. The people that I know who read Agatha Christie—for example, the woman who does my hair—every time a new Christie book came out, she got it at the library. But she gets all kinds of books. I know two or three schoolteachers who've read every Agatha Christie book that came out. Women. A lot of older women would always read the latest Agatha Christie book when it came out. They would probably forget it as soon as they read it, but it enthralled them to read it.

Christie could tell a story and it helped pass the time. I have never had enough time to let it lie heavy on my hands, but a lot of older people do. For those kinds of people she was great. She was great anyway, in my opinion.

EDITOR

Why do you think that Agatha Christie has been read in places that are not at all like England, like the Orient and Africa? Why was she so popular?

DENTON

She was a master storyteller. People love to be lifted above, over, beyond, out of themselves, and get absorbed in a real fast-moving story. She had a knowledge of human nature, which is basically the same anywhere you go. She traveled widely and that was to her advantage. The more you travel, the more you realize that people are pretty much the same all over. A mystery novel is a microcosm of life, because as you grow older you really do see that life is a puzzle. It really is.

EDITOR

Has mystery reading affected your life, or the way you think about people or the way you solve your own problems?

DENTON

Yes it has. I was brought up in a very proper manner, to believe that if you just did the right thing somehow everything would come out all right. Well, basically I knew that wasn't so. Miss Marple's admonitions, "Be careful about your first impressions" and "Things are never what they seem," are valuable words of wisdom to anybody. I realized, instinctively, years ago that that was exactly right. I am much more wary now. But when I am convinced that something is the right thing to do, I'm much quicker to do it. I don't know if that's true from reading mysteries or just living but since I do read them . . .

EDITOR

Would you like to say a few closing words about Agatha Christie?

DENTON

Well, she's gone and there's nobody, there was never anybody, who wrote like Agatha Christie wrote. She really was a great storyteller.

The fact that she had such a rich, full life in addition to her prolific writing shows she was a genius in her own way. It's very hard to be a prolific writer, for one thing, and to turn out prose that will consistently be published. You can turn out a lot of stuff but only the tip of the iceberg will get published.

EDITOR

The publishing miracle, they call her.

DENTON

Yes. And she was. But there was a reason she was and there was nothing in her background to portend the fact that she would be the way she was. It was just one of those freaks. Just like Shakespeare. Of course, they're all saying that he didn't really write all that stuff, but they really don't know. We know that Agatha Christie wrote her stuff.

A FAN LETTER
FROM LILLIAN CARTER

Lillian G. Carter
PLAINS, GEORGIA 31780

Feb. 26th 1979.

Dear Pamela –

Yes! I have been an
admirer of Agatha Christie
for years – all of her books.
I have every one of her
books, and will have them
for my grandchildren.

Yours Sincerely
Lillian G. Carter

The Mysterious Affair at Styles (1920)

The place: Styles Court, an English country estate set in the flat fields of Essex, only a few miles from the coast.

The time: summer, during the Great War.

The event: the murder, in the dead of night, by poison, of Emily Inglethorp, owner of Styles Court.

The Mysterious Affair at Styles, which came out in 1920, is Agatha Christie's first published novel. It is also the first appearance of the soon-to-be-renowned Belgian detective, Hercule Poirot.

The action, if one may call it that, begins when our narrator, Hastings, recovering from wounds he suffered at the Front, runs into an old acquaintance, John Cavendish. Though they are fifteen years apart in age, they have much to talk about, and Hastings is invited down to Styles, where Cavendish lives.

It is but a few miles from the country railroad station to the house itself, where most of the cast is assembled. The center of attention, alive as well as dead, is Emily Inglethorp, John Cavendish's stepmother, since remarried. She had married the father of the Cavendish boys when their own mother died. Cavendish *père* eventually died also, apparently of natural causes, and the house was left to Emily. John Cavendish refers to her as "the mater."

Hastings has his own memory of Emily. He recalls her as "an energetic, autocratic personality" with a fondness for "playing the Lady Bountiful." She was devoted to the charitable life of society, forever involved in bazaars and other functions.

She hasn't changed much, and there is no question of who is running the show at Styles. Emily Inglethorp's presence and conversation dominate the scene from the first teatime, spread under the shade of a sycamore near the French doors leading into the house. Her husband, fetching and carrying for her, is an obvious sycophant. Even her ward leaps to obey her orders, which are but lightly masked as requests.

All right, one might say. Rich woman in her seventies, deeply involved in the life of her community. A bit strong-minded and somewhat old-fashioned, especially from the perspective of sixty years later. Still, who would want to kill the old dear?

One obvious answer is Alfred Inglethorp, the man for whom no one has a kind word. He started out being the old lady's secretary and got promoted to husband, though still acting as secretary and general creature. "Rotten little bounder" is how John Cavendish describes him. Inglethorp is years younger than his wife and has no apparent antecedents, other than a distant blood relationship with Mrs. Inglethorp's companion. "A bad lot," says one character of Inglethorp; "bare-faced fortune hunting" is another description of his wooing of the lady of the house. John Cavendish sums it all up. Inglethorp, he notes, is "an absolute outsider." The man, if it can be believed, "wears patent leather boots in all weathers!"

John Cavendish we have met already. The older of the two Cavendish sons, he was a practicing barrister who has since settled down to the life of a country squire. As far as we can tell, his duties are not onerous. "I drill with the volunteers twice a week, and lend a hand at the farms."

John's distaste for life at Styles is obvious from the first. The situation between Inglethorp and his stepmother is "making life jolly difficult for us," he tells Hastings. John and his wife of two years, Mary Cavendish, haven't the funds to move to their own place. "The mater" controls all the money, and it apparently never occurs to John to go back to working for a living.

If John is less than thrilled with life at Styles, Mary is far from enthralled herself. We find out later that she was the daughter of a consular official who took her with him on his travels after his wife died. When he passed away she was placed in the hands of some aunts in Yorkshire. "The narrowness, the deadly monotony of it, almost drove me mad," she recalls. John Cavendish rescued her from the Yorkshire aunts, but the two are now estranged. She claims to arise at five every day to help with the milking, but the only interest we can see in her life is an occasional *tête-à-tête* with the mysterious, not to say sinister, Dr.

Bauerstein, of whom more anon. Mary is also virtually the only character allowed to have much sensuality. Hastings sees her as "a wild untamed spirit in an exquisitely civilized body." We never learn just what an "exquisitely civilized body" is, but it certainly sounds interesting.

Winning the prize for ineffectuality in the family is John's brother Lawrence who had been "a delicate youth." He had qualified as a doctor but early relinquished the profession of medicine, and lived at home while pursuing literary ambitions. As we never see John practicing law or Mary with the cows, neither do we encounter Lawrence in the act of writing. "His verses had never had any marked success," according to Hastings. John Cavendish was less charitable. "He's gone through every penny he ever had, publishing rotten verses in fancy bindings." The sons are obviously free of the need to overachieve.

"I had been dared to write a detective story; I had written a detective story; it had been accepted, and was going to appear in print. There, as far as I was concerned, the matter ended. Certainly at that moment I did not envisage writing any more books." —*An Autobiography*

The Mysterious Affair at Styles (1920)

Free of the need to be diplomatic is Evelyn Howard, Mrs. Inglethorp's companion, assistant, and general busybody. She was "a pleasant-looking woman of about forty, with a deep voice, almost manly in its stentorian tones, and had a large sensible square body...." Evelyn, or Evie as she is known, often disdains the complete English sentence. "Weeds grow like a house afire. Can't keep up with 'em." But she makes herself more than clear when, soon after Hastings's arrival at Styles, she leaves her employment with Mrs. Inglethorp. "You're an old woman, Emily, and there's no fool like an old fool. The man's twenty years younger than you, and don't you fool yourself as to what he married you for. Money!...I'm going to warn you, whether you like it or not. That man would as soon murder you in your bed as look at you."

Can it be any surprise then, when Emily Inglethorp succumbs to strychnine poisoning?

Included in the household is Cynthia Murdoch, to Hastings's not unjaundiced eye "a fresh-looking young creature" who refers to Mrs. Inglethorp as "Aunt Emily" though they have no blood relationship. Cynthia was the daughter of an old friend of Emily's and was left a penniless orphan when her parents died. "The mater" took her in. Cynthia is the only one we see doing anything that could be called productive—she works in the dispensary of a nearby hospital.

Also cluttering the landscape is Dr. Bauerstein, allegedly a specialist in toxicology who is in the village recovering from a nervous breakdown. But why is it that he is seen wandering through the neighborhood at all hours, appearing after dinner at Styles completely covered with mud? How is it that he is conveniently passing the house before dawn on the day that Mrs. Inglethorp is taken to her reward?

Rounding out the cast are the servants, the sturdy gardener Manning and the redoubtable Dorcas, respectable, respectful, and devoted. "Dear old Dorcas," Hastings says at one point, echoing, we may assume, Dame Agatha's thought, "as she stood there with her honest face turned up to mine, I thought what a fine specimen she was of the old-fashioned servant that is so fast dying out."

Then we have Poirot, the retired Belgian detective, now a refugee from the war and by coincidence settled at the Village of Styles St. Mary. "He was hardly five feet, four inches, but carried himself with great dignity. His head was exactly the shape of an egg, and he always perched it a little on one side. His moustache was very stiff and military. The neatness of his attire was almost incredible. I believe a speck of dust would have caused him more pain than a bullet wound."

Though Poirot has retired, the quiet village life has apparently left him bored. He moves with alacrity into the case, partially, at least, because Mrs. Inglethorp had been instrumental in settling the Belgians in the village.

The clues are far from sparse. There is the crushed coffee cup in Mrs. Inglethorp's room, the remains of the cocoa in another cup, the stain on the carpet, the locked despatch case, the thread on the door bolt, the candle grease on the floor, the burned fragments of paper in the fireplace.

The authorities have their hands quite busy with suspects. First, of course, is the execrable Alfred Inglethorp. But his alibi is convincing. Then there is John Cavendish, but does not the evidence also point to his brother? Even Dr. Bauerstein is taken into custody.

It falls, of course, to Poirot to capture the miscreant.

DICK RILEY

The Secret Adversary (1922)

SCENARIO

Fade in on life preserver with *Lusitania* stenciled on it, smoke intermittently obscuring the name. Camera tilts up to catch man standing in middle of frame as he looks toward group of women and children waiting to board lifeboats. It pans to discover an eighteen-year-old girl standing apart from the group. The man approaches her, ascertains her American citizenship, explains that he has a packet of secret papers vital to the Allied cause and that she must take them because of "women and children first." If they both survive, he will place an advertisement in the personal column of the *Times*; if no ad appears, she is to take the packet to the American Embassy and give it personally to the ambassador.

A high-angle shot reveals a person lurking behind and over the man's shoulder as shrieks and related noises obscure some of his instructions. Cut to shot of girl getting into lifeboat; as she is lowered toward the water, camera tilts up to the man leaning over the railing and then pans to reveal the second person who watches him for a moment and then approaches him as the smoke once again obscures the picture. Fade out. The girl's name is Jane Finn.

Fade in. Miss Prudence Cowley, known to her friends as Tuppence, runs into an old friend, Thomas (Tommy) Beresford, whom she has not seen for five years. They are both suffering from the postwar unemployment blues, he having been wounded during the Great War and she having served in several volunteer capacities.

They pool their meager resources for a lunch neither can afford, during which they decide to throw in with each other and to place an ad in the

Times: "Two young adventurers for hire. Willing to do anything, go anywhere. Pay must be good. No reasonable offer refused." Henceforth, they will be known as The Young Adventurers, Ltd.

Tuppence is followed by a Mr. Whittington who has overheard the restaurant talk and who, at his office the next day, offers her a job. The job: she is to go to Paris and impersonate an American. When Whittington asks her name, she replies, "Jane Finn." This takes him aback as he suddenly realizes she knows more than she lets on; it is Jane Finn he is looking for.

What he doesn't know is that it is a name Tuppence has chosen as an alias, having heard it the day before from Tommy, who had himself overheard Whittington and an accomplice mention it. Tommy thought it was a peculiar name.

Whittington accuses her of extortion and mentions the name "Rita," but before he can extract information from her, the meeting is interrupted by his assistant, Mr. Brown, who says he has an important phone message. Tuppence is asked to return the next day.

When she returns with Tommy in tow the next day, the office no longer exists and the two place a second ad in the *Times*: "Wanted, any information respecting Jane Finn. Apply Y.A."

The second ad yields two replies: one from an American millionaire, Julius P. Hersheimmer, who claims to be looking for Jane Finn, his long-lost cousin, and the second from a Mr. A. Carter who happens to be a secret service operative and who explains the truth about Miss Finn.

It seems in the post-war climate that the document carried by Miss Finn, who disappeared after landing with other survivors, could be used by

The Secret Adversary (1922)

revolutionists to foment unrest. Neither side, it seems, has the document or knows who Miss Finn is, but one thing is sure: the opposition is led by an identity-less master criminal who calls himself Brown and who takes pride in being able to fade into the woodwork. And Whittington is actually only an accomplice; his innocuous clerk, whom neither Tuppence nor Tommy can remember, is really the brains of the operation.

Figuring that they might do no worse than other of his operatives, Carter puts the Young Adventurers on the payroll.

Marguerite Vandemeyer, a fortyish, hard-looking beauty who once must have been truly lovely, is a survivor of the *Lusitania* and turns out to be the Rita mentioned by Whittington. Tuppence becomes her parlormaid with a cover story supplied by Mr. Carter.

In the meantime, Tommy runs across Whittington and a fellow named Boris. Enlisting the aid of the millionaire Julius in trailing Whittington, he himself trails Boris to a house where he is able to spy on a secret meeting of various foreign types. He overhears bits and pieces of conversation, which include references to revolution, Mr. Brown, Jane Finn, and the secret document. But he is captured and held prisoner.

Later, Boris turns up as a guest at Rita's house, as does a very distinguished gentleman, Sir James Peel Edgerton, who takes a paternalistic shine to Tuppence and gains her everlasting trust by suggesting that there are many more savory people to work for than Mrs. Vandemeyer.

Julius has followed Whittington to a private hospital in Bournemouth, where it is possible Jane is being kept on the second floor. Having fallen out of a tree he climbed to get a better look, Julius awakens under the medical care of a little black-bearded man with gold glasses, Dr. Hall. Whittington et al. have made their escape, and Julius returns to London and Tuppence.

Distraught at not hearing from Tommy for several days, Tuppence and Julius confide everything to Sir James, who, knowing Mrs. Vandemeyer quite well, suggest that they all show up at her place later that evening and confront her with the facts to get at the truth and recover Tommy.

When Tuppence arrives early, Rita, packing to leave, pulls a gun and says she is going to drug Tuppence and go on her way. Tuppence manages to get the gun from her and proposes a deal wherein Julius will pay her a large sum of money to recover Jane Finn. At that point Julius and Sir James arrive, and upon seeing them, Mrs. Vandemeyer faints.

Terribly distraught and frightened, Mrs. Vandemeyer deliriously expresses many fears as she lies in her bed and is given a sleeping potion to calm her. Sir James recalls that Dr. Hall is in London and suggests that the next morning Rita be put in his care. The problem is that the next morning, Rita Vandemeyer is found dead from an overdose of chloral, the sleeping potion she was given in the proper dosage the night before.

When they talk with Dr. Hall, they learn that Rita came to him in June or July of 1915 with a young woman she represented to be her niece suffering from amnesia. Unfortunately the young woman—Jane Finn—is no longer under his care.

Meanwhile, Tommy is able to put off his execution through clever answers and references to Mr. Brown as he is interrogated by his captors. His prison is an almost escape-proof room with a single heavy door, no windows, and some heavily framed pictures on the wall. He decides to smash Conrad, his jailer, with one of the pictures and try his escape, but instead, his next meal is brought by a French girl named Annette.

In a particularly perilous moment, Tommy is able to make an escape with Annette's help. As he runs from the house, she calls after him: "This is a

"That, I thought, would make a good beginning to a story — a name overheard at a tea shop — an unusual name, so that whoever heard it remembered it."
—An Autobiography

terrible house. I want to go back to Marguerite. To Marguerite. To *Marguerite*." Does she mean Rita, or does she mean something else?

Tommy confides in Carter. Time is running short to find Jane and the document because Labor Day is fast approaching, and a Russian official, Kramenin, is visiting England and surely plans to use the document to foment unrest.

Brown is responsible for all of this, and he will be found out. He has slipped up ever so slightly but more than enough for Tommy and Tuppece to bag him. Which one is he? Dr. Hall? Mr. Carter? Conrad? Julius? Annette? Sir James? Boris? Kramenin? And, who is Jane Finn?

GERALD M. KLINE

Murder on the Links (1923)

The year is 1923, and the great Hercule Poirot, Detective Extraordinary (Ret.), is leafing through his mail. One after another he tosses the letters aside. How boring they are these days! Nothing but banal requests—"recovering lost lap dogs for fashionable ladies" and the like. Nothing, absolutely nothing, of interest.

But wait: here is something out of the ordinary. "For God's sake, come!" writes Paul Renauld from his villa at Merlinville, in the south of France. He is in danger of his life, he fears...he hints at mysterious agents, and a deadly secret he mustn't reveal. He cannot go to the police, but he has heard of Poirot's abilities. Please! —

Poirot's interest is aroused. He will go, immediately. Has not M. Renauld requested haste? Quickly the dapper little Belgian gathers all he will need — neatly packed, of course — into a small suitcase, persuades his friend Hastings to accompany him, and heads for the boat-train.

The next day the two arrive at Merlinville, only to be repulsed at the gate of Renauld's villa by an unflappable *sergent de ville*. They cannot see M. Renauld, appointment or not. When they insist on knowing why, they are told:

"M. Renauld was murdered this morning!"

Too late, then — the feared assassins have struck. But having come this far, Poirot will see the thing through. He may not have been able to save the man's life, but he will assuredly find his murderer.

The local police are happy to have his assistance, and Poirot begins his investigations. Certain facts come immediately to light. Renauld and his wife had a good marriage, say the servants — though there is no denying that the attractive lady next door, a certain Madame Daubreuil, was a frequent visitor when Madame Renauld was not at home. In fact, she had been in only the night before. And there had been another female visitor too, an attractive young lady who seemed to be very upset about something. M. Renauld had tried to be rid of her, and was in fact overheard pleading with her, "For God's sake, go!" Who was she? No one questioned seemed to know.

Madame Renauld is not immediately available for questioning. She has been a victim, too, the previous night — cruelly bound and gagged by the thugs who, she says, forced her husband out into the night clad only in underwear and overcoat, to be stabbed in the back and buried in a shallow grave on the golf course. Her wrists are badly cut and she appears to be in shock, but as soon as she is able she agrees to see Poirot, and relates to him the events of the night just passed.

Then, trembling, she accompanies the investigators outside to identify the body. Dear God, she cries, it is he, and falls away in a faint. Poirot rushes to her side. Is this a ruse, he wonders? Did she, as the only beneficiary of her millionaire husband's estate, somehow engineer the whole thing? But no — the collapse is genuine, Poirot can see; her skin is clammy, her pulse faint. The servants are right: this is a woman who genuinely loved her husband, whatever the truth of his relationships with other women. She is truly in distress over his death.

Who, then, can be suspected? Madame Daubreuil, the neighbor—was she a spurned mistress, killing in revenge? Or had she been visiting for other purposes — perhaps blackmail? Her bank account, the police discover, has grown steadily since the arrival of Renauld to the area several months before.

> **"I think *Murder on the Links* was a moderately good example of its kind — though rather melodramatic. This time I provided a love affair for Hastings.... Truth to tell, I think I was getting a little tired of him."**
> —*An Autobiography*

If it is blackmail it is undoubtedly tied to the "secret" Renauld had alluded to in his summons to Poirot. It may have had something to do with his previous life in Argentina, and with the making of his fortune there. He was, alas, very hazy about his past.

The identity of the other lady has police puzzled until they discover a note in the overcoat Renauld was wearing, a passionate love note signed "Bella Duveen." Another mistress! Parbleu! How does this square with the loving wife?

The checking goes on. There is a son, Jack, who is away; he returns. His father had sent him orders to go to Santiago, Chile, just prior to his death. He would be at sea now, in fact, but the sailing was cancelled at the last moment. No, he doesn't know why his father wanted him to go; he was to receive complete instructions upon arrival. Does he know why his father's will had been changed just two weeks previously, leaving all to his mother instead of half to him, as an earlier will had done? Indeed not; he is not aware of the change. Until this very moment he had thought himself an heir...

Aha — motive. Had father and son not been heard to quarrel violently a short time ago? Had Jack not slammed out of the house, uttering threats?

It looks bad for Jack, but Poirot wonders...

That story of Madame Renauld's, it is strange, no? It reminds him of something, though he cannot think what. No matter: it is impossible to think of her being involved; she loved her husband, he is sure, and could not wish him dead. If only he could find Bella Duveen...and then there is the matter of the footprints in the flower bed.

There are no footprints in the flower bed, says Hastings, ever the foil.

Exactly, replies Poirot. *There ought to be* —

Pressed, Jack Renauld explains the fight he had with his father: it concerned Marthe Daubreuil, beautiful young daughter of the household next door. They planned to marry, but the senior Re-

nauld became infuriated when he learned of it, for reasons the younger man could not fathom. So what if her family's background was obscure! So, indeed, was his own. As for the relationship between his father and Madame Daubreuil, Jack knows nothing, but he is sure they were not lovers—far from it. Renauld had seethed at the mention of the Daubreuil name, so much so that he forbade his son to see Marthe any more.

Which of course was impossible. They were in love; they would marry, blessing or no. Now, of course, with his father dead, there is no impediment to the marriage...

Aha — more motive. Jack is getting in deeper with every twist of the plot. Curiously, he makes no effort to disentangle himself, other than to say that he is innocent. One might almost suspect that he *wanted* to be arrested. Why, for example, if he was out of town, does he not produce evidence to that effect? Could it be that he cannot?

It is so. Worse — the railroad attendant at Merlinville has come forth to say that Jack Renauld arrived on the 11:40 P.M. train the night his father was killed. To the police it is clear as crystal — they are sure the case is solved. Only Poirot knows that someone is lying, probably to protect someone else. But who is the liar, and who the beneficiary?

The threads are still far from unraveled when a second body is discovered, in the same place as the first, and stabbed with the same dagger. Isn't one enough?

Hardly. Victims and villains leap out in seemingly endless succession; no one is what he seems — or even who he seems — to be. But the little gray cells rush to the rescue, just in time to prevent still another tragedy. Past sins are avenged, justice is done, and even love is triumphant, and if the reader is left a little breathless at the end, could anyone wish it another way?

Certainly not I.

NORMA SIEBENHELLER

The Man in the Brown Suit (1924)

You like your Christie straight and are proud of it. Lord knows anything the good lady does is fine with you. Once in a while, though...tell the truth ... you find Miss Marple's stolid good sense and Poirot's eternal fastidiousness a bit wearing. Again, those stuffy English country houses, with their supply of fresh corpses and fresher nephews, are interesting but not always your cup of tea. Nothing serious, of course; just that it would be nice, once in a while, to match wits with a sleuth who was effervescent and attractive, as well as sharp-eyed and keen-witted. And a change of scene — say, an ocean voyage, or a train ride through Africa, or a small revolution — would leave you none the worse for wear, either.

Meet, then, Anne Beddingfeld, recently orphaned daughter of the late Professor Charles Beddingfeld, the eminent authority on Neanderthal man. Anne is a young woman of many talents. She is not only levelheaded, having had to administer her father's meager fortunes throughout his absentminded life, and aggressive, having had the pluck to wangle a coveted special correspondent's job on the *Daily Budget*, and poor, having been left only £87 by her father's estate, but she is also fabulously beautiful, friendless, restless, adventuresome, courageous, and curious as a cat. All told, Anne's personality is a lucky break for the readers of *The Man in the Brown Suit*. If she had been content to marry the doctor in Little Hampsly and settle ingloriously down, we would have been deprived of a tale of international intrigue, diamond thefts, murder, shipboard shenanigans, bomb-throwing revolutionaries, island idylls, and at least three more marriage proposals.

Anne is on the lookout for adventures but is introduced to her mystery simply because she is in the right place at the right time. Who says there is no such thing as Fate? As she waits for a train on the platform of the Hyde Park Corner tube station, a small, thin, bearded man, whose overcoat reeks of mothballs, accidentally falls to his death.

Only Anne, of all the officialdom in attendance, realizes that the doctor who checks the body is no doctor at all. Only she finds the message "17.122 Kilmorden Castle" which the doctor rifles from the pockets of the dead man and then accidentally drops. And only she connects this "doctor" with the Man in the Brown Suit who is wanted for the murder of a beautiful foreign woman in the unoccupied Mill House of Sir Eustace Pedlar.

Since the obvious key to all this is the mysterious message, Anne sets to decoding "17.122 Kilmorden Castle." Using all her deductive talents, though, she can't decipher "17.122." She can't even find Kilmorden Castle—until she happens to walk past a London steamship office. She realizes that the castle is actually a cruise ship bound for Cape Town, Africa. Auspiciously, the ship will be sailing on 1/17/22. Like any self-respecting heroine, she manages to be on board, paying for her passage with all of her inheritance.

No doubt some of the financially practical among you are shaking your heads and muttering about legislation to protect orphans from themselves, but Anne's passage turns out to be a solid

"It is, I think, the only time I have tried to put a real person whom I knew well into a book, and I don't think it succeeded. Belcher didn't come to life, but someone called Sir Eustace Pedlar did." —*An Autobiography*

investment. She is on the ship for no more than two days (discounting the time she is seasick and prays for a merciful end) when she discovers that she is only peripherally investigating the beautiful foreign woman's murder and the small thin man's accidental but mysterious demise. These two deaths are the symptoms, so to speak, of an ugly and more widespread disease.

Anne learns that the woman, Nadina, spent part of her young life as an agent for an elusive but powerful Colonel, a Napoleon-gone-wrong who heads an international organization of criminals. Jewel robberies, forgery, wartime espionage, sabotage, and discreet assassinations are all part of a busy and rewarding day for him.

Before the war, Nadina, using her husband as accomplice, had stolen £100,000 of DeBeers diamonds for the Colonel. The Colonel, being the mastermind that he is, had a ready scapegoat for the blame. Two young prospectors had been making a hoopla about discovering a new diamond source in the jungles of British Guiana. Beautiful Nadina easily substituted a few of the DeBeers diamonds for their samples and kept back a few of the prospectors' diamonds for her own "protection." If the Colonel ever forgot his old friends, she intended to use these diamonds to substantiate the prospectors' story of substitution and to pin the blame squarely on the Colonel. Needless to say, the Colonel did not approve of her plan and took ready steps to stay its execution.

Anne finds this information easily enough, but to her everlasting delight, realizes that the two major points are still at loose ends, namely, who is the Colonel and where are the diamonds located now?

The Kilmorden Castle is a neat treasure trove of suspects. All Anne has to do is find the right one.

Could Colonel Race be her man? A strong, silent Rhodesian rumored to be in the government's Secret Service, he certainly seems to know a great deal about the high spots of the Colonel's

career and about the jewel robbery. And, after all, the rank is right.

Or, perhaps beautiful and regal Mrs. Suzanne Blair disguises a razor-sharp criminal brain with a facade of concern for social happenings and new clothes. Why should it be she who winds up with the missing diamonds unceremoniously dumped on her stomach at 1 A.M. in cabin 71 on 22 January? (Remember? 17.122 Kilmorden Castle.)

Include Sir Eustace Pedlar, M.P., on Anne's list. Sure, he's a jovial, well-respected middle-aged man with a certain girth, but why won't he talk about how he made his money?

Guy Pagett, Sir Eustace's resident secretary, has the face of a fifteenth-century poisoner — someone the Borgias would send on odd jobs. Still, he has the morals of a mid-Victorian. Or does he? The man obviously harbors a guilty secret.

Harry Rayburn, traveling as another secretary to Sir Eustace, is no one's man but his own. Clearly, he's the Man in the Brown Suit who, on the strength of circumstantial evidence, is wanted for the murder of Nadina. The question in Anne's mind is, "Did he kill her?" She hopes not because she is madly in love with him.

Finally, Rev. Edward Chichester, a returning missionary, is someone who bears watching, if only because he says he spent several years in Africa working among the natives. This is admirable, of course, but why doesn't he have a tan? He's not even sunburned pink around the edges.

While Anne struggles to name the Colonel, the Colonel struggles to eliminate Anne. It's a match of wits of the most exciting kind, with Anne and the elusive Colonel sparring on the Kilmorden Castle and up and down the coast of Africa. Who wins? It's a near thing, and it's no comfort that Anne tells the story herself. After all, many tales wander into print posthumously.

JANICE CURRY

Poirot Investigates (1924)

England's Prime Minister disappears hours before he is to negotiate an end to the "Big War." Archaeologists drop like flies upon excavating the tomb of King Men-her-Ra near Cairo. People die and disappear in various circumstances in many places, jewels are stolen and recovered, clues are followed around the world.

Mystery after mystery unfolds within the 200 pages of this sampler of thrillers. Two things bind these fourteen stories together—the brilliance of the diminuitive Poirot, and the stupidity of his Watson-like partner, Captain Hastings.

Beyond narrating the stories, Hastings serves only one purpose—to highlight Poirot's brilliance by displaying his own stupidity. Hastings seems to hold no grudge after being used as a whipping boy, despite the fact that Poirot shows no reluctance to degrade him at every opportunity.

When the great lords of Britain come seeking Poirot's help in "The Kidnapped Prime Minister," they are reluctant to tell their state secrets in front of Hastings. Poirot graciously calms them by saying, "He has not all the gifts, no! But I answer for his discretion." When the lords admit the disappearance of the Prime Minister, Hastings exclaims, "Impossible!" Poirot shoots him a withering glance that "enjoined me to keep my mouth shut."

The amazing fact is that we mere mortal readers can finish a story with our self-respect intact. Hastings's opinions about the clues usually seem quite correct, and his conclusions are often similar to our own. So when Poirot shoots a withering glance at Hastings, we too wince. Recovery for the injured ego comes only by conceding preeminence to the gray cells of the superhuman logic machine, Poirot.

Poirot always solves the crime, but if you expect him to take out his spyglass and follow tire tracks, you've got the wrong guy. Others may rush to and fro recovering cigarette butts and taking lipstick samples, but we are dealing here with the academician of the detective business. Seeking the lost Prime Minister, Poirot taps his head and says:

> I need not have left London. It would have been sufficient for me to sit quietly in my rooms there. All that matters is the little gray cells within. Secretly and silently they do their part, until suddenly I call for a map, and I lay my finger on a spot and I say: the Prime Minister is *there!* ...With logic one can accomplish anything!

But what happens to Poirot's logic as he seemingly succumbs to the superstition of Men-her-Ra in "The Adventure of the Egyptian Tomb"? The facts are clear. Sir John Willard, a famed archaeologist, opens the king's tomb and promptly dies. The news media begin buzzing about the curse of death on those who disturb the ancient tombs. Before the ink is dry, the rich Mr. Bleibner, another excavation team member, passes on to greater glory. Within days, Bleibner's nephew shoots himself. The unfortunate young man had just visited the tomb while trying to scrounge some money out of his rich uncle.

Sir Willard's widow aptly points out that three deaths are more than mere coincidence. Since the widow's son has taken his father's place at the excavation site, the woman is reasonably distraught, and seeks Poirot's help. Can he protect her son against an occult influence? The master of logic responds, "In volumes of the Middle Ages,

Lady. Willard, you will find many ways of counteracting black magic."

Poirot and Hastings go trotting off to Egypt. As Poirot battles the sand that he curses for spoiling his usual neatness, Hastings proposes a theory: The nephew wants to poison his rich uncle but gives the dose to Willard by mistake. Willard dies of poisoning, the uncle dies naturally, the nephew realizes how unnecessary his crime was, is stricken with remorse, and kills himself.

That may satisfy the reader who doesn't know that Hastings is always wrong, but it doesn't satisfy Poirot. He, in a rare complimentary mood, admits the theory is ingenious, but chides Hastings for leaving out of the count the "fatal influence of the Tomb."

Hastings's theory is further damaged upon arrival at the excavation site—there has been yet another death. This time, an expert from the Metropolitan Museum, Mr. Schneider, lies in state. Now, this is a very small excavation team, and more than half of its original members are gone. Furthermore, as the number of victims increases, the number of suspects necessarily decreases. All that are left are Willard's son, recently arrived after most of the deaths; the site doctor, Dr. Ames; the British expert, Mr. Tosswill; and the faithful Willard servant, Hassan. Of course we must not let out the prime suspect, the dead king himself.

Poirot himself admits to feeling evil in the air. As if pervasive evil were not bad enough, all present must endure endless discourse on Egyptian antiquities from Mr. Tosswill. Despite the fear aroused from a shadowy figure seen moving among the tents, one can sense relief that the lecture has been interrupted. This interruption is a dog-headed figure like the ones carved on the walls of King Men-her-Ra's tomb!

Poirot, taking no chances, draws inscriptions and diagrams around his tent, presumably to ward off evil spirits. He thereby draws the

contempt of the learned Mr. Tosswill. Has Poirot taken leave of the logic he so proudly espouses? If there is an evil spirit at work, can Poirot's incantations ward it off?

CINDY LOOSE

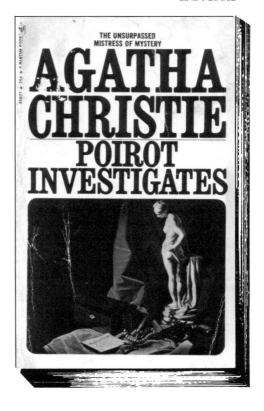

THE UNSURPASSED
MISTRESS OF MYSTERY

AGATHA
CHRISTIE
POIROT
INVESTIGATES

"An English Family at Tea,"
18th-century British School
(National Gallery, London)

A NICE CUPPA
The English Tea Ritual

by Joanna Milton

The cup of tea arrived almost as the thought came to her. Brought on a tray with four sweet biscuits on a little plate...
—from *The Mirror Crack'd*

Webster's Dictionary defines *tea* as "an aromatic beverage prepared by infusion with boiling water of the leaves from a shrub of the family Theaceae, cultivated especially in China, Japan, and the East Indies." But it is much more than such an academic definition would indicate. It is also the name of an English social ritual referred to again and again in the pages of Dame Agatha's mysteries.

The first printed reference to tea in England, calling it *chau*, appeared in 1598 in *Linschooten's Travels,* an English translation of a work originally published in Holland. Since that time, it has virtually become a part of English letters, for what English novelist can resist the significance,

the patriotism, the aesthetic appeal, and the sociability offered by the custom of "tea"? In fact, according to a report in *The Cooking of the British Isles* by Adrian Bailey, it is estimated that the population of Britain purchases 475 million pounds of tea a year, which translates into about six cups a day per head.

Tea may have been known in England as far back as the reign of James I, but it is unlikely, as it is not mentioned in the literature of this period. According to William Ukers in *All About Tea,* the earliest importation of tea into England occurred in the seventeenth century. The first reference to it by an Englishman appeared in 1615, when one tea agent wrote another requesting him to send "a pot of the best sort of chaw." It was referred to as the China drink, tcha, chaw, tay, tee, and tea, and was at first regarded more as a medicine than a fashionable drink.

Garraways, a coffee house which began selling tea publicly in 1657, advertised the notable qualities of the fragrant leaf thusly:

> It maketh the body active and lusty,
> It helpeth the Headache,
> It removeth the obstructions of the Spleen...

In all there were sixteen virtues listed in the Garraways ad, which recommended tea for everything from cleaning kidneys to "overcoming superfluous Sleep." Such advertisements, evidently, had their value, for at Garraways men prominent in business gathered to socialize and refresh their spirits with ale, punch, brandy, coffee—and now tea.

The government soon realized that the demand for tea could be put to its advantage, and subsequently high import duties were levied. This, in turn, led to smuggling and worse. According to *To Think of Tea!* by Agnes Repplier, the beverage was sometimes prepared "in large quantities" and drawn off when called for "like so much ale or beer." Repplier concludes: "That English tea should have survived its early handling is one of the kindly miracles which from time to time restore our confidence in a seemingly unkind world."

> On their arrival at Diana's house, she had at once rung up Admiral Chandler, and they had forthwith gone over to Lyde Manor where they found tea waiting on the terrace...
> —from *The Labors of Hercules*

Tea became a fashionable drink for ladies when Charles II married Princess Catherine of Braganza in 1662. Catherine was England's first tea-drinking queen, and she introduced "tea manners": when a lady had sipped enough tea, she laid her spoon across the top of her cup or else tapped on her cup with a spoon for one of the gentlemen present to relieve her of the cup. Or, if the tea-drinking woman was really adamant about not having any more tea, she turned her cup upside down in the saucer, a custom that still prevails although now it is considered not smart, but gauche.

Further stimulus was given to the occupation of tea drinking as a chic entertainment at Court in 1666, when court officials returned from The Hague with an abundance of rich tea, and the ladies at Court began to serve the beverage in the elegant style of the Continent. At this time the Netherlands represented the height of fashion in tea serving, and every well-to-do home in that country had its own exclusive tearoom.

In 1717 Thomas Twining converted Tom's Coffee House into the Golden Lyon, the first tea shop in London. Unlike coffee houses, the Golden Lyon was frequented by women as well as men. Twining's of course, has kept up the tradition of great tea, and its leaf can now be purchased at almost any grocery in England or America, although drinking the beverage at home isn't quite the same as sipping tea in Devereaux Court, where Twining's house was situated.

She murmured something about changing for tea and left them…

—from *Mr. Parker Pyne, Detective*

The general term *tea* was used almost from the start to designate an occasion where tea would be served, and *teatime* was the hour for such a repast. The first written references to tea as a light evening meal was in 1780, when the religious reformer John Wesley wrote that he met all of the society "at breakfast and at tea," signifying that tea was by that time a recognized custom.

"Afternoon tea" was started by Anna, wife of the Duke of Bedford, who began to serve tea and cakes at 5 P.M., because she had "a sinking feeling" at that hour. In the nineteenth century, people ate large, meaty breakfasts, and luncheon was a light sort of picnic with no servants present. Dinner was not served until 8 P.M., so it was no wonder the duchess (and everybody else, we can assume) felt a need for something in the late afternoon. The afternoon tea of the upper classes is now served about 4 P.M., and consists of cake, pastry, or biscuits with the tea.

Will you have a hot scone or a sandwich, or this cake? We have an Italian cook and she makes quite good pastry and cakes. You see, we have taken to your English afternoon tea…

—from *The Mirror Crack'd*

"High tea," or "meat tea," is a meal with meats and other more substantial delicacies served with the tea. High tea at Court became quite filling, as it consisted of whole roast hams and turkeys along with every kind of pastry imaginable. However, it was followed two hours later by a dinner twice as large. For most of England, however, tea "meats" were to be found primarily as fillings for sandwiches and canapes, just as they are now. Some favorites are sandwich loaves stuffed with chicken, shrimp, egg, or salmon salad, liver sausage canapes, caviar and onion canapes, crab or lobster puffballs, hot creamed

A NICE CUPPA

oyster canapes, tomato or cucumber sandwiches, and quiche. These can be served with pastries and "tea breads" such as date-nut bread, banana bread, honey cake, kugelhopf, or prune, apricot, or cranberry bread. And, of course, your favorite tea.

The tea of the middle and working classes, taken at 6 P.M. upon the worker's return from business, was also a high, or meat, tea, as it was the main evening meal. Such a tea, at the turn of the century, might consist of a venison pastry, a large cut ham, eggs, watercress, red beetroot, medlars, apple tart, and tea.

Nibbling delicately at a scone and balancing a cup of tea on his knee, Hercule Poirot allowed himself to become confidential with his hostess.
—from *The Labors of Hercules*

In the England of yesteryear, Poirot would have balanced "a dish of tea" on his knee, because that is how the English referred to the custom of tea drinking. The saying is probably a carry-over from the Elizabethan habit of asking for "a dish of milk," but it lasted all the way up until the mid-nineteenth century. Or the concept may

have stemmed from the tea tasters, of which there are only a hundred or so left in London. Tea tasters sipped tea from bowls, but after they had tasted the brew, they spat it out into spitoons standing handily nearby.

Nowadays, London businessmen can expect to be interrupted about 4 P.M. every day by the entrance of a typist or secretary bringing two cups of tea. "Teatime" is not about to die out, regardless of Miss Marple's worries:

> "Perhaps if you have time," said Miss Marple, "you might come and have tea with me one day. If you still drink tea," she added, rather wistfully. "I know that so many young people nowadays only go out to drinks and things. They think that afternoon tea is a very out-moded affair."
>
> "I'm not as young as all that," said Dermot Craddock. "Yes, I'll come and have tea with you one day. We'll have tea and gossip, and talk about the village..."
> —from *The Mirror Crack'd*

Come to think of it, *chaw* was a very good name for the brew, wasn't it?

JOANNA MILTON

I WOULDN'T GO IN THERE IF I WERE YOU

Rooms to Avoid in an English Country House

by Dick Riley

Whitehaven Mansions
London

Cher Monsieur,

I have received your letter begging my assistance in this matter. You have the trepidations, the fears, is it not so? You have been invited to a "week-end" in Sussex but you are not an ignorant person, n'est-ce pas? You know how dangerous it is, the lurking strangler, the poisoned cup, the gunshot in the middle of the night. Do I take my life in my hands, you ask?

Do not derange yourself, monsieur, I pray you! Than Hercule Poirot, no one knows better the evil ways of your countrymen at such times. It is true that one must have a care, but with the proper caution, I have been assured that one may have a perfectly splendid time on such a holiday.

Ecoutez! I, Hercule Poirot, will instruct you.

Avoid, if you can, all bedrooms — mos dangerous places. From my first case in your country, the regrettable affair at Styles, the boudoir has been the place of the murder. Poor Mrs. Inglethorp. A woman of good heart. But she was only the first. Could we forget Cora Lansquenet, murdered in her bed, poor woman, in After the Funeral? Or Laura Welman in Sad Cypress, Miss Blanche in Cat Among the Pigeons?

Ah, you English. So cold! What countryman of mine would contemplate the homicide over Christmas? But Simeon Lee — "done in" in his bedroom. A Holiday for Murder indeed. The names — the names go on and on. Rosaleen, Celia, Pat—from my own experience alone. And if one keeps up with the literature in my métier—

astonishing. A certain Mona Symmington in The Moving Finger, solved by the estimable Miss Marple; Lady Tressilian in Towards Zero; M. Leonides in Crooked House.

You comprehend? Bon. Avoid the bedroom.

Now, be careful of the parlor, the sitting room. Why, you ask? I will tell you. Do you recall the case of M. Shaitana in Cards on the Table? Quietly he sits in his favorite chair and then—voilà—he is dead, stabbed. Most regrettable. You recall the parlor in The Clocks—just where the poor victim died. And Mrs. McGinty, humble cottage, humble parlor—no protection. We know, do we not, that Mrs. McGinty's Dead?

Of the library one must also be wary. Who can forget Miss Marple's Body in the Library? The poor woman is constantly finding the remains among the volumes. Col. Protheroe, not so nice a

person perhaps, but even so, dead in the library in *Murder at the Vicarage*. Most unseemly. Do not take tea in the library, whatever you do. Recall, if you will, Adele Fortescue in *Pocket Full of Rye*. And her scone only half-eaten!

Relax not your vigilance, I pray you, at dinner. Be careful of what you eat and drink. Never, never ask for a sleeping draught or a cup of chocolate before bedtime—you are, as you say, asking for trouble. Someone is nearly always trying to poison someone else at these affairs and you know what servants are — the cups could easily be switched by mistake.

I know those who take their own food on such a weekend and keep it under lock and key in their rooms, trusting their host only for an occasional cup of chamomile tea. A bit excessive, you say? Perhaps. But one must judge for oneself, *non*?

At any rate, never allow yourself to be in the parlor, sitting room, or library with less than three other people, though of course this is no guarantee of safety. Try not to go outside — remember the death near the swimming pool in *Murder after Hours*, the body on the lawn in *Peril at End House*, the corpses in the boathouse and the river in *Dead Man's Folly*, and on the rocky cliffs in *Elephants Can Remember*.

Need I warn you to be careful on the train on your way there? We have always before us the example of the notorious Ratchett, who met his fate on the Orient Express, and Ruth Kettering, whose murder you recall from *The Mystery of the Blue Train*.

As you can see, monsieur, this country weekend is not a thing to be entered upon lightly. I well know, but little comprehend, your English passion for things rural. It is a strange characteristic of your people, quite curious. Vicious insects, unpredictable weathers, those great, drafty rooms—I shudder to think of them. And then, to literally risk one's life in those dreary piles of masonry!

I personally much prefer London. But if you, my dear sir, insist on such adventures, I can only wish you *bonne chance*.

With all sincerity,

Hercule Poirot

HERCULE POIROT

The Secret of Chimneys (1925)

Bulawayo. Of all places for Anthony Cade to run into his old friend Jimmy McGrath! But then again, for men with as much in common as they had—both adventurers and soldiers of fortune, both sharing a taste for good whiskey, lovely women, and all things exotic—maybe a chance meeting in the Rhodesian bush was not quite as astonishing as it at first seemed.

Always ready with an interesting yarn or an intriguing offer, McGrath had one of each for his friend Anthony Cade. Paris, a few years back: Jimmy McGrath was walking alone in a deserted area of the city when he happened upon a group of French toughs beating up a helpless old gentleman. Just to even the odds, Jimmy took the old gent's cause, thrashed the attackers, and sent them running. He was then amazed to find that the old man was none other than Count Stylptitch of Herzoslovakia. Why, even those who had never heard of Herzoslovakia had heard of the Count—master diplomat and kingmaker, the "Grand Old Man of the Balkans."

Jimmy had thought the chapter ended, but he recently read that Count Stylptitch had died in Paris and received in the mail a parcel containing the old man's memoirs. Along with the manuscript came an advisory stating that a thousand pounds would be awarded him upon delivery of it to a certain publisher in London.

So much for the story, now for the offer: Even though Jimmy McGrath could put the extra loot to good use, he had it from a good source that there was gold to be found at a particular location in the African interior. When compared with a lode of gold, a thousand pounds paled to a paltry sum. But rather than drop the deal, how would Anthony Cade like to act in Jimmy's stead?

Cade reflects momentarily. Why would anyone want a package sent from Paris to London via Africa? The tale and the proposal are just enigmatic enough to court his attention. They toast to the deal.

Herzoslovakia. Though it was not a great power, Cade knows enough of its recent history to find it an interesting parcel of real estate. The last of the Obolovitch rulers, King Nicholas IV, had fallen in love with a Parisian actress named Angèle Mory — a woman of alleged moral turpitude—and had tried to dupe his people into believing that she was of Romanoff descent. The final affront came when the king had the temerity to marry this parvenu tart and proclaim her Queen Varaga of Herzoslovakia. That little maneuver not only cost the royal couple their thrones (by way of a republican revolution), but it also cost them their lives (both were mutilated beyond recognition on the palace steps).

Though he was put out of work along with the Obolovitch dynasty, Count Stylptitch continued to wield considerable influence over world affairs and pined for the day when the monarchy would be returned to Herzoslovakia. If one believed what one read in the newspapers, the Herzoslovakian romance with republicanism had quickly soured and there was a strong movement within the country to find another king. Poor Count Stylptitch — dead barely months before seeing his dream realized. The injustice of it all!

Before the two friends parted company, Jimmy McGrath had a small favor to ask of his old friend. It seems that several months ago, in Uganda, Jimmy had saved the life of one "Dutch Pedro," which was a pointless thing to do since Pedro died of fever shortly thereafter anyway.

However, before he died, he managed to repay his debt to Jimmy by passing on to him the letters with which he had been blackmailing an Englishwoman by the name of Virginia Revel. Blackmail was too foul a business for Jimmy's sensibilities and he asked his friend Cade to relieve the poor lady's mind by giving her the letters.

Well, Cade would be in the neighborhood anyway. It was only a small favor to ask of a friend. Done, then.

All goes swimmingly until Cade arrives in London and is met at his hotel by the man with the unpronounceable name: Baron Lolopretjzyl ("lollipop" is Cade's best approximation). The Baron claims to represent a Herzoslovakian royalist faction in London and is concerned that publication of the memoirs would prove to be an encumbrance to their plan of putting Prince Michael Obolovitch on the throne. Prince Michael, he explains, already had been assured of Britain's backing in his bid. Beyond his simple appeal to Cade's patriotism, the baron tries to sweeten the deal by offering Cade twice what he would receive from the publisher. Attractive as

the deal might have been, Cade has to turn it down; after all, he has given a promise to his friend Jimmy McGrath. There is his honor as an Englishman to consider, as the baron is fond of stating.

Cade's next visitor is less courtly. He is not even polite enough to identify himself by name. Announcing himself simply as a member of the Comrades of the Red Hand, he invades Cade's suite and plainly demands the manuscript.

The Comrades of the Red Hand are a picturesque, if by and large ineffectual, radical political group. Having done their feeble best to oust the Obolovitch dynasty, they are determined to see that it does not reappear in Herzoslovakia. But, Anthony Cade is not a man to take anyone's *demands* seriously, and when the ill-mannered intruder draws a revolver to back up his threats Cade answers it with a well-aimed kick. Hardly worth the effort of a chase, the man is left to flee in pain down the hotel corridor.

That night, Cade awakens to the sound of a rustling in his hotel room. He springs from his bed, switching on the light as he does so. The

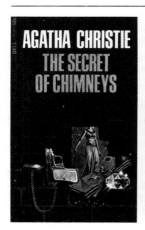

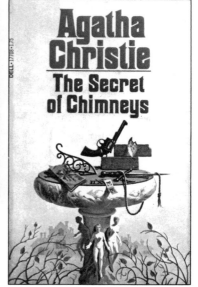

The Secret of Chimneys (1925)

man kneeling by his suitcase he recognizes as a hotel waiter named Giuseppe, and before Cade can demand an explanation, Giuseppe is at him with a knife. Once again, someone has underestimated Anthony Cade, and after a brief scuffle the attacker is disarmed. However, before Cade can immobilize him, Giuseppe escapes—not only with his life, but with the letters meant for Virginia Revel.

After depositing the manuscript with the appropriate publishing company, Cade thinks himself duty-bound to at least proffer an explanation to the poor lady at 487 Pont Street. Virginia Revel is a tall, statuesque woman of twenty-seven. Bright, charming, and vital, she is also self-possessed and utterly in charge of her life. Had he known her beforehand, Cade might not have been surprised when, before he can explain the purpose of his mission, she vexes him with a polite request. Would he care to help her dispose of the dead body slumped in a chair in her study?

Does she recognize the deceased? Certainly she does. It is the same fellow who had tried to negotiate a blackmailing scheme with her only days before. Cade also recognizes him; it is the rascal who had tried to knife him while burgling his hotel room. Poor Giuseppe.

Whoever did him in saw to it that he was picked clean of any identification. All Cade can find is a small scrap of paper caught in the lining of one pocket. The message scrawled on it is terse enough: "Chimneys 11:45 Thursday."

How positively extraordinary. Virginia Revel has an appointment to visit Chimneys this very evening. Could it be possible that somebody, or some persons, intend to prevent her from keeping that appointment?.

There is another curious item — the murder weapon on the floor next to the chair. Though Virginia Revel disclaims any knowledge of weaponry, the pistol used clearly has the name *Virginia* engraved on it. It is too obvious a clue for

a man used to dealing in the most Byzantine intrigues, and anyway, it is bad form to turn one's back on a lady in distress—especially a beautiful lady. Anthony Cade has no choice but to accept Virginia Revel's entreaty to become her bodyguard. Off to Chimneys.

A formidable country estate nestled into the Berks countryside, Chimneys is a place where kings and queens could frolic on the weekends. It is 11:45 in the evening when Anthony Cade arrives at Chimneys (after having first disposed of Giuseppe's body and the murder weapon as professionally as he can). Everything is dark and quiet. Suddenly, a shot. It seems to come from the room occupied by Count Stanislaus of Herzoslovakia, but Cade cannot be sure. Maybe he has just imagined the shot—quite understandable in view of his adventures these last few days. Cade notices a light go on, then off, in the room of Mademoiselle Brun, the French maid.

Morning. The tinkle of silverware mixes with the buzz of earnest conversation as the visiting notables gather for breakfast and discuss the scandalous events of the previous night. Someone has, in fact, potted Count Stanislaus.

Superintendent Battle of Scotland Yard, an unflappable veteran detective, assures Lord Caterham that he will be discreet in his investigation. Aiding Battle will be Inspector Lemoine of the French Sûreté, who has crossed the Channel in search of the infamous jewel thief "King Victor."

However, a most startling revelation is made by a member of the foreign office, the Honorable George Lomax. It seems that Count Stanislaus was merely an incognito; the murdered man was in truth none other than Prince Michael Obolovitch, pretender to the throne of Herzoslovokia.

The plot is thickening for Anthony Cade but he is determined to stick around until the end. It appears there is more to these Chimneys than just a few whiffs of smoke.   PETER J. FITZPATRICK

The Murder of Roger Ackroyd (1926)

The Murder of Roger Ackroyd is a landmark in the history of detective fiction—but you won't know why until you've read the last page.

When it was published in 1926 a few critics labeled the final twist a "dirty trick," but in the years since it has come to be seen for what it was—a stroke of genius. Almost no one, unless he or she has been forewarned, would suspect what Christie is up to. The end, when it is revealed, is quite a shocker.

The facts are simple, on the surface: Mrs. Ferrars, a wealthy widow living in the village of King's Abbot, was found dead in her bed on a Thursday night, the victim of an overdose of veronal. The following evening Roger Ackroyd, a widower who everyone thought hoped to marry Mrs. Ferrars, was murdered in the study of his home, Fernly Glen. The two deaths are related, and thereby hangs the tale.

The first death, the village gossipers said, was definitely a suicide. Dr. Sheppard feared as much when he first examined the body, though with true country doctor discretion he refrained from saying so publicly. After all, it could never be proved, so what would be the point? He thought he'd rather not know.

Ackroyd, however, did know. "I've got to talk to you," he said to Sheppard the next day. "This is a terrible business... worse than you know." He looked haggard and worn. The doctor agreed to come to dinner that night, and they parted.

After the meal — during which they were joined by the usual company of family, friends, and employees so common to every "great house" in Christie fiction — the two friends withdrew for coffee and conversation. Ackroyd unburdened himself. He was, unfairly or not, blaming himself for Mrs. Ferrars's death.

They had, he said, planned to marry, though they had not yet announced the fact, preferring to follow convention and wait until a year had passed since her husband's death. That anniversary had finally arrived, however, and he began urging her to let their secret out. She stalled for a while, then finally, yesterday, announced that she could not do it—could not marry him at all. She had a terrible thing on her mind. She had, she confessed, poisoned her husband, a drunken lout whom she had never loved!

"My God!" cried Ackroyd to Sheppard, his voice breaking as he related the story. "It was murder in cold blood!"

His tone left no doubt that such a man as he—honest, straightforward, and true — could never forgive such a crime, even for a woman he loved. Mrs. Ferrars had known this too, known that with her confession she was writing an end to their affair. Perhaps she could have carried it off, could have remained silent and kept her guilty secret to herself, were it not for one thing: the secret was not hers alone. Someone else knew—and that someone had been blackmailing her for a year, with ever-increasing demands that had driven her, finally, to the point of desperation.

And Ackroyd, instead of offering sympathy, had clearly shown his horror at her revelation. Could he have foreseen that she would kill herself that night? If only she had told who the blackmailer was...

Sheppard was uttering doctorly words of reassurance when the butler arrived with the evening post. Hullo, what's this? A letter—in her

The Murder of Roger Ackroyd (1926)

handwriting! So she did leave a message after all!

Sheppard is curious, but Ackroyd is first: the letter was meant for his eyes alone; he will read it later, and then will decide what, if anything, to do. He puts the blue envelope down. It can wait.

After satisfying himself that his friend will take no rash action Sheppard leaves, returning to the home he shares with his sister nearby.

Alas, revenge is not to be Ackroyd's. Less than two hours later the doctor is called back to Fernly Glen. Ackroyd has been murdered!

The blue letter, needless to say, has disappeared.

Who can have done it? Almost anyone in the house — they all had motives of one sort or another, and they all had the opportunity. For example, there's his housekeeper, Miss Russell, an intelligent woman in early middle age, a bit pursed about the lips but otherwise quite handsome. Until Mrs. Ferrars came along, she herself had hoped to marry Ackroyd. And she was clearly flustered when the doctor had first

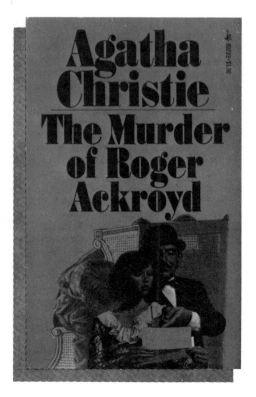

> **"I think it is possible that Miss Marple arose from the pleasure I had taken in portraying Dr. Sheppard's sister in *The Murder of Roger Ackroyd*. She had been my favorite character in the book — an acidulated spinster, full of curiosity, knowing everything, hearing everything: the complete detective service in the home."**
> —*An Autobiography*

entered the house before dinner. As if his coming might have upset some of her plans...

Or Major Blunt, big-game hunter and adventurer, a house guest and old acquaintance of Ackroyd's. That Blunt had something on his mind was very clear. He stumbled over his words all through dinner. And who would know better than he the lethal powers of the murder weapon, a small dagger from Tunis? He had, after all, given the blade to Ackroyd himself, on his last visit.

Mrs. Cecil Ackroyd, a widowed sister-in-law, and her daughter, Flora, could be suspected from a different angle. They made their home at Fernly Glen, but although they lived in the midst of luxury they were nonetheless poor. They hadn't a penny to call their own, and Ackroyd was uncommonly niggardly for one so rich. Demanded an accounting of everything, and questioned the necessity of such items as ball gowns and velvet wraps. Oh, it was so difficult! If only he would settle a sum on his niece now, when she needed it—but no, he said, she would have to wait. She'd be well fixed after his death, to be sure, but until then he would control the purse strings.

It was enough to drive a woman to drink. Or murder.

There's still more: the butler—now, there's a suspicious character. Sheppard caught him eavesdropping at the study door when he left. What was he trying to hear?

And Geoffrey Raymond, the young secretary, who really did appear too good to be true. Took charge of unpleasant details after the death with such aplomb, almost as if — as if he'd known ahead of time...

Ursula Bourne, too, is an enigma. Much too smart for a parlormaid. Simple enough to check on her references, of course, but when they do, the police find only muddy water. Who is she, really? And why is she at Fernly Glen?

And who is the mysterious stranger who had been seen approaching the house just as the doctor left? He had asked several townspeople for directions, surely not something he would do if he had his mind on murder, but still...

Finally there is Ralph Paton. Twenty-five years old, charming, handsome, he is Ackroyd's adopted son. His gambling debts have so enraged his father that the two have not spoken in some time. Ackroyd, in fact, was not even aware that Ralph was in the village, but he was; he'd slipped in the day before and was staying at the Three Boars. Slipped out, too, just before nine Friday night, and disappeared into thin air. He is the prime suspect, particularly since his footprints have been found on the window ledge leading into Ackroyd's room.

Flora disagrees. She and Ralph, she says, are engaged to be married, and she *knows* he cannot have killed his father, though the police seem to think he has. She does the only thing she can think of to save him: she goes to Hercule Poirot.

How fortunate — Poirot, newly retired, had come to live in King's Abbot less than a year before. Already he is growing tired of cultivating vegetable marrows. He welcomes the chance to practice his old profession once again.

"I want the truth," says Flora the day after the crime.

"I hope," replies the dapper Belgian, smoothing his mustache, "that you will not regret those words!"

Immediately he sets to work. The insignificant suddenly gains importance with the aid of his little gray cells. No matter about Ralph Paton and his money troubles—no, nor even his mysterious disappearance. What matters is a discarded ring, and a chair out of place, and a telephone call.

We follow, but always a step behind. No one but Poirot could work this puzzle: the pieces don't fit. And then, finally, he shows us—

Oh, Agatha! How *could* you?

NORMA SIEBENHELLER

The Big Four (1927)

What a fine irony this is! Hastings, Hercule Poirot's longtime friend, is just back in London after a year and a half in Argentina and has plans for surprising the little Belgian. But what should he find Poirot doing but packing for a trip to South America? What a strikingly curious coincidence! Or is it?

Poirot claims to have been, for the first time in his life, "tempted by mere money" and to be on his way to do some investigating for the richest man in the world, Abe Ryland, "The American Soap King." His train leaves within the hour and, having given his word, nothing can detain him— not even the mud-covered man who stumbles into his flat and passes out.

Given a little brandy, the man revives. But he is obviously suffering from some shock and for the longest time is only able to mutter Poirot's name and address. When offered pencil and paper, he scrawls the figure 4 a dozen times, each one larger than the last. Finally regaining his senses, he says clearly "Li Chang Yen" and then begins to speak quickly in a flat tone as if reciting a report. He says that Li Chang Yen is the brains of the Big Four; he is Number One. Number Two is an American and is represented by a dollar sign. Number Three is a Frenchwoman. And Number Four is . . . the destroyer. And he passes out again.

Curiously, Poirot has just been telling Hastings that he has recently become interested in something called the "Big Four"—about which he knows little except that they are evidently "a gang of international criminals or something of that kind."

But Poirot must be off to the train and on to South America, and he hurries off with Hastings

(who is accompanying him to the port) leaving the stranger in the care of his housekeeper, Mrs. Pearson.

On the train Poirot is restless. When the train is delayed unexpectedly in the countryside, he decides that it is "undoubtedly the blessed saints" sending him a sign. He commands Hastings to jump.

Hurrying back to London, they find their mysterious visitor dead. And thus begins a long trail of murders leading to the final showdown with the Big Four.

The Big Four (1927) is no novel of country manor gentility and drawing room murder. It is the story of a secret, global organization bent on the "disintegration of civilization" and possessing control of "some scientific force" (perhaps the secrets of gravitation, perhaps atomic power) which renders its threat particularly insidious. In opposition to this threat stand only "the little gray cells" of Hercule Poirot.

One especially sinister agent of the Big Four goes so far as to recommend that Poirot "return to your former avocations, and solve the problems of London society ladies." Once on the trail of a challenge, however, the "delicately plump," green-eyed, moderately egotistical detective with the egg-shaped head is not to be easily deterred.

Given the basic clue that there is something essentially Chinese about this menace known as the Big Four, Poirot begins by consulting Britain's leading authority on the inner workings of China, John Ingles. Ingles has recently heard from an old seafaring friend, John Whalley of Hoppaton, who claims to fear for his life because

"Ever since my mother's death I had been unable to write a word. A book was due this year, and having spent so much on Styles I had no money on hand; ... my brother-in-law, Archie's brother Campbell Christie, who had always been a great friend and was a kind and lovable person, helped me here. He suggested that the last twelve stories published in *The Sketch* should be run together, so that they would have the appearance of a book. That would be a stop-gap. He helped me with the work — I was still unable to tackle anything of the kind. In the end it was published under the title of *The Big Four*, and turned out to be quite popular."
—*An Autobiography*

of the Big Four. A quick trip to Hoppaton proves not quite quick enough; Whalley has been murdered by a blunt instrument applied to the skull and a knife run from ear to ear. The local inspector has already proved the manservant did it; he is an ex-felon, after all. But Poirot is not so easily convinced. What could possibly be the motive for killing such a kindly old retired drunk? He *had* traveled to Shanghai, of course. Who knows what sort of evil Chineseness he might have encountered there?

So now there are two mysterious deaths tenuously linked to the Big Four. And whose interest should this arouse but that of Poirot's old friend, Inspector Japp of Scotland Yard? Japp has begun to take an interest in this Big Four matter himself and comes to Poirot for his assistance with other bizarre cases which seem to have a possible connection or which are so unusual as to admit of virtually no explanation at all.

The first of these concerns the death of a Mr. Paynter, a rich, cultured, globe-trotting gentleman of the estate of Croftlands. Paynter was discovered dead in his study under rather curious circumstances. After complaining of feeling poorly after dinner, Paynter had retired and summoned his doctor. The doctor gave him an injection for his weak heart and departed. Next morning, Paynter was discovered with his head and shoulders charred beyond recognition. Apparently he weakened and fell headlong into the fireplace. But one odd piece of evidence casts a shadow over that simple explanation. A newspaper is found with the words "Yellow Jasmine" scrawled across it in ink. Paynter's index finger is covered with ink. The inky message also shows two straight lines at right angles. Could these be the initial strokes of the figure 4? But what could be the motive for murder here? Even Japp has overlooked the obvious answer; Paynter was

The Big Four (1927)

writing a book called *The Hidden Hand in China*!

About a month later, Hastings and Poirot encounter Inspector Japp at a restaurant. While gently ribbing Poirot about his single-minded dedication to the Big Four case, he admits that there is another recent incident which totally baffles him. A young American chess player has died, apparently from heart failure, in the very midst of a match with the reigning Russian champion, Dr. Savaronoff. Certainly there's nothing to connect this death with the notorious Big Four—unless you can make something of the small burn on the victim's left hand or the white bishop clasped so tightly in his dead hand that his fingers had to be pried apart to remove it.

If anyone is to make sense of scattered, seemingly disparate clues, of course, the man is Hercule Poirot. And the man who shares the reader's confusion over Poirot's clairvoyant style and his apparent inaction in the face of pressing danger is his ever-present companion (and narrator), Hastings.

The delicate tension between the styles and manners of Hastings and Poirot weaves a teasing thread beneath the plot. Consistently, Hastings is for "energetic proceedings" and "taking the offensive" while Poirot is convinced that "every day they [the Big Four] fear me the more for my chosen inactivity." Hastings is particularly upset by Poirot's reaction to an incident in Paris — where they've gone to research the disappearance of a young British scientist who had been conducting experiments concerning the nature of magnetism. As they depart the house of one suspect, a tree crashes across the sidewalk—very nearly crushing them. Hardly a coincidence!

"And what are we going to do now?" Hastings asks coldly. "'Do?'" cried Poirot. "We are going to think. Yes, here and now, we are going to exercise our little gray cells."

Ultimately, Hastings gains the opportunity to exercise his own initiative, but hardly under pleasant circumstances. After a particularly nasty explosion (and one to which Hastings himself contributed by not acting with Poirot's meticulous care), Hastings revives in the quarters of Dr. Ridgeway and is told: Poirot is dead.

Within a day, confirmation arrives in the form of a letter held by Poirot's solicitors for release only upon his death. It reads:

> Mon Cher Ami—when you receive this I shall be no more. Do not shed tears about me, but follow my orders. Immediately upon receipt of this, return to South America. Do not be pig-headed about this. It is not for sentimental reasons that I bid you undertake the journey. *It is necessary*. It is part of the plan of Hercule Poirot! To say more is unnecessary, to any one who has the acute intelligence of my friend Hastings.
>
> *A bas* the Big Four! I salute you, my friend, from beyond the grave.
>
> Ever thine,
> HERCULE POIROT

And what does one do in this situation? Go back to South America? Contrive some new "energetic proceeding" for stalking the Big Four?

Perhaps the best plan might be to remember Poirot's earlier admonition: "In a case of this kind, you have got to make up your mind who is lying."

JERRY SPEIR

The Mystery of the Blue Train (1928)

The flawless ruby known as the Heart of Fire and its companion stones had accumulated a long history of tragedy and violence, but neither their ominous legend nor their fabulous prices bothered the American millionaire Rufus Van Aldin. A man used to having his own way, Van Aldin loved only one thing in this life — his daughter, Ruth. He would pay any sum, brave any danger, if the jewels would take her mind off her floundering marriage.

Like the Heart of Fire, the ancient family of Leconbury had an unsavory history, or at least a recklessly romantic one. Derek Kettering, the future Lord of Leconbury, was no exception. When he married Ruth, he had seemed willing to turn over a new leaf, to give up the mad gambling and wild ways that had squandered his family's wealth. But in a few years his early resolve faded and now Derek is very publicly involved with the exotic and notorious dancer, Mirelle.

When Van Aldin, bearing his gift of rubies, suggests that it is time Ruth admit her mistake and divorce her wayward husband, he finds her strangely hesitant, but he eventually convinces her that Derek married her for her money and gains her consent to begin divorce proceedings.

The Heart of Fire thus has its intended effect. And so, while Van Aldin neglects to mention that within ten minutes of purchasing the gems in France from a rather nervous Russian diplomat he was attacked by two "apaches," he simply warns his daughter to put them in her bank vault before leaving London for the winter season on the Riviera.

Unknown even to Van Aldin, the apaches were the first ploy of Monsieur le Marquis, an international jewel thief whose French is very good indeed for an Englishman and whose white hair might very well be a wig. Undaunted by the apaches' bungled attack, he tells Demetrius Papopolous, a well-respected dealer in "unique antiques," that his real plan will not fail.

Derek Kettering, when confronted by his rich father-in-law, hints that Ruth is to blame for their failed marriage, that she married him only for his title and position. Despite what seems to be an open-and-shut case against him, Derek also hints that he has grounds to contest the divorce which, he readily admits, would be his financial ruin. Suddenly Ruth's reluctance to rid herself of her worthless husband takes on a new significance for Van Aldin.

Derek is not optimistic about his chances of avoiding financial ruin, however. As he tells Mirelle, "On the one side, the man with unlimited money; on the other side, the man with unlimited debts. There is no question as to who will come out on top."

Adding to his misery, Mirelle makes it clear that she is a rich man's luxury. Since she is fond of Derek, however, she does have a few suggestions. Ruth, a rich woman even without the millions she will inherit from her father, could have an "accident." When Derek's only response to that suggestion is a sharp look, she counsels blackmail. A woman with many friends, Mirelle has learned that Ruth is not going to the Riviera as she says, but is heading for an assignation in Paris with an infamous scoundrel and ladies' man known as Comte de la Roche. Considering that the Comte was Ruth's lover before her father ended the affair ten years ago and she married

The Mystery of the Blue Train (1928)

Derek, "You can make things very awkward for her," she tells the shocked husband. Strangely enough, Derek is infuriated by Mirelle's information and storms out of her flat.

But cooling down quickly, Derek considers the hopelessness of his situation and reluctantly books a berth on the Blue Train to Nice, the same train Ruth will board for the Riviera and ride at least as far as Paris.

Returning to his own flat, Derek finds Van Aldin's private secretary, the young and able Major Richard Knighton, waiting uneasily. Now also aware of his daughter's renewed acquaintance with the Comte, Van Aldin has instructed Knighton to offer his son-in-law £100,000 if the divorce is not contested. Much to the relief of fellow Englishman Knighton, Derek refuses the offer and challenges the American millionaire to do his best to break him.

The "best" train to Nice, the Blue Train fills with England's leisured rich every January as they head to the Riviera for the two-month "season." Among them for the first time is Katherine Grey, a former paid companion with a brand-new fortune left to her by her old employer. Although pretty and possessing both serenity and a fine sense of humor, Katherine feels that at the age of thirty-three her first bloom of youth has faded and has decided to enjoy her new and unexpected fortune. She realizes that an invitation to spend a few months in the Riviera with her long-lost cousin Lady Tamplin is directly related to that new fortune but has accepted knowing "there would be profit on both sides."

Entering the Blue Train's dining car for lunch, Katherine is seated next to Ruth Kettering. For the first time in her life, Ruth feels her self-control slipping away as she considers the madness of her rendezvous. Before the train has even reached Paris, the unusually self-assured Ruth has confided her problem and misgivings to Katherine as the former companion ruefully muses that people always want to tell her things she doesn't want to hear.

The worst thing about such confidences is that the person never wants to see you again, and much to Katherine's relief she shares her table at dinner that evening with a different stranger, the semi-retired Belgian detective Hercule Poirot, whom she finds amusing, if a bit pompous.

The rest of the trip passes without incident, but when the train pulls into Nice, Katherine is suddenly thrust into events far more exciting and frightening than those in her favorite *roman policier*

The Mystery Of The Blue Train

"...I had changed from an amateur to a professional. I assumed the burden of a profession, which is to write even when you don't want to, don't much like what you are writing, and aren't writing particularly well. I have always hated *The Mystery of the Blue Train*, but I got it written, and sent it off to the publishers. It sold just as well as my last book had done. So I had to content myself with that — though I cannot say I have ever been proud of it."—*An Autobiography*

— Ruth Kettering has been murdered, strangled in her sleep, her face then disfigured by a heavy blow.

Since Ruth's maid has disappeared, the police ask Katherine to identify the body. And, of course, since he is on the spot, the world's most famous detective offers his assistance to the grateful commissary of police.

Back in the murdered woman's compartment, Katherine notices that a large, conspicuous jewel case she had seen the day before is missing. Despite her father's instructions, Ruth had taken the Heart of Fire with her and, apparently, had paid for her stubbornness with her life.

And so the entire cast is assembled in Nice.

The maid, Ada Mason, is found in Paris and brought to the Riviera. For some unexplained reason, she testifies, Ruth suddenly ordered her to get off the train when it pulled into Paris and to wait for her at the Ritz.

Van Aldin and his young secretary rush to Nice, where the millionaire asks Poirot to find his daughter's murderer and damns the day he became involved with the Heart of Fire.

The Comte, already known to the police, had conveniently arrived in Nice the day before the murder, according to the testimony of his well-rehearsed servants. A letter reveals, however, that he had persuaded Ruth to bring the famous ruby to help him finish "his book on jewels."

The dealer in unique antiques, Papopolous, is found visiting the resort town "at his doctor's order." Although noted for his discretion, he is in debt to M. Poirot for helping him through an unpleasant moment seventeen years ago. Disavowing all knowledge of the missing gems, he suggests that if M. Poirot is interested in racing he keep his eye on the English horse, the Marquis.

Unknown to everyone, Mirelle has come to Nice to the very same Blue Train as her lover and her lover's estranged wife. Rebuffed by Derek, she hints she will reveal what she saw on the Blue Train if he doesn't return to her.

Derek, who openly admits that his wife's murder has saved him from ruin and made him a rich man, stays on in Nice after he is introduced to Katherine by her cousin. Though still reckless, he vows he will marry the former companion.

And Katherine, blossoming in the Mediterranean climate, finds herself romantically entwined with two very different men — Derek Kettering and the shy, reserved Major Knighton.

JIM MELE

The Seven Dials Mystery (1929)

Lady Eileen "Bundle" Brent loves adventure. She is unperturbed when she learns that during the time her father has let their estate, Chimneys, to Sir Oswald and Lady Cootes, a houseguest has died in her very room. When the apparent suicide turns out very possibly to be a murder, Bundle is intrigued. Her curiosity mounts when she comes across a letter that the dead man, Gerry Wade, wrote his half-sister, suggesting that she "forget" about a secret society called the Seven Dials. But when a second victim, Ronny Devereux, stumbles onto the road and into Bundle's speeding car, she is moved to action. Ronny has time only to utter "Seven Dials ... tell ... Jimmy Thesiger ... " before he expires, and Bundle is off to cajole and confront her old friends Bill Eversveigh and Superintendent Battle into providing her with relevant information.

It seems that Eversveigh, Thesiger, Devereux, and Wade, young, upper-class Britishers, had all made each other's acquaintance in some "gentlemanly" capacity in the Foreign Office. All were vacuous, lazy, and cheerfully inefficient. And all were present on the weekend Gerry Wade was killed.

Bundle, Jimmy Thesiger, and Loraine Wade (Gerry Wade's half-sister) come together to investigate the mysterious Seven Dials and to find Gerry's and Ronny's murderer. Bundle's adventures lead her to the rather seedy Seven Dials Club where, after having herself locked into a closet by a trusted servant so as to better observe the goings-on, Bundle learns that this society has international political goals and that an important document is going to be stolen in the near future. She also learns, from her cramped vantage point,

that an integral member of the Seven Dials is missing. Who is the mysterious number seven, and why are even his fellow members unaware of his true identity?

Bundle and Jimmy must connive an invitation to the upcoming political meeting at Wyvern Abbey and prevent the theft of plans of an invention by one Herr Eberhard.

At Wyvern Abbey Bundle has her first real chance to meet the powerful, rich, but somewhat crass Sir Oswald. Is there a connection between Sir Oswald Coote's steelworks and Herr Eberhard's formula? And why, oh why, did Jimmy have to let the well-intentioned, but apparently slow-witted, Bill Eversveigh in on their plan? Bill is becoming more and more attentive to the beautiful but rather distant Hungarian, Countess Radzky. Who knows what he might inadvertently reveal ...? Also curious is the presence of Superintendent Battle in a disguise so easily detected that the most inept criminal could see through it and be put on guard.

At 2 A.M. Bundle's contemplations are shattered by the sound of a violent struggle down below. The noise of furniture breaking has drawn all the guests to the library, and finally the fight is punctuated by two gunshots fired in rapid succession. When the door is opened to reveal a slightly wounded Jimmy Thesiger, an unconscious Countess Radzky, and no sign of the documents or the thief, Bundle's speculations and our own are aroused.

Bundle's suspicions become our own, as the resourceful and brave young woman functions as the real sleuth in our story. But as we allow for Bundle's deductions in solving the case, we are

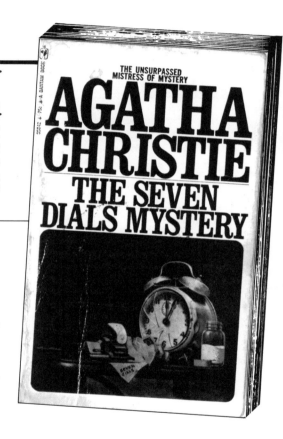

THE UNSURPASSED
MISTRESS OF MYSTERY

AGATHA
CHRISTIE
THE SEVEN
DIALS MYSTERY

"I had followed up *The Murder of Roger Ackroyd* with *The Seven Dials Mystery*. This was a sequel to my earlier book *The Secret of Chimneys*, and was one of what I called 'the light-hearted thriller type.' These were always easy to write, not requiring too much plotting and planning."
—*An Autobiography*

drawn to a variety of conclusions about the night of the theft at Wyvern Abbey. What timing brought Loraine Wade to Wyvern Abbey just in time to rescue the documents? What prompted Sir Oswald's 2 A.M. stroll? What was Countess Radzky doing in the darkened library *before* the fight occurred?

Bundle is determined to keep up her explorations until all of her suspicions are quite unexpectedly answered and so, of course, will we.

LISA MERRILL

A Little Diversion: A Christie Crossword
by Dale G. Copps

DOWN

1 Sgt.
2 Suffixes for drag and buff
3 Sacred Buddhist mountain
4 Cologne, in Cologne
5 Et ___
6 Dome, in Houston
7 *Monthly* and Ocean: Abbr.
8 Born
9 ___ Lanka
10 Rubber or ink
11 Rage
12 Winglike parts
13 Sally or McNally
18 Kind of worm
19 Henrik Ibsen, for one
23 Theater awards
24 "Million-Dollar ___"
25 Tired Titan
26 Often found on the faces of dead men
27 H'a'azard, to h'a Cockney
28 Little one
29 Curtain of a sort
30 ___ nothing
31 Artillery discharge
32 Put into something
34 Nash or Utah
37 Pea
38 *NY Times* critic Richard
39 Yaley
45 Pol
46 Soup green
47 Fashion
48 "Al and ___": Sherman song parody
49 Hart
50 Over, for short
51 Homer's "tradition"
52 Bodkin wound
53 Petrie culture
54 Theme, in music
55 Bowdlerize, sometimes
57 King of Judah
58 Relative pronoun: Fr.
59 Last word in *Ulysses*

ACROSS

1 Cranny partner
5 Actor James & family
10 Girder
14 Lake north of Milan
15 Acid/alcohol compound
16 She's "like a dream come true"
17 He choked his little self
20 Murderers, among others
21 Did a lube job
22 ___ Magnon Man
23 Labor, in Madrid
25 Our Lady of Mystery
29 "I'm ___ boy!": Lou Costello plaint
30 "___ Lay Dying": Faulkner
33 Three Blind Mice, for one
34 Pygmy antelope
35 County, in Stockholm
36 Aids to 45 Across
40 Aux.; subord.
41 Iceland epics
42 Often a motive for murder
43 Quieting sound
44 Preceders of 27 Down
45 The Master
47 Veer
48 Tibetan ox
49 Hurricane
52 Having sawlike notches
56 *All My Sons* or a Christie title
60 Flaherty's "Man of ___"
61 Defunct Asian org.
62 Girlfriend, in Nice
63 Midas metal
64 Offense position, in baseball
65 Piper quarry

(Solution to puzzle on page 161.)

Partners in Crime (1929)

Mrs. Thomas Beresford shifted her position on the divan and looked gloomily out of the window of the flat ...

"I wish," she said, "something would happen."

So begins the title story in this Tommy-and-Tuppence collection, and needless to say Tuppence soon gets her wish. Before too many weeks have elapsed she and her husband find themselves in not one but a whole series of adventures, and amass a stockpile of excitement sufficient to carry them to the beginning of World War II.

The year is 1929. The Beresfords, married six years, have what appears to be everything they need in life — a comfortable apartment, enough money, and each other. Yet something is missing. Life is too settled, too dull. Tuppence, especially, feels stirrings of unease, and finds herself longing for the excitement and danger of their earlier life. "Think of the wild days of peril we went through once!" she exclaims one day. She craves that kind of adventure again.

Enter the Good Fairy, in the person of Mr. Carter, chief of the Secret Service, with which Tommy still has some vague and unexplained ties. What a stroke of luck — Carter just happens to have a difficult assignment that will take the cooperative efforts of two people. It's a bit risky, but as he so engagingly puts it, "I don't think you are the kind who shrinks from risks, are you, Mrs. Tommy?"

Quite the reverse, as he well knows. "Mrs. Tommy" can be downright foolhardy when she gets caught up in a good cause. She is delighted to be caught up in this one.

The stage is set for some play-acting: the Beresfords take over the running of the International Detective Agency, Inc., suspected by His Majesty's government of acting as an information drop for Bolshevik spies. Tommy slips into the role of Theodore Blunt, private detective, with his wife playing Miss Robinson, secretary, Girl Friday, and all-around First Assistant.

They are, says Mr. Carter, to take genuine cases and act in every way like professional private eyes. In this sense they will be devoting their full time to the business. But in addition they are to watch for those telltale blue letters with Russian postmarks, or for any visitor who initiates a conversation by using the code word *sixteen* in the first sentence. At either of these signals they are to communicate with British Intelligence immediately.

Other than that they're on their own. Tuppence is elated at the thought of playing detective. Purpose has come back into her life.

How, exactly, does one go about being a private investigator? Tommy has a novel idea, born of the indolence of their first few days, before clients begin to respond to their advertising. He assembles a library of great mystery literature ("I've read every detective novel that's been published in the last ten years") and begins to assume the roles of the great fictional sleuths. He even collects a few props — a violin, a Turkish slipper, a pipe — the better to resemble the characters he will play.

"I intend," he says, "to try different styles, and compare results."

Tuppence has a few caustic comments to make about this, but before she can get into full swing they are interrupted with the news that their first

Partners in Crime (1929)

real client has arrived. It seems that a very valuable pink pearl has disappeared during a quiet evening at the Laurels, the fashionable estate of the Kingston Bruces at Wimbledon. Who can have pinched it? There were only a few guests, and the usual trusted servants. Of course there is Mr. Rennie, that awful Socialist boyfriend of the daughter of the house, a natural thief if there ever was one, according to Mr. Kingston Bruce ("I'm sure, holding the views that he does, he can have no principles whatever"). Mr. Rennie is a likely candidate, but it is odd, isn't it, that one of the honored guests has been visiting at so many great houses when something of value was stolen? Not that

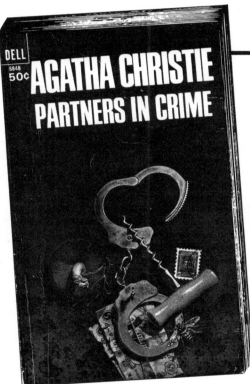

"Each story here was written in the manner of some particular detective of the time.... I remember Thornley Colton, the blind detective — Austin Freeman, of course; Freeman Wills Croft with his wonderful turntables; and inevitably Sherlock Holmes ....some are household words, others have more or less perished in oblivion....*Partners in Crime* featured in it my two young sleuths, Tommy and Tuppence, who had been the principal characters in my second book, *The Secret Adversary*. It was fun to get back to them for a change."
—An Autobiography

she — perish the thought. Still, one must investigate every angle ...

This is a Dr. Thorndike case, says Tommy, likening it to those of a famous contemporary fictional detective. He proceeds to solve it with lightning speed, leaving even his wife in the dark until the last minute.

She soon gets even with him, however, beating him to the punch a time or two in later adventures. Tuppence doesn't stay in the dark long.

New cases arrive almost daily and lead to a series of triumphs and near-escapes, all heavily laced with sarcasm and wit. Tommy and Tuppence can't seem to take anything seriously — certainly not danger. They are engaged in a cleverly devised spoof in which they manage to parody not only all the better-known fictional detectives of the day but themselves as well.

"This is decidedly a Sherlock Holmes case," says Tommy after a Mr. Stavansson, just back from a polar expedition, finds his fiancee, Hermione, is inexplicably missing. There is a definite similarity, he adds, between this situation and the disappearance of Lady Francis Carfax.

True, replies Tuppence, but if he must portray Sherlock he'd better not overdo it. "For God's sake leave that violin alone!" she pleads. Luckily the explorer was a little simple, "or he'd have seen right through you."

She plays Watson, though, as they travel down to Surrey to get to the root of the disappearance. When they do, the laugh is on them. "We have made blithering idiots of ourselves!"

says Tuppence at the conclusion of the case.

So much for Sherlock Holmes. They have better luck with Thornley Colton (Tommy wears an eyeshade, the better to impersonate the "Blind Problemist"), and as McCarty and Riordan they neatly discover who stabbed the Queen of Hearts at a fancy dress party. Then comes a Father Brown problem. ("Are you really a priest?" asks Gilda Glen, her beautiful brown eyes totally bewildered. "Very few of us are what we seem," responds Tommy, gently.)

There are a couple of murders, real enough to the victims, but otherwise rather — uninvolving. No one really *cares*. And the other cases, the missing lady friends, the unbreakable alibis, the smugglers and counterfeiters, and yes, even the spies who eventually do drop in, all seem to be copybook exercises, workbook problems, if you will. Flights of imagination for Christie, and for Tuppence and Tommy too, into the fictional worlds of the other great detectives.

So the play-acting instincts that lead the two to assume the identities of Theodore Blunt and Miss Robinson at the beginning of the book lead them further into role-playing, with different personalities according to the case that presents itself.

Even Poirot doesn't escape their clutches, and more than once Tommy urges Tuppence to "use your little gray cells." In the end it is the great Belgian's methods that lead to the capture of the elusive Number Sixteen and the dramatic rescue of ... well, that would be telling.

NORMA SIEBENHELLER

Murder at the Vicarage (1930)

Over lunch one Wednesday afternoon, Vicar Leonard Clement remarks to his wife, Griselda, and nephew, Dennis, that the world would be a better place if someone — anyone — were to hurry Col. Lucius Protheroe along to his just reward. Protheroe is a churchwarden who particularly enjoys upsetting the vicar.

Dennis warns his uncle that he shall be accused when the old man turns up bathed in blood, and also suggests that the maid, Mary, will give evidence against him.

The vicar is upset because Protheroe has scheduled a meeting with him the next afternoon to discuss the purported theft of a one-pound note from the church collection, bag.

Shortly thereafter Lettice Protheroe, daughter of the colonel, drifts into the vicarage for some talk — these folks do a lot of visiting — and remarks how nice it would be if daddy were dead. After all, he's rather tight with his money, and if he were gone she'd inherit her little pile. She also says that her father has barred the portrait painter who is visiting town, Lawrence Redding, from their estate, Old Hall, because he was discovered painting the lovely Miss Protheroe while she was clad in only her bathing suit. And no swimming pool in sight.

It is a full day at the vicarage — though not as full as some to come — and a number of village biddies drop by to chat with the young vicar's wife and malign a few reputations.

And now, for the first time in fiction, appears Miss Jane Marple, as unlikely a detective as ever fondled a clue. The white-haired spinster knows everything that happens in the tiny hamlet of St. Mary Mead. As she later tells the vicar, her hobby

Agatha Christie
The Murder at the Vicarage

> **"Murder at the Vicarage** was published in 1930, but I cannot remember where, when or how I wrote it, why I came to write it, or even what suggested to me that I should select a new character — Miss Marple — to act as the sleuth in the story."—*An Autobiography*

is "human nature," and she is willing to devote an inordinate amount of time and energy to its study. The main topic of the church ladies this day is Redding and the speculation as to which of the village women sitting for him is doing a bit more that sitting.

Later the vicar wanders down to the painter's studio, which is in a shed at the corner of the vicarage yard, and happens upon Redding and Mrs. Anne Protheroe, the colonel's wife, kissing

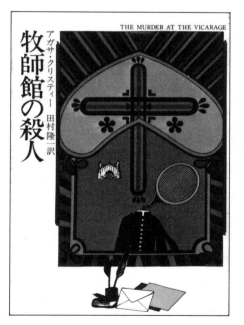

passionately. They disentangle, embarrassed, and the colonel's lady trails the vicar back to his study where she informs him how miserable she is with the old coot and how happy the young artist has made her. Well, this being a 1930 novel, not *that* happy; she tells the vicar that Nothing Else Has Happened. Despite her assurances, the vicar is adamant that she must end her little fling. Perhaps significantly, while telling her to give up the extracurricular sport, the vicar notices for the first time what a fine-looking woman this Mrs. Protheroe is.

Quite by chance, Redding is to be a dinner guest at the vicarage that evening, and after the meal the painter and the vicar retire to the study. Redding anguishes while the vicar reads him the riot act. The only honorable thing to do, says the churchman, is for the painter to leave town before he brings disgrace on the married lady. Redding says he just can't. Love and all that, don't you see. He also notes it would be awfully decent of the old fellow to die and later casually remarks that he is the owner of a pistol, a 25-caliber Mauser.

The next morning, the vicar encounters old Protheroe on the main and only street of St. Mary Mead. Like many people who are losing their hearing, Protheroe assumes everyone else is also, and he reminds the vicar at the top of his lungs about their important appointment that afternoon, adjusting the time to 6:15.

Soon thereafter, Redding drops by the vicarage to tell Vicar Clement that he was right. Redding vows he'll end the affair and leave town the next day.

About 5:30, the vicar gets a call asking him to come to Lower Farm, about two miles away, to

Murder at the Vicarage (1930)

attend to Mr. Abbott, who is dying. He decides he will be unable to keep the 6:15 appointment with Protheroe and tells his servant to ask the colonel to wait.

The call turns out to be a fake — Mr. Abbott is quite well, thank you — and on returning to the vicarage, Clement encounters a distraught Redding, who is leaving quickly. Inside, the vicar finds the late colonel, slumped on the writing desk with his blood dripping onto the rug.

With a victim so universally disliked, Christie has left us a rather large surplus of suspects. In addition to the vicar, the colonel's daughter, his wife and her lover, numerous other people wished the colonel ill.

Inspector Slack of the local constabulary is the first lawman on the case, and he is soon joined by Colonel Melchett. Their first puzzle is a note found beneath the body. Not for nothing was the late colonel at the writing desk. The note is headed 6:20 and reads, "Dear Clement: Sorry I cannot wait any longer but," ending apparently at the writer's death.

The next morning comes the word: Redding has given himself up and confessed to the crime. But Miss Marple, who happens by the vicarage this morning, is skeptical. And while Redding has confessed to killing the colonel about 6:45, Dr. Haydock, the town's physician, tells the police the old man could not have been killed later than 6:35.

When the vicar gets to the police station, he gets a note from Mrs. Protheroe asking him to come quickly. Sure enough, she also confesses to the murder. After bringing both confessors to the scene of the crime, they each shamefacedly admit they were only confessing to protect the other. Redding found his gun near the body when he went to say good-bye to the vicar and assumed his lover had killed her husband. Mrs. Protheroe assumed Redding was telling the truth about the murder and confessed because she felt it was actually her fault.

But if not them, then who?

Daughter Lettice Protheroe? She disliked the old man, hated her stepmother, and was smitten

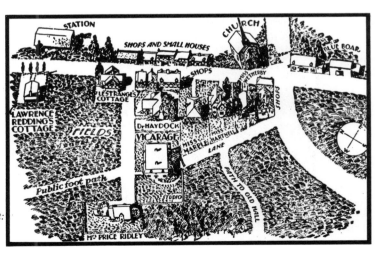

Left: St. Mary Mead, as described in its first appearance in Murder at the Vicarage. *Opposite left: from a 1950 production of* Murder at the Vicarage, *Barbara Mullen as Miss Marple, Jack Lambert as the Rev. Leonard Clement, Andrea Lea as Lettice Protheroe, and Betty Sinclair as Mary. Opposite right: poster of the most recent production.*

by Redding. Did she do it and then try to pin the blame on Mrs. Protheroe?

The mysterious Estelle Lestrange? No one seemed to know why she had moved to town or where she had come from. And the police established that she had visited the colonel on the evening before his demise and had been most secretive in manner.

The poacher, Archer, whom the colonel had sent to jail in his role as town magistrate? Archer had just recently been released.

What about Mary, the Clements' cook and maid? She had been going round with Archer when he wasn't busy poaching or doing time. And Archer's mother, who cleaned Redding's cottage, could have stolen the gun for her. To make matters worse, Mary insists she had heard no gunshot in the house.

The vicar's wife? Griselda admits to the vicar late in the game that she had gone round with Redding in London before she was wed. She is much younger than the vicar, twenty-five to his apparent fifty. If Protheroe had discovered some dark secret of her past, she may have acted to guarantee secrecy.

Dennis, the vicar's nephew? He was head over heels for Lettice, and young men in love have been known to do impetuous things.

More suspects? Dr. Stone passes himself off as an anthropologist digging in a barrow on the Protheroe estate and has an assistant named Miss Cram. He is discovered to be a thief, and has argued publicly with the colonel.

And Hawes, the pathetic curate to the vicar, is the one suspected of taking the one-pound note. Did he also wish to keep the colonel silent?

Just as the police believe they have their murderer, Miss Marple arrives to explain the case to them. She suggests a plan to trap the killer, and of course it succeeds.

JACK MURPHY

FORTURE THEATRE
RUSSELL STREET, COVENT GARDEN

Box Office 01-836 2238

DONALD BODLEY   &   RAY COONEY
for Scotia Theatrical Ltd.   for Ray Cooney Productions Ltd.

present

AGATHA CHRISTIE'S

Murder AT THE VICARAGE

GABRIELLE HAMILTON   MIKE MURRAY

JOHN HART DYKE   JOHN RUDLING

Adapted by
MOIE CHARLES
and
BARBARA TOY

ELIZABETH WADE
BRIDGET McCONNEL
CLIVE HORNBY
WILLIAM GRIEVES
DIANA MARTIN
ROBERT GRAY
DEBBY MARTIN
and
BARBARA ASHCROFT

DIRECTED BY
DONALD BODLEY

Designed by
NEVILLE DEWIS

Evenings 8 pm   Matinees Thursdays 3 pm
Saturdays 5 and 8 pm

'I enjoyed every minute of it.' Lynda Lee-Potter, Daily Mail
'... Dame Agatha, always ingenious and exciting.'
—Harold Hobson, Sunday Times

The Mysterious Mr. Quin
(1930)

In these twelve short stories, a Mr. Satterthwaite observes the drama of human affairs. He is an elfin, elderly, desiccated man who has held himself aloof from the stormy emotions of mankind, especially love and greed, but he has developed his intuition and his ability to know the hearts of others.

Mr. Satterthwaite is intrigued, led, and guided in his thinking by the slim, saturnine Mr. Harley Quin, who "comes and goes," often in a most peculiar and unpredictable manner. Mr. Quin carries with him, the motifs of his origin. In commedia dell'arte, Harlequin, dressed in motley (a suit of many colors or of black and red diamonds), appears to lead people in odd paths. In Mr. Quin's first appearance, the stained glass throws a light on him that makes him appear to be dressed in a rainbow of colors. In other stories, the light shining on him again casts a glow, particularly reddish. When he must stay at an inn, he chooses the Bells and Motley, reflecting the belled cap and varicolored garb of his talisman.

Each of the stories involves a different cast of characters aside from Mr. Satterthwaite and Mr. Quin. Half of the stories are murder mysteries. The others involve disappearances and missing jewels. A favorite theme is the reuniting of old lovers. Most frequently, the stories are triangles complicated by the presence of additional parties.

Mr. Satterthwaite has a soft spot for young women ill-used by fortune, and he is intrigued by little mysteries around them. He wonders why Eleanor Portal dyes her light hair black and sits on the stairs listening and sighing; he enters imaginatively into Gillian's romantic difficulties; his heart is moved by sad Mabelle.

Mr. Quin also can interfere when he deems it necessary. He prevents Naomi Carlton-Smith from leaving the room just before she hears something she needs to know. He sends Mr. Satterthwaite a message by the spiritual medium of the table-tapping alphabet.

Mr. Quin, however, is not the only mysterious personage in the stories. There is the Cavalier in the large hat, and the Weeping Lady with the Silver Ewer.

In "The Coming of Mr. Quin," the men at a country house party, including Mr. Satterthwaite, are discussing the story of Derek Capel, the previous owner of Royston. Everyone is intrigued with the problem of why Derek Capel would shoot himself when he has revealed that he is on the verge of announcing his engagement. He simply left the table, picked up his mail, and retired to his room to do away with himself.

Mr. Quin arrives at the party immediately after midnight, calling to mind the old superstition that if a dark man is the first person to step over a threshold after midnight on New Year's Eve, good luck will come to the house. His car has broken down and he is seeking a temporary asylum. Through his questions, Mr. Quin focuses the attention of the group on the news of the day and unravels the old mystery.

In "The Shadow on the Glass," Greenways House has a stain on a glass — appearing in the likeness of a previous owner, a Cavalier who watched his wife run away with her lover. No matter how often the glass is replaced, the stain reappears, and the window has had to be specially walled off. An unfortunately constituted house party brings together Richard Scott and his lovely bride, Moira Scott, with Mrs. Iris Staverton, who, before the marriage, had gone on an African trip with Scott and his friend Major John Porter. Iris and Richard are thought to have had somewhat too close a relationship, and Iris is heard warning Richard about the results of jealousy. Not long thereafter, two shots are heard and Iris is discovered in the garden holding a pistol and standing over the corpses of Moira and Captain Jimmy Allenson. Fortunately, Mr. Quin has arrived to consult with the host, Mr. Unkerton, about a picture, and he and Mr. Satterthwaite save the day.

In "The Face of Helen," Gillian West is much in need of Mr. Satterthwaite's aid, for she possesses that face. Her friend and aide, Phil Eastern, is disturbed by her growing attachment to the clerk, Mr. Burns. The men's animosity erupts into a fight after the opera where they have heard the new tenor, Yoaschbim. Mr. Eastern recovers enough to give Gillian two wedding presents, a handsome wireless set and an unusual beaker with a glass bubble. He sentimentally asks her to listen to a certain broadcast. What would have happened had he not met Mr. Satterthwaite later at the Arlecchino and had a lengthly conversation about Eastern's various interests?

More questions arise when Mr. Satterthwaite visits an art gallery and buys a painting. Why was the artist, Frank Bristow, moved to paint the dead Harlequin on the floor of the Terrace Room at Charnley? And why is Mr. Quin's face that of the Harlequin looking in the window? Even more, why does the actress, Aspasia Glen, want so much to get that painting for herself? It is understandable that Alix Charnley, the widow of the dead owner of the house, should want the picture, even though reminders of her husband's suicide are so painful. Her life has been blighted.

Mr. Satterthwaite and Mr. Quin attend to all with concern and compassion, rescuing lovers when they can and enjoying the suspense and drama of it all to the hilt.

GAILA PERKINS

"Mr. Quin was a figure who just entered into a story — a catalyst, to me — his mere presence affected human beings. There would be some little fact, some apparently irrelevant phrase, to point him out for what he was: a man shown in a harlequin-colored light that fell on him through a glass window; a sudden appearance or disappearance. Always he stood for the same things: he was a friend of lovers, and connected with death." —*An Autobiography*

Murder at Hazelmoor (1931)

(Alternate title: *The Sittaford Mystery*)

As winter's bitter winds sweep across Devon County's moorland, the villagers of Sittaford gather in the elegant mansion built by Captain Joseph Trevelyan upon his retirement from the navy ten years earlier. They are greeted by the gracious Widow Willett and her lovely daughter Violet, both of whom had recently arrived from South Africa to pass the winter months as tenants of Sittaford House.

After the guests warm up with a spot of tea, it is young Ronnie Garfield who suggests that the night is perfect for a round of table turning. Mr. Rycroft, who considers himself an expert in psychic research, says the idea is super, naturally, while the mysterious Mr. Duke agrees to whatever would amuse Miss Violet. Even Major Burnaby finally gets into the spirit of things, although he'd clearly have preferred his habitual Friday visit to Captain Trevelyan, who has rented a small house, Hazelmoor, in Exhampton for the duration of the Willett's lease on the mansion.

The lights are lowered and the séance begins. It isn't long before the table obliges the delighted guests by answering their questions with a variety of rocks, raps, and jerks. Spirits are high until the table spells out a ghastly message: "T-R-E-V-E-L-Y-A-N D-E-A-D." The guests grow grave. "M-U-R-D-E-R," the table adds as an afterthought.

"Tommyrot," growls the Major, who nevertheless pulls on his boots and overcoat and announces his intention to walk the six miles into Exhampton to check on his old friend, despite the pending blizzard.

Arriving through the blinding snowstorm two and a half hours later, Major Burnaby summons the local constable and a doctor after Trevelyan fails to answer his knocks. Without trying the door, the trio plods around to the back of the house, enters the study through an open window, and immediately stumbles over the body of the wealthy captain. Pronouncing Trevelyan dead of a fractured skull, Dr. Graves gravely indicates the murder weapon lying beside the victim — a green baize tube used as a sandbag to keep drafts from blowing under the door.

Trevelyan's athletic achievements and preoccupation with solving acrostics were as familiar to his neighbors as his fondness for money and his distaste for women. Trevelyan's resentment of his sister's marriage to an invalid and his refusal to permit his faithful servant's bride in the house were common knowledge around the town. Much to everyone's amusement, the captain had even moved his beloved trophies and sporting equipment out of Sittaford House before the Willett women moved in. "Lock things up as you will," he explained, "a woman will always find a way of getting in." The Dartmoor area natives took special delight in Widow Willett's persistent dinner invitations to the captain, which were invariably declined. Couldn't she see that the wealthy bachelor much preferred the company of his old friend Major Burnaby?

Enter Inspector Narracott. Trevelyan's impoverished nephew, James Pearson, is quickly identified as the stranger who had registered at the Three Crowns Inn, disappeared for a few hours, then left on the first train the morning after the murder. Although the Inspector arrests Pearson, he is so unimpressed by the ineffectual lad that he continues searching for a more likely villain.

Since the captain seems to have had no enemies among his neighbors, the Inspector turns his attention to Trevelyan's four heirs. There is the estranged sister who had been refused financial assistance for her demanding, bed-ridden husband. Her reaction to the news of Trevelyan's death is relief that finally she will have the money needed to cure her husband. Then there is James Pearson, and his brother Brian, who is away in Australia—or is he? Finally there is a niece, Sylvia Pearson Dering, wife of a moderately successful author.

Conducting her own investigation into the murder is Miss Emily Trefusis, who is convinced that her clumsy fiancé, James Pearson, is innocent. "He simply couldn't pick up a sandbag and hit an old man on the back of the neck with it. He would make a bosh shot and hit him in the wrong place if he did," she says of her beloved.

Aided by the easily flattered and ambitious reporter Charles Enderby, Emily zeros in on the newcomers to the Dartmoor area. Who is Mr. Duke, the man who "leads a blameless life," and what branch of criminology did he indulge in? Who are the Willetts, why are they so nervous, and who was Violet meeting at midnight on the barren moor?

Charmed by Emily's hazel eyes and liquid voice, Enderby agrees to spend the night shivering in the bushes outside Sittaford House to learn the answer. Much to everyone's surprise, he flushes out Brian Pearson, the nephew believed to be in Australia. What is he doing in England, and what is his connection with the Willetts?

The Dartmoor natives have never had too much to gossip about. A murder in the village is disgraceful enough, but the way Emily keeps running from house to house asking questions and charming the men (even though she's engaged to the murder suspect), well, it's all too scandalous! On top of that, there's the matter of the convict who escaped from the nearby prison

right after Trevelyan was murdered.

While the Inspector and Emily follow each other around the countryside interviewing the same people over and over, the original group returns to Sittaford House for another séance, hoping to learn the true identity of the murderer. The lights are lowered, apprehension fills the air. A sharp rap breaks the spell, and the murder at Hazelmoor is solved.

ANITA McALLISTER

Peril at End House (1932)

When we discover Hercule Poirot holidaying blissfully at the Hotel Majestic near the idyllic village of St. Loo on the Cornish Riviera, we also know that evil impends. And indeed it does, in the form of a spent bullet the dapper Belgian sleuth comes across and picks up in the hotel garden, just before tea.

Nor are we particularly surprised when Nick Buckley, a frothy, comely girl despite her name, rounds the corner, a bullet hole in her floppy sun hat.

Thus does Agatha Christie quickly get off the mark in this early mystery, set not too long after World War I. Poirot is not alone in resort country. He has Hastings with him, not only as a companion but as foil. As the detective puts it repeatedly, Hastings is so Britishly decent and dumb that when he suggests a direction of inquiry, Poirot tends to do exactly the opposite to get on the correct track.

Nick is quick to blurt that this is not the first time her pretty life has been imperiled recently. No indeed. Only the other day the brakes failed on her car and, but for turning back home for a forgotten item (she's a scatterbrain) and her crash into a nearby hedge, she might have done a serious number on the St. Loo Town Hall itself as she sped downhill toward it.

And then there was the remarkable affair of the loosened boulder. Nick's country home, End House, a mere grapefruit's throw from the Majestic, overlooks what is probably the English Channel, although it could equally be the Irish Sea. At any rate, Nick had descended her path to the beach for a bath when the boulder came crashing down the hill and narrowly missed her. Hast-

ings fingers a man as the probable boulder dislodger. Poirot points out a lot can be done by a woman with leverage. Too true, too true.

And what about the painting? Nick sleeps in a large bed, over the headboard of which hangs a large oil painting. One night, the wire holding the painting broke and down it crashed. It might have killed her, had the timing been better, Poirot deduced. But a banging door had awakened her and she had left her bed moments earlier. She has since had the wire replaced, and the detective cannot find the old one to determine whether it was cut or just tired.

Other characters crowd the stage, lending a note of pretty confusion. Nick's lunch and drink companions: Frederica Rice, pale, wan, but beautiful; Jim Lazarus, apparently heir to an art dealer's fortune; George Challenger, a bluff, heart-of-oak commander in the Royal Navy, who seems to lust in an ineffectual way for Nick; the Crofts, a semimysterious but friendly Australian couple who have rented the lodge at End House; the dim-witted (but is he?) gardener and his possibly evil ten-year-old son; Ellen, the maid who suspects something is up and whose knowledge of a secret compartment in the house is noted by Poirot; Charles Vyse, lawyer in town, Nick's cousin; and another cousin of Nick's, Maggie Buckley, the simple, straightforward daughter of a Yorkshire parson.

Poirot is at the end of his considerable wits. Early on, he explains patiently to the dense but decent Hastings that the task facing him here is considerably more difficult than the run of cases. Because, he says, until a murderer commits his murder, his footprints are faint, if they exist at all.

After the fact, though, it is a piece of cake to the skilled detective because the killer always signs his work, even as does the artist. And to carry that parallel further, the amateurs sign their work in the largest hands.

No, his job in the forepart of the book is simply to protect Nick Buckley until he can single out the would-be murderer. And it is to this end that he has Nick invite her cousin Maggie down for a visit, which leads to Maggie's untimely demise. She is killed, it seems, through mistaken identity. She goes from the lawn to End House to fetch a coat because it is chilly. Nick goes with her, but they cannot find Maggie's coat. She borrows Nick's flaming red Chinese silk shawl. The killer thinks Maggie is Nick — and bang, bang, bang.

Poirot's dilemma deepens, as does his gloom. He has failed. Mon Dieu! He strikes his forehead in a gesture of Gallic frustration. Where have I gone wrong? He ponders into the night, indeed even into the dawn. Hastings keeps waking up— he can sleep anytime, anywhere— to find the detective compiling and refining lists of suspects (everybody around) and motives (the usual).

How can greed play a part, he wonders, when Nick is obviously out of pocket and saddled with the heavily mortgaged End House?

Is it simple love or the old triangle? Apparently not.

Who would benefit from Nick's death? Freddie Rice, to whom Nick leaves everything in a hasty will made (but not received by her solicitor) just before Nick has her appendix out? But is there much to inherit?

"*Peril at End House* was another of my books which left so little impression on my mind that I cannot even remember writing it." —*An Autobiography*

Yes, by jingo, quite a bit, Poirot discovers. Because our girl has been secretly engaged to Mad Michael Seton, the now-dead round-the-world flier! And heir to the fortune of the second-richest man in all England! And Seton has willed it all to Magdala Buckley, which is Nick's real first name. Nick is just a nickname.

Good grief! This puts another color on the matter!

So Poirot stuffs Nick into a nursing home where she will be guarded. No visitors, no outside food to be eaten, nothing without the detective's permission. She will be safe, no? No! Somebody tries to poison her with a chocolate full of cocaine, and, clever devil, from a box bearing Hercule Poirot's personally autographed calling card.

Well, you may be certain the detective now is properly baffled, but not for long. In a masterful session of sifting tiny clues and further refining his list of suspects, plus welcome help from old cronies in Scotland Yard, the malefactor is identified.

RUSS KANE

THE CRUDER METHODS
Knives, Guns, and a Concerto for Blunt Instruments
by Dick Riley

Quick — what do an ancient grain mill, a bronze figure of Venus, and a marble paperweight have in common? How about a kitchen skewer, a nylon stocking, part of a musical instrument, and a chessboard? Or a block of white marble, a fireplace poker, stilettos, surgical knives, and the ever-reliable revolver?

Even the most casual of Christie fans can guess the answer. All the above were used at one time or another by Dame Agatha to dispatch her victims.

However delicate Agatha Christie's sensibilities, however Victorian her social attitudes, she never lacked for invention in the methods of murder. Poison, traditionally a lady's weapon, certainly got its due from her. But she didn't neglect the equally efficient, if a trifle cruder, methods.

Any listing of knives and other sharp instruments in the Christie cutlery drawer must include the dagger that ended the days of the execrable Ratchett, the scoundrel who kidnapped little Daisy Armstrong and caused the deaths of the child and members of her family and household. Ratchett has escaped the law's punishment, but justice was served by a blade as Ratchett was the victim in *Murder on the Orient Express*.

When Poirot and a companion discover the body of Louise Bourget under her bed in her cabin on the *Karnak* in *Death on the Nile*, there seems to be little doubt as to the cause of her demise. "Stabbed to the heart. Death pretty well instantaneous, I should imagine," says Race.

It is left to Dr. Bessner to pinpoint the murder weapon. "Not a common table knife," he says. "It was something very sharp, very thin, very del-

icate." He brings out one of his own surgical knives, saying, "It was something like that."

He denies, however, that any of his knives are missing. Dare we believe him?

A gleaming stiletto with a jeweled head and, need we mention, a very sharp point, ended the life of Mr. Shaitana in *Cards on the Table*; either a razor or an extremely sharp knife severed the jugular vein of Mr. Lee in *Murder for Christmas*; a hatchet came in handy for the murderer in *Funerals Are Fatal*; and poor Agnes, stunned first by a blow to the head, succumbed to a kitchen skewer thrust into the base of her skull in *The Moving Finger*.

We are told that firearms are difficult to obtain in the British Isles, at least according to criminologists who compare the rate of death by gunshot wound in the United States and in England.

This may be true, but one certainly wouldn't know it from Agatha Christie's books. Ask, for instance, Philip Lombard, Dr. Morley, Michael Gorman, Richard Warwick, Maggie Buckley, Salome Otterbourne, or Lucius Protheroe, among others.

All met their end through gunfire.

Lombard was shot through the heart in *Ten Little Indians*; Dr. Morley, a dentist in *The Patriotic Murders*, perished as the result of a bullet from a pistol "of foreign make," which entered just below his right temple; Michael Gorman, the doorman in *At Bertram's Hotel*, and Richard Warwick, the crippled and frustrated big-game hunter of the play *The Unexpected Guest*, were shot to death; a small caliber Mauser served to dispatch Maggie Buckley and confirmed that there was indeed *Peril at End House*; *Death on the Nile* came

for Salome Otterbourne at the wrong end of a colt revolver; and we saw the Mauser again (there's nothing like that Teutonic craftsmanship) in *Murder at the Vicarage*. This time it was equipped with a silencer and aimed at poor Lucius Protheroe—if one can muster any sympathy for that almost universally disliked magistrate.

A pearl-handled .22, highly decorated, plays an important part in *Death on the Nile*, along with the Colt that did in Maggie Buckley. As Poirot says of that ornamental gun: "It is an *article de luxe*, a very feminine production, but it is none the less a lethal weapon."

So much for the gun and the knife. But let us not neglect death by strangulation, and a wide choice of items not usually regarded as weapons. Chief among these must be the various items of feminine apparel that come so easily to hand when the murderous mood strikes. There is the nylon stocking that disposes of Gladys in *Pocket Full of Rye*; Mrs. Bland's scarf, which proves her own undoing in *The Clocks*; a silk belt does in Betty Barnard in *The A.B.C. Murders*, while a raincoat belt serves for Mrs. Boyd as she sits listening to the radio in "Three Blind Mice."

One thing must be said about articles of women's clothing as murder weapons—they are certainly accessible. The murderer had to look no farther than the end of his arms for the strong

hands that strangled the victim in *What Mrs. McGillicuddy Saw!*, but the murder weapon in "The Bird with the Broken Wing," one of the stories in *The Mysterious Mr. Quin*, was considerably more bizarre.

"That rope that was round her neck wasn't the rope she was strangled with," says Inspector Winkfield, clearing up some points about the death, first taken to be suicide, of Maybelle Annesley. "It was something much thinner that did the job, something more like a wire."

Though the police are baffled, Mr. Satterthwaite knows an out-of-tune musical instrument when he hears one—which leads to the discovery that the murder weapon was a ukelele string.

Causes of death in Christie's books are almost infinitely various: falls from cliffs play a role in *The Boomerang Clue* and *Death Comes As the End*; it is a poison dart from a blowgun that gives us the body in *Death in the Air*; and in a miracle of modern electrocution, the white bishop of a particular chess set is connected to a "hot" chessboard and in turn to an electrical device in a flat below in *The Big Four*.

THE CRUDER METHODS

But Christie never forgot the good old reliable blunt instrument. Sports were a source for some of them: Costello, in *Spider's Web*, perished as the result of being struck over the head with a golf club; Lady Camilla in *Towards Zero* was the victim of a somewhat modified tennis racquet — into its handle had been screwed the heavy left-hand knob of an old-fashioned fireplace fender. (She died of a backhand to the skull.)

Of course, the fireplace-fender–tennis-racquet combination might also come under the category of furniture, another part of the Christie armory. A marble paperweight slipped into a woolen sock (*Hickory, Dickory, Death*), a fireplace poker (*Ordeal by Innocence*), and a green baize sandbag tube, used along doorsills to keep out drafts (*Murder at Hazelmoor*) fit into this category.

Looking out the window can be dangerous in a Christie book. Louise Leidner certainly found it so in *Murder in Mesopotamia*. When she looked out the window of her bedroom in the archaeologists' compound in Iraq, she saw descending on her a cuern, an ancient grain mill. Not that being outside is much better — a heavy granite boulder

had much the same effect on Elizabeth Temple in *Nemesis*.

The cosh, sometimes known as a blackjack in America, also had its place in the Christie arsenal. "Well and truly coshed," says Dr. Corrigan of Father Gorman, the deceased in *The Pale Horse*. "First blow probably killed him, but whoever it was made sure. Quite a nasty business."

But perhaps the most charming of Dame Agatha's blunt instruments is that which dispatched Sir James Dwighton in "The Love Detectives," a short story in which lovers play an important role, and which is included in *The Mousetrap* collection. Sir James, sitting at his writing table in the library of his estate, Alderway, was struck from behind.

> The weapon lay on the floor — a bronze figure about two feet high, the base of it stained and wet. Mr. Satterthwaite bent over it curiously.
>
> "A Venus," he said softly. "So he was struck down by a Venus."
>
> He found food for poetic meditation in the thought.

A MACABRE TEA PARTY

by Joanna Milton (with compliments to Lewis Carroll)

There was a table set out under a tree in front of the house, and Miss Marple and M. Poirot were having tea at it: Harley Quin was sitting between them, fast asleep, and the other two were using him as a cushion, resting their elbows on him, and talking over his head. "Very uncomfortable for the poor fellow," thought Alice, "only, as he's asleep, I suppose he doesn't mind."

The table was a large one, but the three were all crowded together at one corner of it. "No room! No room!" they cried out when they saw Alice coming. "There's *plenty* of room!" said Alice indignantly, and she sat down in a large armchair at one end of the table.

"Have some Devonshire cream," Poirot said in an encouraging tone.

Alice looked all around the table, but there was nothing on it but tea. "I don't see any Devonshire cream," she remarked.

"There isn't any," said Poirot, wiping a drop of tea from his impeccable black mustache.

"Then it wasn't very civil of you to offer it," said Alice angrily.

"It wasn't very civil of you to sit down without being invited," said Hercule Poirot.

"I didn't know it was *your* table," said Alice. "It's laid for a great many more than three."

"Don't you have a second cousin named Mary Bain," said Miss Marple, "who once lived in St. Mary Mead? Rumored to have eloped with Arthur Babcock after his wife's rather untimely death?" The elderly, white-haired lady had been looking at Alice for some time with great curiosity, and this was her first speech.

"You should learn not to ask personal questions," said Alice with some severity. "It's very rude."

Miss Marple opened her china blue eyes very wide on hearing this, but all she said was, "Why is a first impression like a knitting needle?"

Come, we shall have some fun now! thought Alice. I'm glad they've begun asking riddles. "I believe I can guess that," she added aloud.

"Do you mean that you think you can solve the mystery?" said Poirot.

"Exactly so," said Alice.

"Then you should say what you mean," Hercule Poirot went on, stooping under the table to buff the shine on his smart patent leather shoes.

"I do," Alice hastily replied; "at least — at least I

A MACABRE TEA PARTY

mean what I say. That's the same thing, you know."

"Not the same thing a bit!" said Poirot. "Why, you might just as well say that a murder committed by the Queen of England is the same thing as two spoons and a teapot stolen by a serving wench!"

"You might just as well say," added Jane Marple, "that your second cousin Mary Bain of St. Mary Mead never eloped with Mr. Babcock at all, when as a matter of fact rumor has it *you sent her trunk on to her at Beldover!*"

"You might just as well say," added Mr. Quin, who seemed to be talking in his sleep, "that, 'those who tell a faulty story don't want to be believed,' eh, young lady?"

"It *is* the same thing with you," said Poirot, and here the conversation dropped, and the party sat silent for a moment, while Alice thought over all she could remember about first impressions and knitting needles, which wasn't much.

"Mr. Quin is asleep again," said Poirot, and he poured a little hot tea upon the young man's nose.

Harley Quin shook his head dreamily and said, without opening his eyes, "Of course, of course, just what I was going to remark myself."

"Have you solved the mystery yet?" Miss Marple said, turning to Alice again.

"No, I give it up," Alice replied. "What's the answer?"

"Now, you remind me of old Mrs. Bantry from the village," said Miss Marple musingly. "Always ready to give up on a puzzle before she's made a good stab at the solution."

"Beware of those too willing to give up on the answers," said Mr. Quin sleepily, from his position half in, half out of the teapot, "for they may have answers they don't want to give up!"

"Yes," said Miss Marple, contemplating, "there really is no limit to the depravity of the human character. Dear me," she added, picking up her binoculars, "isn't that Colonel Armbruster

running off there in the distance?" She squinted into the glasses intently, then passed them over to Alice.

"Where? I don't see anyone," said Alice, staring into the binoculars with a puzzled expression on her face.

"Of course you don't," said Poirot. "Colonel Armbruster's dead." Here Poirot and Miss Marple exchanged a meaningful look, which Alice barely caught as she lowered the glasses onto the tea table.

"See here," the girl exclaimed crossly, "you two are trying to blame me for some crime I haven't yet committed — I mean, that I don't *intend* to commit!"

"How do you know you don't?" asked Miss Marple gently. "You *are* Mary Bain's second cousin, and human nature running true to form —"

"Perhaps we should ask Mr. Quin to sing a song for us," Poirot interrupted delicately, setting his teacup in his saucer with a flourish, "and then Miss Marple can continue her review of your relatives and their crimes when he's finished."

Mr. Quin opened his wide, dreamy eyes and began to sing:

Twinkle, twinkle, little tot!
How I wonder who you've shot!

"You know the song, perhaps?" he asked Alice.

"I've heard something like it," said Alice.

"It goes on, you know," Mr. Quin continued, "in this way:

Underneath your childish gabbing,
You plan a robbery, or a stabbing —
Twinkle, twinkle …

Here Mr. Quin shook himself, and began singing in his sleep "Twinkle, twinkle, twinkle, twinkle … " and went on so long they had to pinch him to make him stop.

"Well, I'd hardly finished my first case," said

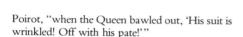

Poirot, "when the Queen bawled out, 'His suit is wrinkled! Off with his pate!'"

"How dreadfully savage!" exclaimed Alice.

"And ever since then," Poirot went on mournfully, "I can't solve a single mystery unless my suit's been pressed. And my shoes shined too!"

A bright idea came into Alice's head. "Is that why you can't answer Miss Marple's riddle?" she said. "Because your suit isn't pressed?"

"Yes, I'm afraid so," said Poirot with a sigh. "It's so hard to get good help these days, and since Georges died my crime-solving quotient has gone down considerably."

"Because of the suit," Miss Marple put in wisely.

"Why don't you get an iron and an ironing board," suggested Alice, "and press it yourself?"

"Suppose we change the subject," Poirot interrupted, yawning, "I'm getting tired of this. I vote the young lady tell us a story."

"I'm afraid I don't know one," said Alice, rather alarmed at the proposal.

"Then Mr. Quin shall!" they both cried. "Wake up, Mr. Quin!" And they pinched him on both sides at once.

Harley Quin slowly opened his eyes. "I wasn't asleep, I was meditating," he said. "I heard every word you two were saying."

"Tell us a story!" said Jane Marple.

"Yes, please do!" pleaded Alice.

"And be quick about it," added Poirot, "or you'll be asleep before it's done."

"Once upon a time there were three little children," Mr. Quin began in a great hurry, "and their names were Georgie, Susan, and Jimmy, and they lived on a farm—"

"What did they live on?" said Alice, who always took a great interest in questions of eating and drinking.

Mr. Quin considered a moment before answering, "They didn't live on much, you see, and that was the problem: a bit of treacle, a cup of tea once in a while—"

"They couldn't have lived on just that, you know," Alice gently remarked, "They'd have been ill."

"So they were," said Mr. Quin. "*Very* ill. In fact, it wasn't too long before one of the children —Georgie, I believe it was—died from malnutrition and criminal neglect."

"Take some more tea," said Miss Marple to Alice, very earnestly.

"I've had nothing yet," Alice replied in an offended tone, "so I can't take more."

"You mean you can't take *less*," said Poirot, "it's very easy to take more than nothing."

"Nobody asked *your* opinion," said Alice.

"Who's making personal remarks now!" Miss Marple asked triumphantly, picking up her knitting and whipping off a row at a very fast clip.

Alice did not quite know what to say to this; so she helped herself to some tea, and then turned to Mr. Quin and asked: "What happened to the other two children? Susan and Jim?"

Mr. Quin again took a minute or two to think about it, then answered in his dreamy voice, "We thought perhaps *you* could tell us."

"What!—" Alice was beginning very angrily,

A MACABRE TEA PARTY

but Miss Marple and Poirot went "Sh! Sh!" and Mr. Quin sulkily remarked, "If you can't be civil you'd better finish the story for yourself."

"No, please go on," Alice said very humbly. "I won't interrupt again. I can't tell you what happened to Susan and Jimmy — how should I know?"

"How, indeed," said Mr. Quin meaningfully. "Two murders have already been committed, and Susan and Jimmy may well have the answers, as well as the meaning of "Three Blind Mice," the only evidence we've got on the case!" he finished enthusiastically.

"Three blind mice?" said Alice, quite forgetting her promise to keep quiet.

"Might as well confess, dear," said Miss Marple, knitting happily. "Criminal tendencies run in the family. As my great-uncle Louis used to say, 'when in doubt check the family tree—'"

"I want a clean cup," interrupted Poirot, "let's all move one place on."

He moved on as he spoke and Mr. Quin followed him; Miss Marple moved into Mr. Quin's place and Alice rather unwillingly took the place of Miss Marple. Poirot was the only one who got any advantage from the change; and Alice was a good deal worse off than before, as Miss Marple had just upset the milk jug onto her plate with one of the knitting needles.

Alice did not wish to offend Mr. Quin again so she began very cautiously: "But I don't understand. Why would Susan and Jimmy know about the murders? And what have they to do with three blind mice?"

"If you would just calm down and look at the facts," remarked Poirot primly, "you would see what they have to do with it."

"Were Georgie, Susan, and Jimmy the three blind mice?" said Alice to Mr. Quin, not choosing to notice Poirot's last remark.

"Of course they were," said Mr. Quin. "Blinder."

This answer so confused poor Alice that she let Mr. Quin go on for some time without interrupting him.

"The whole thing came to a boil, you see," said Mr. Quin, yawning and rubbing his eyes, for he was getting very tired, "at Monkswell Manor, when one of the mice—I mean, children—tried to complete the avenging of his brother's death. He tried all methods of murder, everything that begins with an *S* —"

"Why with an *S*?" said Alice.

"Why not?" said Miss Marple.

Alice was silent.

Mr. Quin had closed his eyes by this time, and was going off into a doze, but on being pinched by Poirot, he woke up again with a little shriek and went on. "That begins with an *S*, such as stabbing, and shooting, and strangulation, and strychnine poisoning — now, why didn't he try that, Miss Marple?" said Mr. Quin, turning to the elderly knitting woman with a puzzled frown, "So much neater than a revolver, to say nothing of that awful *raincoat belt* —"

"People of that profession don't normally carry strychnine," said Miss Marple, clacking her knitting needles, "so I suppose he thought he'd be suspected."

"Who?" said Alice, by this time very much confused. "What profession? I can't follow the story!" she protested crossly.

"Then you shouldn't listen," said Poirot, picking a small piece of lint from his clean, albeit not very well-pressed, brown tweed suit.

This bit of rudeness was more than Alice could bear; she got up in great disgust and walked off; Mr. Quin fell asleep instantly, and neither of the others took the least notice of her going, though she looked back once or twice, half hoping they would call after her.

The last time she saw them, Miss Marple was trying to teach Poirot how to knit, and the mustached detective was failing miserably.

The Tuesday Club Murders (1932)

(Alternate title: *The Thirteen Problems*)

In this collection of related episodes, Miss Marple solves one case of smuggling, one case of poltergeists, and ten cases of murder; in addition, she prevents a respectable young girl from entering into a life of crime for the sake of revenge. And these remarkable feats are all done in two evenings, as Miss Marple sits knitting by the fire in her home in St. Mary Mead.

Over the years Miss Marple has learned to keep her eyes open, spending her time making observations on such mundane matters as the fact that gardeners don't work on Whit Monday, the shape of digitalin leaves, and the litmus paper carried by nurses. "People are mostly the same everywhere," Miss Marple remarks at one point, and her observations on human nature in St. Mary Mead have given her an amazing source of lore for solving heinous and sinister crimes anywhere in the world.

Consider, for example, the case of the "Grove of Astarte." A well-to-do English lord invites some friends to his country place for the weekend. He shows them around the estate, pausing at a strange grove of trees. All the guests feel a particular eeriness upon entering the grove, which was a place of pagan worship in the time of the Phoenicians.

In the evening, however, madcap Diana Ashley dresses herself as the goddess Astarte and goes out to the grove. Everyone is delighted with her flamboyance and originality, until she appears to go into a trance. One of the men comes too close to her and she strikes him dead with a wave of her hand. Diana then faints and is carried back to the house. Later, another guest returns to the grove to investigate the death of his friend and he

is found with a knife wound in his shoulder. The police cannot explain these events, but Miss Marple is reminded of something and consequently the goddess Astarte murder is solved.

In the case of Simon Clode and Eurydice Spragg, Mrs. Spragg, a medium, has promised to put Mr. Clode in touch with his deceased granddaughter. Mr. Clode's nieces and nephews and everyone around him realize that Mrs. Spragg is a fraud, but Mr. Clode persists in believing in her, to the point of making her the major beneficiary of his will. Mr. Clode writes out the will in front of his lawyer and hands it to him. On the way out of the house, the lawyer stops to have tea with Mr. Clode's niece, and as he puts on his coat to leave, he finds Mrs. Spragg on her knees beside the chair where his coat has lain. She appears to be straightening the chair's chintz cover. A few days later, Mrs. Spragg comes to see the lawyer, who unthinkingly leaves her alone in his office with the will for a few minutes.

Two months later, when the will is opened, it turns out to be a blank piece of paper, though the lawyer saw Mr. Clode writing it. Mrs. Spragg gets nothing and the estate goes entirely to Mr. Clode's nephew. How did this happen, since the only persons who had an opportunity to tamper with the will were the beneficiaries?

Miss Marple chuckles at hearing this story. It reminds her of naughty little Tommy Symonds, who bemused his Sunday-school teacher with the question, "Teacher, do you say yolk of eggs is white or yolk of eggs are white?" When the teacher replies that one says yolk of eggs is white and yolks of egg are white, Tommy says, "Well, I should say that yolk of egg is yellow!"

The Tuesday Club Murders (1932)

This kind of low humor impresses no one, but Miss Marple uses it to illustrate a technical kind of point that, naturally, leads to solving the case.

Another day Miss Marple is summoned to visit her niece in a nearby village. The niece has just been widowed, and people are talking because they say she murdered her husband. It seems that the marriage had not been happy. One day, the niece bought some arsenic, ostensibly to do herself in. That night her husband died in great agony, muttering something about a "heap of fish." An autopsy showed no trace of arsenic poisoning, but neither did it show any other cause for death. The doctor suggests the possibility of a strong vegetable alkaloid poison, which would be very difficult to detect.

Miss Marple considers the suspects. Aside from her niece, there are the cook, the maid, the husband's father, who lives in the house, and the father's nurse. The niece alone seems to have a motive—unless the husband committed suicide.

Walking down the street the next day, Miss Marple sees a fresh haddock in a shop window. Eureka! The case is solved. From seeing the haddock, and in particular the marks upon its gills, Miss Marple becomes quite clear on the whole nasty business of the heap-of-fish murder.

And how does Miss Marple feel about her amazing ability to solve crimes while she sits knitting? After solving three murders and two extortion schemes, she says, in her modest fashion, "It is true, of course, that I have lived what is called a very uneventful life, but I have had a lot of experiences in solving different little problems that have arisen." She drops a stitch, then goes on to solve another seven murders.

ROBERT SMITHER

The Hound of Death (1933)

To put it bluntly, these are not really murder mystery stories. They are something else entirely —bizarre fantasies, ghost stories, haunted house tales, stories of the macabre and the occult.

The most famous story in this collection is "Witness for the Prosecution" (reviewed elsewhere in this book). In fact "Witness" and five other of the stories from this 1933 collection were later regrouped into a (1948) collection with "Witness" as the title story.

These are stories that begin with sentences like: "Macfarlane had often noticed that his friend, Dickie Carpenter, had a strange aversion to gypsies," or "Silas Hamer heard it first on a wintry night in February."

Premonitions and second sight are the predominant talents of our protagonists though a few of the characters are bluffers and deceivers, using the props of the psychic world with dry-eyed calculation.

In "Wireless" for example, a not-so-nice trick is played on old Aunt Mary Harter who has a "certain cardiac weakness." Her nephew, Charles Ridgeway, is concerned. He is reassured by the doctor that his aunt could live for years but that "a shock or over-exertion might carry her off like that!" Shortly after this conversation, while concerned Charles is out to a bridge game, Mrs. Harter is cuddled up for the evening program on the wireless. Suddenly the program is interrupted by a familiar male voice saying, "Mary — can you hear me, Mary? It is Patrick speaking...I am coming for you soon. You will be ready, won't you Mary?" Patrick, of course, is Mary's dead husband. A few days later he repeats his promise and Mary sends for her will. And finally the ghostly

Patrick gets specific in his wireless message: he is coming for her on Friday at precisely half-past nine.

Before we know it, it is Friday at half past nine and suddenly there is a "fumbling at the front door" and poor Mary is quite appropriately terrified. Something slips from her fingers "into the grate" as she slumps to the floor, dead.

But that's not really the end of the story. Concerned Charlie, who has spent his time either playing bridge or fussing with the wireless, has occasion to be even more concerned and ends the story feeling as though Somebody (with a capital S) "must be laughing..."

There are other stories in this collection in which psychic phenomena, mysticism and sorcery are used most dishonestly (even murderously) by imposters. But in most of the stories these phenomena hold their own in the world of the bizarre.

The title story "The Hound of Death" is about a nun who once called down the lightning to blast away some impious Huns during W.W.I, and the whole convent blew up leaving only two walls. On one of the walls was left a black powder mark that was the exact shape of a great hound — The Hound of Death.

The nun turns out to be Sister Marie Angelique, still kicking and pursued, not only by our benevolent but curious protagonist, but by the sinister young Dr. Rose. The poor nun explains everything she knows to the doctor while she is in a trance. What she knows is that "He Who Was Guardian of the Crystal" revealed the "Sixth Sign to the People too soon." Evidently the Sixth Sign concerns power and destruction, and the one who

The Hound of Death (1933)

calls it forth must remember *not* to close the Circle. Oops. Too late. Dr. Rose finally gets the secret of the Sixth Sign but forgets not to close the Circle. After the debris of his cottage is washed to the beach it all piles up in a fantastic mass which "from a distance looks like a great hound."

"The Strange Case of Sir Andrew Carmichael" is, in fact, very strange. (Agatha wasn't kidding when she chose that adjective.) Sir Arthur, soon to be married to the lovely Miss Paterson, goes to bed one night and wakes up the next morning with a personality resembling a . . . well, to give you a hint, he will only drink milk from a saucer on the table. He laps it with his tongue, but not before he stretchs and yawns. And when he isn't drinking from a saucer, he is sitting on the window sill watching everything from under immovable lids.

Then there's the cat. Oh, it is not really a cat, but the ghost of one that yowls viciously outside the bedroom of Arthur's very possessive mother. Arthur's mother should have kept her hands off that ancient and curious work on "the possibilities of the metamorphosis of human beings into animals!"

In "The Last Seance" poor, delicate Madame Simone Daubreuil is ill from the mental, emotional and physical strain of being the most wonderful medium in Paris. She is in no shape to face the session with Madame Exe, the grieving mother dressed in the heavy black of French mourning. But Simone has promised to work the miracle one last time — calling forth not only the spirit of the child Amelie, but the flesh and blood. It is explained to Madame Exe again that she must not try to touch the materialization of her little Amelie lest she place the medium, Simone, in gravest danger. But why should Madame Exe care about the medium if this is to be the very last seance anyway? Hint: the ending to this story is not upbeat.

"The Lamp" is a story of a house haunted by the sobbing ghost of a boy who had starved to death there all alone. And then little Geoffrey and his family move into the haunted house despite the warnings of local residents. They hear the strange, forlorn sobbing of the little ghost . . . but so what? And when little Geoff wants to know if he can play with the "little boy" in the attic, his grandfather says sure, why not. (You'd think little Geoff would wonder why there's a little boy living in his family's attic, but he doesn't.) Needless to say, little Geoff falls ill and eventually gets to play with his little friend in the great attic in the sky.

This volume is the perfect gift for your palm reader or for someone planning to spend a stormy winter's night on a lonely moor with the gypsies.

PAM McALLISTER

Thirteen at Dinner (1933)

(Alternate title: *Lord Edgware Dies*)

George Alfred St. Vincent March, fourth Baron Edgware, is found in the library of his London home by a housemaid — dead of a very precise stab wound in the back of the neck. Although Hercule Poirot considered this case one of his failures, it is he alone who manages to untangle the web of possible suspects and uncover the truth of Lord Edgware's death.

The confusion by no means results from a lack of clues, or of people with good reason to have done Lord Edgware in. As a matter of fact, things in this case always seem very obvious, so obvious that Poirot's analytic mind is disturbed.

> "But frankly, the case as you present it, re-volts the intelligence .... Here is a young woman who wishes, you say, to get rid of her husband. That point I do not dispute. She told me so frankly. Eh bien, how does she set about it? She repeats several times in the loud clear voice before witnesses that she is think-ing of killing him. She then goes away. What do you call that, my good friend? Has it even the common sense?"

The woman in question is the American actress Jane Wilkinson, Lord Edgware's estranged sec-ond wife. Poirot first meets her shortly before the murder, when she attempts to enlist his aid in convincing Lord Edgware to divorce her so that she can marry the Duke of Merton. Poirot's mis-sion is only to visit and talk with Lord Edgware, but Jane Wilkinson proclaims over and over how she wishes her husband were dead. "Of course if we were only in Chicago I could get him bumped off quite easily, but you don't seem to run to gunmen over here," she tells Poiret. And she is

identified by two witnesses as having been to see her husband the night of his murder.

But wait, Jane Wilkinson is also identified as having been at a formal dinner party at the house of Sir Montague Corner that same night. Some-one failed to show at the last minute, so an un-lucky thirteen were seated at the table; not only was Jane Wilkinson among those thirteen, but she was not out of the company except for the few minutes her meal was interrupted by a phone call. And the butler was with her for the length of that call.

If Jane Wilkinson could not be two places at once, then who did stab Lord Edgware? Some-one who looked enough like Jane to fool not only the butler, who had never actually met her before, but also Miss Carroll, Lord Edgeware's secretary. Miss Carroll, "neatness and precision per-sonified," heard Jane Wilkinson speak to the but-ler, watched her walk along the hall, and saw her on the phone through the open library door. But Poirot discovers that from where Miss Carroll said she was standing, the face of a visitor would not have been visible.

It would have been someone, then, who could copy Jane Wilkinson's walk, manner, and voice. Someone like Carlotta Adams, a young actress whose smashingly successful "Some Imitations" included miming not only famous politicians and society beauties but also well-known actresses — including Jane Wilkinson. Poirot had seen her perform, as had Jane herself, and the sketch was deemed uncannily accurate, "clever but perhaps slightly malicious."

Carlotta Adams had struck Poirot as shrewd but with a love of money that "might lead such a

Thirteen at Dinner (1933)

one from the prudent and cautious path." Was Carolotta the murderer, or a part of the real murderer's cover? Poirot rushes to her lodgings, only to find that she has died in the night from a supposedly accidental overdose of the sleeping drug Veronal. And in the bag that her maid said she'd had with her the evening before, Poirot finds a box of makeup, two shoe elevators, and a wig of gold hair the shade and style of Jane Wilkinson's.

Murder may have seemed somewhat out of context with Carlotta's character, but something was obviously going on. She had told her friend Jenny Driver that she was to be involved in a giant hoax from which she would become rich, and she further detailed the hoax in a letter to her sister.

Who, then, other than Jane Wilkinson, could have wished Lord Edgware dead and enlisted Carlotta's aid? Well, Ronald Marsh, Lord Edgware's nephew, who inherited the title after the murder, is certainly a prime suspect. His uncle had quarreled bitterly with him over money and had thrown him out of the house three years earlier. The day before the murder, Ronald, by his own admission, had called to ask again for financial assistance. As a matter of fact, he details to Poirot how likely his guilt is, "the well-known Wicked Ne'er-Do-Well Nephew," while also proclaiming his alibi of having been at Covent

> "I had another idea that came to me after going to a performance by Ruth Draper. I thought how clever she was and how good her impersonations were; the wonderful way she could transform herself from a nagging wife to a peasant girl kneeling in a cathedral. Thinking about her led me to the book [*Thirteen at Dinner*]."
> —*An Autobiography*

Garden at the time of the murder.

Alibis are not always what they seem, however, and aside from his own motives, Ronald is linked with Geraldine Marsh, Lord Edgware's daughter. Geraldine hysterically tells Poirot how much she hated her father, how she is glad that he's dead. And it seems Geraldine was also at Covent Garden the night of the murder. Carlotta's letter to her sister also seems to implicate Ronald.

Of course, if the Duke of Merton is to marry Jane Wilkinson, he is a prime beneficiary of Lord Edgware's death. Though to Poirot the duke "looked more like a weedy young haberdasher than like a duke," his fabulous wealth and social position keep him from early suspicion as the actual murderer. But he is cold and uncooperative, to say the least, when Poirot tries to interview him.

The Dowager Duchess of Merton, the duke's mother, can also be seen as suspicious. She makes only one appearance, but that is a powerful one, when she calls on Poirot to demand that he stop the impending marriage between her son and Jane Wilkinson. "There is nothing I would not do, M. Poirot, to save my son from this marriage." She reiterated the word emphatically. "Nothing." Could that nothing have included arranging Lord Edgware's death so as to implicate Jane, to the point of having her convicted of murder? The duchess certainly knew some strange details about the circumstances of the crime.

In classic mystery fashion, there is also the problem of the potentially culpable staff. Lord Edgware's secretary, Miss Carroll, is certainly caught in a lie about Jane Wilkinson's appearance the night of the murder and , as Poirot says, one must always distrust the totally positive witness. Too, Miss Carroll is the only wearer of pince-nez among the suspects, and a pair of pince-nez were found in Carlotta's bag along with the box of Veronal that killed her.

Nor can we ignore the matter of the missing butler. Soon after the murder, Lord Edgware's butler disappears, and although the police can't locate him they determine that he's "mixed up with a couple of rather disreputable nightclubs. Not the usual thing. Something a great deal more recherché and nasty. In fact, he's a real bad hat."

With such a field of suspects and clues, Hercule Poirot has plenty of work to do in unraveling this mystery. Many people seem clearly guilty — so we assume they probably aren't guilty — so maybe that means they *are* guilty—and so on and so on. And in the end, it is a chance conversation overheard at a bus stop that leads Poirot to the last layer of this tangle, to once more finding a truth in the old suspicion that thirteen at dinner is more than merely unluckly.

CYNTHIA A. READ

The Boomerang Clue (1934)
(Alternate title: *Why Didn't They Ask Evans?*)

Bobby Jones plays golf the way he does a lot of things, with a kind of bold impulsiveness that makes up in drama what it lacks in precision. On this particular day his method, applied to the seventeenth hole, lands his ball at the bottom of a chasm.

It's a familiarly vexing problem for young Jones, who often plays this seaside course set along a cliff on the Welsh coastline. In hopes that his ball may still be in sight if not in play, Bobby and his golf partner, Dr. Thomas, peer into the chasm. And there, on some rocks about forty feet down, they see the crumpled body of a man.

The two golfers scramble down the rocks and find the victim still breathing, though unconscious. "His number's up," diagnoses the doctor after a quick examination. "His back's broken. He'll last another twenty minutes at most." Bobby nervously volunteers to stay with the unfortunate fellow while the doctor goes off for help. A few minutes later the doomed man opens his eyes. "Why didn't they ask Evans?" he says and dies.

"Why didn't they ask Evans?" If Bobby knew that these last words would be the so-called boomerang clue and that overhearing this would bring him close to death more than once, would he wish he had had a better golf swing so that he wouldn't be in this mess?

Never having seen a dead body before, Bobby feels he should "do something." He searches the man's pocket and, finding a silk handkerchief, lays it reverently over the lifeless face. In so doing a small photograph falls out of the pocket. Bobby looks at it and gasps. It's the most hauntingly beautiful woman he's ever seen. He places the

photograph reverently back in the man's pocket. All this reverence makes him remember that he's supposed to be playing the organ at his father's church this very moment! By a stroke of luck a man in plus fours walks up and offers to stay with the body until help arrives. Grateful, Bobby leaves the responsibility to the agreeable Mr. Roger Bassington–ffrench.

The next few days do not find Bobby deep in thought about his experience. He accepts without question the coroner's verdict of accidental death: the man had walked over a cliff concealed by the mist. When Bobby meets the victim's sister, who's supposed to be the woman in the photograph, he chalks up to "aging" the fact that this woman doesn't look anything like the one in the photogaph. And as for the dying man's curious last words, Bobby doesn't remember them.

With a protagonist like this the story threatens to fizzle out unless some drastic action is taken. And so it is. Someone tries to poison Bobby with a huge dose of morphia.

Enter Lady Frances Derwent, also known as Frankie, the spunky young woman who lives in the town castle. She and Bobby had been childhood buddies but as they got older the difference in their class status drew them apart. They've recently renewed their acquaintance; Frankie genuinely seems to have nothing of the snob in her and Bobby, suspicious at first, sees this and warms to her again.

Frankie had taken the view that perhaps there was more to the golf course death than mist and Fate. Now with Bobby in the hospital recovering she is vindicated, though she wisely doesn't rub it in.

They go over the odd occurrences since the "accident." The sister and brother-in-law of the dead man (whom they identified as Alex Pritchard) had asked Bobby if there were any last words. Bobby said no, honestly not remembering, but later he did remember and wrote to them about the "Evans" remark. Very shortly after that Bobby gets a letter from an unknown firm in South America offering him a high-paying job if he would be willing to leave for Buenos Aires that week. Come to think of it, that is a little odd, isn't it? Bobby's father thinks they may have written to him because they especially wanted an Englishman, but as Bobby astutely points out, "There are a lot of Englishmen in England."

What clinches their suspicion is a newspaper reproduction of the photograph taken from the dead man's pocket. It is *not* the photograph that Bobby saw!

Frankie draws the obvious conclusions: the dead man was pushed over the cliff. Whoever did it did not want the victim identified, and so switched the photographs. The only one who could have accomplished the switch was Mr. Roger Bassington-ffrench. The "sister" and "brother-in-law" were in on it too. They think Bobby knows too much (downright unfair under the circumstances).

Frankie wants to get right on the trail, and comes up with something original. She finds out where Roger Bassington-ffrench lives and arranges to smash her car into the outer wall of his home (no, not the Bentley; she buys a heap from Bobby's friend for the occasion). Then, with the help of a doctor friend, she stages a mild concussion that can only be treated with three days of

The Boomerang Clue (1934)

bed rest in the guest room of the Bassington-ffrench manor.

Lady Frances makes a big hit among the Bassington-ffrench's. She is even invited to stay on after she has "recovered" by Sylvia, wife of Henry Bassington-ffrench and Roger's sister-in-law. Frankie decides that Roger seems altogether decent and genuine—and innocent. Henry, with the pinpoint pupils, is a little strange however. In fact, he's a dope fiend, hooked on . . . morphia.

The head of a local hospital for nerve and drug cases, a Dr. Nicholson, comes with his wife for dinner. He questions Frankie closely about the details of her car accident, pointing out little discrepancies in her story. This, naturally, shakes her up a bit. When she hears rumors that Nicholson's sanitorium is a virtual prison where helpless people are kept against their will, she becomes downright nervous. And not only that, Nicholson looks nasty too.

Bobby comes back into the action posing as Lady Frances's chauffeur, Hawkins. He splits his time between mastering the proper use of "'m' lady" as opposed to "your ladyship" and looking for clues. One night, on the grounds of Nichol-son's sanitorium, he runs smack into a vision—the haunting woman in the original photograph: she turns out to be Jaspar Nicholson's wife, Moira, who is mortally frightened that her husband is trying to murder her.

At the same time Frankie thinks she has discovered the true identity of the dead man. He's Alan Carstairs, a Canadian naturalist who went in for big game hunting. What he was doing in March-bolt, a small seaside town in the south of Wales, remains a question.

But Frankie, the brains behind this operation, is full of clever schemes for pursuing information and suspects. In addition to the car accident/chauffeur ruse, she impersonates a pamphleteer for the Conservative party and a mildly philanthropic heiress and has Bobby pose as the junior partner in a solicitor firm.

Even so, it's too late to prevent the "suicide" of Henry Bassington-ffrench and the disappearance of Moira Nicholson. Will it also be too late for Bobby and Frankie? The reader is sped to the thrilling conculsion of this book and the unexpected meaning of the phrase, "the boomerang clue."   JAN OXENBERG

Black Coffee (1934)

How do you take your coffee? Black? With sugar? Cream? How about with hyosine hydrobromide, like Sir Claud Amory? Of course, Sir Claud didn't request it this way, but someone obliged him anyway. Sir Claud, a scientist engaged in atomic research, had just discovered the formula for Amorite, whose force "is such that where we have hitherto killed by thousands, we can now kill by hundreds of thousands." Now, who would want to do away with such a shining example of humanity?

It wasn't called Amorite, of course, it was called nuclear fission. But then, how could Dame Agatha know that? She was writing in 1930. Uncanny.

The uncanny, of course, is quite at home on the Christie stage. Isn't it uncanny how Miss Amory's niece, who had trained as a dispenser during the war, had unearthed a box full of all sorts of poisonous drugs just as she was leaving for India? Isn't it amazing that at least four people were involved at some point along the chain that delivered Sir Claud his fatal cup? And isn't it absolutely stupefying that Hercule Poirot is on his way to Abbot's Cleve this very moment, summoned by Sir Claud to flush out the person (a pacifist, no doubt) who has stolen the Amorite formula.

Before Poirot arrives, however, Sir Claud, sporting man that he is, enacts a little drama of his own. With all the members of the household gathered in the library—Miss Amory, Sir Claud's sister; Richard, his son; his wife, Lucia; his niece, Barbara; Dr. Carelli, a foreigner who has arrived quite unexpectedly for dinner; Tredwell, the butler; and Raynor, Sir Claud's secretary—Sir Claud douses the lights to give the culprit a chance to return the formula undiscovered.

After a moment or two, the lights come back on—for everyone but Sir Claud, that is. In the dark, we have heard, as Miss Amory later describes it to Poirot: "Gasps—a lot of little gasps—and then the noise of a chair falling—and a metallic kind of chink...Lucia's scream, a knock on the door, [Poirot arriving] ... Oh, wait a minute! Right at the beginning there was a curious noise, like the tearing of silk. Somebody's dress, I suppose." Suppose not?

The clues begin to mount up. A duplicate key to the safe is found under the fallen chair, previously occupied by Raynor. Lucia is seen emptying the fatal cup of coffee into a planter, but not before Poirot has surreptitiously drained a sample into a test tube—how uncanny that he had one on him. Raynor produces a letter to Sir Claud warning of a "viper in your bosom. Beware of Selma Goetz and her brood." Who's Selma Goetz? Just the greatest international spy ever known, Poirot informs us. Alas, she is dead. But she had a daughter, since disappeared...

And then there is that box of drugs. Why is there no dust on it, when the top of the bureau where it has lain for some time is covered with dust? And why is Poirot forever having to straighten the spill vase on the mantlepiece? (Spills, for those of you raised in the days of gas heat, electric lights, and plentiful matches, are rolls of paper used for lighting fireplaces, oil lamps, or pipes.) Cleanliness is not only next to godliness, it's also damned helpful in sleuthing, it turns out.

As for motive, well, everybody knows Sir Claud was "an old skinflint" as Barbara calls him.

Black Coffee (1934)

And he and Richard had quarrelled about Richard's debts. "Of course, all young men have debts!" says Miss Amory understandingly. And then there's that mysterious Dr. Corelli, about whom nothing whatsoever is known, except that he is an acquaintance of Lucia's. Even Miss Amory herself might have wanted revenge for enduring years of her brother's miserly ways. And what about Tredwell? The butler? "I've been brought up to suspect the least likely person," says Barbara.

Black Coffee is, of course, sweetened with typical Christie humor. There is that wonderfully snobbish English matron she paints so well. "You know what servants are, M. Poirot," observes Miss Amory. "They positively delight in funerals!" Going on, she makes another point about Lucia, an Italian, adding confidentially to the Belgian detective, "After all, you know what foreigners are — Oh, I didn't mean ..." Poirot himself has some wonderful scenes with his dull-witted aide, Captain Arthur Hastings,

O.B.E. He concludes one explanation of a possible sequence of events:

> *Poirot:* You see what that gives to our thief?
> *Hastings:* Yes.
> *Poirot:* What?
> *Hastings:* What?
> *Poirot:* Security. He can dispose of his booty. Even if the existence of the formula is known, he has plenty of time to cover his tracks.
> *Hastings:* It's an idea ... Yes.
> *Poirot:* But naturally it is an idea. Am I not Hercule Poirot?

He is, indeed. Who else could dupe the murderer into believing he or she has poisoned Poirot? Watching him slowly fall asleep, the murderer laughingly confesses and is confidently making off with the formula when Poirot calmly speaks from the dead: "Wouldn't you like the envelope [for the formula]?" The classic trap. But who was caught?

GRANVILLE BURGESS

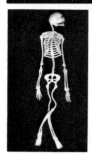

HOW TO TRACE YOUR FAMILY MYSTERY— IF YOU DARE

by Anita McAllister in the Marple spirit

My goodness...I don't quite know how to begin. You see, this dear girl asked me to discuss how one should go about uncovering the skeleton in one's own family closet. Oh, I suppose I've unraveled many a family line along with my knitting, but it's not quite as simple as one might think. Raymond (that's my nephew, you know —a very dear boy), he says that the trouble with tracing family trees is that you're apt to find there's been some monkeying around. (He's so clever.)

In a way Raymond is right, you know. You must be very cautious in your personal investigations or you may very well uncover some things that could distress you and your family. My advice is to let well enough alone. That's my advice. Murder isn't a thing to tamper with, I've always said. Now, of course, there are times when it's a person's duty to dig up the past...when someone has been falsely accused, for example.

However, if you are set upon uncovering your own family mysteries, the first step is to talk with old relatives and family friends. It's quite amazing what you can learn just by chatting with folks. Why, I recollect the time Raymond sent me on a lovely trip to St. Honore in the Caribbean and just by talking and listening to the stories of poor Major Palgrave (God rest his soul) I eventually was able to identify his dreadful murderer. Then there was the time Jason Rafiel (who delighted in calling me Nemesis) financed my tour of famous homes and gardens and I discovered the truth about his son by chatting with shopkeepers, schoolmates, and clergymen in the village of Jocelyn St. Mary. Then again, you may recall that strange murder case which occurred on the

Orient Express some years back. M. Hercule Poirot succeeded in reconstructing not only the Armstrong family tree, but also the composition of the entire household, servants included, at the time of little Daisy's kidnapping, merely by chatting with folks who had known them.

But don't think it's quite this easy. Check everything before you believe any of it. I myself make it a rule to take nothing that is told me as true. Call me distrustful. As I told Giles Reed [in *Sleeping Murder*], "It really is very dangerous to believe people. I never have for years." Yes, that's what I said then and I'd say it again as a warning to you now. You can find out a lot from people's stories, but remember at the same time that there's a lot of queerness about, more than you might imagine.

But to continue...Sometimes it's just plain impossible to speak diectly with a relative who lives a great distance away (Raymond calls them "Distant Relatives"). You see, it used to be quite simple when folks lived and died in the same little village. But nowadays people move about so. Gracious! When I think of how St. Mary Mead has changed over the years. It becomes most difficult to keep up with folks nowadays. In such a case it is necessary to post a letter to the relative requesting the desired information. This reminds me of the time I helped sweet Gwenda Reed and her husband Giles [again in *Sleeping Murder*] find out the truth about her family. Gwennie learned all about her folks and her own early childhood by writing to an aunt down in New Zealand. She was also most fortunate to come across some old diaries and notebooks written by Major Halliday (her poor father) prior to his death in the

HOW TO TRACE YOUR FAMILY MYSTERY

sanitorium. Gwen even went to the trouble of searching the parish death register—a most helpful resource.

Gracious, I do believe that Agatha often gave Hercule and myself a little too much credit for solving various mysteries of family relationships. (I hope you don't think I'm trying to belittle M. Poirot's great abilities.) It's just that, in many ways, you can solve your own mysteries as readily as Hercule and I have. For example, do you recall that case at the Nasse estate in Devonshire where Ariadne Oliver's little Murder Hunt for the fete turned into the real thing [in *Dead Man's Folly*]? Well, Hercule succeeded in discovering Sir George Stubb's family—not merely by using his "little gray cells," but by looking through the local marriage records.

Now let me see. Once you have interviewed friends and relatives (in person or by mail); have examined family diaries, Bibles, and letters; and have checked for birth-death-marriage records, you should be well on your way to uncovering the bones of your own dear departed. Raymond says that the best place to dig up one's ancestors is in the cemetery. (Such a sweet, clever boy, my Raymond.) Actually, you *can* learn a good deal from family tombstones if you know in which cemetery to look. Probate records (wills, that is)

also may contain genealogical information. I recollect that Inspector Narracott readily discovered the names of the unfortunate Captain Trevelyan's relatives in his will after he was found murdered at Hazelmoor. Where there's a will, there's a way!

Another excellent method of finding out about your family mystery is to examine jewelry, silverware, and other heirlooms that may be stored away in the attic. Do you remember the murder of poor Roger Ackroyd? By merely examining a ring fished out of a pond Hercule established that a marriage had taken place in the family. Likewise, that clever Belgian confirmed another kinship after inspecting the empty goose quill and a scrap of cambric found in the summer house of Fernly Park. In a similar vein, when the murder occurred on the Orient Express, Hercule discovered the victim's identity through examining the fragment of a burned letter. And after scrutinizing the wet label on Countess Andrenyi's suitcase and her diplomatic passport, he deduced her true identity.

Mercy me! I've rambled on so that my tea has grown quite cold. Just remember what Raymond always says: if you trace your family tree back far enough, you're certain to find a horse thief. Now, my dear, you'll please excuse me if I take my leave.

CRIME, CLASS, AND COUNTRY IN CHRISTIE'S MYSTERIES

by Sue Ellen York and Pam McAllister

"How tiresome they [servants] are and what curious things they say. How can one have pleasant relations with a garden? It sounds improper in a pagan kind of way."
—Clarissa in *Spider's Web*

Agatha Christie's eye for intrigue was continually winking at her characters' preoccupation with class and money—not to mention at their prejudices regarding national origin. And well she might know these preoccupations, being a well-bred, upper-class lady herself. "My idea of bliss," she is reported to have said, "would be to be surrounded by legions of well-trained servants." On another occasion she told a reporter that what she would most like to have was a mink and a brand-new Bentley.

Little wonder, then, that her stories are set in the hushed elegance of upper-class tea parlors where, as poet and critic Ralph Tyler wrote, "a housemaid will always answer the bell-pull—unless she has been strangled...."

In these stories, where brains, sophistication, and wealth are all the same thing—or appear to be—the servants are easily fooled by their employers. Miss Marple demonstrates this in the very beginning of *The Mirror Crack'd* when she sends her obnoxious nurse-attendant, Miss Knight, on a useless errand in order to have an independent morning. After musing how "devoted maidservants had gone out of fashion," Miss Marple makes a request:

"And if it isn't too far for you, perhaps you wouldn't mind going as far as Halletts and see if they have one of those up-and-down egg whisks—not the turn-the-handle kind."

(She knew very well they had nothing of the kind, but Halletts was the farthest shop possible.)

Miss Knight takes the bait of course, thinking she is lucky to have an excuse to shop and gossip. She hurries to make her "abortive inquiries" just as the foxy Marple had planned.

The maids and butlers are also easily gotten rid of if they've seen too much, but then just about everyone in these stories is easily gotten rid of.

And occasionally the servants have enough intelligence or personality to be suspected of the dastardly deed itself—though, in fact, none of them ever quite manage to pull it off. They are doomed to the realm of the red herring. Horbury rates suspicion in *Murder for Christmas* because he walks noiselessly and drops a coffee cup at the wrong moment—just as the arrival of the police is announced.

"I hate that beastly man-servant."
"Old Tressilian?"
"No, Horbury. Sneaking round like a cat and smirking."

And of course Horbury has only been employed a year: an outsider is always under suspicion. The superintendent concludes that Horbury is either a thief and a murderer or a thief and not a murderer or... um, innocent.

In "The Case of the Perfect Maid," from *The Mousetrap and Other Stories*, Miss Marple has a chance to reflect on the problem of servants—which is the main topic of conversation in St. Mary Mead. It is generally agreed that "if one has no domestic worries, it takes such a load off one's mind." Here we are privileged to glimpse "the perfect maid" through Miss Marple's eyes:

CRIME, CLASS, AND COUNTRY

She was certainly a most superior-looking maid, at a guess forty years of age, with neat black hair, rosy cheeks, a plump figure discreetly arrayed in black with a white apron and cap — "quite the good, old-fashioned type of servant," as Miss Marple explained afterward, and with the proper, inaudible, respectful voice, so different from the loud but adenoidal accents of Gladys.

Perfect maids aside, most servants are thought a bit...uncivilized, if you please. "You know what servants are, M. Poirot. They positively delight in funerals," contends Mrs. Amory in *Black Coffee*.

The "working class" is generally quite childish, naive, and honest in the Christie plots. They are unsure of themselves and fawning before their "betters." The clearest example of this is in "The Mousetrap" when two men come into the police station with information about the recent murder on Culver Street:

In his room at Scotland Yard, Inspector Parminter said to Detective Sergeant Kane, "I'll see those two workmen now."

"Yes, sir."

"What are they like?"

"Decent class workingmen. Rather slow reactions. Dependable."

Two "embarrassed-looking" men are then ushered in to tell their story and find themselves almost overwhelmed by the "difficulties of narration." The inspector is as condescendingly patient as he can bear to be while the two men actually shuffle and cough and use excited gestures in painful contrast to the well-educated, calm inspector:

His questions became brisk and professional. He got places, times, dates — the only thing he did not get was a description of the man who had dropped the notebook.

And if anything distinguishes the upper class

from the rest, it is understatement, both literal and figurative. Understatement is the ace in the deck of the upper class, and the working class just doesn't have it. Miss Marple knows.

"The sensible thing to do would be to change into trousers and a pullover, or into tweeds. That, of course — I don't want to be snobbish, but I'm afraid it's unavoidable—that's what a girl of—of our class would do.

"A well-bred girl," continued Miss Marple, warming to her subject, "is always very particular to wear the right clothes for the right occasion. I mean, however hot the day was, a well-bred girl would never turn up at a point-to-point in a silk flowered frock."

"Ruby, of course, wasn't — well, to put it bluntly, Ruby wasn't a lady. She belonged to the class that wear their best clothes, however unsuitable to the occasion."

—from *The Body in the Library*

There is just that one area of grim excess ... greed. Without the distractions of sex or career, the leisure class is free to obsess about money — who has it, who wants it, and who just got murdered because of it. Christie spells out the caste system as clearly as she describes the chosen weapon and, inevitably, the social scheme leads us down the garden path. Preoccupation with class is not a clue but a subplot in the Christie tale as it blinds the smug and snobbish from seeing the truth—until it's too late. They fall, ever so often, into the trap of assigning guilt by social position, their social prejudices shrouding not only the motive for murder, but the identity of the guilty party as well.

Nothing is valued as highly as keeping the wealth in the thin fingers of upper-class relatives. On the second page of Christie's first story, *The Mysterious Affair at Styles*, we are introduced to Alfred Inglethorp, a proverbial gold digger:

"Oh, this fellow! He turned up from nowhere, on the pretext of being a second cousin or something of Evie's, though she didn't seem particularly keen to acknowledge the relationship. The fellow is an absolute outsider, anyone can see that. He's got a great black beard, and wears patent leather boots in all weathers! ... It's simply bare-faced fortune hunting but there you are— she is her own mistress, and she's married him."

The gravedigger, in the mind of the Christie character, never held a candle to a gold digger slipping into the small English town and threatening the status quo of the long-established residents. A female is more dangerous in this role since such a woman could easily latch on to a wealthy, elderly man and endanger the legacy of an entire proper English family.

In *There Is a Tide*, for example, Rosaleen, the quiet farm girl, is destined to inherit her ex-husband's fortune to the utter horror of the dead man's blood relatives. She is besieged by class criticism; all of the would-be inheritors notice how awkward Rosaleen appears in her newly acquired, expensive clothing. They assume she is half-witted and openly question her past, narrow-ing in on the thought that it must contain some seedy elements—undoubtedly of a sexual nature.

Coming from the wrong side of the tracks could get you into a lot trouble in a Christie mystery. Suspicions overflow when it is remembered that the murdered Helen Kennedy was once involved with the seedy J. J. Afflick in *Sleeping Murder*:

> "An undesirable young fellow, shifty—and of course not her class, not her class at all. He got into trouble here afterwards ..."

CRIME, CLASS, AND COUNTRY

Helen's brother, Dr. Kennedy, explains why he discouraged his beloved, misguided sister from seeing J. J.:

> "I'm old-fashioned, young man. In the modern gospel, one man is as good as another. That holds morally, no doubt. But I'm a believer in the fact that there is a state of life into which you are born—and I believe you're happiest staying in it. Besides," he added, "I thought the fellow was a wrong 'un. As he proved to be."

But the lower classes and the threat they represent are a flash in the pan compared to *any* foreigner, regardless of age or circumstance. Christie's characters, who stand on the edge of imminent murder, face foreigners and outsiders with a fear far greater than that with which they face death.

Poirot, for example, never meets another Christie character without hearing some comment related to his Belgian roots:

> Again Major Porter paused. His eyes traveled up from the patent-leather shoes—striped trousers — black coat — egg-shaped head and colossal mustache. Foreign, of course! That explained the shoes. Really, thought Major Porter, what's the club coming to? Can't get away from foreigners even here.
> — from *There Is a Tide*

And in *Murder for Christmas* one irreverent character says of Poirot: "Then there's that lunatic foreigner prowling about. I don't suppose he's any good but he makes me feel jumpy."

Poirot is not the only foreigner to bear the brunt of the English xenophobia. As the Orient Express heads toward its destination, M. Bouc becomes more and more anxious to pin the crime on the Italian passenger: "He has been a long time in America, and he is an Italian, and Italians use

the knife! And they are great liars! I do not like Italians."

Mrs. Boyle, of "Three Blind Mice," expounds on the subject — lecturing as an expert in the field: "You are young and inexperienced and should welcome advice from someone more knowledgeable than yourself. And what about this queer foreigner? When did *he* arrive?"

After this same "queer foreigner," the Italian Mr. Paravicini, compliments Molly, the hostess, by saying, "You are without a doubt an enchanting cook," Molly unashamedly thinks what a "nuisance" foreigners are!

Magdelene Lee, in *Murder for Christmas*, openly voices her suspicions of the hot-blooded Spanish beauty, Pilar Estravados, who is also unfortunately new to the household:

> "I can't help feeling that the manner of my father-in-law's death was somehow *significant*. It —it was so very *un-English*."
> Hercule Poirot turned slowly. His grave eyes met hers in innocent inquiry.
> "Ah," he said, "The Spanish touch, you think?"
> "Well, they *are* cruel, aren't they?...All those bull fights and things!"

In *Murder at Hazelmoor* Mrs. Curtis sighs:

> "It's Captain Wyatt as could do with a spring cleaning." she observed. "That nasty native of his —what does he know about cleaning. I should like to know? Nasty black fellow."

To which Major Burnaby replies:

> "Nothing better than a native servant. They know their job and they don't talk."

Anglophiles, however, are not alone in their preoccupation with prejudicial observations. They are, in fact, the common object of the overt stereotypical comments that seethe out of Christie's work.

The aforementioned Italian, Mr. Paravicini, bears his own burden of judgment:

> "'Three Blind Mice'—so it was! The tune has got into my head. Now I come to think of it, it is a gruesome little rhyme. Not a nice little rhyme at all. But children like gruesome things. You may have noticed that? That rhyme is very English— the bucolic, cruel English countryside. 'She cut off their tails with a carving-knife.'"

Pilar Estravados, about whom so much suspicion was cast in *Murder for Christmas*, doesn't think much of her English relatives, deciding that they are not "gay" and that they smell bad:

> How very odd the English smelled ... It was what had struck her so far most forcibly about England—the difference of smell. There was no garlic and no dust and very little perfume. In this carriage now there was a smell of cold stuffiness —the sulphur smell of the trains—the smell of soap and another very unpleasant smell — it came, she thought, from the fur collar of the stout woman sitting beside her. Pilar sniffed delicately, imbibing the odour of moth balls reluctantly. It was a funny scent to choose to put on yourself, she thought.

Poirot himself, who has patiently borne the brunt of English xenophobia, sharply retaliates in *Curtain*:

> "Very well, then. You will not look through key-holes. You will remain the English gentleman and someone will be killed. It does not matter, that. Honor comes first with an Englishman. Your honor is more important than somebody else's life. Bien! It is understood."

It is difficult to sort out from under the pile of attitudes just when Dame Christie had her tongue in her cheek and when she was slipping in signs of her own opinions. For a woman who handled murder with such finesse, she barely hesitated when it came to conversational knife-throwing.

> "Egyptian children stare and stare, and their eyes are simply disgusting, and so are their noses, and I don't believe I really like children—not unless they're more or less washed..."
> — Mrs. Allerton in *Death on the Nile*

Trapped in the web of prejudice and misdirected blame, the "nice" people of Christie's upper crust fret about the outsider and in doing so miss the bloodied fingers of their nearest and dearest curling ever so delicately around the finest china teacup.

Murder on the Orient Express (1934)

(Alternate title: *Murder in the Calais Coach*)

All aboard in Syria on the Taurus Express. Awaiting you is a journey through many countries, to many intrigues. Don't worry that there are only three passengers at present — more will board, each with his or her own story to tell.

Poirot, the Belgian detective with a large mustache and an egg-shaped head, is aboard. Excitement cannot be far behind. In the meantime, he amuses himself studying the other passengers—a pastime that pays off.

Mary Debenham and Colonel Arbuthnot are not so keen on their fellow sojourner. They take a glance and pass him off quickly as just "some darn foreigner." Mary is a cool, efficient young lady and the Colonel has a tour of India behind him— and both will soon be forced to raise their estimation of the little foreigner.

Poirot's journey is long, and after changing trains, we find him on the Orient Express, Istanbul-Calais coach. Mary and the Colonel tag along, and we are introduced to a whole new cast.

There are princesses, a lady's maid, Russians, Americans, Hungarians, Frenchmen, Englishmen, and for good measure, an Italian, a Swede, and a German. Nearly every ethnic group represented holds the other in disdain. As the conductor notes, traveling is a strange phenomenon — on a train, total strangers live together in intimacy for a few days or weeks, then part, perhaps never to meet again. Well, maybe on most trains. The passengers of the Orient Express are soon to experience an event that will not soon let them forget one another.

For now, they sit calmly, chatting in the dining room. Well, at least the boisterous American matron chats. Mrs. Hubbard bores everyone in earshot with tales of her wonderful daughter. The

handsome Hungarian couple, Count and Countess Andrenyi, have the good sense to leave the dining car, and others fleeing Mrs. Hubbard are not far behind. Slow to take a hint, Mrs. Hubbard follows the crowd, and Poirot is left alone with Ratchett and his secretary, Hector McQueen.

Ratchett is another prime example of the Ugly American, and he corners Poirot. Apparently, Ratchett has enemies fierce enough to kill him, and he appeals to Poirot for help, offering big money. But an offer of $20,000 for a couple days' work doesn't interest Poirot. He refuses the case with brutal frankness. "I do not like your face, M. Ratchett," he says.

Poirot never regrets that decision. Ratchett doesn't live long enough to regret anything.

At twenty-three minutes before one, Poirot is awakened by a cry. He thinks immediately of Ratchett, but, peeking out, he hears a voice from Ratchett's compartment speaking calmly to the conductor. Within moments, the indomitable Mrs. Hubbard is insisting that there is a man in her compartment; a search, however, turns up nothing but a conductor's suit button. Dropping off to sleep, Poirot hears something heavy falling with a thud against his door. Springing up, he sees nothing in the hall but a woman wrapped in a scarlet kimono. Poirot decides he is just suffering from nerves.

Morning finds the train stuck in a Yugoslavian snowbank. As if that were not enough to fray already bad nerves, Ratchett is found in bed, dead. At least a dozen knife wounds pierce his body— some delivered with great force, others little more than scratches. All are seemingly delivered haphazardly and at random.

We already know that Poirot will not protect

anyone whose face he doesn't like. Apparently he suffers no such compunction when asked to track down the killers of a rotten-faced person. Besides, as he himself admits, he is now bored. An unsolved crime is to Poirot a gift.

The gray cells he is so proud of go to work. A doctor advises that Ratchett died around 1 A.M. The train has been stuck in snow since 12:30, and there are no footprints leading to or from the compartment window. Obviously, the murderer is still on the train, and can be only from the Istanbul-Calais coach. That fact dwindles the list of suspects down to little more than a dozen people — all of them perfectly respectable-looking. It is a case tailor-made for Poirot.

A tour of Ratchett's compartment turns up many clues, none of which escape the eagle eyes of Poirot. First of all, several wounds on the corpse are deep, yet the edges do not gape and have not bled—suggesting that at least several of the blows were delivered to an already dead man. Secondly, some blows were obviously thrust by a right-handed person, others by someone using the left hand. Poirot is exasperated—"The matter clears itself up wonderfully! The murderer was a man of great strength—he was feeble—it was a

"All my life I had wanted to go on the Orient Express. When I had travelled to France or Spain or Italy, the Orient Express had often been standing at Calais, and I had longed to climb up into it."
—*An Autobiography*

Murder on the Orient Express (1934)

woman—it was a right-handed person—it was a left-handed person. Ah!"

But clues abound. A sniff of an empty glass shows that the victim was drugged into sleep. Burnt matches do not correspond with the ones in Ratchett's pocket. A dainty handkerchief embroidered with the initial *H* lies on the floor, as does a pipe cleaner. The dented watch in Ratchett's pocket points to 1:15. The abundance of clues seem to Poirot to be too convenient — perhaps red herrings drawn by a clever killer.

But one clue does interest Poirot — a charred fragment of paper. Through an elaborate system that involves putting the fragment between wire netting and burning it even further, he can make out a few words: "— member little Daisy Armstrong." Ah! This is a crime Poirot remembers. Obviously Ratchett was really Cassetti, the ignoble American kidnapper who killed the Armstrong child some years before. The killed is a killer. Who is the killer of the killed killer?

Colonel Arbuthnot is the only pipe smoker on board. Ratchett's valet, Masterman, had the easiest access for giving his master a sleeping draught. Two women have the initial *H* in their names—Mrs. Hubbard and Hildegarde Schmidt, the maid of the frail Russian lady, Princess Dragomiroff.

But the train conductor is anxious to pin the dirty deed on the only Italian on board: Antonio Foscarelli, usually referred to simply as the Italian. The only thing worse than being an American, according to most characters in this book, is being an Italian who has spent time in America. Poor Antonio seems a decent young man, but M. Bouc, the conductor, thinks otherwise. "He has been a long time in America, and he is an Italian, and Italians use the knife! And they are great liars! I do not like Italians," says M. Bouc.

Luckily for Antonio, Poirot has a different set of prejudices: "I have a little idea that this is a crime very carefully planned and staged. It is a long-sighted, long-headed crime. It is not—how shall I express it—a *Latin* crime. It is a crime that shows traces of a cool, resourceful, deliberate brain—I think an Anglo-Saxon brain."

Eventually the little gray cells save the day, if not the victim, and the puzzle aboard the Orient Express is solved.

CINDY LOOSE

Mr. Parker Pyne, Detective (1934)

(Alternate title: *Parker Pyne Investigates*)

The personal advertisement appeared on the front page of the daily newspaper each morning.

"ARE YOU HAPPY?" it asked in discreet, six-point type. "IF NOT, CONSULT MR. PARKER PYNE, 17 Richmond Street."

In this collection of a dozen short stories, the forlorn, the worried, and the curious take Mr. Pyne's odd offer, and wind up sitting opposite the detective, spewing forth their tales of woe. Like an aging, overweight magician, Mr. Pyne, a former government clerk and statistician-turned-detective, makes their trouble disappear and turns their fantasies into realities.

It is really quite simple, claims Pyne, adding that the causes of unhappiness can be categorized under five simple headings: ill health, wives having troubles with husbands, husbands having troubles with wives, boredom, and miscellaneous. Like a doctor attending to a disease, says Pyne, once the diagnosis is made, the prescription is easily filled out.

Assisting Pyne is a small group of talented, loyal, and valued employees, who can assume a variety of roles tailored to each situation. They include Claude Luttrell, the leading-man type who is usually cast as a dancer or gigolo; Madeleine de Sara, the vamp; Mrs. Ariadne Oliver, a detective-story writer (wonder who that could be?) who devises plots for Pyne; and Dr. Constantine, who is available to administer drugs when the need arises.

A perfect example of the "boredom" category is "The Case of the Discontented Soldier." The story also gives Parker Pyne and Mrs. Oliver a chance to demonstrate their talents.

Major Wilbraham is bored. After many years of service with the British military in East Africa, he is now retired and objects to "the boredom and endless tittle-tattle about petty village matters." He tells Mr. Parker Pyne so. Pyne then tells Wilbraham that his wish for danger and excitement will come true . . . for fifty pounds, payable in advance.

The next day, Wilbraham receives a note requesting him to go to Eaglemont, Friars Lane, Hampstead. He complies, but before he gets there, he comes upon two men accosting a young woman. Wilbraham's sense of chivalry forces him to stave off the attack, and also introduces him to Miss Freda Clegg and those trying to kill her.

Wilbraham learns that Freda's father had been involved in a financial transaction several years earlier, and certain men are now trying to obtain papers which they believe Freda possesses. Wilbraham decides to help the young lady, and winds up on the floor of a cold cellar, bound hand and foot, as is his companion, with water slowly trickling in.

Here is the adventure he yearned for. But will he survive?

In "The Case of the Distressed Lady," Mrs. Daphne St. John is upset. Heavily in debt, she is also in trouble.

Daphne has taken her friend's platinum ring with a large solitaire diamond, and instead of bringing it to the jeweler's to be repaired, she has a duplicate made and keeps the original.

Now feeling guilty about her actions, she wants to give the ring back, but cannot think of a

Mr. Parker Pyne, Detective (1934)

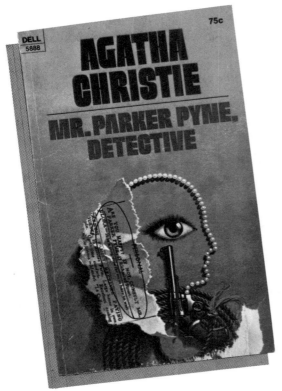

tactful way to do so. She explains her predicament to Parker Pyne. This is a case for Claude Luttrell and Madeleine de Sara.

Luttrell and de Sara, posing as dancers, attend a party at which the real ring's owner, Lady Dortheimer, will be a guest.

After their performance, they mingle with the guests, and Luttrell dances with Lady Dortheimer. Suddenly the lights go out and then back on again. Claude is standing next to Lady Dortheimer with a platinum ring with a solitaire diamond. "Your ring," he said. "It slipped off."

But was it the real ring, or just the imitation? Would Claude and Madeleine get caught? Would Daphne find happiness?

And then what about the wife in "Middle-Aged Wife" whose husband is having an affair, or the husband in "The City Clerk" who wanted some adventure while his wife and kids were on holiday? What would become of the title character in the "Rich Woman" who longed for a simpler life?

All these and more visit Mr. Parker Pyne, detective. How many find true happiness, and how many get their money back?

RICHARD REGIS

Murder in Three Acts (1935)

(Alternate title: *Three-Act Tragedy*)

CASTING NOTICE

From a noted producer, a project dramatizing Agatha Christie's *Murder in Three Acts*. Actors are needed for the following roles:

Sir Charles Cartwright, a distinguished actor, retired, now living at Crow's Nest, his "modern bungalow of the better type," in Loomouth, Cornwall. He is a well-built, sunburned man of middle age. A consummate performer, even in retirement he is always acting.

Mr. Satterthwaite, of the same age, a man appearing invariably at the tail end of guest lists; a determined but pleasant snob of considerable intelligence who is a shrewd observer of people and things.

Sir Bartholomew "Tollie" Strange, an Oxford classmate of Sir Charles and a distinguished Harley Street Doctor, a well-known specialist in nervous disorders.

Miss Milray, Sir Charles's secretary, a superefficient "glorified housekeeper," a tall and exceedingly ugly woman of rugged countenance, possessed of a "kind of hideous respectability."

Angela Sutcliffe, a well-known actress, no longer young but with a strong hold on the public, celebrated for her wit and charm.

Cynthia Dacres, proprietress of Ambrosine, Ltd., a successful dressmaking establishment. A tall woman with a perfect figure, greenish bronze hair superbly coiffed, and an exquisitely madeup face. "What Mrs. Dacres really looked like, it was impossible to tell."

Freddie Dacres, her husband. A former jockey, there is something not quite right about him. He

has spent a lot of time on and about race courses, and although nothing untoward has ever been proved, eyebrows rise at the mention of his name.

Miss Wills, better known as the playwright Anthony Astor, is tall, with a receding chin, pincenez, wrinkled stockings, and a high and undistinguished voice. She is "cut off by success from her spiritual home — a boarding house in Bournemouth." Singularly intelligent, she tends to poke and pry.

Hermione Lytton Gore, known as Egg. Possessed of abounding vitality, this young lady can sometimes be galling — the callowness, one presumes, of youth. This is mitigated by her undeniable attractiveness.

Lady Mary Lytton Gore, Egg's mother, a sweet and rather timid woman of fifty-five, she was left a widow when Egg was three years old. She adores her child but is a little alarmed by her.

Oliver Manders, a somewhat impulsive and sometimes insecure young man in his midtwenties with something "un-English" about him. He has talked of things like communism and could be a beau of Egg's if she would just allow it.

The Reverend Stephen Babbington, rector of Loomouth, a man "of sixty-odd, with kind, faded eyes and a disarming, diffident manner."

Mrs. Babbington, a big, untidy woman, full of energy and free of petty-mindedness.

John Ellis, a butler hired by Dr. Strange two weeks before a fateful party at his estate. Ellis is somewhat nondescript, white-haired, and in his mid-sixties.

Hercule Poirot, a detective.

There are various bit parts available as servants,

Murder in Three Acts (1935)

a police inspector, and other necessary function-aries. The actors playing these roles may double in other roles and will most certainly understudy the major roles.

SYNOPSIS OF ACTS
Act I

At a dinner party given by Sir Charles and at-tended by all the major characters save Ellis, the Reverend Mr. Babbington indulges in an unac-customed cocktail and dies. Diagnosis: some kind of seizure. Even though an analysis of the glass yields nothing, Sir Charles suspects murder and presses for an investigation. Since nothing war-rants one, however, everyone goes his separate way, and Sir Charles, distraught, heads for the Continent.

Some time later, while spending a day in Monte Carlo, Satterthwaite reads of Dr. Strange's death under similar circumstances while entertaining friends at his house in Yorkshire.

This time it is murder. Although his glass, too, yielded nothing suspicious, a toxicologist estab-lishes the cause of his death as nicotine poisoning.

The guest list at this party was identical to the first, with the addition of Dr. Stange's staff, his new butler, Ellis, and a few other guests. Sir Charles, Satterthwaite, and Poirot were not there but do happen to meet quite by chance in Monte Carlo as Satterthwaite gets the news about Tollie.

Did the butler do it? He came out of nowhere and disappeared the day after his master's death.

Act II

Sir Charles relishes his new role as detective. En-listing the aid of Satterthwaite and Egg while Poirot stays out of the spotlight, he directs the ef-forts to solve both murders. (It seems exhuma-tion of Babbington discovers nicotine poisoning also.) Ellis is not found, but incriminating letters appear that indicate he knew something about who killed Dr. Strange.

As the trio investigates the people who were guests at both parties, it is discovered that most of them had something to gain from Dr. Strange's death, but the real problem remains—why any-one would want to kill dear, sweet Babbington. The two crimes must be related, but how?

Act III

Poirot, with Sir Charles's aid, stages one more party where another death occurs. This one is only play-acting, and it produces almost every-thing Poirot needs to know. He could have been aided by a Mrs. de Rushbridger, a patient at Dr. Strange's sanatorium, but she too suffered an un-timely demise from nicotine-injected candy. Hers is the third death and as hard to fathom as Bab-bington's.

Needless to say, the murderer is found out, and Poirot marvels at how closely he and others at the first dinner party escaped death.

NOTE: The title of this work indicates precisely how it is to be staged. A flare for the theatrical in

AGATHA CHRISTIE | TRAGEDIA EN TRES ACTOS

each of the characters, the motives, the murders, and in the denouement will be maintained.

Following is a list of the roles and the actors we have in mind for them. We have tentatively contacted their agents, but nothing is firm at this moment. Sue Mengers and others are invited to submit actors for the following major and unnamed minor roles:

Sir Charles Cartwright	Sir Laurence Olivier
Mr. Satterthwaite	Alistair Cooke
Sir Bartholomew	
Strange	John Houseman
Miss Milray	Maggie Smith
Angela Sutcliffe	Jean Simmons
Cynthia Dacres	Jane Fonda or Cher
Freddie Dacres	Dirk Bogarde
Miss Wills	Glenda Jackson
Oliver Manders	Cliff Gorman
Mary Lytton Gore	Jessica Tandy
Egg Lytton Gore	undecided, maybe
	Marie Osmond
Babbington	Robert Morley
Mrs. Babbington	Jean Stapleton
John Ellis	George Spelvin
Hercule Poirot	**Dustin Hoffman**

For the producer,
GERALD M. KLINE

Death in the Air (1935)

(Alternate title: *Death in the Clouds*)

The noon flight of the "Prometheus" is a typical lunchtime run from Paris to London. Yet this day, one of the nine passengers seated in the rear section will change the plane's simple course forever. The "Prometheus" is about to fly straight on a course to murder.

Madame Giselle, a French moneylender, is fast asleep in her seat just opposite the entrance door. It is a sleep from which she will never awaken. On her neck is a small red mark, and it wasn't caused by the sandman.

Could it be a bite left by the wasp that was killed a few minutes earlier by Jean Dupont as he and his father, Armand, argued heatedly about archaeology? Or was the mark left by the little dart with the teased orange and black silk thread knotted around it, which is found by her feet?

If it is the latter—which, of course, it is—who then is the murderer?

Aboard the luxurious plane is an odd mix of beautiful people and seedy characters. Not one can prove his or her innocence.

Either of the Duponts could have had access to a blowpipe and poison dart. As noted archaeologists, they travel to all corners of the globe. In the corner where they are seated — across the gangway from Madame Giselle—only James Ryder, a British businessman, could have seen them lift the pipe and fire the lethal thorn.

And what about Ryder? A letter in his pocket, written by his business partner, states that if he does not secure the loan which he has been negotiating in Paris, "We're on Queer Street." Could Giselle have turned him down? Or did Ryder get his loan and decide that the interest rate was a bit too high? One way to keep the wolf from the door is to kill it.

Perhaps, though, it is Mr. Clancy, the writer of detective novels, just confirming a plot idea for his next book. When questioned by the English police and the French Sureté, he admits to owning a blowpipe, the same as the type found aboard the "Prometheus" under seat No. 9.

The occupant of seat No. 9, however, is beyond reproach. You see, sitting there, bundled up from his head to the tips of his patent leather shoes, is M. Hercule Poirot, the "little Belgian" detective. Although the finger of guilt points directly at him — even the verdict at the coroner's inquest charges Poirot—all good Christie readers know that he, above everyone else, is innocent.

But what about his traveling mate, the man seated beside him, softly playing the flute? Couldn't Dr. Bryant's instrument have been used to fire the dart with the snake venom on its tip? And couldn't the soothing music have been used to create the *moment psychologique* that Poirot so fervently searches for?

Still, the clouds grow thicker. The fog that hangs within the plane is almost as heavy as the one that covers London like a blanket.

Venetia Kerr, a member of the British aristocracy, seems above suspicion, but her companion, Lady Horbury, is not.

Lady Horbury, the wife of a wealthy and titled British landowner, has a taste for cocaine and gambling — two favorite pastimes of the leisure class—and often gets in above her head...and, at times, out of it. But this time her husband, who usually wishes to avoid a scandal at all costs, refuses to bail out his high-rolling wife. Did she visit Giselle to borrow a few francs to pay off her debts? Or did the innocent Venetia set her up?

Venetia is madly in love with Lord Horbury

and has been since her schooldays, but the scandal-shy Horbury won't give his wife the divorce she wants. However, if the good lady is in jail, Venetia can have the lord and his castle all to herself.

Both Jane Grey and Norman Gale are assisting Poirot in his kingdom-to-continent investigation, so it wouldn't be either of them who slayed the napping Giselle. Or would it?

Grey, a hairdresser in one of London's poshest salons, was on holiday in the South of France, a vacation paid for by a winning Irish Sweepstakes ticket. Did the life of the social class, whose heads she has been styling, finally go to hers? Did she flip her wig while gambling away all her money at the roulette wheel in Le Pinet?

Would the death of Madame Giselle help Norman Gale? Gale had been a dentist who followed in his uncle's footsteps, fulfilling his dream of leaving behind the practice that he vehemently hated.

And what of Giselle's long-estranged daughter? Could she have found out about an inheritance and had her careerwoman mother killed off by one of the debt-ridden passengers?

Perhaps Giselle committed suicide. She had left strict orders with her maid to burn all her files in the event of her sudden or questionable demise. Did she discover some information about one of her clients which she could no longer live with? What about the two spoons found in her coffee cup aboard the plane?

Clouds of suspicion accumulate faster than a summer thunderstorm, and it is up to Poirot to soar through those clouds and shed some light upon a most complicated murder mystery.

BRIAN REGIS

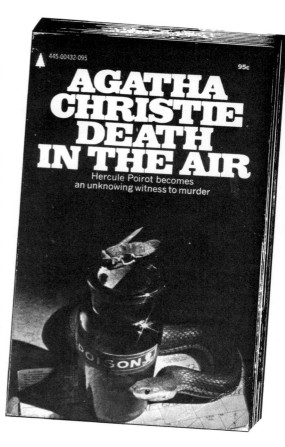

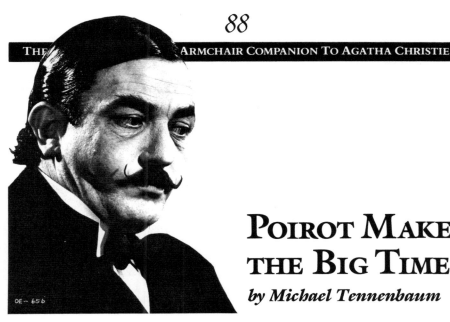

OE- 656

POIROT MAKES THE BIG TIME

by Michael Tennenbaum

When the moviegoer is asked to shell out four or five dollars to see a first-run film, he grumbles about inflation and high salaries for name stars, but rarely does he think about where most of his money goes. Certainly actors' earnings eat up a chunk of a movie's budget, but the rest of the jillions are used to make the film a pleasure to watch — whether it be for some stupendous special effects a la *Star Wars*, or the intricate detail of period authenticity in lush movies like *Murder on the Orient Express*.

Director Sidney Lumet knew exactly how to make this project a success — he was fully aware that previous Christie adaptations had been less than substantial hits (with one or two exceptions). He reasoned that the Christie magic that works so well on the printed page cannot be transferred to the screen, which some critics maintain is true for any good novel. Therefore, another "hook" had to be found, something besides the basic whodunit of the plot. The answer was style. Lumet proceeded to put on the classiest act in town, using only internationally known stars (even in the smallest roles) and bathing the entire film in the warm glow of nostalgia, making it a paean not only to a time remembered, but to an entire way of life that no longer exists.

One would imagine that assembling a cast of such magnitude would create untold headaches for the poor director. But this was not to be the case. Most of the actors were thrilled at the prospect of being in this film — Richard Widmark made no secret of the fact that he took the role of Ratchett, the American gangster, simply because he wanted to meet the other actors involved. For Lauren Bacall it was an opportunity to revive her film career after her successful return to Broadway in the hit musical *Applause*. For Ingrid Bergman, John Gielgud, and Wendy Hiller it provided a chance to play rich character roles that actors of their stature are rarely offered. For Sean Connery it was a favor he willingly repaid to friend Lumet, who had rescued the actor from his James Bond image in such films as *The Hill* and *The Offence*. In fact, the entire cast was unanimous in their praise of the director — so much so that press conferences became meetings of the Sidney Lumet Appreciation Society.

A festive mood prevailed on the set and it became the in spot for socially prominent types, including members of the royal family who were squired around the studio by the stars. Only Vanessa Redgrave, her radical politics very much intact offscreen, disapproved of such pampering of

the ruling class. She, too, had a guest visit the set — Gary Healy of the Workers' Revolutionary party.

Most of the attention was focused on Albert Finney, whose portrayal of Poirot was perfect down to the last detail. (We all noticed the limp—but did anyone catch the ring made from the bullet that wounded him? It's there.) Finney spoke to a reporter about the characterization: "In order to get the short, solid look I needed as Agatha Christie's elder statesman of criminologists, I wore body padding — a t-shirt draped with cotton wool. I also had to have padded thighs to make me look wide so that my height appeared less. Fa-

Among the passengers on the Orient Express (from left): Wendy Hiller, Rachel Roberts, Lauren Bacall, Sean Connery, Anthony Perkins, Martin Balsam. Opposite page, top: Albert Finney as Poirot.

POIROT MAKES THE BIG TIME

cially the transformation [by makeup artist Stuart Freeborn] was achieved with a false nose and padded cheeks to achieve the egg-shaped look. By far the most important part of the makeup was the gleaming black hair and the meticulously trimmed, trained, and waxed period moustache." Hair stylist Ramon Gow provided the following recipe for Finney's character coiffure: Cherry Blossom boot polish and Vaseline, set every morning, half an hour under the dryer, and a finger wave at the back. Perfect.

The other luminaries in the cast certainly understood all the fuss made over Finney, even though Connery was heard to grumble that "the rest of us are only glorified extras." But at least they knew that they were not buried under pounds of makeup and would be recognized by their fans; Finney was not so sure. During a break in filming Lauren Bacall spoke of the difficulty of these leading actors assuming secondary roles: "It was so frustrating, everything revolves around Albie [Finney] who talks all the time, we just react. The other day when he left early for his matinee, we all went absolutely bananas and couldn't stop speaking. It was complete chaos."

But to return to the original question, where does the rest of that money go? People often assume that movies are shot where they take place in the story, but this is rarely the case. In any event, it becomes an incredible impracticability to shoot movies in real locations, let alone the cramped quarters of a real railway car, so adaptable set pieces, called mock-ups, must be built on the sound stage of a film studio. At the Elstree Studio stages outside London designer Tony Walton not only re-created the Orient Express, but improved upon it. Lumet wanted the look of elegance to dominate the film and Walton responded by adding to his authentic set (based on original plans and existing cars) some totally inaccurate, but absolutely convincing, lamps, upholstery, and floral patterns. To heighten the effect, a studio artist was brought in to paint minutely detailed wood "inlays" along the newly built train corridor panels. The entire set was built on rubber wheels so that it could be rocked and rolled by the crew to give the illusion of motion.

Details. Here is a partial breakdown of some of the costs for only one area of props—printing:

Menus—$100 (only one was used)

Newspapers—$350

Hungarian passports, railway tickets, Poirot's stationery—$400

The list goes on. The expense was great, but the rewards were enormous. *Murder on the Orient Express* went on to become the most successful wholly British-financed film ever. Yet, some rewards are more elusive than others, and there is a paradox involved. Lumet took on this project because of increased public interest in nostalgia, and he set out to make the perfect memory trip. But the film was released late in a year when every major producer seemed to have the same idea. When the Academy Awards were handed out, period films ruled the competition and the Oscars for best art direction and costume design went to *The Godfather Part Two* and *The Great Gatsby*, respectively. Which goes to show you that crime and glamorous nostalgia can be taken separately, but not in combination.

The "What's in a Name" Word Find

by Dale G. Copps

Find the entries below in the Word Find Grid. Each entry is in a straight line—horizontal, vertical, or diagonal — though some read backward (right to left or bottom to top). After you've done this, transcribe the leftover letters, starting at the top left and going across each line to the bottom, onto the spaces provided below the grid, and find yourself with another puzzle.

FIND THESE ENTRIES...
Agatha
Blood
Grey cells
Hastings
Hercule
Heroism
Mysterious
Novelist
Terror
Trials
Villain
AND THESE TITLES:
A.B.C. Murders
Appointment with Death
Big Four
Cat Among the Pigeons
Clocks
Curtain
Dead Man's Folly
Dead Man's Mirror
Death in the Air
Death on the Nile
Elephants Can Remember
Evil Under the Sun
Halloween Party
Hickory Dickory Death
Murder at the Gallop
Murder for Christmas
Murder in Mesopotamia
Murder in the Calais Coach
Murder of Roger Ackroyd
Mystery of the Blue Train
Patriotic Murders
Peril at End House
Poirot Investigates
Poirot Loses a Client
Sad Cypress
There is a Tide
Third Girl
Thirteen at Dinner
(Solution on page 185.)

```
M Y S T E R Y O F T H E B L U E T R A I N T M
U H T A E D H T I W T N E M T N I O P P A U H
R E F R A I M A T O P O S E M N I R E D R U M
D O L P A T R I O T I C M U R D E R S D L H R
E S S E R P Y C D A S M O W E I I N E G T S E
R A N O C R N R D L G I Y A T L G R I A N P B
I E A P L A U E L E A A T S A S O N E A O O M
N G N R O O T E E S A H T T T F I D A I M I E
T U I N F L C A G W O D E H R E Y L R T R R M
H S S G I Y L N M N O N M O A R R O E O H O E
E D I E E D I A T O D L G A O E T I R V E T R
C B E R H T T H G H N E L K N L S R O D O I N
A A G A S T E A O E R G C A O S I L I U R N A
L H B A T N R U N A H I T S H M F T A L S V C
A E H C I H S E C E D T E H S E A O R I N E S
I R N L M E I K D Y E S T N E S R I L I R S T
S C E I F U R N R N A T A A I P G O A L I T N
C U D R A O R O T C U M R E R D I T I S Y I A
O L O T Y L K D L H D L R I R E R G L S Y G H
A E O D F C L I E A E E I I H U D A E M M A P
C O L C I U E I E R H A H V C T E R R O R T E
H S B H K N Y D V T S T I S E E E T U A N E L
T S A M T S I R H C R O F R E D R U M M A S E
```

LEFTOVER LETTERS: _ _ _ _ _ _ _ _ _ _ _ _ ,_
_ _ _ _ _ _ _ _ _ _ _ _ _ _ _ _ _ _ :
_ _ ,_ _ _ _ _ _ _ _ _ _ _
_ _ _ _ _ , _,_ _ _ ? _ _ _ _ _ .

The A.B.C. Murders (1935)

"If you could order crime as one orders a dinner, what would you choose?"

Hercule Poirot: "A very simple crime. A crime with no complications. A crime of quiet domestic life...very unimpassioned...very intime. Supposing that four people sit down to play bridge and one, the odd man out, sits in a chair by the fire. At the end of the evening the man by the fire is found dead. One of the four, while he is a dummy, has gone over and killed him, and, intent on the play of the hand, the other three have not noticed. Ah, there would be a crime for you! Which of the four was it?"

The phone rings, ending Poirot's musing about simple domestic mayhem. Scotland Yard is on the line reporting the murder of Alice Ascher of Andover, a poor, elderly shopkeeper. Poirot's worst fears are realized. A few days earlier he had received this letter:

Mr. Hercule Poirot—
You fancy yourself, don't you, at solving mysteries that are too difficult for your poor thick-headed British police? Let us see, Mr. Clever Poirot, just how clever you can be. Perhaps you'll find this nut too hard to crack. Look out for Andover on the 21st of the month.
Yours, etc.
A.B.C.

A madman.

More letters, more murders.

Betty Barnard, a flirty young waitress, strangled with her own belt on the beach at Bexhill. Sir Carmichael Clarke, wealthy collector of a Chinese art, clubbed to death in Churston. But at Doncaster in the dark of the Regal Cinema, perhaps our alliterative assassin errs, for the man fatally stabbed is named George Earlsfield.

The A.B.C. murderer leaves no physical clues except those he chooses to leave...an A.B.C. railway guide beside each body and the letters to Poirot announcing the date and city of each murder. The letters also taunt our proud little Belgian detective for not solving the mystery of A.B.C.

The English public is terrified and titillated by the A.B.C. maniac. Newspapers sprout headlines like "HE MAY BE IN *YOUR* TOWN." As Poirot noted at the Andover murder site, "What we saw was a mess of average human beings looking with intense interest at the spot where another human being had been done to death."

Poirot does little but think. A policeman observes that "Mr. Poirot done some good stuff in his time, but I think he's a bit ga ga now, sir."

But Poirot knows luck turns. "The gambler (and the murderer, who is, after all, only a supreme kind of gambler since what he risks is not money, but his life) often lacks intelligent anticipation. Because he has won he thinks he will continue to win! He does not leave the table in good time with his pockets full. So, in crime the murderer who is successful cannot conceive the possibility of not being successful! He takes to himself all the credit for a successful performance but...however carefully planned, no crime can be successful without luck."

And Poirot knows that it is just a matter of time. "Crime is terribly revealing. Try and vary your methods as you will your tastes, your habits, your attitude of mind, and your soul is revealed by your actions."

Of course Poirot separates incredible truth

93

from plausible falsehood, delighting his beanbag, Captain Hastings, and us with such bon mots as "Speech, so a wise old Frenchman said to me, is an invention of man's to prevent him from thinking."

"Murder, I have often noticed, is a great matchmaker."

"You yourself are English and yet you do not seem to appreciate the quality of the English reaction to a direct question. It is invariably one of suspicion and the natural result of reticence."

"Anonymous letters are written by women rather than by men."

"I am better than the police."

Dame Agatha gives us characters named Nurse Capstick, Witness Strange, and Alexander Bonaparte Cust. Her people say things like, "What's wrong with being an orphan? Sometimes it's a blessing in disguise. You might have a good-for-nothing father and a mother who drank..."

"It's all the noise and the speed nowadays — people can't stand it. I've always been sorry for mad people...their heads must feel so queer."

Poirot indignantly confronts the killer. "I consider your crime not an English crime at all...not above-board...not sporting..."

PHIL CLENDENEN

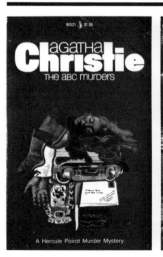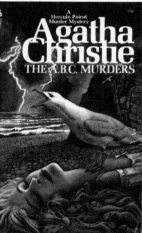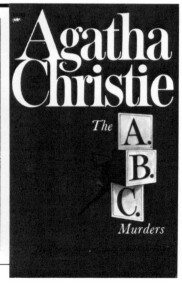

Murder in Mesopotamia
(1936)

Amy Leatheran, thirty-two, an English nurse who is in Baghdad wrapping up a case, is hired by an American archaeologist, Eric Leidner, who is leading a dig in Iraq. He wants a nurse to look after his wife, Louise, who is having "fancies." Nurse Leatheran agrees to come to the compound at Tell Yarimjah, on the banks of the Tigris River in Old Mesopotamia.

At the compound she meets Louise Leidner and the other members of the University of Pittstown expedition to Iraq. Mrs. Leidner is a gracious, charming, beautiful woman approaching forty, but she is badly overwrought, nervous to the point of exhaustion.

She confides in her nurse that she expects to be killed, and soon. Mrs. Leidner explains that she was first married when she was twenty, during World War I. She soon discovered that her husband, Frederick Bosner, was a German spy; she reported him and he was taken away to be executed.

At least she thought he would be executed. When she became seriously interested in another man, she got a letter from her husband, warning her to break off the romance. Her father, who had been in the War Department, told her that Bosner had escaped, but had been later found dead in a train crash. Her father admitted that Bosner's body had been rather badly mutilated, but he insisted her husband was dead. But the letters continued, arriving each time she met a new young man. But she was never certain whether they were a cruel hoax, or from Bosner himself, or possibly from Bosner's adoring younger brother. Her present husband, Leidner, and Nurse Leatheran, suspect that Mrs. Leidner has written the letters to herself.

The only time the letter writer missed was when Louise met and married Leidner. But soon after the wedding another missive came from "Frederick," telling her that she had disobeyed and she must die. Soon after, she and Leidner were almost poisoned by gas in their home. They decided to live abroad while not working in Iraq, and for almost two years no notes came. Then, this year at the dig, the notes started again. The last bore no postmark, arrived the day after Nurse Leatheran, and said simply "I have arrived."

Mrs. Leidner is satisfied the nurse is not the killer, but she is very upset, as one expecting death's nod at any moment might well be. One afternoon she lies down after lunch at 12:45. At twenty minutes before three, her husband finds her dead on the floor in her bedroom, apparently killed by a blow from a heavy object to the right side of her forehead. The weapon is not found.

Hercule Poirot, who is passing through the region on his way to Baghdad, agrees to work on the case at the request of the local police, who agree it is out of their league.

Mrs. Leidner's room could only be entered through a door opening onto the courtyard of the compound, and the compound could only be entered through the front gate where the native servants gathered to gossip. Since the natives say no stranger entered the compound, Poirot decides the killer is a member of the expedition. He sets out to find what kind of a woman Mrs. Leidner was, and who would want her dead.

He quickly rules out Nurse Leatheran, and she becomes his informal assistant. Poirot discovers Mrs. Leidner was not only beautiful but a magical sort of egoist, the kind of woman who feels it is her birthright to be the center of the universe, or at least the part of it that enters her gravitational pull. And largely because of that, Poirot decides she has given virtually every member of the expedition a reason to kill her.

The New York archaeologist Mercado, with whom she played as a cat might with a mouse, may have wanted to kill her to hide some unnamed secret of his past, or to hide his current drug addiction. And his wife, Poirot decides, would have killed to protect her husband and his secret.

Carl Reiter, one of the three young assistants at the dig, was continually needled by Mrs. Leidner. William Coleman, another assistant, was a good forger and could have been responsible for resuming the threatening correspondence. The third assistant, David Emmott, is the calmest and coolest of the lot and, Poirot judges, the best equipped to plan and carry through a complex crime.

Richard Carey, Leidner's friend and associate, was attracted to Mrs. Leidner, and she to him. He loved her, but he also hated her for "making" him love her.

Father Lavigny, who is supposed to be a French monk, is revealed an imposter. Did he kill Mrs. Leidner to insure her silence?

Finally we have Anne Johnson, Eric Leidner's devoted spinster assistant. She was obviously in love with Leidner. Did she kill her mentor's wife, thinking the woman was ruining his life? On the night of the murder, Miss Leatheran had discovered Miss Johnson weeping bitterly in Leidner's office. And later Miss Johnson hurriedly burned a piece of paper that the nurse found in the room, though not before Miss Leatheran noticed that the writing on it was remarkably similar to that on the threatening letters.

A day or so later, Misses Johnson and Leatheran are on the roof of the compound together at sunset when Miss Johnson suddenly looks terrified. She says something about seeing how the murderer could have gotten in, but when the nurse presses her for details, Miss Johnson rushes off.

That night Miss Leatheran hears a strangled cry and rushes to Miss Johnson's room. She finds the woman has drunk hydrochloric acid. The nurse works quickly but it is too late, and the dying woman can only utter, "The window. Nurse, the window." Beneath her bed is found the Leidner murder weapon, a heavy ancient quern, or grinder.

Did Miss Johnson kill Mrs. Leidner and then take her own life in grief? Poirot and Miss Leatheran decide not. They believe the murderer knew Miss Johnson had discovered him, and he substituted the glass of acid for her customary bedside glass of water.

It is left to Poirot to assemble the suspects and then, in a classic scene, take them on a journey through the case until he brings them to the inescapable conclusion, and the murderer's confession.

JACK MURPHY

Cards on the Table (1936)

It is for Friday, the eighteenth, that Dr. Shaitana, a well-known London socialite and giver of spectacular and fascinating parties, arranges a dinner party to introduce Hercule Poirot, reowned Belgian detective, to his "Black Museum" to view his collection of murderers—"the ones who have got away with it, the successes!" Included on Shaitana's guest list are Mrs. Ariadne Oliver, famous author of detective and sensational stories; Superintendent Battle, reputedly the best of Scotland Yard's representatives; and Colonel Race, a handsome and esteemed member of His Majesty's foreign secret service. To complete his curious guest list, Mr. Shaitana invites Mrs. Lorrimer, a well-dressed, well-mannered woman of sixty; Major Despard, a lean, handsome man who travels a great deal to out-of-the-way and dangerous places; shy, pretty Anne Meredith; and the garrulous, hearty, brisk-bedside-mannered Dr. Roberts. An interesting party of nine.

In keeping with his reputation, an elegant, gracious dinner is served, complete with a mousse foie gras in gleaming blue Irish glassware. Mr. Shaitana presides, his Mephistophelean features accented by the candlelight, as conversations revolve around poisons, the possibility of a woman director of Scotland Yard, accidents, books, and world politics.

Bridge is the evening's after-dinner entertainment, with the "sleuths" competing at one table, and Mrs. Lorrimer, Anne Meredith, Dr. Roberts, and Major Despard at the parlor table. Shaitana himself demurs, preferring to spend the evening by the fire. At 12:10, as Colonel Race, Poirot, and the others are ending their game and

saying good-bye to their host, the colonel discovers that Mr. Shaitana is dead, stabbed in the chest in his chair by the fire.

Who did it? Four sleuths were present, and four people who had reason to want Shaitana dead—he knew too much about their pasts.

Together and individually the four sleuths attempt to unravel the mystery, interviewing each suspect and his or her friends, neighbors, and employers. Carefully following hunches and clues they add information, patterns of behavior, motivations.

Miss Anne Meredith, a young woman in her early twenties, daughter of an army officer, has made her way as a companion and housekeeper (she had noticed that the water in the flowers in Mr. Shaitana's parlor needed changing). She moved from job to job—from the Isle of Wight to Switzerland to Devonshire (which she fails to mention), always receiving good recommendations from her previous employers. Mrs. Oliver, bolstered up by cups of hot black coffee and buttered toast discovers the time gap in Miss Meredith's employment — about four to five years before. While Anne was employed in Devonshire, her employer, Mrs. Elton, had accidentally taken poison stored in a Syrup of Figs bottle and had died. Very interesting.

Dr. Roberts, it is discovered, had been slightly indiscreet in his attentions to a Mrs. Craddock. Her husband found out. Shortly thereafter Mr. Craddock was dead, by infection from an anthrax-contaminated shaving brush of cheap manufacture, which in turn precipitated a major public scare. Mrs. Craddock, inoculated against

typhoid prior to traveling in the Near East, died in Egypt some time later from an obscure strain of blood poisoning. Purely coincidental.

Mrs. Lorrimer, the superb bridge player with enormous powers of concentration, has been a widow for twenty years. She has often traveled during the damp English winters to civilized places like the Riviera and Egypt where she had occasion to meet Mr. Shaitana. She was held in the highest esteem by her friends and associates. But she was a widow whose husband died under suspicious circumstances.

And there is Major Despard, a trained and successful hunter in Africa, known as Pukka Sahib by the natives who knew and trusted him. A cool-headed gentleman. Some time before, in Africa, he had killed a tiger and saved a man's life. But also in his past was his position as guide for Professor Luxmore, noted botanist, and his wife on an expedition to South America. The professor, who never returned, was said to have died of a fever somewhere along the Amazon. Mrs. Luxmore still lives in London.

These, then, are the four people Shaitana had chosen from his collection. Four people who played cards in the same room where Mr. Shaitana was found dead. Four people who claim innocence. Four people associated with deaths of mysterious or dubious circumstance. Four

people about whom the sleuths are assembling information gleaned from the past, their words, their behavior, and their bridge scores.

No suspect can lead the great Poirot down the garden path, because whether one tries to hinder or help the progress of his search, each suspect will necessarily provide the cards for the ultimate deck that Poirot so skillfully shuffles and deals.

HELENE VON ROSENSTIEL

Poirot Loses a Client (1937)

**(Alternate titles: *Dumb Witness,*
Murder at Littlegreen House,
Mystery at Littlegreen House)**

It was an intriguing little missive. The writing style was a poor attempt at elegance that tended to obscure the meaning, and the penmanship suggested the trail of a spider that had fallen out of an inkpot and wandered across the paper. Yet, it was precisely what was obscured or left unsaid that seized the attention of Hercule Poirot. That and the fact that the letter had been mailed to him two months after it had been written, impelled him to take old Emily Arundell's case.

> In the circumstances, as I am sure you will be the first to appreciate, it is quite impossible for me to consult any one in Market Basing, but at the same time you will naturally understand that I feel uneasy...It is actually preying on my mind and affecting my health, and naturally I am in a difficult position as I can say nothing to any one.

What had motivated the old lady to write the letter? Did she feel that her life was in danger? Or, as Poirot's associate Captain Hastings would suggest, was the letter merely the paranoid ramblings of a senile dowager? The most obvious way to determine the facts would be for Poirot and Hastings to take a short ride in the country to the town of Market Basing—a mere hour and a half ride from London.

When Poirot and Hastings arrive to inspect the Arundell estate, they discover a sign posted in front of the manor, indicating that the place is for sale. Miss Emily Arundell, as fate would have it, has been dead for over a month.

Did the old lady meet an untimely end? Were her morbid fears realized? And if so, who mailed the letter to M. Poirot?

Rumors about Miss Arundell's death prolifer-

ate around Market Basing, seeded by the curious truth that the old lady had revised her will only days before her death. Her entire estate had been left to her companion, Minnie Lawson, while nary a bob was awarded to her immediate family. There was little doubt in the minds of the townsfolk that foul work had been done.

The last of three sisters, Emily had been heir to a fortune left her by her father, General Arundell. Yet, since she herself had no children to whom to pass the estate, it seemed a matter of course that the fortune would one day be divided among her nieces and nephews.

The likelihood of one day being made rich by their aunt's demise was not lost on the would-be heirs. Indeed, it tended to temper their feelings toward her. One, or some, may have even contemplated encouraging nature's inexorable process. They had gathered two months earlier to celebrate what was to be Aunt Emily's last Easter.

Niece Theresa Arundell is an adventurous, occasionally reckless, young woman. She belongs to that wild young London set whose *carpe diem* philosophy breeds scandalous parties and who are a constant embarrassment to their families. Theresa's brother Charles, though less ostentatious, is no more respectable. In his better moments he might be considered a rake. In his worst, he is a thieving scoundrel.

Bella Winter Tanios, another niece, imitates her cousin Theresa's taste for chic and expensive clothes. Poor Bella, however, never developed good clothes sense to complement her taste. Consequently, nothing on her is ever properly matched. Her lack of taste, many feel, is reflected in her domestic life, for, though she is a commendable mother to her children, she had them by a foreigner — and not just a foreigner, but a Greek.

The prejudice that Emily Arundell had harbored for Dr. Tanios tended to be exacerbated by his good manners and charm. Not a people to be trusted, these Greeks; somewhere on a par with Argentines and Turks.

Then there is Minnie Lawson, Emily's companion. Though basically well meaning and good-hearted, Mrs. Lawson tends to be full of the empty-headed chatter that Emily had found so tiresome. She also has an interest in the occult and attends séances with those bizarre Tripp sisters.

Emily had been under no illusions as to what was on the minds of those gathered around her. They were not the ideal group to be trusted with the Arundell fortune, and the fact that some of them were in a hurry to collect it had made Emily uneasy. Why, Charles had even suggested that if Emily entertained notions of changing the will, it would be so much the worse for her. Best to be guarded.

On those nights when sleep evaded her, Emily had been fond of wandering about the manor, walking with the phantasms of past Arundells. It was one o'clock in the morning when she got out of bed to go downstairs and check over the weekly books. The only person awake in the great house, she made her way to the head of the stairs and started down. Suddenly she found herself propelled headfirst down the staircase.

Summoned by the clamor of the fall and Emily's cry, the family gathered around her. She was lucky, Dr. Tanios said, there were no broken bones. What had caused her to fall? The dog's

Poirot Loses a Client (1937)

ball, Charles insisted, holding it in his hand; Emily must have stumbled over the damn thing when it was left at the top of the stairs.

Oh, really? Emily was quite sure that the ball had been left in the bureau drawer where she always kept it. Also, her dog, Bob, was out for the night. Emily said nothing, but she knew that, first thing in the morning, she had a letter to write—to Hercule Poirot.

Where to begin the inquiries?

First, there is the nail driven into the skirting board at the top of the stairs where Emily had fallen. Minnie Lawson claims to have seen a woman kneeling there one night. And though her eyesight was too impaired to recognize the face, she did notice the woman's brooch with the initials *T.A.* on it.

T.A. — Theresa Arundell? Wild as she is, was she impetuous enough to try murder? She might have had a motive in the guise of her new beau, Dr. Rex Donaldson. A colorless sort, Donaldson could have used the inheritance to further his scientific research.

Speaking of things scientific, let us not forget Dr. Tanios. It was rumored that he had lost through unwise investing the little money Bella had at the time of their marriage. Too, he had prescribed nostrums for Emily's ailments on any number of occasions. Could he have used his office toward some evil end?

In addition to having threatened his aunt, Charles Arundell had offered to the gardener the idea of poisoning her. The gardener thought nothing of it until he discovered that a goodly portion of the arsenic he used in his work was missing.

Poison. Emily's last meal had been in the company of Minnie Lawson and the weird Tripps. The meal had been so heavily curried that it could easily have masked a lethal dose of any number of poisons. Both Minnie and the Tripps claim to have had an omen of dire happenings to come when, that same evening, they persuaded Emily to take part in a séance and saw an evanescent glow appear around the old woman's head.

The Home Office will certainly require more than a lot of assumptions and circumstantial evidence before permitting an exhumation. Yet Poirot is not a man easily daunted. Although he might have lost a client, his investigation is just beginning.

PETER J. FITZPATRICK

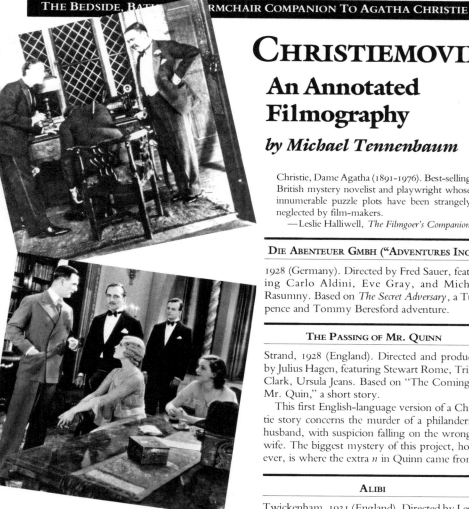

CHRISTIEMOVIE
An Annotated Filmography
by Michael Tennenbaum

Christie, Dame Agatha (1891-1976). Best-selling British mystery novelist and playwright whose innumerable puzzle plots have been strangely neglected by film-makers.
—Leslie Halliwell, *The Filmgoer's Companion*

DIE ABENTEUER GMBH ("ADVENTURES INC.")

1928 (Germany). Directed by Fred Sauer, featuring Carlo Aldini, Eve Gray, and Michael Rasumny. Based on *The Secret Adversary*, a Tuppence and Tommy Beresford adventure.

THE PASSING OF MR. QUINN

Strand, 1928 (England). Directed and produced by Julius Hagen, featuring Stewart Rome, Trilby Clark, Ursula Jeans. Based on "The Coming of Mr. Quin," a short story.

This first English-language version of a Christie story concerns the murder of a philandering husband, with suspicion falling on the wronged wife. The biggest mystery of this project, however, is where the extra *n* in Quinn came from.

ALIBI

Twickenham, 1931 (England). Directed by Leslie Hiscott, featuring Austin Trevor, Franklin Dyall, Elizabeth Allan. From *The Murder of Roger Ackroyd*.

This is the first in a series of three films to feature Austin Trevor as Hercule Poirot. Trevor, a dapper character actor, was totally wrong for the role, physically. He once suggested that he was cast for his ability to do a French accent. The story revolves around Poirot's investigation of a suspicious suicide on a country estate.

The first Poirots: Charles Laughton (right, top) played Hercule Poirot in the first stage treatment of a Christie work: Alibi *(1928) by Michael Morton, based on* The Murder of Roger Ackroyd. *Dr. Sheppard (left) was played by J. H. Roberts. Austin Trevor (below, left) was the first on-screen Poirot, starring in three Christie mysteries in the early '30s. With him are (from left) C. V. France, Elizabeth Allan, Philip Strange, Adrianne Allen.*

BLACK COFFEE

Twickenham, 1931 (England). Directed by Leslie Hiscott, featuring Austin Trevor, Richard Cooper, Adrienne Allen, Melville Cooper. Based on the stage play of the same name.

This film suffered from being stage-bound, and Trevor's portrayal was completely overshadowed by the true-to-Christie characterizations of Poirot by Charles Laughton and Francis Sullivan on stage. In the story, Poirot unmasks a murderer who has also stolen a secret formula.

LORD EDGWARE DIES

Real Art, 1934 (England). Directed by Henry Edwards, featuring Austin Trevor, Jane Carr, Richard Cooper, John Turnbull. From the novel.

In this final film in the Trevor-Poirot series, the detective investigates the murder of the husband of a vain American actress.

There seems to be no trace of these films left today, and records indicate that they were never released in the United States, even though the stage version of *Alibi* was a fairly successful Broadway venture. Poirot was not attempted again by film-makers for more than thirty years.

Left: Austin Trevor (Poirot) and Richard Cooper (Hastings) in Lord Edgware Dies, *with Jane Carr as Lady Edgware.*

Above, from left: Louis Hayward, C. Aubrey Smith, Barry Fitzgerald, Richard Haydn, Mischa Auer, and Walter Huston in And Then There Were None.

CHRISTIEMOVIE

LOVE FROM A STRANGER

United Artists, 1937 (filmed in England). Directed by Rowland V. Lee, featuring Basil Rathbone, Ann Harding. From the play based on the story "Philomel Cottage."

A bride becomes justifiably suspicious of her new husband when she realizes he has probably murdered his last three wives. But he has a heart condition, and if she can get him before he gets her.... This chestnut was a successful play that was improved on screen with the stylish direction of Lee and the suave yet menacing presence of Rathbone. A piercing scream from Miss Harding was the high point in the film's thrilling climax.

This was the first film version of a Christie work to be seen in the United States—seventeen years after her first book was published.

AND THEN THERE WERE NONE

Twentieth Century-Fox, 1945. Directed by Rene Clair, featuring Louis Hayward, Barry Fitzgerald, Walter Huston, June Duprez, Roland Young, C. Aubrey Smith, Judith Anderson, Mischa Auer, Richard Haydn. From the play *Ten Little Indians* based on the novel *Ten Little Niggers*.

Ten strangers are assembled on an island, are accused of murder by their unseen host, and are themselves bumped off, one at a time, as in the famous children's rhyme.

LOVE FROM A STRANGER

Eagle Lion, 1947. Directed by Richard Whorf, featuring Sylvia Sidney and John Hodiak.

This remake of the thriller of a decade earlier changed the time and place of the original to America at the start of the century. Unfortunately, none of the mystery remained. If the story was old-fashioned in 1937.... The review in the *New York Times* summed it up: "The thrill has gone from 'Love from a Stranger.'"

Left: Basil Rathbone and Ann Harding in Love from a Stranger *(1937); below: Sylvia Sidney, John Hodiak, John Howard in the 1947 remake.*

WITNESS FOR THE PROSECUTION

United Artists, 1957. Directed by Billy Wilder, featuring Charles Laughton, Marlene Dietrich, and Tyrone Power. From the play and short story of the same name.

Likeable Leonard Vole is accused of the murder of a rich old lady, and barrister Sir Wilfrid Robarts takes his case, in spite of his own failing health. The surprise comes when the witness of the title turns out to be none other than Vole's own wife, Christine, and Sir Wilfrid begins to doubt everyone involved. There is a plot twist, then another, and another.

THE SPIDER'S WEB

United Artists, 1960 (England). Directed by Godfrey Grayson, featuring Glynis Johns, John Justin, and Ronald Howard. From the 1954 play.

It is surprising that this modest domestic murder drama, involving blackmail and a disappearing corpse (a la Hitchcock's *The Trouble With Harry*), was the only follow-up film after the success of *Witness for the Prosecution*. Nowhere is Hollywood's reticence about Christie more apparent; the film wasn't even released in this country.

CHRISTIEMOVIE

MURDER SHE SAID

MGM, 1962 (England). Directed by George Pollock, featuring Margaret Rutherford, Arthur Kennedy, Muriel Pavlow, James Robertson Justice, Charles Tingwell, Stringer Davis, Ronald Howard. Based on *What Mrs. McGillicuddy Saw!*

In the first of four Miss Marple mysteries produced by MGM's British unit, the indefatigable amateur sleuth sees a murder being committed on a passing train, but can get no one to believe her. So she begins an investigation on her own by posing as a maid on the estate where she believes the body must have been hidden.

Starting left, counterclockwise: Marlene Dietrich, Elsa Lanchester, and Charles Laughton in Witness for the Prosecution; *Agatha Christie with director Godfrey Grayson on the set of* The Spider's Web; *Margaret Rutherford as Miss Marple in* Murder She Said *and* Murder Ahoy.

MURDER AT THE GALLOP

MGM, 1963 (England). Directed by Pollock, featuring Rutherford, Tingwell, Davis, Robert Morley, and Flora Robson. Based on *Funerals Are Fatal*, a Poirot novel.

Miss Marple joins a riding academy (the Gallop) to investigate the death of an old recluse.

MURDER MOST FOUL

MGM, 1964 (England). Directed by Pollock. With Rutherford, Tingwell, Davis, and Ron Moody. Based on *Mrs. McGinty's Dead*, another Poirot novel.

Miss Marple becomes a thespian to track down a killer and clear an innocent man in the death of a blackmailing actress.

MURDER AHOY!

MGM, 1964 (England). Directed by Pollock. With Rutherford, Tingwell, Davis, and Lionel Jeffries. An original screenplay, not based on a Christie work, by David Pursall and Jack Seddon.

Miss Marple investigates blackmail, embezzlement and, of course, murder on a training ship that has become a school for young criminals.

CHRISTIEMOVIE

TEN LITTLE INDIANS

Seven Arts, 1965 (filmed in England). Directed by George Pollock. With Hugh O'Brian, Shirley Eaton, Fabian, Leo Genn, Wilfrid Hyde-White, Stanley Holloway, Daliah Lavi, Dennis Price. A remake of *And Then There Were None*.

Ten strangers are assembled in an isolated hotel in the Austrian Alps, and...

THE ALPHABET MURDERS

MGM, 1966 (England). Directed by Frank Tashlin. With Tony Randall, Robert Morley, Anita Ekberg. Based on *The A.B.C. Murders*.

Originally intended as a vehicle for Zero Mostel, the project was held up for two years because of Miss Christie's objections to the script. Eventually the problems were ironed out, with a heavily madeup Tony Randall assuming the role of the Belgian detective. Under the direction of Frank Tashlin, known for his work with Bugs Bunny cartoons and Jerry Lewis vehicles, the film became an exercise in visual humor, with Poirot and his abilities relegated to background.

The far from coherent story involves Poirot's interest in a series of seemingly unrelated murders. Margaret Rutherford and Stringer Davis make guest appearances in the film. Another guest, at least on the set, was Austin Trevor, the screen's original Poirot, who is pictured below with his first successor in the role.

ENDLESS NIGHT

United Artists, 1972 (England). Directed by Sidney Gilliat. With Hayley Mills, Hywel Bennett, Britt Ekland, Per Oscarson, George Sanders. Based on the novel *Endless Night*.

The permutations of a romantic triangle result in murder. When this film was screened for the press in London, the critics surrounded the studio's press representative demanding answers to plot questions that had been left dangling as a result of the movie's sloppy editing. In the parlance of Hollywood flacks, this movie wasn't released—it escaped.

MURDER ON THE ORIENT EXPRESS

EMI-Paramount, 1974. Directed by Sidney Lumet. With Albert Finney, Lauren Bacall, Martin Balsam, Ingrid Bergman, Jacqueline Bisset, Jean-Pierre Cassel, Sean Connery, John Gielgud, Wendy Hiller, Anthony Perkins, Vanessa Redgrave, Rachel Roberts, Richard Widmark, Michael York. Based on the 1934 novel (U.S. title *Murder in the Calais Coach*).

In this, the most successful British film ever made, all the passengers on the famous European train are suspected of the murder of an American gangster. Poirot is determined to find the culprit. (See "Poirot Makes the Big Time" for details about the film's opulence.)

TEN LITTLE INDIANS

Avco–Embassy, 1975. Directed by Peter Collinson. With Oliver Reed, Elke Sommer, Richard Attenborough, Gert Frobe, Charles Aznavour. A remake of the 1965 remake.

There's these ten strangers, see? And they're called to this isolated hotel in the Iranian desert...

DEATH ON THE NILE

EMI–Paramount, 1978 (filmed on location in Egypt and England). Directed by John Guillerman. With Peter Ustinov, Bette Davis, Mia Farrow, Lois Chiles, David Niven, George Kennedy, Jack Warden, Maggie Smith, Angela Lansbury. Based on the 1937 novel.

While on vacation in Egypt, Poirot investigates the murder of a beautiful young heiress. Filming on location caused many interesting developments. (See "Life on the Nile" for details.)

*Below, starting left: Dennis Price discovers another corpse, as Hugh O'Brian and Shirley Eaton look on (*Ten Little Indians, *1965); Anita Ekberg and Robert Morley attempt to revive Tony Randall (Poirot) in* The Alphabet Murders; *Herbert Lom and Oliver Reed discover the corpse this time, as Elke Sommer, Gert Frobe, and Stephane Audran look on (*Ten Little Indians, *1975). At right: David Niven and Angela Lansbury do the tango in* Death on the Nile.

THE CONDEMNED ATE A HEARTY MEAL
Some Favorite English Dishes
by Joanna Milton

They were all huddled in the kitchen. On the gas cooker the potatoes bubbled merrily. The savory smell from the oven of steak and kidney pie was stronger than ever....
— from "Three Blind Mice"

One of the delicious things about reading Agatha Christie is that her books stimulate your appetite. Steak and kidney pie, kippers, Yorkshire pudding, and Devonshire cream are not very familiar to a Florida-raised gourmet, but after reading my first mysteries I became curious to try these dishes. What, exactly, *was* a Yorkshire pudding? What did it taste like? Could a hush puppy fancier from the Deep South attempt a treacle tart?

Christie used her favorite dishes in more than a functional or aesthetic way. Certain foods were rituals, evoking poignant memories of tradition and even womanhood. For instance, Molly, the baker of the steak and kidney pie mentioned above, finds solace in her pudding while she tries to locate a murderer in the house:

Molly stood very straight and still, a red flush burning in her cheeks. After standing rigid for a moment or two, she moved slowly toward the stove, knelt down, and opened the oven door. A savory, familiar smell came toward her. Her heart lightened. It was as though suddenly she had been wafted back into the dear, familiar world of everyday things. Cooking, housework, homemaking, ordinary prosaic living. So, from time immemorial women had cooked food for their men. The world of danger — of madness, receded. Woman, in her kitchen, was safe — eternally safe.

Nor was Hercule Poirot oblivious to the delights of the steak and kidney combination:

Poirot had been at the inn for about an hour and had just finished a hearty lunch of steak and kidney pudding, washed down by beer, when word was brought to him that a lady was waiting to see him...
— from *The Labors of Hercules*

Here, then, is one of Christie's favorites.

STEAK AND KIDNEY PIE

1 ½ lbs. round steak	2 cups meat stock
¾ lb. lamb or veal kidneys	1 cup red wine
3 tbs. butter or fat	pie dough
flour	

Preheat oven to 350°

While one can use beef kidneys in this dish, they should be blanched to make them as tender as possible. You should have enough pie dough to cover the top of the ovenproof baker in which the dish is made.

Cut the round steak into small slices about half an inch thick. Wash, skin, and slice the kidneys. Melt the butter in a skillet, saute the kidneys for about two minutes, shaking all the time. Then take the kidneys out and shake them inside a paper bag with seasoned flour until they are coated.

Put the steak slices in a greased baking dish, then add the kidneys, the stock and the wine. Bake, covered for 90 minutes to two hours. Remove and cool slightly, then raise oven heat to 400°, cover the dish with pie dough, and bake 15 more minutes, or until brown.

THE BEDSIDE, BATHTUB & ARMCHAIR COMPANION TO AGATHA CHRISTIE

Those who find steak and kidney pie a little intimidating may satisfy their Christie-induced cravings for an English pudding with the Yorkshire. Yorkshire pudding is the equivalent of a pasta or starch course, but it is considered rather elegant as well as traditional. In one example, Christie has it prepared by Lucy Eyelesbarrow, a detective who functions as a cook in *What Mrs. McGillicuddy Saw!* She also serves, in the course of the book, such specialties as apple meringue, roast beef of Old England, peach flan, ginger cake, curried chicken with rice, and syllabub, so the Yorkshire pudding is in good company. Below are two of Detective Eyelesbarrow's favorites, which should give anyone a taste of merry old England.

YORKSHIRE PUDDING

(6 servings)

| 2 eggs | 1 cup milk | salt |
| 1 cup flour | 1 tsp. olive oil | pepper |

Preheat oven to 400°.

The ingredients must be at room temperature when mixed or they will not puff. Make the batter for the Yorkshire pudding when you first put in the meat and let it stand to get the air into it.

First separate the yolks from whites of the eggs

and beat the yolks well. Add the flour gradually to the yolks, then thin it down with the oil and milk and add the salt. Beat well until like thick cream. Leave to stand until the meat is about ½ hour from being cooked.

Stir in the stiffly beaten whites and mix well. Have ready a pan with about 1 inch of piping hot beef drippings in it, and pour in the batter. It should sizzle when it goes in. Put the meat on a lower shelf and the pudding on the top one. Cook for about ½ hour, until it is golden brown and well risen. Serve the pudding at once with the meat and with horseradish sauce.

It was customary to cook this dish in the pan with the roast or under the roast. As many of us now cook roast beef in a slow oven, it is best to cook it separately in the hot oven required to puff it up and brown it quickly. In Yorkshire it is served before the meat course as a hefty pudding.

SYLLABUB, OR MILK PUNCH

(4 servings)

| 1 tbs. sugar | a pinch of nutmeg |
| 1 cup Madeira or sherry | 2 cups heavy cream |

Mix together the sugar, wine, and nutmeg, then divide the liquid among 4 long glasses and pour it

THE CONDEMNED ATE A HEARTY MEAL

into the bottom. Whip the cream and likewise divide this among the glasses, pouring it slowly on top of the wine mixture. Leave in a cool place for several hours or overnight before serving.

Poultry à la Christie is also a dish that conjures up images of elegance and good taste. In "Four and Twenty Blackbirds," the waitress at the Gallant Endeavor greets Poirot's friend Henry Bonnington in this manner:

> Good evening, sir...you're in luck today—turkey stuffed with chestnuts—that's your favorite, isn't it?
> —from "Four and Twenty Blackbirds,"
> in *The Mousetrap*

And Poirot himself is not averse to a bit of the old bird. In *Death in the Air* he states candidly that "the stomach rules the mind," and orders, during the course of the book, an example of what he considers excellent "mind food," a *chaud-froid* of chicken. Like to try it?

SAUCE CHAUD-FROID

2 cups bechamel or other cream sauce
3 or 4 tbs. stock

The name *chaud-froid* is derived from the fact that this sauce is made over heat, but served cold. Basically, one uses the stock from a particular dish to flavor the cream sauce. Thus, for a chicken one would use chicken stock, for fish a fish stock.

Prepare the cream sauce, perhaps overseasoning a bit, and add the stock. Stir constantly over medium heat until combined, then cool, still stirring occasionally. When it coats a spoon but has not yet set, pour or spoon it over the chicken or fish and put it in the refrigerator until it sets.

Sometimes a dish may take more than one coat.

CHESTNUT DRESSING FOR TURKEY

2½ cups boiled chestnuts	1 cup dry breadcrumbs
	1 tsp. salt
2 tbs. chopped parsley	⅛ tsp. pepper
½ cup chopped celery	½ cup melted butter
1 tbs. grated onion	¼ cup cream

Dice the chestnuts and combine with all other ingredients.

Among other things, one can add various kinds of sausage or a small amount of raisins.

Miss Marple loves Devonshire cream and so, evidently, did Agatha Christie, according to her biography. In fact, Devonshire cream is mentioned with such reverence in Christie's books one would think it must be some rare variety of Old English chocolate, served only on special occasions. But no, even the working class had Devonshire cream with their fruit, and it's really just ...cream.

DEVONSHIRE OR CLOTTED CREAM

Put a quantity of cream out to stand in a casserole or cooking dish. Let stand 12 hours in winter, six in summer, then heat very slowly on the stove, never allowing it to boil. When small rings form on the surface, remove and refrigerate for 12 hours. Skim the clotted cream and serve, cold, on berries.

Food items are often used by Christie to show a subtle English patriotism, usually at the expense of Americans. For example, at Bertram's Hotel, the Americans are served cereal and juice for breakfast, while the British can choose eggs and bacon or kippers (salmon), cold grouse, kidneys and bacon or York ham).

However, you don't have to be British to like souffle au kipper.

SOUFFLÉ AU KIPPER

8 oz. kipper	1 tbs. cream (optional)
3 eggs, separated	½ oz. flour
¼ pint kipper stock	seasoning
1 oz. butter	

Preheat oven to 400°.

Simmer the kipper in boiling water until tender, drain (retaining the stock) and flake the fish. Then, using a wooden spoon, pound it into a paste.

Stir the butter into the hot kipper stock, beat this sauce into the fish paste, and cook for one minute. Remove from heat and add cream and seasoning, and the egg yolks one at a time, being careful not to scramble them.

Beat the egg whites until stiff, fold them into the mixture. Turn the whole into a buttered souffle dish and bake for about 30 minutes.

Bertram's Hotel was also justly famous for its muffins. Colonel Luscombe, for instance, compared them with those in the former colonies:

> Only place in London you can still get muffins. Real muffins. Do you know when I went to America last year they had something called muffins on the breakfast menu. Not real muffins at all. Kind of teacake with raisins in them. I mean, why call them muffins?
> —from *At Bertram's Hotel*

See if these are the real thing for you.

MUFFINS

(About 2 dozen 2-inch muffins)

1¾ cup all-purpose flour	2 beaten eggs
¾ tsp. salt	4 tbs. melted butter
¼ cup sugar	¾ cup milk
2 tsp. double-acting baking powder	

Preheat oven to 400°.

All ingredients should be at room temperature, and the flour should be sifted before measuring.

Sift the flour again, this time with the salt, sugar, and baking powder. Then add the eggs, butter, and milk, and mix only about 20 seconds, which will leave some lumps.

Grease the tins, and fill each about 2/3 full, bake at once for 20 to 25 minutes. Eat immediately.

Finally, a study of Christie reveals a food item every Southern girl knows: blackberry jam. This international specialty could be either friend or foe in Christie's delicacy lineup. Tuppence, in *By the Pricking of My Thumbs,* loves blackberry jam, but the victim in "Four and Twenty Blackbirds" never eats blackberries. His murderer caught — by ordering everything the poor fellow hated.

BLACKBERRY JAM

4 cups blackberries (or raspberries, etc.)

3 cups of sugar (approximately)

Prepare hot, sterilized jars.

The amount of sugar should vary with the tartness of the berries. Use your own judgment. Combine the berries and sugar, and cook over low heat, stirring to prevent sticking. Cook until sugar is dissolved and a small amount of the berry mixture dropped on a plate will stay in place. Pack immediately in the jars.

Where there are blackberries, can treacle be far behind? Treacle, in England, means molasses — specifically, molasses that drains from sugar-refining molds. Treacle, sometimes called golden syrup, is milder in flavor than molasses and, according to *Joy of Cooking*, does not substitute well for it; therefore, it should be used only where specified.

I'm afraid I haven't got any recipes for treacle, nor any treacle at all, for that matter. Anyone for apple tarts?

Death on the Nile
(1937)

A scarlet Rolls Royce pulls up in front of the country post office and a girl jumps out. Her golden-girl manner is the envy of one imbiber at the Three Crowns: "It seems all wrong to me — her looking like that. Money *and* looks — it's too much! If a girl's as rich as that, she's no right to be a good looker as well. And she is a good looker. Got everything, that girl has. Doesn't seem fair."

Linnet Ridgeway, at twenty, is perhaps the richest girl in England. And she knows how to use all her assets to get what she wants. She believes that what's best for her is generally best for all.

Linnet's old school chum Jacqueline de Bellefort calls. She must see Linnet at once. Jackie's had a tough time since her family lost its money two years before and now, she tells Linnet, her fiancé, Simon Doyle, has just lost his job. Please, she pleads, couldn't Simon be Linnet's estate manager, and they could all live happily ever after. "Oh, Linnet," Jackie begs, "you will give him a job.... I shall *die* if I can't marry him! I shall die! I shall die!"

Linnet laughs. "Bring along your young man and let me have a look at him." When Jackie returns with Simon the following day, Linnet takes one look at the way Simon returns her look — and hires him on the spot.

Hercule Poirot is on holiday in Egypt. The little Belgian detective with a moustache nearly as big as his opinion of himself has found a pretty young companion, Rosalie Otterbourne, for his stroll along the Nile at Assuan. Soon they will be taking a steamer cruise to the second cataract at Wadi Halfa. They are diverted from their shopping as a large steamer from Luxor moors just below them. They are joined by Tim Allerton, who also will travel with them. As the steamer's passengers disembark, Tim starts: "Hullo, I'm damned if that isn't Linnet Ridgeway.... There with the tall man. He's the new husband, I suppose. Can't remember his name now."

"Doyle," Rosalie says, "Simon Doyle. It was in all the newspapers.... Some people have got everything."

Poirot sees what they don't. "Something is not right," he notes. He has noticed the lines under Linnet's eyes and that her hand holds the sunshade so tight her knuckles are white. What could conceivably bother the golden girl?

The warm darkness of the Egyptian evening has brought a mysterious hush to every table on the terrace of the Cataract Hotel. There is almost a sense of expectancy as the guests sip coffee and gaze at the prehistoric rocks of Elephantine Island.

Everyone turns as the swinging door revolves. A dark-haired girl in a wine-red dress crosses the terrace deliberately, sits, and stares at Linnet Doyle. Linnet changes her seat and the girl, Jackie de Bellefort, moves too — always so that she has a clear view of Linnet and so that Linnet can always see her.

It is driving Linnet to distraction. Later that evening she asks Hercule Poirot if there is any way to stop this "intolerable persecution." Jackie has been following them everywhere, from Venice to Brindisi, to Cairo and now.... But, Poirot points out, there is nothing illegal in traveling to the same places.

Poirot looks for Jacqueline de Bellefort and finds her sitting on the rocks high above the river. "Mademoiselle," he pleads, "bury your dead.

Turn to the future. I beseech you, do not open your heart to evil."

Jackie says she cannot stop, will not stop, not now when her revenge is working so well.

Simon Doyle is disgusted with his former fiancée: "Why can't Jackie take it like a man? Decent girls don't behave like this! I admit I was entirely to blame. I treated her damned badly and all that.... But this following me round—it's—it's *indecent*! I'd understand better if she'd tried to do something melodramatic—like taking a pot shot at me."

It's upsetting Linnet so much, she and Simon devise a ruse. They announce they will stay in Assuan instead of going on the Nile cruise—and that morning they head off by donkey for Philae (as their luggage is spirited to the steamer).

A radiant Linnet Doyle emerges with Simon from their cabins. They are free. Laughter meets them. Linnet whips around: Jackie! Linnet is stunned; Doyle looks furious.

"Monsieur Poirot," Linnet confides as the sun sets over the rocky Nile of Nubia, "I'm afraid. Everyone hates me.... I feel that everything's unsafe all around me.... There's no way out."

Rosalie Otterbourne (Olivia Hussey) attempts to calm the hysterical Jacqueline de Bellefort (Mia Farrow) in the recent film adaptation of Death on the Nile.

Death on the Nile (1937)

Just how unsafe, Linnet has no idea. Two days later a boulder from the top of Abu Simbel hurtles down toward her. She is pulled out from under by Simon just a split second before it hits.

And now they are back in Abu Simbel, after their turn-around at Wadi Halfa. The day has been terribly hot, and Poirot is unusually sleepy. He does not suspect it yet, but it is not the heat that is affecting him. As he leaves the ship's saloon, he almost collides with Jacqueline de Bellefort. She apologizes, "It's been the sort of day when things — snap! Break! When one can't go on...."

Jacqueline orders a double gin. The more she drinks, the less Simon is able to concentrate on his bridge game with Linnet and two other passengers. Simon's calls become absentminded as Jackie tosses off one drink and orders another. The other players call it an evening, but Doyle stays.

Jackie latches on to ingenuous Cornelia Robson. "Don't leave," she orders. "We girls must stick together." In the corner, a young English lawyer, Jim Fanthorp, is so embarrassed by the growing theatricality of the scene that he feigns absorption in his reading.

Jackie wants another drink and orders Simon to get it. "You've had quite enough," Simon responds. So Jackie tells Cornelia, rather loudly, the story of her broken heart. Simon protests, and Jacqueline hisses in anger, "I told you that I'd kill you sooner than see you go to another woman...and I meant it." Her hand holds something that flashes and gleams. Simon springs to his feet. And Jackie pulls the trigger.

A crimson stain seeps through the handkerchief Simon holds to his trouser leg. Jacqueline is hysterical; she drops the gun and kicks it away. "Get her out of here," Simon yells. Cornelia and Fanthorp drag her away and get her settled under the care of a nurse. Then they rouse Dr. Bessner and take him to bind Simon's leg.

Poirot sleeps right through it.

"Linnet Doyle's dead," Poirot is told next morning, "shot through the head last night." And written next to her in blood, the letter *J*. For Jacqueline? But the murder was done after Jackie had been sedated by Nurse Bowers, who stayed with her all night. Who was trying to accuse Jacqueline de Bellefort? Who had written that *J*? Who killed Linnet Doyle?

There were others besides Jackie de Bellefort who wanted Linnet dead: her American trustee who was about to be caught with his hand in the till; sweet Cornelia Robson whose father was destroyed by Linnet's father; the ship's engineer who lost a lover through Linnet's "good efforts"; and there is the person who stole Linnet's perfect pearls from her beside table the night she was murdered.

Before Poirot deduces the truth, Linnet's blackmailing maid is stabbed to death with a surgeon's knife, and Rosalie's mother, the flamboyant author Salome Otterbourne ("There is no God but Sex and Salome Otterbourne is its Prophet") is shot dead just as she is about to reveal the maid's murderer.

Piecing together the most unlikely clues — nail polish, a velvet stole, a hand-carved rosary — Poirot, against all odds, finally comes up with the only logical solution even though, *naturellement*, it is the most surprising: a petit tragedy played by the ephemeral people and artifacts of Edwardian England against the ageless panorama of the Nile Valley.

LIBBY BASSETT

Dead Man's Mirror (1937)

(Alternate title: *Murder in the Mews*)

Dead Man's Mirror is a collection of three stories—"Dead Man's Mirror," "Murder in the Mews," and "Triangle at Rhodes"—which were first published in the 1930s.

DEAD MAN'S MIRROR

It is September 1936. Hercule Poirot, detective extraordinaire, is sitting in his flat, puzzling over a letter he has just received. His correspondent is Sir Gervase Chevenix-Gore, who believes himself to be the victim of fraud. He tells Poirot to be prepared to go down to Hamborough Close, Chevenix-Gore's country house, upon receipt of a telegram, and not to answer the letter.

Poirot is incensed. "It did not seem to occur to this Sir Gervase...that it was extremely unlikely that I should be able to fling everything aside and come hastening like ... a mere nobody!" However, he is also curious. He seeks out his acquaintance Mr. Satterthwaite, an encyclopedia of aristocratic gossip, and learns that Sir Gervase Chevenix-Gore is an elderly baronet, the last of a line dating back at least to the first crusade. He is fabulously wealthy, fabulously eccentric, and fabulously arrogant. Poirot suspects that a man so encased in an armor of egoism could very well be vulnerable to attack, and he decides to see Chevenix-Gore if summoned.

Sure enough, the telegram arrives and Poirot travels to Hamborough Close (following the instructions to have the express stopped at Whimperley: now *that's* privilege!). He arrives just before dinner and is ushered into a room filled with people in evening dress. Lady Chevenix-Gore greets him. She obviously has no idea who he is,

and everyone else is equally mystified.

Snell, the butler, announces dinner. Suddenly everyone is *really* in a dither; Sir Gervase is late. Snell goes to the study to fetch him, but reports that the door is locked. Poirot assumes command of the situation, and orders the door broken down. There they find Sir Gervase, slumped in a chair. On the floor, beside his dangling right hand, lies a small pistol. Sir Gervase has shot himself.

Or has he? Why did he turn the chair away from the desk and why did he lean a little to the right before he fired? And if the bullet that killed him also shattered the mirror behind him, as everyone supposes, why is a sliver of looking-glass stuck to the base of a bronze statuette? And that's not all. *"It is wrong psychologically,"* Poirot insists. Could an egomaniac like Sir Gervase imagine that the world be able to get on without him?

Poirot decides it is time to meet the household. Lady Vanda Chevenix-Gore is rather less than helpful. She dresses in oriental robes and claims to be a reincarnation of an Egyptian queen. ("Before that, I was a priestess in Atlantis," she adds.) Most of the time "she's the vaguest creature that ever lived," although she occasionally displays uncanny shrewdness.

Ruth Chevenix-Gore is Sir Gervase and Lady Vanda's adopted daughter. (We learn—in confidence—that she is really the illegitimate child of Gervase's dead brother Anthony.) She is exceptionally beautiful, and she stands to inherit the bulk of the estate. ("She inherits the temper, too," someone comments.) Sir Gervase was about to alter his will so that she would inherit only if she

Dead Man's Mirror (1937)

married her cousin Hugo Trento (the son of Gervase's sister). Ruth and Hugo both have other fish to fry, but this was no consequence to Sir Gervase.

Two old friends are staying at Hamborough Close. Ogilvie Forbes is a tight-lipped lawyer whose firm has represented the Chevenix-Gores for over a century. Colonel Bury is an old admirer of Vanda's who still follows her about "like a dog." Bury unwisely persuaded Sir Gervase to invest heavily in the Paragon Synthetic Rubberine Company, which caused Chevenix-Gore to lose a great deal, though he was still "an extremely rich man." Another guest is Susan Cardwell, Hugo's clever, red-headed girlfriend. They want to get married, but neither has any money.

Rounding out the household are Captain Lake, Sir Gervase's well-liked estate manager; Godfrey Burrows, Gervase's secretary (who is judged to belong to a "definitely inferior social class" largely on the basis of his "sleek brushed-back hair and a rather obvious style of good looks"); and Miss Lingard, a "funny old thing" who was researching Sir Gervase's family history for a book he was writing. (She was careful not to bring any undesirable forebears to his attention.) After questioning all of these people, Poirot finds less and less likelihood of suicide—because he finds more and more motives for murder.

MURDER IN THE MEWS

London, November fifth. It is Guy Fawkes Day, and fireworks light up the evening sky. Hercule Poirot and Inspector Japp of Scotland Yard are taking an after-dinner stroll through Bardsley Gardens Mews, a quiet side street. "Good night for a murder," Japp comments as a firecracker goes off. "Nobody would hear a shot on a night like this." Astute Agatha Christie readers will probably have guessed by now that this remark

heralds just such a crime—committed (by sheer coincidence, of course) in the aforementioned Bardsley Gardens Mews.

The victim is Mrs. Barbara Allen, a young widow. At first it appears that she has shot herself, but certain details are suspicious. The pistol is in her right hand, but she is not actually holding it — and the shot was fired just above the *left* ear. *Another* murder made to look like suicide! But what motive could anyone possibly have? Barbara was, by all accounts, a "real lady"— well-bred, sweet, and considerate.

Mrs. Allen had shared her house with Jane Plenderleith, a dark-haired young woman of twenty-seven or twenty-eight. One officer describes Jane as a "very cool, efficient young lady," but Japp complains that she is "too cocky by half." Jane had been away in the country when the shooting occurred. But she is oddly reluctant to show Poirot and Japp the cupboard under the stairs, which has nothing in it but some umbrellas, golf clubs, and a briefcase.

Barbara had been engaged to Charles Laverton-West, an ambitious and pompous Member of Parliament (who seems critical of his late fiancée's "horror of being snobbish!"). His alibi for the night of the murder is flimsy at best. "In fact, it wasn't an alibi at all," Japp notes.

Finally, there is the man who was seen leaving the house on the night in question. From the description, Jane identifies him as Major Eustace, a "doubtful customer" who had known Mrs. Allen in India. Barbara had been withdrawing large sums of cash from the bank, and it seems probable that Major Eustace had been blackmailing her. But would he kill her and cut off such a steady source of income?

Can Poirot solve this one? Japp is dubious. After all, the aging Belgian has done little but poke around in all the wastepaper baskets and dustbins.

TRIANGLE AT RHODES

Poirot has gone to the sunny Greek island of Rhodes for a holiday. There, he finds—for starters—Pamela Lyall, an English girl "whose principal interests in life were the observation of people . . . and the sound of her own voice." The present subject of Pamela's attention — and monologue—is Valentine Chantry, "a woman of thirty-nine who had been famous since sixteen for her beauty." Valentine is on her fifth marriage. (She has been for six months—and they said it wouldn't last!) This husband is a commander in the Navy, "pugnacious . . . sullen . . . a touch of the primeval ape about him." He mistreats his wife, but Poirot thinks that "she probably likes that."

Another vacationing couple are Marjorie and Douglas Gold. She is not bad-looking but "liable to be overlooked." He is "extremely good-looking . . . natural and unaffected . . . perhaps a little stupid." Valentine's ever-roving eye falls upon Douglas, and he is immediately bewitched. Poirot traces a triangle in the hot sand.

The situation becomes obvious to everyone. One day Mrs. Gold finds Poirot on the Mount of the Prophet (where he had gone to be "far above the petty wrangling and squabbling of human beings"). She confesses her desperation. Poirot advises her to leave the island at once. But she can't as long as Douglas wants to stay. They stay.

One evening, everyone is having a suspiciously jolly time—even Commander Chantry tries to be sociable. Gold offers to buy a round of drinks and Chantry asks for a pink gin. Valentine enters the room and takes a sip of his still untouched drink. Five minutes later she is dead. Chantry realizes the drink was intended for him, and the case seems sewn up when a packet of heart poison is found in Gold's dinner jacket pocket. Poirot, however, has anticipated murder and has watched *everyone* very closely. Surely, the murderer will not elude him . . .

JOHN STURMAN

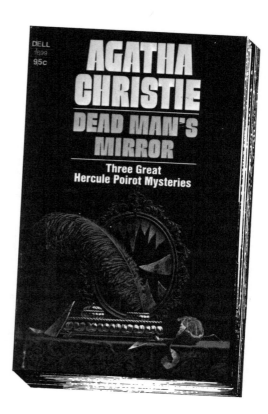

Appointment with Death (1938)

Interesting place, Jerusalem: the City of Peace; holy place to three great religions; melting pot of Judaic, Islamic, and Christian culture; the Wailing Wall, Mosque of Omar, the Church of the Holy Sepulcher. Exotic, ancient, vital, exciting.

A perfect place for Hercule Poirot to vacation, escape the grim work which is his *métier*. Jerusalem, where one can contemplate the aesthetic in an atmosphere that is spiritually moving and where one can ignore anything that reminds one of humanity's darker side.

"You see, don't you, that she's got to be killed?"

His first night in the holy city those words seem to drift into his room out of the stillness of the night. No matter where he goes, there are always things to remind him of crime. To shield himself from any further base intrusions, Poirot gets up and closes the shutters, insulating himself. Yet he cannot help but wonder what has occasioned such an ominous declaration. He decides to remember the nervous male voice that uttered it, should subsequent events give those words more dire import.

The Boynton family are a queer lot, and wherever they go they attract attention because of the strange way they comport themselves. All activity seems to revolve around the mother, and when compared with her needs, all other human wants pale to insignificance. So tight a rein does she hold over her family that virtually any social contact with other human beings, except for the most necessary, are nonexistent.

This fat, grotesque woman called Mrs. Boynton would sit Buddha-like in the midst of her ménage, supervising and criticizing every detail of their lives. She is an emotional sadist who delights in cruelty for its own sake, and whose family serves as a convenient vent for her perversities.

The oppressive atmosphere that the family exudes attracts the attention of medical student Sarah King and Dr. Theodore Gerard, the celebrated French authority on schizophrenia. Sarah has managed to have a clandestine conversation with Raymond Boynton and is distressed that such a handsome, intelligent young man would never see any of his potential realized as long as he remains under the matriarch's influence. Even now, Raymond is obviously avoiding Sarah, pretending that their previous encounter had never happened.

While Sarah has a personal interest in the family, Gerard's is more professional. Yes, he notices Raymond's and sister Carol's nervousness, but he diagnoses something more — fear. Younger sister, Jinny, is obviously schizoid, staring blankly into space while mindlessly tearing her handkerchief into shreds. And then there is Lennox, a man too exhausted from suffering to care about anything, who is married to the quiet woman with the thoughtful gray eyes, Nadine.

From the King Solomon Hotel there will be a side tour to Petra, and maybe there Sarah and Dr. Gerard will be able to study the family closely and make a prescription for whatever it is that ails them.

Petra, capital city of the ancient Nabataeans. Rose-colored sandstone cliffs surround the valley in which the city rests, protecting it from the surrounding desert and the world without. From the

119

cliffs it is necessary to take a donkey ride down to the valley floor where one finds the glorious ruins and the Place of Sacrifice. Place of Sacrifice?

The campsite at Petra is shared by Sarah and Dr. Gerard, the Boynton family, an American tourist named Cope, a twit of a woman named Miss Pierce, and Lady Westholme. Well, certainly everyone knows Lady Westholme; she is an American who married into her title, ran successfully for Parliament, and frequently made the papers championing the causes of family life and slum clearance. In all, an interesting quorum.

At Petra, Raymond does a daring thing—he actually initiates a conversation with Sarah wherein he declares his love for her. Stranger still, when it comes time for the tour to climb to the Place of Sacrifice atop one of the summits, Mrs. Boynton permits her family to go on without her.

After they have been to the summit and seen the awesome view of the rose-colored valley and the ruins below, the party begins to file back down. They find Mrs. Boynton just where they had left her, sitting immobile in a chair at the mouth of a cave. She declines offers to join the group for lunch. There is some concern for her heart condition, but mother knows best, and remains intractable.

Dr. Gerard suffers a malaria seizure and retires to his tent, and the rest of the group settle down for dinner. A Bedouin goes to assist Mrs. Boynton, then returns with the news that she is ill and cannot move. Sarah goes to check Mrs. Boynton's situation herself.

Correction: Mrs. Boynton is not ill, rather she is dead.

At first,. there seems to be nothing unusual about the death — Mrs. Boynton had been afflicted by heart trouble. But then it is revealed that Dr. Gerard's hypodermic syringe had been missing at the time he wanted to use it (for his malaria), along with a quantity of digitoxin, a drug that, if used in an improper amount, could be a deadly poison. Then, the body of the late Mrs. Boynton is found to have a needle mark on the wrist.

Hercule Poirot's ominous premonition is validated.

Further, the master detective recognizes Raymond's voice as the one to have uttered those threatening words outside his window. Although Raymond claims to have spoken to his mother forty minutes before her body was discovered, Sarah King, trained in such matters, puts the time of death as much earlier than that. Why would Raymond lie about such a thing?

During her interrogation Miss Pierce makes a startling revelation. After the death, she saw Carol Boynton sneak away from the group and throw something into a stream. Retrieving it, Miss Pierce is perplexed to find it to be a box containing Sarah King's syringe. When it is confirmed that Raymond had been speaking with his sister Carol when Poirot overheard their plot, Poirot seems to have a good case for conspiracy. But if the brother and sister were acting in concert, they certainly would not have had a use for *two* syringes.

Miss Pierce also claims, as does Lady Westholme, to have seen Mrs. Boynton chastise one of the Arab servants. Yet Lady Westholme's description of the Bedouin's puttees seems to be inordinately detailed to have been perceived from two hundred yards off. It is doubtful that a Bedouin would have thought to use a syringe full of digitoxin, should he want to kill someone. But what could the ladies' motive be in creating such a fabrication?

It would seem that the more things begin to make sense, the more questions arise, and the more questions, the more dogged is Poirot in his quest for the truth. And as Colonel Carbury, the chief law enforcement officer in Amman, knows — Hercule Poirot is a good man for the job.

PETER J. FITZPATRICK

Murder for Christmas (1938)

(Alternate titles: *Hercule Poirot's Christmas, A Holiday for Murder*)

A raucous clamor. A bloodcurdling scream. Then silence. Murder, of course. But not a typical Agatha Christie liquidation. *Murder for Christmas* is special, written for Christie's brother-in-law James, who complained that her killings were getting "too refined—anaemic in fact." For him she wrote a "good, violent murder with lots of blood."

Blood, in fact, is one of the keys to the solution of this 1938 mystery featuring the inimitable sleuthing of Hercule Poirot.

The scene: A typical English millionaire's estate, Gorston Hall, a mansion in Longdale, Addlesfield.

The cast: a not-so-typical English millionaire and his oddly mismatched family.

Simeon Lee is a very old upper-class British millionaire, who made his fortune as a young man mining diamonds in South Africa. Often he brings back the past by looking at and touching a quantity of uncut diamonds that he keeps in a safe in his room. He is thin and shriveled, white-haired and yellow-skinned, but his proud nose and dark intense eyes reveal fire, life, and vigor still stirring within. He is a widower, his wife having died young of a "broken heart" because of his cruelty and constant womanizing.

He is a ruthless, tyrannical person who detests weakness. Yet he is generous with his money, admires strength and spirit, and enjoys a good joke. His sense of humor, however, tends to be sadistic, as he amuses himself by playing on the cupidity and greed of others and stirring up their emotions and passions.

His latest game is to invite his far-flung family home to Gorston Hall for Christmas to see how much he can stir them up. Unfortunately for Mr. Lee he creates so much of a stir that he is murdered on Christmas Eve!

And murdered in the most un-British and ungentlemanly way—his throat slit like a pig's, almost a ritual killing, a bloodletting.

But by whom? As expected, the list of suspects leaves out almost no one but M. Poirot himself!

Was it Alfred Lee, Simeon's devoted eldest son, who has spent all his life at Gorston Hall sacrificing his own life's pleasures to his father's? Is Alfred beginning to think that devotion does not always pay off?

Was it Lydia, Alfred's wife, who hates the old man because she knows the price of her husband's devotion?

Could it be George Lee or his wife, Magdalene, who have been taking the old man's allowance for years and won't be content with less than luxury?

What about David Lee, the youngest son, who despises his father for "killing" his mother, or his wife, Hilda, who sees Simeon's cruelty and judges him for it?

Was it Harry Lee, the black sheep of the family, who has returned to the homestead after many years away? Even in his absence he had managed to get plenty of money from his father, but now did he want more?

Did the hand that struck the blow belong to Pilar Estravados, Simeon's hot-blooded, half-Spanish granddaughter, orphaned and impoverished, who has traveled to England to get what she is entitled to, and perhaps what she is not?

And what about Stephen Farr, the mysterious stranger—or is he—who has come uninvited all the way from South Africa on a special errand?

We must not forget Horbury, Mr. Lee's personal valet, who was always there when needed to assist his invalid charge, except that Christmas Eve.

This varied crowd is gathered at the estate for Christmas, each looking for his own special answer. Before dinner the patriarch summons them to his room, where he purposely has them overhear a telephone conversation with his lawyer concerning the changing of his will. As if this doesn't upset the apparent heirs enough, he rants at them all, telling them they are stupid and weak, that he probably has children "born on the wrong side of the blanket" who turned out better than they. He even goes so far as to defile the memory of their mother. Only Pilar, to whom he has taken a liking because of her beauty, youth, and vitality, escapes the wickedness of his tongue.

He then dismisses them to enjoy their dinner downstairs, which they do, to the best of their ability, until they hear a crashing din from above, followed by a chilling, inhuman scream. When they run upstairs en masse and break down the locked door, they discover Simeon Lee, surrounded by destruction and blood, silent at last.

Enter Hercule Poirot, that renowned Belgian on holiday in England, but never on holiday when duty calls. Assisting Superintendent of Police Sugden, Poirot uncovers the clues with his famous sense of detail and imagination.

He gets to know the victim posthumously and the suspects intimately as he juggles the pieces of the puzzle. Why was there so much blood all around the room? How did a weak old man put up such a struggle against his attacker? How did the murderer get out of the room so fast, and how did he lock the door from the inside? Where were Mr. Lee's missing diamonds, and did they figure in the murder? What was the meaning of a small piece of rubber and a wood peg found on the floor of the room? What was the motive — robbery, hate, greed, revenge, or all of these things?

Poirot deftly unravels the mystery of this most un-Christmasy violent night.

JOAN GERSTEL

Easy to Kill (1939)

(Alternate title: *Murder Is Easy*)

Luke Fitzwilliam, a retired police officer returning to England from his service in the Mayang Straits, becomes involved in a train-ride conversation with "a nice old tabby" who reminds him of his Aunt Mildred. Aunt Mildred never had this old lady's concerns, however; Luke discovers that Lavinia Fullerton is convinced that there is a murderer at work in her village of Wychwood-under-Ashe, thirty-five miles from London. Accidental or natural deaths have been occurring with what seems to her to be more-than-normal frequency, and Miss Fullerton has satisfied herself that she knows who the murderer is. The entire matter being more than she thinks the local constable can handle, she is off to Scotland Yard to tell them what she suspects. And she is in rather a hurry, because, as she tells Luke, she has reason to believe that Dr. Humbleby, one of the village's two general practitioners, will be the next victim. After listening to Miss Fullerton's rather vague and rambling account of her thoughts, Luke hopes that Scotland Yard's Department for Dealing with Impressionable Old Ladies will be able to let her down lightly. She seems "rather an old dear," though possessing a vivid imagination.

Within a week, however, Luke Fitzwilliam finds himself on his way to Wychwood-under-Ashe to conduct an informal investigation into the situation there. His interest is piqued by two newspaper accounts that appear in the intervening days. First he reads that Miss Fullerton was killed in a hit-and-run accident while on her way to Scotland Yard. A few days later, there is an announcement of the death of Dr. Humbleby. These two events are enough to make the policeman in Luke think that even if Miss Fullerton's

story was not altogether true, there are nevertheless things that bear looking into in Wychwood-under-Ashe.

Luke decides to pose as an anthropologist writing a book on local superstitions, and a friend of his persuades his cousin Bridget Conway, who lives in Wychwood, to present Luke as her cousin so that the locals will talk more freely to him.

Thus set up, Luke begins his inquiries. The recent deaths in Wychwood under Ashe seem totally unrelated to each other; furthermore, they do not even seem to be the result of murder: Harry Carter, the drunken landlord of a nasty local pub, lost his footing on a footbridge one night; Amy Gibbs was a sloppy housemaid who perhaps intentionally drank a bottle of paint instead of cough medicine; Tommy Pierce, a no-account mischief-maker, died after a fall from a third-story window he was washing; Dr. Humbleby died of blood poisoning from a badly dressed scratch, doctors being so careless of their own health; and of course Miss Fullerton's automobile mishap was no doubt accidental.

If the deaths are thought of as murders, however, it becomes apparent that there are several people who might have had motives for one or more of them. Dr. Humbleby's partner, Dr. Thomas, certainly benefited from the former's demise, getting not only the entire practice for himself but the good doctor's daughter as well, Dr. Humbleby having opposed the match. Moreover, Dr. Thomas had given Amy Gibbs the cough mixture the day she died.

Mr. Abbot, the local attorney, had been publicly abused by Harry Carter for paying too much attention to the latter's wife; he had dismissed

Tommy Pierce for reading his personal papers; and he had fought fiercely with Dr. Humbleby over a new village water distribution scheme.

Bluff Major Horton had no apparent reason for doing in any of the victims previously enumerated, but the fortunate (and ambiguous) death of his overbearing wife a year before did seem to make a new man of him, and blackmail might be involved.

Mr. Ellsworthy, the distinctly odd antique dealer, might be some sort of blood-lust killer, with his nasty temperament and his reputation for dabbling in black magic. Amy Gibbs and Tommy Pierce had both taken part in the strange rites he conducted in Witches' Meadow.

Lord Easterfield, a self-made newspaper magnate and self-centered pompous fool, had his differences with all the dead, but seems too busy grinding out trash for his weekly papers and playing *nouveau riche* lord of the manor in his native village to be a diabolical murderer.

Honoria Waynflete, a friend of Miss Fullerton's who took charge of the latter's cat after her accident, thinks she knows the name of the person her friend suspected, but since she is not sure, she is unwilling to pass the name on to Luke.

Bridget Conway, Lord Easterfield's secretary-turned-fiancée, sees through Luke's anthropologist disguise fairly early on, and as they work together on identifying the murderer, romance grows hesitantly between them.

The investigation goes round in circles—that is to say, nowhere — until another murder forces Luke to come into the open, identify his true purpose, and call in Scotland Yard. At the last possible moment the pieces fall into place for him, and Luke arrives at the scene of what was to be the next murder just in time to foil the murderer's insanely clever designs.

JERRY KEUCHER

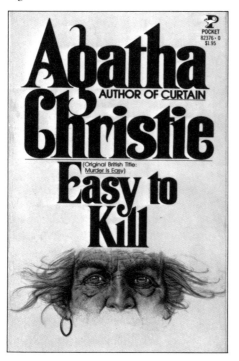

"YOU NEED LOOK NO FARTHER, INSPECTOR – THERE STANDS YOUR CRIMINAL"

Or, How Did the British Police Get By Without Poirot and Marple?

by Elizabeth Leese

Our first encounter with Scotland Yard comes halfway into Agatha Christie's first book, *The Mysterious Affair at Styles,* in the person of Detective Inspector Jimmy Japp.

Japp explains to his companion: "That's where the yard is at a disadvantage in a case of this kind, where the murder's only out, so to speak, after the inquest. A lot depends on being on the spot first thing, and that's where Mr. Poirot's had the start of us."

It was a relationship that was to continue on that basis for more than fifty years. Japp and his fellow fictional officers could defer to Poirot's "gray cells" and his eccentric habits to solve their crimes. But in real life Scotland Yard relies on the more than a thousand detectives, the central criminal records, and the forensic science laboratory to ferret out evildoers.

New Scotland Yard is the headquarters not only of the Metropolitan Police but also the C.I.D. — the Criminal Investigation Department. The name is derived from an old palace in which Scottish royalty was housed when visiting London. On the site of this palace was built the office of the commissioner of police, and the name became so well known that when the time came to move to newer and larger premises the name "New Scotland Yard" was the only possible choice.

The first system for policing Great Britain dates back to the Statute of Winchester in 1285 and lasted, with only minor variations, until the formation of the modern police force in 1829.

Early methods of keeping order put the responsibility on the law-abiding citizen and were amateur operations. A constable was appointed for each area: it was his job to report any illegal activities and to apprehend anyone breaking the law, but it was usually a system of "citizen's arrest." It worked well enough provided criminals stayed more or less in the same area but it couldn't operate successfully in larger towns and cities, particularly in London, with its overcrowded, shifting population and the appalling poverty from which so many of its citizens suffered.

For centuries it had been virtually impossible to keep law and order in London and by the early eighteenth century it was a very dangerous city in which to be abroad. Violence and disorder, so clearly illustrated in the work of Hogarth, were the accepted background to life in the metropolis and the brutal punishments given to transgressors had little effect.

However, in 1748 the novelist Henry Fielding (author of *Tom Jones*) was appointed magistrate at Bow Street Court. Technically, it was the court set up to administer justice in the area of Westminster but the enlightened Fielding began the basis of the present police force during his term of office there.

Fielding started a system of having men, known as the Bow Street Police, patrol the street on foot. He also started the famous Bow Street Runners, consisting of fifteen men who were the detective force of their time. They were really private detectives, since they required payment before undertaking a case. The Bow Street Runners functioned until 1839.

By 1821 the Bow Street Police had extended their patrols to the outskirts of London. This was necessary because of the large areas of unlit and almost deserted parks and heathland in and around London. Places like Hounslow Heath and Hampstead Heath were notorious for their highwaymen, and traveling after dark by coach was a very hazardous business.

In 1785 Prime Minister William Pitt tried unsuccessfully to set up a more national police force but it was not until 1829 that a professional force was begun.

The man responsible for the foundation of the present system was England's Home Secretary Sir Robert Peel, who in 1829 brought together all existing methods of upholding the law and started the Metropolitan Police. It was not a national institution — even today there are in England and Wales alone forty-seven separate police forces. But London's Metropolitan Police is the one they are all based on.

Peel's force was organized by a Colonel Charles Rowan: the pattern was taken from the model of the army. Peel's name was the derivation of one of the first nicknames given to the police. The colloquial expression "the peelers" came from his surname. And "bobbies" comes from his Christian name.

Unfortunately, Sir Robert also specified the wages to be paid to his men—three shillings a day when the average wage for a skilled laborer was much higher. This led to a general dissatisfaction about pay that has been going on ever since. The first police strike (in 1872) was over pay and resulted in 109 constables being dismissed.

A later strike in 1890 was no more successful and, in addition to the seemingly justified complaints about low wages, the men asked for one rest day in seven. This request wasn't granted until 1910.

The C.I.D. and the other special facilities (the Laboratory of Forensic Science is considered to be one of the best in the world) mean that the Yard is often called in to help solve crimes committed outside its area. Provincial police forces will ask the assistance of Scotland Yard detectives to help them with a difficult case and, providing the request is made promptly, the request is never refused. But Poirot, Marple, even Sherlock Holmes or Lord Peter Wimsey notwithstanding, the Yard cannot interfere with a case unless specifically invited by the local police.

LIFE ON THE NILE

by Michael Tennenbaum

The cast: standing, left to right, Simon McCorkindale, I.S. Johan, David Niven, Peter Ustinov, Jane Birken, Jack Warden, Maggie Smith, Jon Finch, and George Kennedy. Seated: Lois Chiles, Mia Farrow, Angela Lansbury, Bette Davis, and Olivia Hussey.

In 1977, producers John Brabourne and Richard Goodwin hoped that lightning would strike twice when they embarked upon their second Agatha Christie venture. Their *Murder on the Orient Express* was the most successful British-produced film ever, and the same formula would be repeated for the new film—a star-studded cast in a story of murder in an exotic locale.

Death on the Nile concerns the murder of a beautiful young heiress on board a steamer filled with suspects. Peter Ustinov was cast as Poirot, actress-model Lois Chiles as the victim, and the list of suspects included Bette Davis, Mia Farrow, David Niven, George Kennedy, Maggie Smith, Angela Lansbury, and Jack Warden. But Brabourne and Goodwin were taking no chances with the public's memory; to insure the link from the first film to the second, the original title for the movie was *Murder on the Nile*.

Of the seven weeks spent shooting on location in Egypt, four were spent on the steamer *Karnak*, some two hundred miles down the Nile between Aswan and Cairo. The remainder of the time was spent among the ruins at Aswan, Abu Simbel, and Luxor, and in Cairo—with filming on top of a pyramid and in the shadow of the Sphinx.

Bette Davis commented on the difference between such location shooting and the studio days in Hollywood, where "they'd have built the Nile for you, and you would never have known the difference. Nowadays, films have become travelogues and actors stuntmen."

Somebody didn't plan ahead. In making all the arrangements for location shooting, someone forgot about hotel reservations for the crew, and they were subsequently shifted from one hotel to another (sometimes on a daily basis) when tourists showed up with prior reservations.

Shooting in the desert has its own rules; makeup must be done at 4 A.M. so that shooting can start promptly at 6. This is necessary because of the two-hour delay in shooting every day around noon when temperatures hover near 130°.

Ustinov and the Sphinx.

THE BEDSIDE, BATHTUB & ARMCHAIR COMPANION TO AGATHA CHRISTIE

Once, during the filming of a love scene with Lois Chiles and Simon MacCorkindale, one of the many hostile flies came to rest on one of Miss Chiles's beautiful teeth. Glassily, the actors carried on, but were relieved when director John Guillerman finally broke up and called for another take.

Guillerman had his own problems — he was never able to see the footage he had shot on any given day. On orders from the producers, exposed film was shipped directly to London from Cairo and into the hands of the editor before anyone on the set had a chance to view the "rushes."

Ever notice a character's shoes in a movie? Pay attention in this one. Costume designer Anthony Powell loves detail. Lois Chiles wears a pair of shoes with diamond heels that came from a millionaire's private collection. And Bette Davis wears a pair of reptile shoes made from the tiny scales of twenty-six python skins.

Two middle-aged ladies on a holiday in Egypt spotted Peter Ustinov lounging in the lobby of their hotel. "You go first," said one, "then I can peek at him. I'll go first tomorrow night."

Ustinov speaks on creating the character of Poirot:

My biggest reservations always were whether I would be able to do justice to M. Poirot's high standard of grooming. Since he is essentially immaculate in his person at all times, and I lean toward untidiness, creased garments and a general lack of sartorial elegance with no effort whatsoever, there were certain major differences between us that needed to be reckoned with.

And on Poirot himself:

The man's sense of logic is quite extraordinary, for sure, but I have become somewhat disturbed, during my examination of Poirot's methods, about his sources of information. He does seem to gather most of his facts from conversations *overheard* in the most unlikely places. He's forever stepping forward and saying knowledgeably, "Ah, but I happened to overhear your conversation with so-and-so," always in the most unlikely places. We do know that he is a bachelor and therefore all his time is pretty much his own, but there surely must be undisciplined moments in his life when he is not constantly on the receiving end of other people's conversations.

LIFE ON THE NILE

As Johnny Carson is fond of saying, "Timing is everything." The *Death on the Nile* advertising art was redesigned for two reasons. The original pre-release publicity prominently featured the steamer *Karnak* surrounded by portraits of the stars, much in the style of the *Murder on the Orient Express* poster. But then artist Richard Amsel, who created the *Orient Express* poster, was commissioned to do the same for *Nile*; he made, however, a substantial change in motif—the *Karnak* disappeared and was replaced with the golden image of a familiar Egyptian King wielding a ceremonial knife and a not-so-ceremonial revolver. Then the film's New York opening coincided with the much heralded sale of tickets to the Metropolitan Museum of Art's exhibit on King Tutankhamen. Two weeks later, the film was mysteriously pulled from distribution only to surface again, two months later, just when the Tut exhibit finally opened. An amazing coincidence? Perhaps. But one that would not have been terribly taxing to someone's little gray cells.

Ten Little Indians (1939)

(Alternate titles: *And Then There Were None, Ten Little Niggers*)

Ten men and women have been invited to stay for one week on Indian Island, off the Devon coast in England, by its owner, Mr. Owen. The ten people are strangers to each other and none of them know Owen, but the mysterious owner, strangely, knows enough about each of his prospective guests to make his invitations appealing. To those in need of employment, he has offered jobs, to those desiring relaxation, he has promised a vacation.

The prospect of staying at Mr. Owen's home has proved so alluring that seven of the invitees are presently aboard a motor launch bound for the island; two of the guests have come to the island ahead of the others; and the last will arrive later that day. "A queer lot" is how the group impresses Fred Narracott as he pilots their boat to the island; they're not at all as classy as he had expected the guests of Mr. Owen to be. But, how would Narracott know what they should be like? The boatman has never met Mr. Owen because he has received his orders and payments from Owen's go-between, Mr. Isaac Morris. Narracott thinks this is a bit funny and concludes that "Mr. Owen must be a very different sort of gentleman."

Well, back to the "queer lot." There's the "reptilian old man," and retired judge, Mr. Justice Wargrave; the attractive ex-governess, Vera Claythorne, who appears "a bit schoolmistressy"; the arrogant Philip Lombard, who brings a gun with him to the island; and the old woman, Emily Brent, with her air of righteousness and unflinching morals. Anthony Marston, the handsome young man, looks "not a man, but a young god"; past police detective, Mr. Blore,

disguises himself as a Mr. Davis of South Africa; and retired General Macarthur appears soldierly and shrewd. Already on Indian Island are the reticent manservant, Mr. Rogers, and his wife. The successful Dr. Armstrong, who is en route to Owen's home apart from the other guests, appears in need of a rest.

First impressions of Indian Island and the Owen home, the only building on the island, are enthusiastic — the house is modern and exciting, the rooms provide beautiful views of the sea, and the larder is stocked with fine food and drink. In each guest's room, displayed in a frame, is the old nursery rhyme which begins

> Ten little Indian boys went out to dine;
> One choked his little self and then there were nine.
> Nine little Indian boys sat up very late;
> One overslept himself and then there were eight

and continues its account of the dissolution of the ten little Indians until its final lines read

> One little Indian boy left all alone;
> He went and hanged himself and then there
> were none."

The Indian theme is carried out further in the ten little china figures of Indians that grace a table in the dining room. The figures are the Indians referred to in the nursery rhyme, Vera reasons, and all the guests find the idea quite quaint and amusing.

First impressions don't prove too lasting on Indian Island though, for before long, things are far from amusing. "Ha, delightful spot!" General Macarthur had exclaimed upon his arrival at the

Ten Little Indians (1939)

island, but he feels uneasy and thinks it an odd sort of place. Mr. and Mrs. Rogers announce that the Owens have been delayed and will not arrive until tomorrow, and Mrs. Rogers reveals that she and her husband have never met the Owens.

Following dinner the first evening, everybody is in better spirits. They have eaten well, begun to chat with each other, and are content as they enter the drawing room — until the Voice comes "without warning, inhuman, penetrating," charging each guest, in a high, clear voice, with the murders of one or several people. "A mean practical joke," some say, but people faint, drop serving trays, mop perspiring faces, and age ten years within minutes. The uneasy guests find the source of the Voice in a gramophone hidden behind the drawing room wall, which, the Rogers admit, they had been instructed by Owen to put on following dinner.

After comparing their letters from Owen and recounting the uncanny events that have occurred since their arrival, the ten guests resolve to leave the island tomorrow wnen Fred Narracott comes on his daily delivery visit. They consider it the only way to free themselves from the grasp of a man Justice Wargrave describes as "a madman — probably a dangerous homicidal lunatic."

Anthony Marston, oblivious to the gravity of the situation, finds it positively thrilling, "like a detective story," drinks his whisky and soda down in a gulp, and chokes to death. Dr. Armstrong determines the cause of his death to be cyanide poisoning. Though Marston was too vigorous a person to commit suicide, no one has the nerve to label the death a murder.

In the background of the action, Mr. Rogers notices that one china figure is missing.

The next morning, the beginning of the supposed day of deliverance from the lunatic's island, Mrs. Rogers never awakens, and one more china figure is missing. Two suicides within twelve hours is a bit unlikely, so the deaths are presumed to be the handiwork of Mr. Owen. Soon the terrifying realization dawns that the manners of death of the two victims are exactly those depicted in the "Ten Little Indians" nursery rhyme. A search of the house and the entire island reveals that "there is no one on the island but their eight selves." Suddenly, they know that Fred Narracott won't be coming to the island. Suddenly, the nursery rhyme and china figures aren't quaint: they are miniatures in poetry and glass of the fates of ten Indians imprisoned on Indian Island.

Terror and suspicion among the prisoners mount as the number of china figures dwindles. Despite Justice Wargrave's warnings to "take no risks and be alert to danger," General Macarthur's fatalistic prediction that none were going to leave the island alive becomes more likely.

The deaths of all ten guests are finesse jobs — grotesque and well planned. So well planned, in fact, that Sir Thomas Legge, Assistant Commissioner at Scotland Yard, and Inspector Maine, also of Scotland Yard, can conclude only that the ten guests were victims of murder. How could it be that *all* the bodies appeared to be murder victims, and not a single one showed evidence of being that of a murderer who had committed suicide? The detectives are absolutely certain that the ten guests were the only people on the island (before the police arrived), that no person could have left the island because of rough sea conditions after a storm, and that the murderer was one of the ten guests.

Who, then, was the murderer?

That's the question Legge and Maine are stuck with at the end of their investigation, and it's the question that would have remained forever unanswered — had not the mastermind behind it all cast into the waters surrounding Indian Island a bottle containing the secrets of the "fantastical" murder of the ten little Indians.

MAUREEN STODDARD

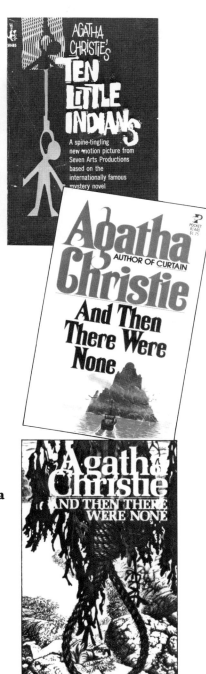

"...it was so difficult to do that the idea had fascinated me. Ten people had to die without it becoming ridiculous or the murderer becoming obvious. I wrote the book after a tremendous amount of planning, and I was pleased with what I had made of it." —*An Autobiography*

Regatta Mystery (1939)

You are, let us say, Mr. Isaac Pointz, a gem dealer and owner of an exquisite diamond called the Morning Star. You have a habit of carrying this diamond around on your person and displaying it at dinner parties. If one of your guests challenged you that she could steal it if you passed it around at one particular gathering, would you take her up on it?

Perhaps you would, if the challenger were fifteen-year-old Eve Leathern, and the stakes were a bet of half a dozen pairs of silk stockings versus a new tobacco pouch.

But, since "The Regatta Mystery" is an Agatha Christie story, we are sure in advance that much more will really be at stake. And of course we are correct. For things do not turn out like a pleasant little dinner party game where everyone's property gets returned — the Morning Star, worth £30,000, disappears.

The diamond was being handed around the table when Eve Leathern, after exclaiming "How perfectly lovely," dropped the stone to the floor. In a moment she and several other guests were crawling about, knocking glassware off the table. But what's this? The stone has disappeared? You don't mean the girl managed to do it?

She submits to a search — and no stone is found. The men search each other, then, the furniture. The ladies even search each other. Still no luck. Mr. Pointz has been bested, fair and square.

"Are the stockings mine?" demanded Eve (confident of winning).

"They're yours, young lady," (said Pointz, amazed).

But when Eve shows the party the clever place she hid the diamond, it appears that someone

cleverer still has found it first, for the Morning Star is missing — this time for real.

Mr. Pointz had thought so well of his companions — his partner, Leo Stein; Sir George and Lady Marroway; the attractive Janet Rustington; even the faintly wolfish Evan Llewellyn; not to mention Samuel Leathern and his daughter, the now tearful Eve.

Thank heavens for the perspicacity of Parker Pyne, detective, who knows the significance of the sound of breaking glass.

"The safest place to commit murder is in the middle of a crowd," opines Hercule Poirot in "Yellow Iris." Poirot has been summoned to a nightclub by an anonymous female voice on the phone, which tells him to come to the table that bears yellow irises. At that table in the club Jardin Des Cygnes Poirot finds only an acquaintance, Tony Chappell, who is drowning in self-pity because his girl, Pauline, is angry with him.

Poirot's first job is to deduce which of the women present likes yellow flowers. Pauline Weatherby is his first choice, but she claims to prefer lillies of the valley. The other woman in the party of five, Lola Valdez, a South American dancer, also states that the irises cannot have been meant for her.

"Yellow flowers — no — they do not accord with my temperament," says the fiery Lola, disappointed because Poirot has claimed to be too old to dance with her.

But it develops that the irises are in honor of someone deceased—the wife of host Barton Russell. Russell's wife, Iris, died four years before in a New York nightclub and—stranger and stranger

—the party that night was identical to that which has gathered around the table this evening, with the exception of course of Poirot.

On that night Iris, Pauline's sister, was sitting with the rest of the group when the lights went down in the club. When they went up again Iris was dead, having taken cyanide in her cocktail. The remains of a cyanide packet were found in her purse, and the police assumed it was suicide.

This time the lights go down again, the orchestra strikes up the very tune that was playing when Iris died, and suddenly Pauline keels over. Poirot leaps up and feels for her pulse. "Yes, she is dead," he proclaims, "but this time the murderer shall not escape."

Guilty looks shoot around the table. Why would anyone want to do in Pauline, unless perhaps she knew too much about that night four years ago? Did Lola perhaps have designs on Barton Weatherby? Perhaps indeed. But what motive could there have been for Tony Chapell—anger? Or how about for the silent Stephen Carter, reputed to be doing something hush-hush with the foreign office? Some kind of international intrigue, perhaps?

And imagine Poirot's shame—the victim succumbing as she sat beside him, just moments after he had whispered in her ear. Shall this killer escape again? Not if Poirot can help it.

Let us not, however, forget Miss Marple, also represented in this collection in "Miss Marple Tells a Story." How clever she once again demonstrates herself to be, solving this case without ever leaving her dining room, which she occupied rather than the drawing room because "in early spring I think it is so wasteful to have two fires going."

The matter concerned the demise of a certain Mrs. Petherick, stabbed through the heart with a stiletto while she lay, enjoying poor health, in her hotel bedroom.

She had taken to her bed while her husband, in an adjoining room, worked on a book he was writing on prehistoric flints. The chambermaid had come and gone, and by late evening, when her husband looked in to see if she wanted anything, she was dead.

Now, Petherick recalled that his wife had read to him some letters that had accused her of injuring a child in an auto accident and that threatened that the child's death would be avenged. But the accident had happened before their marriage, and Mrs. Petherick had a certain *dramatic* tendency. "If she slipped on a banana peel it was a near escape from death," as Miss Marple put it.

Still, someone *had* done her in. The police had no reason to suspect the chambermaid, a hotel employee of long standing and limited intelligence, with no reason to harm the woman. Mr. Petherick claimed that neither had he any reason to harm her, but who else was there? The hallway doors to both rooms had been under continuous observation by witnesses, and the door to Mrs. Petherick's room had been bolted from the inside.

Who else but her husband could get in there? The coroner's jury had returned a verdict of murder by person or persons unknown, but the police were keeping a sharp eye indeed on Mr. Petherick's whereabouts. Could even Miss Marple come up with an explanation, assuming, of course, that Mr. Petherick is telling the truth?

DICK RILEY

Sad Cypress (1940)

What happens when you blend two lovers, a bed-ridden widow, and an anonymous letter with two seasoned nurses, a fresh doctor, and a beautiful girl? In Agatha Christie's 1939 novel, *Sad Cypress,* the result is murder.

The lovers, Elinor Carlisle and Roddy Welman, lead quietly extravagant lives in London awaiting the death of wealthy Aunt Laura. For the fashionable Elinor, life is an endless struggle to maintain a cool, aloof facade, to appear casual about her feelings for Roddy. Ah, Roddy! Roddy! if only you knew the emotions boiling beneath that sculptured breast! If only you could see behind those deep blue eyes the sudden throb of pleasure that sets the world spinning whenever you appear.

But for the delicate Roddy, Aunt Laura's nephew by marriage, life is an endless pursuit of placidity. Educated at Eton, he abhors display of emotion, and all unpleasantness makes him nervous. Roddy constantly reminds Elinor that "some women are so damned possessive — so dog-like and devoted — their emotions slopping all over the place! With you I never know, I'm never sure. Any minute you might turn around in that cool, detached way of yours and say you'd change your mind—without batting an eyelash!" Roddy is so attached to his detached cousin, as he refers to Elinor, that he plans to marry her just as soon as Aunt Laura dies and leaves her considerable fortune to the two heirs.

When they receive an anonymous letter warning that Aunt Laura might leave her entire fortune to a girl who's "sucking up" to the widowed invalid, Elinor and Roddy agree to take a quick trip to the Hunterbury Estate in Maidensford. Not

that they actually worry about being cut from the will — Aunt Laura's generosity and family pride would never permit her to disinherit her brother's child or her husband's nephew. Still, Roddy says, "We'll go down to protect our interests and because we're fond of the old dear."

Although a stroke has left her left side paralyzed, Aunt Laura's eyes shine with pleasure when Elinor announces her decision to marry Roddy. "I think you'll be happy," says the old lady. "Roddy needs love — but he doesn't like violent emotion. It's not wise to care too much. If Roddy cares for you just a little more than you care for him, well, that's all to the good...To care passionately for another human creature brings always more sorrow than joy, but one would not be without that experience."

In the midst of this philosophical bedside discussion, young Dr. Peter Lord arrives. Upon meeting his patient's lovely niece, "his very eyebrows blushed." "You ought to get married," Aunt Laura tells him.

Roddy, meanwhile, is wandering around in the woods thinking about how wonderfully reserved Elinor is. These lusty meditations are interrupted by the sudden appearance of an "unutterably beautiful" girl with a "long delicate neck, pale golden hair lying close to her exquisitely-shaped head in soft natural waves, and eyes of a deep vivid blue." As the lovely creature with "a wild rose unreality" comes through the trees toward him, Roddy feels the world spinning "topsy-turvy, suddenly and impossibly and gloriously crazy!" Unused to such violent emotion, Roddy stares at the girl "dumb and absurdly fish-like, his mouth open." The young woman introduces herself to him as Mary Gerrard, the lodgekeeper's daughter. At this point Elinor appears and coolly tells Mary that the nurse needs her assistance. Oblivious to Elinor, Roddy gazes starry-eyed at the retreating figure of Mary running gracefully toward the mansion.

Roddy's obvious infatuation with Mary hurts Elinor, who is already disturbed over the girl's devotion to Aunt Laura. She is careful, however, to hide her jealously from Roddy.

Upon receiving a telegram from Dr. Lord the following week, Elinor and Roddy once again rush back to Hunterbury, where Aunt Laura has suffered a second stroke. Though her speech is now almost unintelligible, the paralyzed woman makes Elinor understand that she wants to see her lawyer in the morning so that provisions can be made for Mary. Elinor reassures Aunt Laura and returns downstairs to join Roddy, who barely hears her account of the conversation as he stands gazing dreamily at Mary.

With morning comes word that Aunt Laura has died in her sleep. Both Elinor and Roddy express relief that the proud old woman is finally at peace. When the lawyer arrives, he brings unexpected news: Aunt Laura never made a will. Therefore, as the only blood relation, Elinor inherits everything. Much to her dismay, Roddy stubbornly refuses to accept any share of the money and, in a moment of weakness, confesses to her his love for Mary. True to form, Elinor graciously releases him from their engagement, leaving gentle Roddy to cry out, "what a beast I am! Darling Elinor, you're the best friend anyone ever had!" Darling Elinor takes it like a champ, and even gives Mary £2000, in accordance with

Aunt Laura's last wish.

At this point everyone becomes consumed with the need to make out a will—it's a lawyer's paradise. Mary, assisted by the gossipy but competent Nurse Hopkins, bequeaths her inheritance to an aunt back in New Zealand, while Elinor wills everything to her beloved Roddy.

Unable to face the prospect of living at Hunterbury without Roddy, Elinor sells the estate. Nearly one month after Aunt Laura's death Elinor returns to the mansion to dispose of the furniture. Mary, assisted by the faithful Nurse Hopkins, also arrives to clean out the lodge. Though filled with jealous hatred of the lovely girl, Elinor maintains her characteristically polite facade and invites Mary and Nurse Hopkins to join her for tea and sandwiches. An hour later Mary is dead.

When Elinor is arrested for murder, Dr. Lord pleads with Detective Hercule Poirot to do whatever necessary to have her acquitted. Promising only to discover the truth, Poirot puts his gray cells to work. What is the connection between the old photograph found in Aunt Laura's bedroom and the strange letter regarding Mary's birth? Did Aunt Laura really die a natural death, or was she murdered? What happened to the tube of morphine tablets missing from Nurse Hopkins's case, and where did the German matchbox, found in the shrubs, come from? What about the pharmaceutical label found in the pantry, and the climbing rose bush at the lodge?

With little more than a tilt of his egg-shaped head and a twist of his mustache, the inimitable Poirot resolves the mystery of Sad Cypress.

ANITA McALLISTER

The Patriotic Murders (1940)

(Alternate titles: *An Overdose of Death,* *One, Two, Buckle My Shoe*)

"If you want to catch a man off guard, what better place than at his dentist's?" postulates Hercule Poirot.

The question is not an idle one. For before this book is two chapters old there has been one death in the dentist's office, on the very morning that Poirot himself had undergone the terrors of the half-yearly examination. And then another — a delayed reaction, so to speak, but traceable to that same office, that same morning. Mon Dieu! And one was afraid of the *drill!*

It is a curious assortment of people who are gathered at number 58, Queen Charlotte Street, to await their turn with Dr. Henry Morley; the high and the low are there, the meek and the mighty. Which is which depends entirely on your point of view. There is Poirot himself, of course: perfection personified. And Alistair Blunt, elegant in his Savile Row suit, the rich and powerful financier who single-handedly held the British economy together in the face of the Socialist-Communist-Anarchist threat. Many a radical would like to see *him* out of the way, no mistake.

Then, too, there is Mr. Amberiotis, a large, oily Greek with a shadowy past and no obvious means of support since his recent return from India. How very odd! Miss Maybelle Sainsbury-Seale has just returned from India too, and here she is with a toothache on the very same morning. Funny, they had come back on the same ship, so it was said.

Nor is that all. Mr. Howard Raikes is there, an American, a pseudoradical, a young man who seems to be playing at political intrigue for the sport of it rather than out of conviction. He seems restless, Poirot thinks, and has a dangerous look,

as if he were about to commit a murder.

Gladys Nevill *isn't* there, which is unusual. Dr. Morley's assistant is very conscientious and seldom misses a day of work, but she had been called away suddenly when her old aunt in Somerset suffered a stroke. At least that was what the telegram said. Morley didn't believe it for a minute. A phony excuse, he thought; she'd probably been put up to it by that scoundrel Frank Carter. What she saw in such a rascal he couldn't fathom, but there it was, and they were probably off on a picnic somewhere, at his expense.

Of course he doesn't know Carter is in the building too, hanging around at the back stairs, out of sight, waiting for an opportunity....

Nobody hears the shot. Not Morley's sister Georgina, who lives upstairs, nor any of the patients; not even Morley's partner, Reilly, who is in the next office mixing himself still another drink. After all, it is almost lunchtime.

Even Alfred, the moronic office boy who answers the door and escorts patients to the second-floor offices with each press of the buzzer, hears nothing amiss. He is too busy reading a mystery novel entitled *Death at 11:45*. How prophetic!

So it isn't until well after one o'clock that they finally find the body, and when they do they call it suicide. Poirot shakes his head in disbelief when Scotland Yard calls to tell him. Suicide! Dr. Morley? Impossible! He'd been perfectly normal only hours ago.

Sister Georgina says the same thing. He'd had no worries, she says, no health problems, nothing on his mind. He didn't even own a gun! How could he have shot himself? But if he didn't, who did? And why?

There are so many possibilities. He'd tried to break up Gladys Nevill's romance; did Carter hate him for that? Did Gladys herself? Did she know that she was a beneficiary of his will, and would she kill for money? For that matter, would Georgina? She stood to inherit the bulk of his estate.

Poirot has other ideas. "I never forget a face," the doctor had said. Had he recognized one too many? Or did someone fear that he might?

Ah well, perhaps some of the other patients can throw some light on the matter...

The shadowy Greek, Amberiotis, cannot see anyone; he says he is not feeling well. Fishy, you think, and you are right—but for the wrong reasons. Within hours Amberiotis is dead too, poor old sod. The lab report comes back: an overdose of adrenaline and procaine, a dental anesthetic. Suddenly everything seems clear. Morley accidentally miscalculated the injection, and when he realized, too late, what he'd done, he reached for the pistol no one knew he owned and shot himself. Neat. Scotland Yard wants to tie it all up, but no, Poirot has doubts.

It is not logical, he says. Something is amiss.

Why, for example, did Blunt's niece, Jane Olivera, arrive home and immediately inquire if her uncle had been hurt at the dentist's? It was almost as if she'd expected him to be. And her final remark was really *most* curious. When Poirot said that it was the dentist who was dead, Jane had replied, "How absurd!" If anything was absurd, it was that remark. It made no sense at all, unless...

Maybelle Sainsbury-Seals only adds to the puzzle. Fluttery, dowdy, forever dropping her pince-nez, she is the quintessential silly old maid. Those ridiculous patent leather shoes, for example, all shiny and new—they didn't go at all with the mousy green suit she had on. And she'd broken one of the buckles off when she got out of the cab. Had she really been seen having lunch with Amberiotis?

But before they can question her she ups and disappears. Evaporates. Vanishes. Weeks go by; there is no trace. Then a terrorist tries to kill Alistair Blunt; luckily the shots go wild, but the attempt seems to open a whole new area of inquiry. Possible undercover connections, secret agents, espionage, international organizations, subversive groups—where will it all end?

It will end, thinks Poirot, when Miss Sainsbury-Seale is found. And then it will all fit together: India and old acquaintances; dental charts and size-five shoes; letter bombs and pistol shots. And an overdose of dental anesthetic. An overdose of death.

Ma foi! It arranges itself! One only needs to see it, as it were, right side up...

NORMA SIEBENHELLER

Evil Under the Sun (1941)

The place: The Jolly Roger Hotel, located on picturesque Smuggler's Island, a resort on the coast of England.

The time: August, the month for holidaying at the seashore, when the coastline was a place for sunning and swimming, and a year or two before the skies were darkened by the Luftwaffe.

The event: The untimely departure of Arlena Stuart Marshall, strangled while sunning herself.

Evil Under the Sun provides Hercule Poirot, that master Belgian detective, with yet another opportunity to solve a thoroughly English murder. The victim is the beautiful Arlena Stuart Marshall, a one-time actress who still plays for the attention of a significant audience — the young (and old) men of Great Britain. She is always "on stage," even when on holiday, and Hercule Poirot, as well as his fellow vacationers at the seashore, is quick to notice her charms.

Only one man at the resort seems able to ignore the flirtatious conduct of Arlena, and his apathy is difficult to understand. For Captain Kenneth Marshall, the antics of his wife are tolerable, despite the obvious humiliation he suffers as she courts another young holidaying husband.

Like most men, Patrick Redfern is easily captivated by the lovely performer, and the presence of his young wife, to say nothing of the performer's husband, does nothing to restrict his show of affection. He publicly strolls the beach with Arlena and, in their more private moments, the relationship becomes even more intimate.

Those two men, then, are the principal suspects in the death of the woman they share. But what of Mrs. Christine Redfern, the "poor little wife" who suffers in imperfect silence? She certainly had the motive for disposing of her rival. And how about Linda Marshall, stepdaughter to the deceased? Arlena was not on anyone's most-popular-parent list, and Linda deeply resented the stage lady's attitude toward her father.

Christie, however, doesn't stop with only four suspects. Among the guests at the Jolly Roger Hotel are a dress designer who once had designs on Captain Marshall, an obnoxious Englishman with no visible means of support, and a minister who seems much too preoccupied with the scarlet character of Arlena Marshall. Each could have some motivation for killing the sweet young thing—jealously, money, or divine retribution.

Poirot is not the lawman with actual jurisdiction in the case. He is merely on holiday, a protest he vainly makes when some of his fellow guests probe the reason for his presence at the tranquil Smuggler's Island. But Poirot knows that murder can occur anywhere, even at the Jolly Roger.

As a woman, Christie takes us into the private world of female gossip, where a young lady's sexual habits (and partners) are subject to the traditional English scrutiny. But Christie is sympathetic, too, toward the actress who finds herself used by men, to a certain extent a victim of their calculated attentions.

Poirot, as always, concerns himself with motives and clues. And realist that he is, no one is ruled out in the investigation. As he discovers the whereabouts — and attitudes — of those who knew Arlena Marshall, we are treated to a taste of genteel English life.

An American couple staying at the Jolly Roger for two weeks claim that they've "done England pretty well" and now want to sample the typical British holiday. But did the beautiful Arlena and the philandering Patrick, or any of the men and women at the Jolly Roger, realy come for a typical holiday? Probably not, at least according to that documentarian of British life — and British death—Agatha Christie.   BRIAN HAUGH

N or M? (1941)

Tommy and Tuppence Beresford are bored. During the last war they worked for Intelligence, but now the government considers them too old for dangerous missions against the Nazis. When Mr. Grant from Intelligence does come calling, he offers Tommy only a job shuffling papers in Scotland. Tommy reluctantly accepts, but when Tuppence goes out on an errand, Mr. Grant tells him that the job in Scotland is a cover for a dangerous mission ferreting out spies and Fifth Column saboteurs at a seaside hotel in Leahampton. Mr. Grant insists that Tuppence not be told the true nature of Tommy's assignment.

Mr. Grant gives Tommy the facts. A special agent on the trail of spies within the British government has been murdered. His last words were "N or M Song Susie." Mr. Grant interprets *N or M* to be the code name of the Nazi agent and *Song Susie* as the name of a hotel, the Sans Souci in Leahampton. Although regretful that Tuppence cannot participate, Tommy gratefully accepts the assignment.

After Mr. Grant departs and Tuppence returns, Tommy tells her he will leave for his desk job in Scotland the following morning. The next day Tommy goes to Scotland, then immediately turns around and heads for Leahampton. He takes a room in the Sans Souci and the proprietress, Mrs. Perenna, introduces him to the other guests. Outstanding among them is Mrs. Blenkensop, who happens to be his wife, Tuppence.

Later, when they have a chance to talk alone, Tuppence explains that she was suspicious of Mr. Grant and only pretended to leave the house. After hearing Mr. Grant's plan, she rushed down to Leahampton the next day and started working on the case. She and Tommy agree to keep their identities a secret.

In a short while Tommy and Tuppence are identifying the suspicious people at the Sans Souci. Foremost is Carl von Deinim, a young German refugee given to anger and depression about having left Germany. Several times Tuppence spots him speaking to a mysterious foreign-looking woman who disappears whenever they see Tuppence looking at them.

Major Bletchley, a retired military man who spent many years in the East, becomes Tommy's most frequent associate. The major is a boring, stuffy man, full of stories about the softness of today's youth. He's so British that eventually Tommy comes to question if anyone can be that stereotyped.

Other guests at the hotel are a nondescript lot. Mrs. Sprot is the bland, colorless mother of baby Betty. Mrs. O'Rourke is a mountainous woman who likes to sit in the living room of the hotel watching the guests and figuring out what they're doing. Miss Minton is a spinster who sits on the porch knitting all day. Mr. Cayley, retired to Leahampton for his health, is extremely quarrelsome and condescending to everyone, particularly his wife.

Mrs. Perenna, who treats all her guests with suspicion, is a bit mysterious herself, and her daughter Sheila tells Tuppence that Perenna is not really their name. Further investigation reveals that Mrs. Perenna has been involved in political movements in Spain and Ireland.

Tuppence sets her first trap by telling her fellow boarders that she has three sons in the war and that she communicates with them through a kind of code they use in their letters. A few days after she mentions this, she notices that her room has been searched and one of her letters read. She and Tommy set another trap and discover that young Carl von Deinim has been entering her room when she is absent. But later, Mrs. Perenna lets it

"Now with a grown-up son and daughter, Tommy and Tuppence were bored by finding that nobody wanted them in wartime. However, they made a splendid comeback as a middle-aged pair, and tracked down spies with all their old enthusiasm." —*An Autobiography*

slip that she, too, has been in Tuppence's room while she was away.

Eavesdropping on the telephone, Tuppence hears an unrecognizable voice say that plans are set for the fourth. The Nazi invasion of England, Tuppence wonders?

One evening, as the guests sit around the living room of the Sans Souci talking about the war, baby Betty Sprot disappears. A servant mentions that he saw her going down the road with a foreign-looking woman. In her room, Mrs. Sprot finds a note telling her not to call the police. Mrs. Sprot becomes hysterical and Commander Haydock, the local A.R.P. warden, is called. The boarders decide to go after the kidnapper themselves.

Heading down the road in Commander Haydock's car, they catch up with the woman and the child on a cliff. It is indeed the mysterious woman who had been seen earlier with Carl von Deinim. When they approach the woman and child, the woman speaks in a language no one understands, but she clearly intends to throw the child over the cliff if anyone comes closer. Mrs. Sprot suddenly pulls a revolver from her purse and fires. Luckily, she has struck the woman in the head. Betty is saved.

The kidnapper turns out to have been Polish and living on funds from an unknown source. The next day the police arrest Carl von Deinim. Secret ink and plans for sabotage have been found in his room. Tommy and Tuppence feel the final task remaining is to get the goods on Mrs. Perenna, whom they consider to be the brains of the operation.

The following night, however, on his way back from Commander Haydock's, Tommy disappears. Tuppence is worried, but she figures that Tommy has gone underground to follow some lead. After a few days, however, Tommy still has not returned or sent a message, so Tuppence contacts Mr. Grant. The "fourth" is rapidly approaching, and they still haven't nabbed the head of the operation. Mrs. Perenna is known to be a member of the Irish Republican Army, Mr. Grant tells Tuppence, but her connection to the Nazis remains unclear.

In a final desperate move, Tuppence decides to let the people at the Sans Souci discover that she is an undercover agent. She intends to let it be known that she has uncovered the identity of N or M, hoping that N or M will make an attempt on her life. Protecting her will be her daughter's boyfriend, Anthony, who works in Intelligence, as well as her detective friend Albert.

But everything goes wrong before she can put her plan into action. One of the persons she trusts most completely turns out to be a Nazi agent and Tuppence is led into a trap. Tommy, she finds out, has been held prisoner and is awaiting execution. The Nazis begin to interrogate her—unless she hands over a certain package within three minutes, they will resort to rather unpleasant ways of making her talk. The invasion for the fourth is ready, Tuppence and Tommy are marked for execution. At this point, boredom is the least of the Beresfords' problems.

ROBERT SMITHER

THE ROMANTIC ENGLISHWOMAN
Agatha Christie As Mary Westmacott
by Pat Maida and Nick Spornick

Agatha Christie in 1924

Agatha Christie led a double life as a novelist — one as the well-known writer of detective fiction and the other as the unknown author of romances written under the pseudonym of Mary Westmacott. Her cover was blown by a London *Sunday Times* columnist in 1949. Yet for nineteen years after the publication of her first romance in 1930, Christie had maintained her secret. Six novels were eventually published under the Westmacott name: *Giant's Bread* (1930), *Unfinished Portrait* (1934), *Absent in the Spring* (1944), *The Rose and the Yew Tree* (1947), *A Daughter's a Daughter* (1952), and *The Burden* (1956).

Fans may wonder why the celebrated mystery writer felt it necessary to create a separate and hidden identity as the writer of romances. One obvious reason is related to the form itself — the romance is a different medium, with appeal to a special kind of audience. The romance is sentimental, emotional, and unrealistic; focus is on the spiritual awakening of the central character. Unlike the usual "domestic murder," the romance portrays family strife without the challenge of the mystery puzzle.

The intense personal feeling poured into these novels may well have kept Christie in hiding. A shy, introverted woman, Agatha Christie was never one to expose her emotions. But she may have needed a way to channel this dimension of herself, which could never be expressed within the confines of the detective story.

Giant's Bread, her first romance, recounts the trials of Vernon Deyre, a sensitive boy brought up in a sheltered environment. The walled garden, the nursery, and the ever-present nannie hardly prepare Vernon for the harsh reality of adulthood. when he has to deal with the war and with his young wife's alienation. After he is erroneously reported killed in action, his wife quickly remarries. The news of her remarriage sends Vernon into a suicidal state. In his distress, he is hit by a truck and suffers injuries that lead to amnesia. He then assumes a new identity. Although his memory eventually returns, Vernon chooses not to resume his former identity but to build a new life through his career as a musician.

Vernon's story can be read as a variation on Agatha Christie's plight as a young woman struggling through the breakup of her marriage to Colonel Archibald Christie. The world of Vernon as a child is the recurring one that appears in her fiction — it is modeled after her own experience. Loss of a loved one causes disorientation, suicidal tendencies. Restoration comes through a career, a dedication of self to work. The main events are the same for the fictional Vernon Deyre and for the real Agatha Miller Christie.

While the autobiographical elements are subtle in *Giant's Bread*, Christie's second romance is an almost explicit revelation of self. In fact, Max Mallowan (Christie's second husband) says that *Unfinished Portrait* offers great insight into the

Agatha Christie, as photographed in the '20s (with daughter Rosalind), in the '30s, and in the '40s.

early Christie. *Portrait* is a self-portrait presented through the character of Celia, an imaginative, introverted, and dependent girl. Celia leads a sheltered life in an environment similar to Vernon's with its garden, nursery, and attending nannie. She eventually matures, marries, has a child, begins to write, and then suffers an almost destructive trauma. This romance virtually details the early life of Agatha Miller Christie from her childhood in Torquay to her marriage and eventual divorce from Colonel Christie. Though her recent *Autobiography* (1977) gives the reader certain facts about Christie's life, *Unfinished Portrait* is far more candid.

Celia is dominated by two strong women — her grandmother and her mother. But it is Miriam, Celia's mother, who becomes emotionally essential to Celia. Their relationship is so close that even as a grown woman with a husband and child of her own Celia becomes distraught over Miriam's sudden death. Shortly afterward Celia's world collapses when her husband announces that he is leaving her for another woman. (As the facts bear out, Agatha Christie was faced with the very same situation in 1926.)

Physically ill and fearing her sanity, Celia contemplates suicide as a means of escape. She fears that her husband may try to kill her and senses that suicide might relieve him of the burden of dealing with her. Celia's struggle to cope, her fears of being alone, and her eventual affirmation of life are described in painful detail—perhaps too honestly. For Christie, this romance may have been an exorcism of grief; in a sense, she could have written the past out of her system, saying here what she could never bring herself to reveal in any other form.

Vernon of *Giant's Bread* and Celia of *Unfinished Portrait* are companion portraits — two innocent children forced out of their secure life-styles and thrown upon their spiritual resources to discover who they really are. In values and experience, Vernon and Celia represent dimensions of young

THE ROMANTIC ENGLISHWOMAN

Agatha Christie, the sheltered child of Victorian vintage who survived a major personal crisis and found her place in a changing postwar England.

Ten years later in 1944, Christie published *Absent in the Spring*. This novel may not be autobiographical, but it does reveal Christie's insight into a middle-aged woman's psyche. Joan is experiencing doubts about herself and her family. All her life she has responded to other people's demands, living up to their expectations. Now, stranded on the desert waiting for transportation, she is alone for the first time in years and she begins to do some soul searching. Does her husband really love her? Do the children care for her? Would she live the same life over again?

Here is a classic case of middle-age identity crisis. And one gets the sense that Christie knows exactly what this woman is feeling and why. Christie has the scope in the romances to explore what she can merely touch upon in her detective fiction—the many facets of human relationships, the dynamics of the family, the impact of dependency, and the pain of alienation.

In *The Rose and the Yew Tree* (1947), Christie treats the paradox of the beautiful young woman who is attracted to the "wrong" man. Isabella is torn between a comfortable marriage to her aristocratic cousin and a passion for John Gabriel, an unattractive and coarse opportunist. At one point Gabriel taunts Isabella about her inability to endure pain; to prove a point, he burns her with a lighted cigarette — she endures this without flinching. All are confounded when the fair Isabella gives up cousin and castle to run off with Gabriel. She ultimately gives her life to shield Gabriel; he, ennobled (finally) by her sacrifice, becomes a religious zealot. Farfetched? The story is pure romance — the kind one might find in a Victorian woman's magazine.

Christie is more successful when she leavens romance with common sense and personal experience, as she does in *A Daughter's a Daughter* (1952). Ann, the mother of nineteen-year-old

Sarah, is middle-aged and still attractive. She's torn between making a new life for herself in a second marriage and devoting herself entirely to her daughter. Duty prevails and Ann gives up her opportunity. But this kind of devotion does not bring happiness to either Ann or Sarah. Ann is miserable, and her daughter rebels by entering into a disastrous marriage. Eventually Sarah pulls herself out of this debasing relationship and begins a new life with another man in another country — Ann is left by herself.

This is a cautionary tale liberating mothers and admonishing daughters, and the message is a far cry from *Unfinished Portrait*. Christie has matured and her ideas have mellowed. She does a credible job in this romance of exploring the dimensions of a mother-daughter relationship with its jealousies, its demands, its response to social pressure. Once again, Christie seems to be speaking about people she knows very well.

A similar motif runs through *The Burden* (1956) in the conflict between an older sister's sense of responsibility and a younger sister's freedom. Laura is compulsive about protecting young Shirley—her motivation is guilt. Shirley is a high-spirited individual who is as carefree as her sister is burdened.

Ironically, all Laura's plans for Shirley are ill-conceived. Matching Shirley up with an appropriate mate turns out to be a disaster. The climax is melodramatic, but the message is clear, if overstated: individuals must follow their own courses; no one, not even the well-intentioned sister or mother, can protect a loved one from life.

At the heart of each of these individual odysseys is a message. The early stories were shaped by the blood and tears of disillusionment mingled with the idyllic recollections of childhood and family. The voice that emerged in the subsequent novels was not that of the young, vulnerable Christie, but the mature voice of the older woman who wanted to warn the innocent with a cautionary tale.

TEN LITTLE WHO?

by Pam McAllister

Niggers. That's the word in question here.

One of Dame Agatha's most popular mysteries, *Ten Little Indians* (also titled *And Then There Were None*) was first published as *Ten Little Niggers* in 1939. As G.C. Ramsey explained in his book *Agatha Christie, Mistress of Mystery*:

> No one would have thought that using the word "niggers" in a children's rhyme would suggest any sense of prejudice or condemnation . . . in a country where people of the Negro race had up until the 1960's been so rare as to be curiosities.

Perhaps Christie and Ramsey thought *niggers* to be an innocent word but the etymology doesn't let them off the hook. The word *nigger* originated as a northern English (and Irish) dialect pronunciation of Negro and was first written *neger* in 1587. The first reference to blacks in America dates to John Rolfe's *Journal* of 1619: "A Dutch ship sold us 20 Negars . . . . ."

By the seventeenth century *nigger* was a common word and was considered a variation of *Negro* until about 1825, when the American abolitionists and blacks objected to the word, claiming that it was a derogatory slang reference to people of the Negro race. Since the American Civil War, *nigger* has been considered a contemptuous word. In England since about 1855 it has been commonly used to refer to any member of a dark-skinned race.

Certainly the word is considered offensive in the twentieth century, and so it is somewhat surprising that the questionable term was not only *not* buried on a back page of Christie's story, but put up front where it counts, on the cover—even on a theater marquee.

In Birmingham, England, on October 3, 1966, while eager Christie fans lined up at the box office for the opening of the play based on the novel, a group from the Coordinating Committee Against Racial Discrimination paraded in front of the theater with signs protesting the word *nigger* in the title.

Even before this date, nervous or socially conscious publishers at Dodd, Mead & Company had been trying to bury the offensive title by substituting *Indians* for *Niggers*. Ramsey applauded the title change as an "inspiration," explaining that American Indians are held in curious respect and "valued as a national treasure." Although an altogether different title was tried in *And Then There Were None*, most people still know the book and play by its "Indian" title.

The plot revolves around the "Ten Little Niggers" nursery rhyme of England's lore, not the American "Ten Little Indians," which is a popular counting exercise put to music: "One little, two little, three little Indians," etc. Unknown in America, the English rhyme has no tune.

The "Ten Little Niggers" rhyme tells the plot of the mystery:

Ten little nigger boys going out to dine,
One choked his little self, and then there were nine.
Nine little nigger boys sat up very late,
One overslept himself, and then there were eight.
Eight little nigger boys going down to Devon,
One got left behind and then there were seven.
Seven little nigger boys chopping up sticks,
One chopped himself in half, and then there were six.
Six little nigger boys playing with a hive,
A bumblebee stung one, and then there were five.
Five little nigger boys going in for law,

One got in Chancery, and then there were four.
Four little nigger boys sailing out to sea,
A red herring swallowed one, and then there were
    three.
Three little nigger boys going to the Zoo,
A big bear hugged one, and then there were two.
Two little nigger boys sitting in the sun,
One got frizzled up, and then there was one.
One little nigger boy left all alone,
He went and hanged himself, and then there were
    none.

Evidently there are two endings to this rhyme.
The original rhyme ended with the hanging, but a
later version had the last boy get married... "He
got married, and then there were none." Christie
used the original "hanging" version for her novel
and the later "married" version for the play. Both
endings worked.

*The French edition (left) retains the original title —
inoffensively. The two most recent film versions (1965
and 1975) opted for the American title, whereas the
original screen treatment picked up the last phrase of
the rhyme.*

AND THEN THERE WERE THREE
by Michael Tennenbaum

Cast	1945	1965	1975
The Adventurer	Louis Hayward	Hugh O'Brian	Oliver Reed
The Secretary	June Duprez	Shirley Eaton	Elke Sommer
The Judge	Barry Fitzgerald	Wilfrid Hyde-White	Richard Attenborough
The Doctor	Walter Huston	Dennis Price	Herbert Lom
The General	C. Aubrey Smith	Leo Genn	Adolfo Celli
The Spinster/Actress	Judith Anderson	Daliah Lavi	Stephane Audran
The Private Detective	Roland Young	Stanley Holloway	Gert Frobe
The Playboy	Mischa Auer	Fabian	Charles Aznavour
The Manservant	Richard Haydn	Mario Adorf	Alberto de Mendoza
The Housekeeper	Queenie Leonard	Marrianne Hoppe	Maria Rohm

(NOTE: Individual character names were changed according to the nationality of the actor playing the part, or the screenwriter's whim. Blore and Armstrong are the only names retained from the original novel through 1975, while other characters change only their first names, for no apparent reason. For example, the secretary is either Ann or Vera.)

LOCALE

1945: *Indian Island*. The guests arrive by boat.

1965: *Hotel in the Alps*. The guests arrive by cable car.

1975: *Hotel in the Iranian desert*. The guests arrive by helicopter.

THE TROUBLESOME CHARACTER

In the original novel, the character of the fast-driving, amoral playboy is a snooty British upper-class twit.

In 1945, he becomes an expatriate Russian prince who, as played by Mischa Auer, is a charming rascal whose death is truly shocking, coming right after a rousing toast to crime.

In 1965, we have Mike Raven, pop star, played obnoxiously by Fabian, who, like Mischa Auer before him, gets to sing the title tune before he croaks. Or is that he croaks the title tune before he

dies? At any rate, he doesn't even get to toast anything.

In 1975, Charles Aznavour, as a singer-composer who reminds one very much of Charles Aznavour, gets to sing one of his own songs in addition to the title song, then toasts, then says good-night, then drops. The producer got his money's worth.

CHOOSE YOUR M.O.

In the first version, the housekeeper succumbs to an overdose of barbiturate, just like in the book.

In the second film, she goes in much more spectacular fashion, when the cable car in which she attempts her escape plummets into the valley below.

By 1975 they were back to more conventional methods, as the housekeeper is strangled against a pillar in some convenient nearby ruins.

The first version of Ten Little Indians, *entitled* And Then There Were None, *included (from left) Louis Hayward, Roland Young, Richard Haydn, June Duprez, Walter Huston, and Barry Fitzgerald.*

TAKE CHARGE

Sir C. Aubrey Smith plays General Mandrake (Macarthur in the book) as a doddering old gent, two steps past senility. The picture of the military man was somewhat more respectful by 1965, when the general was given more to do, like organizing the search party for the mysterious Mr. Owen. In 1975, Adolfo Celli's portrayal of the general conformed to the image of the Italian army as told in jokes known all around the world.

THE OTHER WOMAN

In *And Then There Were None*, Judith Anderson played Miss Emily Brent, the rich spinster whose cold, unforgiving attitude caused the suicide of her nephew. The part was changed for the remakes to allow the producer to hire another beautiful woman for the film. Emily became Ilona, the internationally known actress who is accused of causing the death of her husband to further her own career.

Another element was added to the story with this new development — the general had previously met Ilona, a meeting she first denies, because it connects her to her husband's death. The meeting place is made appropriate to the times — in the 1965 film they had met in Berlin; in 1975 it was Saigon.

SEX AND VIOLENCE ANYONE?

The original version of the film conforms pretty much to the standards of the time and is very discreet about the deaths of the various characters. Therefore, it is surprising (not to mention convincing) when we see a full-front view of the poor character with the bullet hole in his head.

By 1965, audiences were demanding a bit more *verismo* in their movies, and *Ten Little Indians* complied. The character of the manservant was changed from a meek type into a full-blown paranoid schizophrenic so that a fight could be provoked between him and he-man Hugh Lombard. The story stands still for about five minutes while these two have it out in the best television tradition of bloodless fisticuffs. After they've rolled up and down a double staircase once or twice, the judge says something like, "Now, now — that's enough," and, sure enough, it is.

AND THEN THERE WERE THREE

Love interest: Hugh O'Brien and Shirley Eaton (top) in a tender moment from the 1965 film; below, Oliver Reed and Elke Sommer as the same couple in 1975.

A much more interesting development is the relationship between Hugh and Ann, the secretary, which was only winked at in 1945. Shirley Eaton portrays the young woman in a manner that can only be described as "in heat" and Hugh O'Brian makes the most of the situation, making for the most provocative love scene to be seen in any Christie adaptation. After all, Miss Eaton had a reputation to live up to—as the golden girl in the previous year's *Goldfinger*, she had attracted more than a small amount of attention.

The 1975 film, although almost a page-by-page copy of the previous one, was fairly tame, especially considering the graphic lengths contemporary films were going to in depicting sex and violence. The fight between Hugh and the butler was still there, but the love scenes between Oliver Reed and Elke Sommer lacked the spark that enlivened the '65 version. A real pity, especially if one is familiar with the early German films of Miss Sommer's career wherein her characters always had the same aversion to outer garments displayed by Miss Eaton in 1965.

THE MYSTERY GUEST

Yes, that is the voice of Orson Welles as "Mr. Owen" in the 1975 film, adding another element of confusion to the muddled version.

THE LAW OF DIMINISHING RETURNS

The 1945 film received uniformly excellent reviews.

The 1965 version was loved by some, rejected by others.

The 1975 version was roundly panned ("Global disaster in Iran"—*N.Y. Times*).

QUOTE WITHOUT COMMENT

From Bosley Crowther's review of *And Then There Were None*, the last line: "As for the murderer's performance—well, you must judge for yourself."

The Body in the Library (1942)

"Oh ma'am, oh ma'am, there's a body in the library" are the first hysterical words of the housemaid Mary when she wakes Colonel and Mrs. Bantry. The peace and quiet of a fine autumn morning at Gossington Hall have been broken by the news that a tall platinum blond, dressed in a white satin and spangle evening gown, has been found strangled with the sash of her dress on the library hearth rug.

Soon numerous police begin questioning the residents of the.estate—the owners, the butler, the maids. For consolation and advice, Mrs. Bantry sends a car to the village to bring her friend, the elderly Miss Marple, to the house. Miss Marple, a keen observer of human nature well known for her curious problem-solving methods, arrives and looks thoughtfully at the body. She makes mental notes of the dress and details of the victim's hands and facial structure. But even she has no immediate explanation.

Why is the body at this staid residence? Who was she? Why has she been strangled? Where was she from? Rumor and speculation travel like wildfire through the small town of St. Mary Mead. Reports of missing persons filter through the police station where Inspector Slack notes that they include a Mrs. Barnard, about sixty-five years old; a dark-haired girl guide, Pamela Reeves; and, oh yes, a newly issued report on a Miss Ruby Keene, eighteen, blond, five foot four inches, dressed in evening clothes — missing from the Majestic Hotel in Danemouth since the evening before. A Mr. Jefferson had notified the police of the disappearance.

A call to the hotel verifies her disappearance, and names Josephine Turner, a cousin, as the nearest kin. Josephine is brought to the mortuary and shakily identifies the body: "It's Ruby, all right."

While Superintendent Harper of the police, Inspector Slack, and Colonel Melchett, chief constable of the county, pursue various leads and plod methodically forward with their investigation, Mrs. Bantry and Miss Marple vacation at the Majestic in order to do a bit of sleuthing on their own. They find plenty to whet their interests.

Among their suspects is Basil Blake, who lives in Chatsworth cottage a mile down the road. He is a flashy, ill-mannered young man associated with a fast crowd from London and involved with the film industry. His most frequent companion is a blond. He is an occasional guest at the Majestic, and his picture is found in the handbag of Ruby Keene.

Other suspects are: Josephine Turner, gracious, able hostess, exhibition dancer and bridge player at the Majestic, well suited by her even temperament and good looks to her position. She often played bridge with the Jeffersons and was one of the first to realize that Ruby was missing.

Conway Jefferson, a powerful, energetic, well-to-do man with a heart condition, confined to a wheelchair as a result of a plane crash in which his two children were killed. He was extremely fond of Ruby Keene, whose youth and looks reminded him of his daughter Rosamund. He lavished attention on her. He provided as well for his grandson Peter Carmody and his daughter-in-law, Adelaide Jefferson, a pleasant young woman who had spent several years caring for Conway, though her interests and activities are now turning toward other men. He also provided

The Body in the Library (1942)

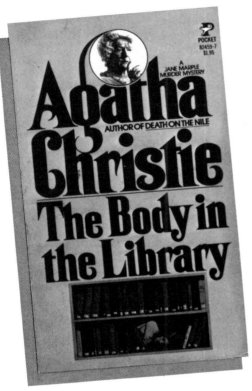

> "I believed that if I wrote two books, and alternated the writing of them, it would keep me fresh at the task. One was *The Body in the Library*, which I had been thinking of writing for some time, and the other one was *N or M?* ..."
> —*An Autobiography*

for his son-in-law Mark Gaskell. Mark is a frank, outspoken man, an inveterate gambler, whose business and friends often take him to London.

The dance and tennis pro, Raymond Starr, of the Devonshire Starrs, a handsome and personable employee of the Majestic. He had danced with Ruby during the evening exhibition dances.

George Bartlett, proud owner of a Minoan 14 automobile, also a guest at the Majestic. George was young, was enchanted with Ruby Keene, and was one of the last people to see her before her unexplained disappearance. He spends considerable time in the bar, which seems to fog his recol-

lective powers and encourages his stutter. His beautiful automobile is found in flames in a quarry, with the remains of a body in it.

Is there but a single murderer—one who would not stop at one death in order to achieve his aim? Is there a conspiracy of hate, greed, revenge, or retribution? Who? Why? Suspicious of everyone, doubting each word and every explanation, Miss Marple slowly creates a trap of evidence, building her theories on parallels of everyday life and events occurring in St. Mary Mead and on her own keen observation of the facts.

HELENE VON ROSENSTIEL

The Moving Finger (1942)

"Good air, quiet life, nothing to do—that's the prescription for you. That sister of yours will look after you. Eat, sleep, and imitate the vegetable kindom." So saith the good doctor. So off to the country for Jerry Burton, under the care of his younger sister, Joanna, to recuperate from a flying accident. They rent a house on a hill overlooking the town of Lymstock, chosen not only for its quiet charm but because neither of them has ever been to the town nor knows anyone in the neighborhood.

Within a week's time they are settled in and their landlady, the elderly Miss Emily Barton, is the first of many to call and leave her card. She is followed in short order by the lawyer's wife, Mrs. Symmington; the doctor's sister, Miss Griffith; the vicar's wife, Mrs. Dane Calthrop; and Mr. Pye of Prior's End.

A week later, following this old-fashioned and auspicious introduction to the community, the first "letter" arrives.

In the morning mail Jerry finds a locally posted letter with a typewritten address. Upon opening the envelope he discovers an obscene note composed of printed words and letters cut out and pasted to the sheet of paper. It expresses rather crudely that he and Joanna are not brother and sister. The letter is unsigned.

Joanna is indignant, then amused, at the letter, and Jerry consigns it to the fireplace as the "correct procedure" for such a piece of trash. But underneath the casual gesture he is disturbed.

Later, during a physical checkup by the local physician, Dr. Owen Griffith, Jerry mentions the anonymous letter. Griffith reacts with immediate excitement; there have been other letters about

town to local residents. Always the letters accuse the receiver of illicit sexual activity. Attorney Symmington was accused of improper relations with his lady clerk, poor old Miss Ginch, who's forty with pince-nez and teeth like a rabbit. The doctor himself was accused of a violation of professional decorum with his lady patients.

The charming old world village of Lymstock, which had its beginning about the time of the Norman Conquest, is now—if one is to believe the writer of the anonymous letters—a seething hotbed of sexual musical chairs.

Among the town's leading citizens are the aforementioned Emily Barton, a spinster and the last of a group of mother-dominated spinster sisters. Refined and gentle, she is fiercely protected by Florence, her former servant, in whose home she now occupies two upstairs rooms.

Meagan Hunter appears as an awkward bicycle-riding young lady of arrested development who attaches herself to Jerry, who in turns finds himself becoming quite protective of her, to the amusement of Joanna.

Solicitor and Mrs. Symmington are the parents of two young sons and sometimes remember that Mrs. Symmington has a daughter — Meagan Hunter—by her previous marriage living in their home. Their sons are efficiently cared for by Elsie Holland, a goddess of breathtaking physical perfection but lacking a matching personality.

Dr. Griffith, who becomes embarrassed and elusive around Joanna, is cared for by his sister, Aimee, to whom idleness in any form is a signal of imminent trouble.

Off to the side is Mr. Pye, to whom beauty is the goal of mankind. In his view Lymstock has

The Moving Finger (1942)

yet to move into the starting gate of competition.

The handsome fifteenth-century church is presided over by the somewhat obscure vicar, Reverend Caleb Dane Calthrop. His wife — of Olympian knowledge and herculean energy — Mrs. Dane Calthrop, is a woman aloof to the business of the parishioners, but she manages to be the conscience of all she touches. A whirlwind of intuition is Mrs. Dane Calthrop.

In the lower echelon of the town are those who serve. There is Agnes, who seems to have seen something; Partridge, who seems to sense that she knows something; Rose, who senses she should have known; and Florence, who will be sensibly on guard, for that is her nature.

On the official side is Superintendent Nash of the local police who approaches the nasty letters with quiet, unemotional probing. To aid him is Inspector Graves, whom Nash has called in. Graves's specialty is anonymous letters and those who pen them.

And finally the fears of the responsible citizens are realized with the suicide of a letter recipient.

Now someone among them is responsible for more than writing accusing letters: someone is responsible for, in effect, a murder. How far will it go? Will there be more deaths? Perhaps the late appearance of Miss Marple as the Calthrops' house guest can bring the mystery letter writer to the surface. Perhaps there is more here than suicide alone. After all, "where there's smoke..."

PAUL AND KADEY KIMPEL

DELL 5861

75¢

AGATHA CHRISTIE

THE MOVING FINGER

"I find that another one I am really pleased with is *The Moving Finger*. It is a great test to reread what one has written some seventeen or eighteen years before. One's view changes. Some do not stand the test of time, others do."
—*An Autobiography*

Murder in Retrospect (1943)
(Alternate title: *Five Little Pigs*)

If you're having nasty thoughts, there's one person you don't want to have them in front of— Hercule Poirot. He reads a face like lesser men read the newspaper.

In the opening scene of *Murder in Retrospect*, Poirot immediately sees that the young Carla Lemarchant is sizing him up, and that she is disappointed.

"You are making up your mind whether I am a mere mountebank or the man you need?" he asks.

Ever honest, Carla admits the indecision. But obviously there's even more disturbing her.

Sparing himself no embarrassment, Poirot pursues the issue. Am I too old, he wants to know.

"Yes, that too." Carla is certainly not one to avoid hurting feelings by telling little white lies. She soon makes it apparent that she is being particular because she needs the best detective money can buy. A man with less self-confidence might have been perturbed by Carla's early doubts of him. Not Poirot. "Rest assured," he says. "I *am* the best."

Carla certainly needs the best, because this case is covered with cobwebs. She was only five years old when her father, Amyas Crale, was poisoned. Her mother was tried and convicted and, a year later, died in prison. Carla was shipped to Canada to live with her uncle and aunt, and her name was changed.

But upon her twenty-first birthday, Caroline Crale, alias Carla Lemarchant, is reminded of the terrible truth — although she is now an heiress, daughter of a famous painter, her father was poisoned by her mother's hand. The mother, also named Caroline Crale, left behind a note to be read on her daughter's twenty-first birthday. The note says she was innocent of the crime.

Carla is convinced. But she is about to be married, and her fiancé sometimes looks a bit askance at his bride-to-be. No one is crude enough to state outright the meaning of the look, but the implication is clear—as the daughter of a husband killer, Carla is suspect. The husband-to-be will perhaps feel obliged to sniff his drinks after a family quarrel. Carla feels that those suspicious glances portend trouble for the marriage, and she wants her mother's innocence proved.

Even if the case weren't so old, innocence would be hard to ascertain. Even Mrs. Crale's best friends still think she was guilty. The prosecutor in the case is long dead, but if Poirot wanted arguments against Mrs. Crale, he didn't have to talk to the prosecutor. Mrs. Crale's own defense council says she was as guilty as a person could be. The defense attorney had pleaded her innocence at the trial and argued that Mr. Crale committed suicide. But Mrs. Crale had failed to put up a real fight to save herself.

The evidence against her was strong. She had a motive — Crale was continually unfaithful, and the couple fought constantly. Crale had the gall to bring one of his lady friends to his home. The lady friend, Elsa Greer, in turn had had the gall to describe, in the middle of lunch with guests present, how she would arrange the furniture "when I am living here."

The ensuing fight was as predictable as it was justified. Mrs. Crale told Elsa, "I'll kill him before I give him up to you." Only hours later, Amyas was dead, shortly after drinking a bottle of beer served by his wife. Yet the bottle had only his

Murder in Retrospect (1943)

fingerprints on it. Apparently she had wiped her own off.

All clues led to Mrs. Crale. Superintendent Hale sorted through Mrs. Crale's underthings and turned up a perfume bottle containing heavy traces of poison. Only her fingerprints were on the bottle. Past history was not in her favor either. When she was younger, in a fit of jealous rage she had slung a heavy paperweight at her baby step-sister, disfiguring her for life.

Mrs. Crale had done penance for that teenage crime, and the battered sister, Angela Warren, became a full-time and beloved member of the Crale household. But the prosecutor made much of that violent precedent.

Motive and means were clearly established — most called the act justifiable homicide. Was the letter claiming innocence left to the daughter in one last act of sentimentality, or was it the truth? Who else could have committed the evil deed?

Elsa Greer, the mistress, wanted not only the house and its rearranged furniture, but the man — presumably alive. If she were to kill anyone, it would most likely be the wife.

Angela Warren had been fighting with her brother-in-law, and had admittedly played a childish prank by putting salt in his beer. But she was a mere naughty child.

Angela's governess was a self-righteous old woman who despised Amyas for his repeated indiscretions. But does one kill to avenge righteous indignation?

Only two other persons were at Alderberry Manor when the fatal drink was quaffed. Meredith Blake was a namby-pamby family friend who, as an aristocrat with no need for a job, dabbled in the herbal arts. He had loved Mrs. Crale from afar since childhood, and no doubt would have loved being cast in the role of faithful friend comforting the bereaved widow. But if Mrs. Crale were innocent, someone must have laid the trial of incriminating clues in the path of the police. As devoted lapdog, Meredith could hardly have done so.

Meredith's brother was something of a rake, and an unlikeable sort at that. He was known to act as a "comforter" to Mrs. Crale during her husband's indiscretions. But he was also Amyas's best friend in a relationship that stretched back into child-hood.

The obvious suspect is still Carla's mother who died in prison for the crime. But leave it to Poirot to vindicate the murderer, in retrospect.

CINDY LOOSE

Towards Zero (1944)

(Alternate title: *Come and Be Hanged*)

A down-and-out would-be suicide complains from his hospital bed about the do-gooders who rescued him...

A tennis pro orchestrates a meeting between his current wife and his former wife...

A police superintendent wonders why his school-age daughter confessed to a crime she didn't commit...

An elderly lawyer with a heart condition is forced to change his vacation plans...

And it all leads to... murder.

"The murder is the *end*," observes the distinguished lawyer Mr. Treves in this departure from the standard murder-investigation-solution format. "The story begins long before that — years before, sometimes — with all the causes and events that bring certain people to a certain place at a certain time on a certain day. All converging towards a given spot... And then, the time comes — over the top! Zero hour."

Readers who feel that their lives, too, are an unfolding of purpose, an inexorable march toward Destiny, will have a special affinity for this book. Readers who have less belief in the idea of order, the ones who are always surprised when their laundry comes back, for instance, may be skeptical but will surely be entertained by this clever puzzle.

The murder is the violent attack upon the head of Lady Camilla Tressilian, matriarch of the seaside estate Gull's Point. September twelfth is the date this unsavory deed is perpetrated, right at the end of a rather unconventional family gathering — the "family" consisting of Lady Tressilian's adopted son, Neville Strange, his new wife, Kay; *and* his ex-wife, Audrey. In addition, Audrey's amorous step-brother, Thomas Royde, has come back from Malaya for the occasion, and Kay's handsome "best friend" Ted Latimer is never far away.

It's a cast of intimates all right, and in various combinations, they know one another pretty well. Nevertheless only one of them knows of an event that took place seven months prior to their September meeting, on February fourteenth, to be exact. This is when a detailed plan for murder was committed to paper. A foolproof plan, someone thought. A plan that was checked and rechecked ... before every evidence of it was burned.

One murder later there is no lack of evidence. A golf club covered with blood, hair, and fingerprints has been found in Lady Tressilian's bedroom, the scene of the crime. A servant reports overhearing a heated argument in that room on the night of the murder. Bloodstains are discovered on the sleeves and cuffs of a dark suit. And all this points to one man—Neville Strange. There's even a motive. On Lady Tresilian's death, Strange stands to inherit £50,000.

Strange seems a personable fellow. A popular, though not really top-notch, tennis pro, he is known by the British public for his sportsmanlike conduct at matches. His plan to unite his current wife and ex-wife at Gull's Point did cause some trouble back in April when it first came up. And besides, Kay Strange thought she'd have a hard enough time just visiting Lady Camilla who, she was sure, took every opportunity to "look down that long nose of hers at me." ("Bad stock" is Kay's problem according to Lady Camilla. "Her father had to resign from all his clubs after that

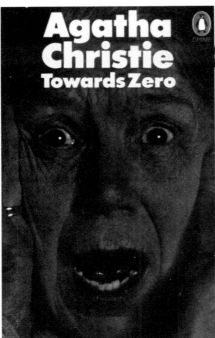

Towards Zero (1944)

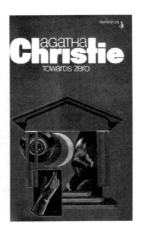

card business," she informs her companion and confidant, Mary Aldin. "Luckily he died shortly after." No such luck for Kay's mother. She, it seems, is actively "notorious on the Riviera.")

For Kay, the idea of combining this unpleasant visit with an attempt to "get to know" Audrey Strange, the woman who has publicly mourned Neville's desertion of her for three years, is madness. Neville insisted it was his idea but it just didn't seem like Neville somehow . . .

Then again, it "just doesn't seem like Neville" to murder his stepmother! But the evidence is there.

Evidence is something Superintendent Battle of Scotland Yard is well acquainted with. He knows that solid physical evidence is hard to refute. He also knows that it's hard to come by. The generous supply of it in this case makes him suspicious. Neville Strange, it seems to him, is being framed.

What a bother! It's one thing to have to figure out who the real murderer is; it's quite another to have to figure out who the real victim is. Are we looking for someone with a motive for the murder of Lady Camilla Tressilian or with a motive for the framing of Neville Strange, or both? Or neither? Are things more, or less, than they seem?

Mr. Treves, the lawyer with the heart condition, seemed to know something the night he visited Gull's Point and told a macabre story of a child who killed a playmate with a bow and arrow. Everyone thought it was an accident, except for one man who had seen the child secretly practicing day after day with a bow and arrow.

Could Treves have been implying that he recognized that child, now grown, here at Gull's Point? He'll never tell—because when he got back to his hotel that night an out-of-order sign on the lift forced him to walk up three flights of stairs—and drop dead of a heart attack. The lift? Not really broken, of course.

There's someone very cunning at work here. Either that or a stupid murderer is having a run of luck. In any case, it's not going to be easy to find the real murderer with trails of evidence leading every which way. But even clever murderers, even murderers who plot far in advance, can slip up. Because, Destiny notwithstanding, things don't always happen according to plan.

JAN OXENBERG

Death Comes As the End (1945)

The lush, fertile Nile Valley of 2000 B.C. was the site of a flourishing civilization. But by the end of this historical novel, one of the few written by Christie, there are more bodies scattered about than there was gold in King Tut's tomb.

Renisenb, after eight years of marriage, has returned to the home of her father, Imhotep, a wealthy businessman, landowner, and ka-priest. Her husband has died, and the young widow is glad to be home, glad that all is peaceful and unchanged.

However, within days the calm surrounding her homecoming is shattered. Her father, back from a lengthy business trip, has brought home a concubine, the beautiful nineteen-year-old Nofret, a sultry she-devil who upsets Renisenb, her three brothers, and their wives.

Quickly, Nofret exerts her power over the aging Imhotep, getting the three brothers — Yahmose, Sobek, and Ipy — dropped from their father's will. She treats the women of the household like the mud on the banks of the Nile and befriends Henet, the maid, and Kameni, a messenger from the north of Egypt, convincing them to join her soon-to-be bloody coup.

But just as Renisenb realizes that she should fear Nofret, the concubine is found dead at the foot of the cliff leading to the tomb on the estate.

Although all agree that her death was accidental, an air of suspicion fills the house. Yahmose, who is normally meek and henpecked by his domineering wife, Satipy, is now powerful. Sobek, the boastful son, is suddenly quiet, and other members of the household also seem strangely changed.

Only Renisenb, Hori the scribe, and Grandmother Esa remain objective, realizing that Nofret's death was no accident, but murder. Even though the three do not voice their suspicions or theories, one by one, members of the household are suddenly, and without outward or apparent motive, murdered.

Satipy, after visiting the burial tomb, falls to her death, landing on precisely the same spot where Nofret's body had been found.

Imhotep, fearful that he may be next, divides the estate and places his two eldest sons in partnership. But while drinking a toast in celebration of their good fortune, both sons, Yahmose and Sobek, become violently ill: the wine was poisoned. Only Yahmose, after weeks of sickness, survives, but he is bedridden, and Sobek is dead. The family is left only with the aged Imhotep and the young Ipy for protection. They become delirious with fear, trusting no one, not even each other.

Adding to that fear is the suggestion that the deaths were the result of a curse left by the concubine Nofret. The family prays to the spirit of Imhotep's dead wife—and have the servants taste the food before eating.

Still, all the precautions are futile. Ipy is found drowned in one of the irrigated fields, and Esa is poisoned through the skin with ointments she uses for massaging her body before going to bed. Henet, who is being suspected more and more by the surviving members of the family, is strangled. Only Imhotep, Renisenb, Yahmose, Hori, Kameni, and Sobek's wife, Kait, are left alive.

The estate has become a mortician's paradise, with funeral directors taking up permanent residence in the house, and sheets disappearing faster

"Stephen [Glanville, an Egyptologist,] argued with me a great deal on one point of my denouement, and I am sorry to say that I gave in to him in the end. I was always annoyed with myself for having done so. ... I still think now, when I reread the book, that I would like to rewrite the end of it — which shows that you should stick to your guns in the first place, or you will be dissatisfied with yourself."
—*An Autobiography*

than at a Macy's white sale.

Hori and Renisenb, who have been relying upon each other for strength and protection, realize that anyone could be next, and they confide in each other. Neither believes in the idea of a curse, saying that the killer must be one in their midst. But who?

One afternoon, Renisenb receives a message to meet Hori by the tomb at sunset. Thinking that he has discovered who the murderer is, she rushes off, climbing the stone path along the cliff to the entrance of the fast-filling tomb.

She waits there until the last ray of sunlight can be seen in the western sky, with no sign of Hori. Then, just as she begins to leave, from out of the shadows comes the killer, a person that she quickly recognizes and whose name she calls.

Was it Imhotep, her father, who is now insane? Or Hori, the man she confided in, the man she loves? Perhaps it was Kameni, the stranger, whose overtures of love she did not respond to? Was it her brother Yahmose, or her sister-in-law Kait? Was it the ghost of Nofret, or one of the others "resurrected" from the dead?

Not only the pyramids hold secrets.

RICHARD REGIS

ALL MY TRIALS
Scenes from the Old Bailey
by Elizabeth Leese

"I couldn't write a court scene," Agatha Christie, in her autobiography, says she told producer Peter Saunders.

"I don't know a thing about legal procedure. I should make a fool of myself," she is alleged to have said.

But the natural drama of an English trial proved too much for her to resist, and before long she was adapting a short story, "Witness for the Prosecution," which had contained no court scene, for the stage.

She chose to set it, as she had chosen to set the brief trial in her first book, *The Mysterious Affair at Styles*, at the Old Bailey, then and now the criminal court for London and its environs.

While the Old Bailey is one of the most famous courts in the world, the title is, more properly, the Central Criminal Court. The site has always been connected with the law — the present building, with its huge domed roof and statue of Justice, was built on the site of the notorious Newgate Prison, whose records date back to 1218. The prison was rebuilt in the fifteenth century and destroyed in the Great Fire of London. Rebuilt again in 1780, it was badly damaged in the Gordon Riots in the same year. The Central Criminal Court was established in 1834 and the present building dates from 1907.

The court deals only with serious crimes; one of the most serious in English law is murder, second only to high treason.

As it is a high court, the advocates must be practicing barristers, unlike the magistrate's court or county court where a solicitor may plead for his client. The counsel, briefed by a solicitor, speaks either for the Crown (prosecuting counsel) or for the defendant (defense counsel), and it is for the Crown to prove its case.

The traditional black robes and white wigs, together with the archaic language of English law, help make the trial theatrical. Any request to the bench is preceded by "If your Lordship

ALL MY TRIALS

pleases" and barristers refer to each other as "my learned friend," even during the most hostile exchanges. Counsels must also put their case forward with great care — the ritual must be observed. It is always "I put it to the court" and "In my submission" and any deviation from this will bring a crushing remark from the judge.

In spite of the restrictions, the Old Bailey has seen some very dramatic scenes — not surprising if one remembers that until a few years ago, the defendant was on trial for his life.

The death penalty was formally abolished in Great Britain in 1969 and before that the most unpleasant task of a High Court Judge was to pronounce the death sentence. A square of black cloth was placed on the judge's head and the sentence passed. "You shall be taken to the place from whence you came and thence to a place of lawful execution, and there you shall be hanged by the neck until you are dead, and that your body be buried within the precincts of the prison wherein your were last confined before your execution and may the Lord have mercy on your soul."

Reactions from the dock to this dreadful pronouncement ranged from complete composure to a dead faint. Christina Edmunds, a Brighton spinster who fell in love with her doctor and tried to eliminate his wife with strychnine-filled chocolates, was condemned to death at the Old Bailey. She then claimed she was expecting a child. Although it was not true, the law declared her insane. She was saved from the gallows.

Frederick Henry Seddon was one of the coolest murderers ever tried at the Old Bailey. Before sentence of the court is passed, it is the duty of an officer of the court to ask the accused if there is anything he or she can say as to why the court should not give judgment of death according to the law. This question is considered a formality, but Seddon was well prepared for a reply. He took out some notes and made an admirable

speech in his defense. Finally, he appealed to the judge, Mr. Justice Bucknill, as a fellow Freemason belonging to the same brotherhood. The judge was so unnerved by this appeal it was a full minute before he could speak; even then he begged Seddon to make his peace with the Great Architect of the Universe before passing the death sentence.

Sir Edward Marshall Hall, who had defended Seddon, appeared many times at the Old Bailey; he was one of the most famous advocates of his day and specialized in criminal cases. Excitable and histrionic, Hall was frequently reprimanded from the bench by judges who found his style somewhat too dramatic for an English court of law. Hall was one of the few advocates who stormed out of court, refusing to continue unless allowed to conduct the case as he wished. But his passionate involvement with his cases frequently helped the client enormously and secured an acquittal when the odds were very much against him.

The case of the *Crown* v. *Madame Fahmy* in 1923 was one of his triumphs and must have been a difficult case for him to defend as the accused did not speak English. Madame Fahmy was accused of murdering her husband and there was no doubt at all that she had fired the shots that killed him.

The murder took place at the Savoy Hotel in London and had all the ingredients to become a criminal *cause célèbre*. The accused was a beautiful Frenchwoman in her early thirties who had been married for six months to Prince Fahmy, a rich and thoroughly degenerate Egyptian. His behavior to her was so cruel that the British public were appalled by the details of her nightmare marriage. Madame Fahmy was terrified of her young husband and wanted to leave him but he constantly threatened to kill her. On the night of July 9, 1923, they had a violent argument and he tried to strangle her. The gun she was holding to defend herself went off and he died instantly.

The defense counsel demonstrated dramatically how the shooting took place, ending his reenactment of the scene by dropping the gun on the floor of the Old Bailey, just as it had fallen to the floor at the Savoy Hotel. When the foreman of the jury announced the verdict as "not guilty" it produced such a storm of cheering that the judge ordered the court to be cleared.

Another celebrated case was the 1932 trial of the *Crown* v. *Elvira Barney*, which filled the galleries with society figures acting as if they were an audience at a play.

Mrs. Barney was a young woman of twenty-seven, divorced from her American singer-husband, and living in an exotically furnished flat off Lowndes Square, Knightsbridge. Elvira was rich and came from a titled family, but according to testimony had devoted herself to drinking and taking drugs with the companion who shared the flat, Michael Scott Stephen.

Parties and nightclubs made up their social life and one night they returned quite drunk and began quarreling about Scott Stephen's interest in another woman. During the argument Elvira shot him, but claimed it was an accident.

What with Elvira's smart set friends in the gallery and the attention of the daily newspapers to the clothes she wore, the trial atmosphere was unusual. In any case she did get off, due to the efforts of her counsel, Sir Patrick Hastings, K.C.

Crown v. *Elvira Barney* was a celebrated case at least in part because it involved the rich, but a search of the records of the Old Bailey, like the courts in America, reveals that such cases are few. The genteel murder, set in an English country house, is to be found more in the detective novel, Agatha Christie's included, than in real life.

A LITTLE DIVERSION (*page 38*)

N	O	O	K	■	C	A	A	N	S	■	I	B	A	R
C	O	M	O	■	E	S	T	E	R	■	N	O	L	A
O	N	E	L	I	T	T	L	E	I	N	D	I	A	N
■	S	I	N	N	E	R	S	■	■	O	I	L	E	D
■	■	■	■	C	R	O	■	O	B	R	A	■	■	■
A	G	A	T	H	A	■	A	B	A	D	■	A	S	I
T	R	I	O	■	■	O	R	I	B	I	■	L	A	N
L	I	T	T	L	E	G	R	E	Y	C	E	L	L	S
A	N	C	■	E	D	D	A	S	■	■	L	O	V	E
S	S	H	■	G	E	E	S	■	P	O	I	R	O	T
■	■	■	T	U	R	N	■	Y	A	K	■	■	■	■
S	T	O	R	M	■	■	S	E	R	R	A	T	E	■
T	H	R	E	E	A	C	T	T	R	A	G	E	D	Y
A	R	A	N	■	S	E	A	T	O	■	A	M	I	E
G	O	L	D	■	A	T	B	A	T	■	R	A	T	S

THE POISON PEN
A Guide to Agatha's Toxic Agents
by Richard Regis

It was late 1914, and England was at war.

The newly married Agatha Christie, wishing to do her bit for the British cause, had begun working in a hospital dispensary in her hometown of Torquay. For two years Christie assisted in the dispensing of drugs to patients and diligently studied for the Apothecaries Hall examination.

"Sometimes I would be on duty alone in the afternoon . . . I began considering what kind of detective story I could write. Since I was surrounded by poisons, perhaps it was natural that death by

During World War II, Agatha Christie again worked as a dispenser, this time at University College Hospital in London.

poisoning should be the method I selected," she wrote in her autobiography.

Her first novel, *The Mysterious Affair at Styles*, includes poison as a murder weapon. And after that success, there was no looking back. She searched near and far for poisonous substances, from the most commonplace of household toxic agents to the most esoteric materials. She employed in her books, plays, and short stories poisons that could be swallowed, poisons that could be injected, poisons that could be inhaled, and poisons that could even be absorbed through the skin.

Her knowledge of fatal powders and deadly liquids was indeed vast, but at the same time she had a few favorites to which she returned time and again.

Cyanide—KCN or NaCN—a white, crystalline compound, most certainly leads the list. At least a half-dozen of her works include death by cyanide poisoning.

Cyanide's most mild side effect is the odor of bitter almonds on the victim's breath. Its more lasting effects include dizziness, convulsions, respiratory failure, collapse, frothing at the mouth, and eventual death.

Cyanide is normally used in extracting gold from lowgrade ores, in electroplating, and in the case-hardening of steel. In Christie's work, it has an altogether different purpose.

In *Endless Night*, a mystery about a gypsy's curse upon a part of the English countryside, it is the bitter almond scent that ultimately gives away the murderer.

Ellie Rogers, a rich American and an accomplished equestrian, is killed in a riding accident.

THE POISON PEN

Most of the town takes the death at face value or passes it off as the old gypsy woman's dirty work, but a second similar death leads to the solution of the mystery.

Ellie's friend Claudia Hardcastle was also an accomplished rider and should not have fallen from her horse. The two women — close enough friends to share everything, right down to Ellie's hay-fever medication — should never have had such accidents.

Dr. Shaw, the village physician, explains:

She died the same way as Ellie did. She fell from her horse in the hunting field. Claudia was a healthy girl, too, but she fell from her horse and died. The time wasn't so long there, you see. They picked her up almost at once and there was still the smell of Cyanide to go by. If she'd lain in the open air like Ellie for a couple of hours, there'd have been nothing — nothing to smell, nothing to find.

Clever, but not clever enough.

Ellie and Claudia are not unique. The list of cyanide victims is long. In *Ten Little Indians*, one of Christie's best-known mysteries, Emily Brent is given chloral hydrate in her coffee, which renders her unconscious, but it is the injection of cyanide that finally does her in. Adele, the stepmother in *A Pocket Full of Rye*, also dies of cyanide poisoning, just as Mona Symmington does in *The Moving Finger*.

Even when the substance is not specifically named, it is the smell of bitter almonds that gives away the cause of death. In *Poirot Investigates*, Ames uses cyanide to commit suicide. While the poison is not mentioned by name, the scent of almonds filled the air.

The methods used to administer cyanide vary. While a few of Christie's cyanide victims either swallow or are injected with the poison by hypodermic needle, the most common method is to mix it with a liquid.

The liquid, of course, varies. In *Remembered Death*, Christie chose champagne. In *A Pocket Full of Rye* it was tea, and in *The Moving Finger*, a glass of water served the purpose.

Morphine was often another Christie choice. A narcotic, morphine — $C_{17}H_{19}O_3NH_2O$ — is the principal derivative of opium. It can cause impairment of mental and physical performance, a reduction in sex and hunger drives, the inability to concentrate, mood changes, and apathy. All the characteristics of a perfect victim. An overdose can, of course, kill.

And in several of Christie's works, kill it does. In *By the Pricking of My Thumbs*, Mrs. Moody knew too much for her own good and an overdose of morphine insured that her knowledge would never be put to use. Both Laura and Mary in *Sad Cypress* learned about morphine's lethal effects. However, their lessons came a bit too late.

Morphine was also put to ill use in *There Is a Tide*. Rosaleen's sleeping powder had been carefully switched, and when she took her nightly dose, she drifted into a dreamy, morphine induced sleep from which she never awakened. Clean, neat, and effective.

Heart medications, too, are used for foul play. The reliance on such drugs as digitoxia and strophanthin by potential victims makes a knowledgeable murderer's work simple.

In both *Appointment with Death* and *Postern of Fate*, digitoxia — $C_{41}H_{64}O_{13}$ — a drug of the digitalis series, is the cause of death. Used by cardiac patients, digitoxia increases the rate and force of heart contractions. However, an overdose can slow the pulse, retard the conduction of nerve impulses in the heart muscle, and increase the amount of blood pumped by the heart. As if that weren't enough, toxic effects include nausea, vomiting, and visual disturbance. It's enough to give someone heart failure.

Strophanthin — $C_{31}H_{48}O_{12}$ — another cardiac drug with effects similar to digitoxia, was used in *Verdict* to dispose of Anya Hendryk, the burdensome wife.

While drugs designed for human consumption certainly get their due, we must not forget another of Christie's favorites — strychnine.

A bitter alkaloid made from a plant named *Strychnos nux vomica,* strychnine — $C_{21}H_{22}N_2O_2$, has been as a rat poison for over five centuries. A potent stimulant of the spinal cord, it causes violent convulsions and difficulty in swallowing.

Almost needless to say, it is the human rats who make use of strychnine in the mysteries and short stories. In *The Mysterious Mr. Quin*, a book littered with the corpses of those who have died from other than natural causes, strychnine is used to dispatch Mr. Appleton. In the short story "How Does Your Garden Grow," from *Poirot's Early Cases*, strychnine is again used as a silent murder weapon.

Christie, however, does not limit herself when using poison. Other substances in her pharmacologic bag of dirty tricks include nicotine — $C_{10}H_{14}N_2$ — a liquid alkaloid that causes respiratory failure and general paralysis, which was used in *Murder in Three Acts;* chloral hydrate — $CCl_3CH(OH)_2$ — a central nervous system depressant (better known as a Mickey Finn) which proved to be quite successful in *Secret Adversary*

and *The Clocks*; hydrogen cyanide, a gas used as an agricultural fumigant and as an effective murder weapon in *The Big Four*; and hyoscine, $C_{17}H_{21}O_4N$ — used in the play *Black Coffee* — an alkaloid that affects the central nervous system by interfering with nerve impulses and causes delirium, delusions, paralysis, and stupor.

There was also the venom of *Dispholidus Typhus,* better known as the boomslang, or tree snake, a South African reptile reputed to be among the most poisonous in existence.

In *Death in the Air*, Madame Giselle, a French moneylender, dies in her seat on an airplane. A red mark is found on her neck, a wasplike object at her feet. She was killed by a dart from a jungle blowgun, the dart having been dipped in the tree-snake venom, a substance that "causes acute hemorrhage under the skin and also acts on the heart, paralysing its action."

In the wealth of Christie novels, short stories, and plays, surely dozens of victims die from the effects of poison — and it all began with the musings of a young woman as she sat alone on quiet afternoons in a hospital pharmacy.

Mrs. Ellis, Christie's supervisor in that dispensary, must have been proud.

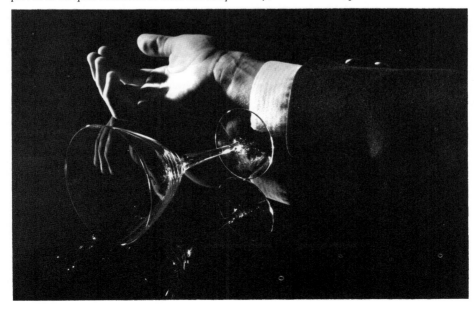

Remembered Death (1945)

(Alternate title: *Sparkling Cyanide*)

Rosemary Barton died as a result of imbibing cyanide-laced champagne upon the occasion of her birthday dinner. For most of the fatal evening, her guests had appeared to be enjoying themselves dancing, drinking, and eating a sumptuous meal. Few of them were truly enamored of the woman in whose honor they'd been gathered; in fact, some held a highly controlled hatred of her in their hearts. As relentlessly civilized, upper-class English folk, however, they'd managed to get smoothly past even this emotional hurdle to the point of proposing a toast to her health: never has a toast been less prophetic and backfired so dismally. Shortly after the toast, the lights went down for the cabaret show to begin, and by the time the lights came back up again, the very beautiful, chestnut-haired Rosemary had become a rather ghastly, convulsed, blue-toned Rosemary slumped over the table at London's exclusive Luxembourg restaurant.

At the time, the police and the coroner put the whole thing down to a case of suicide. Their reasoning? First, given the arrangement of guests at the table, and the certainty that no one had moved so much as an arm out of place during the cabaret, wasn't it virtually impossible for any of them to have dropped the poisonous cyanide crystals into her glass? Second, hadn't Rosemary been unusually depressed after long bout with *influenze* — a type of influenza known to cause depression in its victims? And finally, hadn't they actually found the nearly empty packet of cyanide in Rosemary's own evening bag? After a painstaking investigation and inquiry, death by her own hand was the only conclusion to be reached.

The novel begins one year after the shocking event, at a time when some have reason to doubt the verdict of suicide. One person in particular is absolutely certain it was murder. That person is George Barton, Rosemary's older (though not elderly), somewhat colorless husband, who loved his wife deeply despite her string of social and romantic attachments to men much younger and more dynamic than he. When George married Rosemary, he'd had no illusions that she would ever be a devoted wife. In fact, even as she accepted his proposal of marriage she admitted in the same breath that she didn't love him. "You do understand, don't you?" she said. "I want to feel settled down and happy and safe. I shall with you. I'm so sick of being in love." This, apparently, was enough for dear, humble George — it drove him to ecstasy, not to mention the altar. He'd more or less accepted that there were bound to be what he was wont to refer to as "incidents." But he also knew she'd always come back to his own comfortable arms.

What did alarm him, however, was the prospect of Rosemary's involvement in a *serious* love affair as opposed to the usual short caprice. Thus, when he received, many months after her death, two anonymous and oddly redundant letters saying, "You think your wife committed suicide. She didn't. She was killed," and "Your wife, Rosemary, didn't kill herself. She was murdered," his long-repressed jealousy was roused. Suspicion immediately fell upon the two men who'd received more than the customary portion of Rosemary's attention in her last year of life. George had been hard put to regard these men simply as two more incidents.

And so we come to Anthony Browne and

Stephen Farraday — the glamorous man of mystery and the brilliant but pompous young politician, respectively (Rosemary's taste in men was nothing if not eclectic). George had good reason to believe that one of the two had been, in Rosemary's words, "my own, beloved darling" (yes, one day he'd caught her writing the love letter and, by her reaction, knew she really meant it this time).

Farraday, whose mother drank herself to death on eau de cologne (the breath of death never wafted so sweet), had the most to lose if his affair with Rosemary ever became public: gone would be a political career he'd singlemindely worked most of his life to attain and a fiercely faithful wife whose powerful, aristocratic — and monied — family brought comforts and opportunities he'd never had as a child. Rosemary's lack of understanding, and even downright indifference, where these particular stakes were concerned drove Farraday to desperation. When Rosemary told him that she was going to make their affair known to George and leave the way clear for them to romp around the Continent openly at last, she couldn't fathom in the least Stephen's horrified reaction. We begin to see why most people who knew her agreed with the assessment offered by her black sheep of a cousin, Victor Drake, who said that Rosemary is "lovely as paradise and dumb as a rabbit."

Lest we focus too strongly on Farraday's plight, we should also remain aware that everyone who dined with Rosemary on the last evening of her life had ample motive for wanting her out of the way. There was Iris Marle, her younger sister who stood to inherit a substantial fortune if Rosemary died before leaving a natural heir; Ruth Lessing, George's incredibly efficient and loyal assistant, who despised Rosemary and would have jumped at the chance to become Mrs. George Barton; the previously mentioned Anthony Browne, whose real name (if not identity) had been discovered by the loose-tongued Rosemary — and when this occurred, he lost no time in making it very clear to her that this knowledge, if revealed, could cost her her life (which she didn't understand or take at all seriously); finally, there was Lady Alexandra Farraday, Stephen's proud and haughty wife, whose cool demeanor belied a passionately jealous nature. Did she know of their affair? And if so, did she have it in her to kill the other woman rather than lose her husband?

In order to flush out the murderer, George stages a reenactment, as it were, of the events at the Luxembourg, now one year later. The same guests, the same table, the same flow of champagne. Colonel Race, George's distinguished friend whose career in the service of his country had led him to hunt down all sorts of dastardly characters throughout the world, does not give his blessing to George's plan. And indeed, George lives to regret having taken things into his own hands — actually, he *doesn't* live to regret it, leaving Colonel Race, the police, and even one among our list of suspects, to finally account for the novel's two deaths.   HELENE KENDLER

Murder after Hours (1946)

(Alternate title: *The Hollow*)

The Angkatells are entertaining some family and friends for a late September weekend at their house near London. The guests should find the setting most satisfactory, for the Hollow is run as an English country house should be, with the indispensable butler, Gudgeon, and the requisite number of kitchenmaids, housekeepers, and upstairs maids. The friends are Dr. John Christow, a successful Harley Street surgeon, and his simple-hearted, and simple-minded, wife Gerda. Apart from the Christows, there will be a variety of Angkatell cousins: Midge Hardcastle, the poor relation, who will be coming from her rather horrid job in a London dress shop; Henrietta Savernake, a sculptress living in London; David Angkatell, an intense student; and Edward Angkatell, a quiet, bookish "potterer" who inherited the family's ancestral home, Ainswick. It would not appear that the weekend will be the high point of the season, but in that house, if the weather holds up, it should be fairly enjoyable.

Now, though Lucy Angkatell seems "just a bit batty" (she has a habit of putting teakettles on to boil in the upstairs baths for her guests' tea, then letting the water boil dry, ruining the kettle—the unobtrusive Gudgeon replaces the kettle from a stock he keeps belowstairs for that purpose), she is no novice at entertaining. When Sir Henry was governor of the Hallowene Islands, Lady Angkatell was able to flout the hallowed rules of protocol, thereby making all manner of foreign dignitaries and government officials endure inconvenience and annoyance, because of her extraordinary and pervasive charm. And now, husband, friends, and household staff all fall to do her bidding at a wave of her fragile hand.

Nevertheless, Lady Angkatell has some misgivings about the weekend.

While Dr. Christow is a joy to have as a guest — so strikingly handsome, with such deep blue eyes and such an air of being truly alive—inviting him means inviting Gerda, and that is such a trial. After all, what *can* one do with a person who can't play the simplest parlor games, knits dreadful lettuce-green pullovers, and then *wears* them? So trying. But she adores John, with an attitude almost of worship.

Midge, dark and sturdy, will be good to have present, but she will be tired from her work as shopgirl. Difficult to have to work at a job one doesn't care for, especially if the other branches of one's family are so well-to-do that they think people have jobs because they like to work.

And Cousin David is so stridently intellectual and so young. Lady Angkatell would prefer that boys of that age "put off being intellectual until they were rather older. As it is, they glower at one so and bite their nails and seem to have so many spots and sometimes an Adam's apple as well. And they either won't speak at all, or else are very loud and contradictory."

Edward, on the other hand, gentle, shy, and diffident, seems to become quieter and more self-effacing in groups, especially when Dr. Christow is part of the group. In Lady Angkatell's opinion, "John Christow has always the most unfortunate effect on Edward. John, if you know what I mean, becomes so much *more* so and Edward becomes so much *less* so."

So far the ingredients do not seem promising. But Lucy has two aces in the hole, so to speak. First, Cousin Henrietta. Everything she turns her

"Murder After Hours was a book I always thought I had ruined by the introduction of Poirot. I had got used to having Poirot in my books, and so naturally he had come into this one, but he was all wrong there." —*An Autobiography*

hand to seems to come out splendidly, from her sculpting to her driving. In her interested and concerned way, she takes trouble with the people around her, always knowing what to say and do to bring out their best. Lucy trusts that Henrietta will be able to amuse Sir Henry, be nice to Gerda, keep John and Edward in a good temper, and help with David.

Secondly, it happens that Hercule Poirot, whom Lady Angkatell had met in Baghdad, is renting a cottage near the Hollow. He has been invited for Sunday luncheon to provide a distraction for the somewhat discordant personalities that have been invited.

However, as the guests arrive and the weekend begins, we are led into complications deeper than simply discordant personalities, and Lady Angkatell's misgivings seem well founded. Midge loves Edward and wants him to look her way. But Edward loves Henrietta and wants to make her the mistress of Ainswick. However, Henrietta loves John and has made herself the mistress of the good doctor instead. Lucy disapproves strongly of this liaison, not for reasons of morality, but because she wants Edward and Henrietta to provide an heir for Ainswick to keep it in the family. David hates them all and looks forward to their inevitable demise in the class war, if not before.

Things, in short, are tense. And into the tension comes yet another woman with a claim on John — Veronica Cray, a cool, shrewd, grasping actress with whom John had been in love before his marriage. It seems she is renting the cottage across the way from M. Poirot, and has run out of matches. Could she borrow some? And what a surprise to see dear John after fifteen years! John is again transfixed as he was years before, and he more or less lets himself be led by the nose to accompany the lady home.

Their conversation takes an intimate turn, and they begin to relive old times instead of merely talking about them. John returns to the Hollow at three in the morning, having told Veronica that he is finally free of her spell and that he will not be seeing her again. As he approaches the house, he senses that he is being watched, and it dawns on him, as it has already dawned on us, that there are several people in and around the Hollow who would not be miserable if he were out of the way. When he sees no one, and finds his wife upstairs, he breathes a sigh of relief as he (finally) gets into his own bed.

The next afternoon at one o'clock, as he is being led by the faithful Gudgeon from the house to the pavilion by the swimming pool for drinks before luncheon, Hercule Poirot discovers his hosts and the other guests gathered, not in the pavilion around the bar, but by the pool around the body of John Christow, who has just been shot. At first the artificiality of the scene suggests to the Belgian detective that it is one more example of the tasteless humor of the English to stage a phony murder because Hercule Poirot is coming for luncheon. But he soon sees that it is anything but a joke, and that a murder has been committed almost in his presence.

As Poirot begins to delve beneath the surface civiliy and gentility of the group, he discovers no shortage of possible murderers: the wife — always the first to be suspected, even one as slow-witted as Gerda; one mistres, Veronica Cray, furious over her rejection; the other, Henrietta, strangely detached, and never ready to give herself entirely to anyone; Edward, jealous of John and in love with Henrietta; the embittered Midge; David, the upper-class Marxist with a history of instability in his branch of the family; and Lady Angkatell herself, who shows a technical familiarity with firearms quite surprising in a vague and eccentric gentlewoman.

But in the end, of course, even these knots are not too much for Hercule Poirot to untie.

JERRY KEUCHER

The Labors of Hercules (1947)

Hercule Poirot, a man not known for his modesty, is challenged when a friend scoffs at the detective's lack of resemblance to his namesake. Poirot vows to accept only twelve last cases before his retirement, and these twelve must all, in however obscure a fashion, correspond to the famous labors of the classical Hercules....

Poirot's first "labor" is to tackle a dangerous case involving a missing Pekinese dog. The detective dubs it my "Nemean Lion." (It must be mentioned here that the resemblance between Hercules' labors and Poirot's twelve cases occurs only in our detective's imagination.) Poirot is brought to the trail of the devilish Pekinese upon complaint of Sir Joseph Hoggin, who presents the case on behalf of his wife, Lady Millicent Hoggin. Lady Hoggin's Pekinese, Shan Tung, had mysteriously disappeared, with a ransom note delivered next day threatening dire harm to the little beast if the correct sum of money is not paid immediately.

Poirot's interest perks when he learns of another kidnapped-Pekinese case right down the street from the Hoggins; in fact, similar threats have been made against the lives of several Pekes in the neighborhood. The ladies are all atwitter, and there are really no clues except, in each instance, a sharply severed dog leash. But Poirot manages to solve the crime in such an exemplary way that Sir Hoggin even agrees to let the perpetrators go free, in lieu of Poirot's fee. Such is the satisfaction Hercule Poirot derives from his first "Labor of Hercules."

The second labor is more difficult, involving a well-known ugly monster — rumor. Poirot calls it "The Lernean Hydra," saying that "rumor is the nine-headed Hydra which cannot be exterminated because as fast as one head is cropped off two grow in its place."

The Lernean Hydra case is brought to Poirot by Dr. Charles Oldfield, whom everyone in town thinks has murdered his wife. Tongues are flying, and Oldfield's problem is not helped much by the fact that, as Poirot soon discovers, Oldfield was much younger than his wife, and that she was rich and rather unpleasant. In addition, the good doctor had a pretty girl employed as his dispenser. On the surface, it does look as though the two planned a poisoning, especially when Jean Moncrieffe, the red-headed dispenser, balks at the idea of exhuming Mrs. Oldfield's body. There are the usual suspicious people cluttering the background of the plot, maids and whatnot, but Poirot thinks he's got an airtight case until one of the Hydra's "heads" decides to talk a little too much...

In "The Arcadian Deer," Hercule Poirot's third labor, our well-meaning and competent detective takes on a new role, that of matchmaker for the lovelorn. It all begins when a young garage mechanic consults Poirot, while the latter's car is being fixed, on the matter of a disappearing lady's maid. The maid, by the name of Nita, and, according to her lover, of a description not to be compared, was to rendezvous with him on a certain evening but did not show up and, evidently, has not been heard from since. Poirot, intrigued by the enchanting description of lovely Nita, declares her his Arcadian Deer, and sets out to find her. But alas, his search leads only to the graveyard, for, as our beloved "deer's" family lamentingly exclaims, "she died young." Can

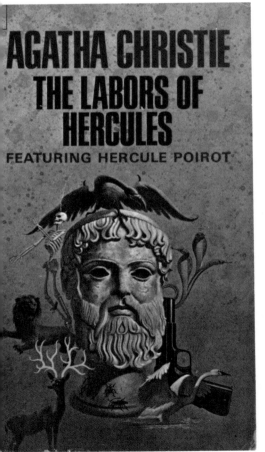

Poirot uncover foul play ... a little hunting out-of-season?

The labor of "The Erymanthian Boar" takes Poirot to the Swiss Alps, to a place called Rochers Neiges, ten thousand feet above sea level, where, in a resort hotel, a dangerous killer is to meet with his partners in crime. Poirot, upon learning this, carefully examines his fellow travelers in the cable car bearing the party up to the hotel: one innocuous American, with the usual American tendency to talk people to death; the renowned Dr. Lutz, a silent type occupied with his books of psychiatric theory; a beautiful woman whose husband died at Rochers Neiges three years ago while climbing; and three cardsharks, who could well be the criminal's gang. But none of the would-be guests, nor the manager or waiters either, fit the description of the killer himself—"a madman and a murderer ... a regular *wild boar*."

Poirot is put on guard when the manager of the hotel is unduly nervous: true, it is off-season, but surely there is enough food in the pantry ...? Then one of the waiters is attacked, and Poirot himself is in danger, with no help forthcoming until the cable-car line, mysteriously cut, can be repaired. It is up to our wily detective to capture the wild boar alive and thus complete the fourth labor of Hercules.

Unfortunately for Poirot, his labors seem to increase in complexity as they multiply in number, as in "The Augean Stables," involving a Prime minister's future and the reputation of his wife, the lovely Dagmar Ferrier, "the proper ideal of English womanhood." Dagmar's image is brutally soiled by photos taken of her, half-unclothed, with a sinister-looking lover, in

The Labors of Hercules (1947)

sophisticated but questionable nightclubs around the world. Can Poirot call forth the purifying floods to cleanse these Augean stables?

Can Poirot handle the Stymphalean birds, who have made life very unpleasant for young Harold Waring, an undersecretary to the Prime Minister, as he vacations in Herzoslovakia — a vacation, one might add, with all the ingredients for illicit love?

Or, can Poirot unlock the mystery in the Cretan bull, a most intriguing case brought to him by none other than the "bull's" fiancée, beautiful Diana Maberly, who suspects that the disintegration of her stalwart young lover is due to something other than the reputed "madness in the family?"

In "The Horses of Diomedes," Poirot encounters cocaine and its innocent victims, four young society girls with wild reputations, out looking for a better-than-average good time. It falls upon Poirot and the kindly young Dr. Michael Stoddart to tame these young fillies.

"The Girdle of Hippolyta" presents two strange cases, a stolen Rubens painting and a missing schoolgirl, which may or may not be the ingredients for an exotic rendezvous in Paris.

Our hero is joined by a former adventurer in crime, now turned sleuth, to unravel the truth in "The Flock of Geryon," a most sinister case involving a secret religion; a rash of lonely women who find themselves, inexplicably,

joining the cult and donating all their worldly goods to its endeavors; and the mesmerizing Dr. Andersen, who almost seduces Poirot's new assistant into his flock. Poirot is worried about his "sacrificial lamb" but there have been three deaths lately of members in the sect, and it is really Poirot's last resort.

"The Apples of the Hesperides" involves an ornate gold cup, stolen from its owner, the wealthy financier, Emery Power. The cup has its own ominous history, but clues to the present disappearance are few, and Poirot is confronted with a tale of chicanery covering half the continents of the world.

Poirot's labors end with a flourish in "The Capture of Cerberus," a tantalizing test for the detective as it involves an old flame, the Countess Vera Rossakoff. Vera now runs a nightclub called Hell, but Poirot is distressed to find, on his very first visit to Hell, that a police inspector, in disguise of course, is also patronizing the club. "What gives?" asks Poirot. Chief Inspector Japp answers with a sordid story of jewel theft and drug traffic; wealthy women claim their jewels have been stolen and substitutions made. The only suspects are Paul Varesco, a ladies-man criminal type, a few other of Hell's more flamboyant clientele — and the countess herself. It breaks Poirot's heart but — he must investigate.

The twelfth labor, you know.

JOANNA MILTON

There Is a Tide (1948)

(Alternate title: *Taken at the Flood*)

Our tale is introduced by a rather distasteful gentleman, Major Porter, who is a reputed bore, but one with an eye for detail and an ear for slander. As Major Porter describes the literally explosive death of Gordon Cloade and the sordid history of Cloade's widow, we catch (through Porter's eye) a glance at one of his listeners, M. Hercule Poirot.

Two years later, a visitor arrives at Poirot's home requesting his services. Mrs. Lionel Cloade (Gordon's sister-in-law) claims that "the spirits" guided her to Poirot's doorstep. She is looking for information on the first husband of Gordon's widow: he had died in Africa shortly before Gordon married his young wife, the now rewidowed Rosaleen.

It isn't long before we learn that the remaining Cloades — Gordon's two brothers, his sister, and his nephew (all of whom reside in Warmsley Vale) — are quite down on their financial luck. Rosaleen alone has inherited Gordon's expansive estate, to the chagrin of his blood relatives. If Rosaleen should die, however, Gordon's wealth would be distributed among his surviving blood relatives.

And, as we enter the homes of Jeremy Cloade, Adela Marchmont, Lionel Cloade, and Rowley (Gordon's nephew), we begin to wonder if dear Rosaleen will live through the first fifty pages of the story. We worry, as well, that our could-be-murderers-to-be will stumble over one another in their haste to remove the one obstacle that stands between destitution and their legacy.

But why is the stranger, who claims to have important information about Robert Underhay (Rosaleen's first husband), murdered instead?

And was the stranger more than just a friend of Underhay's — perhaps Underhay himself? And if the murdered Enoch Arden and Underhay were one and the same, then Rosaleen's claim to Gordon's estate becomes counterfeit. A bigamist can't claim a widow's fortune.

Just as the question of Enoch Arden's identity is beginning to baffle Poirot, Major Porter reenters the story bent on revealing the definitive answer to this question of who is really who. Rosaleen is shipped off to London as the search for Arden's murderer begins.

Arrows of guilt fall just a bit too neatly toward Rosaleen's brother, David. Too neatly, that is, for Poirot. It is true that David's cigarette lighter was found at the scene of the crime. True, as well, that the threat Enoch posed to Rosaleen's inheritance is indeed a respectable motive for murder for David, who rules Rosaleen's every move.

Yet, there is the problem of the lipstick found in the room of the murdered man — the same shade of lipstick worn by Rosaleen and by Lynn Marchmont, as well. And who was the heavily made-up "harpy" who was seen leaving the murder scene an hour after the killing occurred?

There are too many questions left unanswered. Poirot, to the obvious distress of the Cloades, remains at Warmsley Vale. He has taken up gossiping with the locals; he's seeking out the secrets of Gordon's "cheated" heirs. Is he out to solve the Arden murder, in order to free David of suspicion? Or is he attempting to prevent a second death? Rosaleen's safety remains in question. She's still the heir. Poirot has learned that financial desperation is mounting in each Cloade household. Who is capable of planning

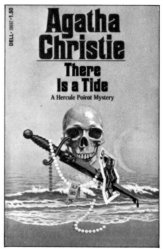

the permanent elimination of the innocent, unassuming Rosaleen?

Would a dedicated doctor, Lionel Cloade, consider murder? Perhaps he would if, as suspected, he was addicted to morphine and in need of the means necessary to support his habit. Indeed, he could have murder on his mind if he learned of the extravagant debts he owed because of his wife's attraction to the occult.

Or would Lionel's brother, Jeremy, a respected lawyer, conjure up the perfect murder of Rosaleen? Maybe not, but his wife, Frances, might in order to save her husband from impending disgrace.

Might Poirot suspect Adela Marchmont, the rather biting lady who has grown used to life's luxuries and who now faces a solitary life of impoverished hardship? And let us not forget that Adela's daughter, Lynn, wears a lipstick shade similar to the one found at the murder scene.

And is Rowley beyond reproach just because Rosaleen finds him so easy to talk with? Rowley, it seems, was counting on using Gordon's fortune to renovate his farm, a farm he is overhauling for his future wife, Lynn Marchmont. Lynn developed a true need for excitement and mystery during her service with the British army; Rowley fears she will desert him for adventures beyond. Wealth might prove the key to Lynn's heart.

With such an array of potential murderers on the brink of bloody action, it seems as if Poirot's stay at Warmsley Vale is quite in order. For, as Poirot wisely quotes from Shakespeare: "There is a tide in the affairs of men, which, taken at the flood, leads on to fortune...."

SUE ELLEN YORK

Witness for the Prosecution
(1948)

"The law, Greta, is a serious business and should be treated accordingly," says Carter, Sir Wilfred Robarts' law clerk, to his secretary. "You wouldn't think so, to hear some of the jokes judges make," she ripostes.

Yes, it is no less than the English judicial system itself that is the touchstone for merriment as the setting of Agatha Christie's classic murder thriller, *Witness for the Prosecution*. And a jolly good time she has with it, too. But, as always — at least, as always in Christie — justice will be served. Only, who's serving?

We begin the play in Robart's chambers, whence his friend, Solicitor Mayhew, brings Leonard Vole, whom the police have questioned about the murder of a certain Emily French. Vole had been in the habit of visiting this wealthy spinster to help with her business affairs, play a game of Double Demon, chat about the theater — that sort of thing. She took quite a fancy to him, Vole admits. Most women do, it seems, and how could they not? He's so open and cheerful and friendly and helpful — a thoroughly engaging young man. Greta can see he's innocent already. Why? "He's far too nice," she says, and everyone agrees. He's even cheery when the police arrive and cart him off to jail.

But his wife, Romaine — now that is another story. First of all, she's foreign. Not that the British are xenophobic, mind you. "Nine out of twelve in a jury box believe a foreigner is lying anyway" is the way Sir Wilfred expresses it. That is indeed unfortunate, for Romaine is Leonard's only alibi. She had already told the police that he was home with her at 9:30 P.M., when the murder occurred. But what's this? She is remarkably calm

about Leonard's having been arrested. And under Sir Wilfred's interrogation, her answers are extremely ambiguous. She seems more interested in whether her alibi will free Leonard than in whether the truth be told. Leonard swears she is devoted to him, but Sir Wilfred's suspicions are aroused. "Never trust a woman," he declares, ringing down the Act 1 curtain.

Act 2 transports us to the Central Criminal Court, London—better known as the Old Bailey — six weeks later. All the majesty of the world's finest judicial system is on display. The Royal Arms and the Sword of Justice hang over the judge's chair. We hear the foreman swear before Almighty God that he will "a true verdict give according to the evidence." Bewigged barristers lend a solemn ear as the parade of witnesses begins. Surely justice will be served here.

An inspector describes the scene of the crime. It looked like a robbery, but then why was the victim left wearing her jewelry? And why should unbroken glass at the window latch be on the ground *outside* the house as well as inside the room? And did the defendant really cut his wrist with this kitchen knife, as he and his wife claim, or did the blood on his jacket cuff once belong inside poor Emily's head? Of course, the blow could have been delivered by a woman, as Dr. Wyatt points out, and it was received at the junction of the parietal, occipital, and temple bones — "behind the left ear," he kindly explains for the laymen. Could it have been delivered by a left-handed person?

It is now Janet MacKenzie, Miss Emily's housekeeper, who takes the stand. She begins to read the oath, holding the Bible in her—in her left

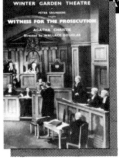

"One night at the theatre stands out in my memory specially; the first night of *Witness for the Prosecution* .... I can safely say that that was the only first night I have enjoyed .... It was one of my plays that I liked best myself. I was as nearly satisfied with that play as I have been with any. I didn't want to write it; I was terrified of writing it." —*An Autobiography*

hand! Oho! She swears she heard Leonard and Miss Emily laughing in the sitting room when she returned home unexpectedly on Friday night. She knows what was going on. Didn't Miss Emily order *The Life of Baroness Burdett Coutts* and that book about Disraeli and his wife from the library, both of them about women who'd married men years younger than themselves? The judge feels constrained to caution the jury that "it is possible for a woman to read the life of Disraeli without contemplating marriage with a man younger than herself." Besides, Janet has her reasons for disliking Leonard. Didn't Miss Emily recently change her will, jilting Janet in favor of Leonard? And what's this about her having recently applied to the National Health Insurance for a hearing apparatus, Sir Wilfred asks in a low voice. "I can no' hear anyone if they mumble," replies the devoted housekeeper.

It is now time for the devoted wife, Romaine, to testify. It turns out, however, that she is devoted not to Leonard, but to truth — imagine a foreigner holding those kinds of ideals! "I cannot come into Court and lie and say that he was there with me at the time it was done. I cannot do it. I cannot *do* it!" she exclaims, getting appropriately dramatic. Sure, Leonard had married her and brought her to England safe from the clutches of Communism. Of course she is grateful. But justice must be done, mustn't it?

Sir Wilfred cannot believe it. Neither can Leonard, who is threatened with explusion from the courtroom for his anguished outbursts.

Under the withering cross-examination of Mr. Myers, Q.C., he slowly and painfully breaks down, until the act 2 curtain leaves us with this pathetic plaint: "I didn't kill her. I've never killed anybody. O, God! It's a nightmare. It's some awful, evil dream."

Act 3 finds us back in Robart's chambers. Sir Wilfred is none too sanguine about his client's chances for acquittal. But then an angel of mercy, or the English equivalent thereof, appears in the form of a blonde-haired woman, cheaply and flamboyantly dressed, violently and crudely made up. She has with her certain letters, written in Romaine's hand, letters that will assure Leonard's freedom. She wants a hundred quid. Robarts and Mayhew, good lawyers both, bargain her down to twenty. But why is she so anxious to interfere in this case? She pulls back her hair to reveal a slashed, badly scarred cheek. Sir Wilfred is shocked. He gives her another fiver.

The denouement takes place in the courtroom the next morning. What is in the letters? Who is the strawberry blonde who is seen with Leonard in a travel agency, mapping out exotic holiday plans? And what kind of woman is Romaine Heigler really? Suffice it to say that Agatha Christie is at her dramatic best here, holding her answers until the very last page of the script, saving her most striking dramatic action until the next-to-the-last line, adding a final line whose ironies reverberate hours after the curtain comes down. Now that, ladies and gentlemen of the jury, is justice!   GRANVILLE BURGESS

THE MAKING OF
WITNESS FOR THE PROSECUTION
by Michael Tennenbaum

Movies are an illusion. They don't really move at all. What we actually see are still pictures, floated quickly before our gullible eyes at the rate of twenty-four times every second. Since our brains can only work so fast, we fail to notice the pauses in between these snapshots and assume that what we are seeing is actually motion on the screen. But the sense of illusion doesn't stop there; moviemakers have always tried to fool us with their art, and the best of them have no trouble succeeding, and we never mind being fooled. Editors do it, art directors do it, and of course, actors do it. But...

Let's go back. In 1957, Agatha Christie's stage adaptation of her short story "Witness for the Prosecution" was a big hit in New York and London, and producer Arthur Hornblow, Jr., thought the time was right to bring it to the screen. Billy Wilder, hot after the successes of *Stalag 17, Sabrina,* and *The Seven Year Itch,* was approached to direct the film. Not one to forget old friends, Wilder remembered that when he had first arrived in Hollywood from his native Austria, Hornblow had given him his first job on a motion picture.

Meanwhile, Wilder's friend Marlene Dietrich had been eyeing the plum role of Christine Vole ever since she had seen the stage production. (In the short story Christine was called Romaine, but her name was changed for the film version in order to avoid confusion with the vegetable.) Here at last, she thought, was the role that would make full use of her acting abilities—abilities that other producers chose to ignore when offering her the usual femme fatale parts. She urged Wilder to accept the job in the hope that his

suggestion of her for the part would not be challenged. She was right. Wilder's other choices were equally good—Charles Laughton was cast as Sir Wilfred Robarts and Tyrone Power became Leonard Vole, the accused murderer.

Wilder may not have had as much faith in Miss Dietrich's qualifications as she. It was very un-Hollywood for Marlene to appear in a film without singing at least one song and offering a glimpse of her justly famous legs. Unwilling to take that much of a risk at the box office, Wilder and screenwriter Harry Kurnitz added a flashback scene where Power and Dietrich meet for the first time: he, a lonely soldier and she—you guessed it — a singer in postwar Berlin entertaining the troops. Marlene got to sing "I'll Never Go Home Any More," and sure enough, she's so sultry and exciting that a fight breaks out among the 145 extras and 38 stuntmen employed just for that scene and poor Marlene gets her pants leg ripped up the seam, exposing one famous beautiful leg.

This is a sight that we jaded filmgoers of the 1970s must never underestimate, for it served as enough impetus for Power to offer her some instant coffee and marriage. Before the audience can become too involved in this silly digression, Wilder, with great wisdom, comically collapses

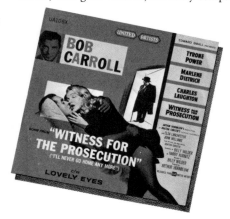

the bed underneath them and the film jumps back to the present and Leonard Vole's serious predicament. However, all the advertising posters for the film prominently show the torrid couple in horizontal harmony, a scene that doesn't really appear in the film at all. More of that illusion?

Witness for the Prosecution was filmed at a time when the words *on location* meant going out on the back lot for an exterior shot. Any place or thing in the entire world could be duplicated within the confines of the studio and all footage shot at home. The enormous cost of set building was justified by weighing it against the cost of transporting cast and crew around the globe and dealing with the enormous problems of a movie company far from home. Wilder's movie was filmed almost entirely on Stage Four on the Sam Goldwyn lot. (If you wonder why all those British character actors in the film appear so familiar, it's because Wilder used all the resident Englishmen he could find in Hollywood — John Williams, Torin Thatcher, Henry Daniell, Ian Wolfe, Una O'Connor, all famous from their many American movies.) At a cost of $75,000, art director Alexander Trauner built an incredible facsimile of London's famous Old Bailey courthouse, where much of the story occurs. Based on original plans and his own sketches (photographs are not permitted in Old Bailey), Trauner constructed a courtroom that was accurate to the last

detail and still flexible enough to accommodate the requirements of a creative director's camera directions. Walls made of Austrian oak moved, flooring in nineteen sections gave way to allow Wilder to film a scene from many different angles, a feat that would not have been possible in the real Old Bailey.

During filming, the publicity people were hard at work on a job that required them to attract attention to the event without revealing anything about the plot. The solution was obvious — the plot became the event. Much was made of the film's surprise ending and the great pains taken to prevent anyone from revealing it: a publicity still shows Wilder denying Sam Goldwyn entry to his own soundstage. But the best bit of all was "The Secrecy Pledge," a huge poster hung outside the studio that everyone entering had to sign:

In faithful compliance with the conspiracy of silence entered into by everyone who has seen Agatha Christie's remarkable play, "Witness for the Prosecution" which is being produced for the screen by Arthur Hornblow for UA Release, I agree to continue this silence by promising not to reveal any of the secrets relating to its electrifying climax. Therefore—if, working on or visiting its set during photography, I discover clues which lead to disclosure of the surprise ending, I promise to let other people enjoy discovering it for themselves — properly, in a theatre.

And it was faithfully signed by all, including, for reasons fathomed only by studio publicity men, Burt Lancaster, Noel Coward, William Holden, and Hedda Hopper.

Back on the set, Wilder had added some life to the script by giving Charles Laughton's Sir Wilfrid a heart condition which added not only another suspenseful element to the script (will he survive the trial?) but another character as well, Elsa Lanchester (Mrs. Laughton) as Sir Wilfrid's naggy nurse. Laughton, consummate actor that he was, was not sure he could skillfully play a man with a weak heart. So one day at home while in the swimming pool he staged a heart attack. Elsa and a houseguest panicked and pulled him from the water, at which point he explained his trick. Mrs. Laughton's reaction has not been recorded. Ironically, the man with the heart condition was Tyrone Power, who died a few months later during the filming of *Solomon and Sheba*.

Still, the illusion in *Witness for the Prosecution* is not in the elaborate set or the skills of the publicity men or the above-mentioned actors. One special segment contains a mystery within the mystery. (At this point, those readers not familiar with the film or short story might consider reading no further — I am about to reveal certain evidence contributing to the film's surprise ending. Can you resist?)

Marlene Dietrich's original interest in the film centered around the idea that Christine Vole must masquerade as a cockney tart as part of the plan to save her husband's life. Dietrich became obsessed with this aspect of the role although at first she

was not sure she could play it. She got considerable help and support from Wilder, Laughton, and Noel Coward. Elsa Lanchester remembered that "Marlene was forever at our house, trying on scarves, shawls, and various wigs and taking lessons in cockney from Charles. She was obsessed with this impersonation." Marlene based the voice characteristics on working-class girls she had known in Berlin, and that made the vocal disguise easier.

But physical disguise was another problem, the solution to which is known to but a few people. When one first sees the film it is easier to accept that Christine and the tart are played by the same person—we do not see the tart again after the revelation is made and we are forced to rely on memory. Knowing the film, and seeing it more than once, it is difficult to believe that Dietrich plays both parts. Vocally, there is no doubt; the telltale *w* substitution for *r* gives her away. But who is that woman? Makeup artists agree that it is difficult to disguise a person's features so completely without affecting facial mobility. So the legend goes that Wilder filmed the scene *twice*, once with Dietrich in makeup and then, disappointed in the results, again with another actress mouthing Dietrich's already-recorded dialogue, and used this second bit of footage in the finished film. This is denied, of course, by everyone involved. And you must decide for yourself.

The price of admission includes the acceptance of the illusion — we check our skepticism at the door if we intend to enjoy the experience within. But how much may the artist tamper with our acceptance?

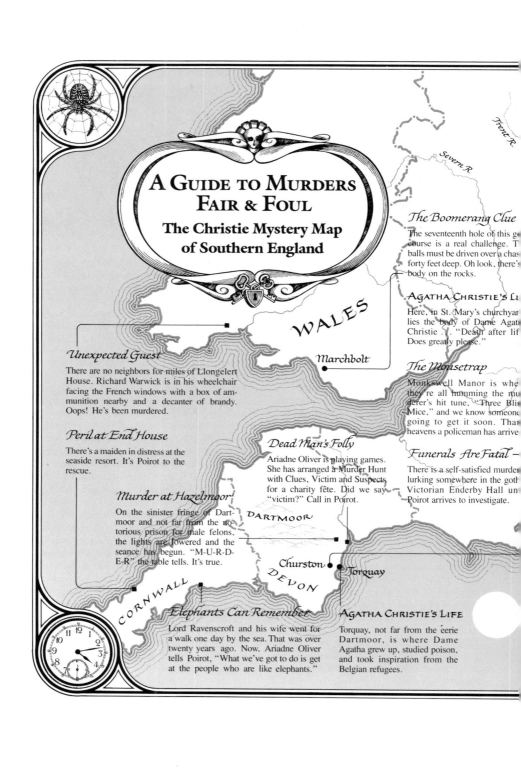

A GUIDE TO MURDERS FAIR & FOUL

The Christie Mystery Map of Southern England

WALES

Marchbolt

DARTMOOR

Churston • *Torquay*

DEVON

CORNWALL

Trent R.

Severn R.

The Boomerang Clue

The seventeenth hole of this g[...]
course is a real challenge. T[...]
balls must be driven over a chas[...]
forty feet deep. Oh look, there'[...]
body on the rocks.

AGATHA CHRISTIE'S LI[...]

Here, in St. Mary's churchyar[...]
lies the body of Dame Agat[...]
Christie . . . "Death after lif[...]
Does greatly please."

The Mousetrap

Monkswell Manor is whe[...]
they're all humming the mu[...]
derer's hit tune, "Three Bli[...]
Mice," and we know someone[...]
going to get it soon. Tha[...]
heavens a policeman has arrive[...]

Funerals Are Fatal —

There is a self-satisfied murder[...]
lurking somewhere in the goth[...]
Victorian Enderby Hall un[...]
Poirot arrives to investigate.

Unexpected Guest

There are no neighbors for miles of Llongelert
House. Richard Warwick is in his wheelchair
facing the French windows with a box of am-
munition nearby and a decanter of brandy.
Oops! He's been murdered.

Peril at End House

There's a maiden in distress at the
seaside resort. It's Poirot to the
rescue.

Murder at Hazelmoor

On the sinister fringe of Dartmoor and not far from the notorious prison for male felons,
the lights are lowered and the
seance has begun. "M-U-R-D-
E-R" the table tells. It's true.

Dead Man's Folly

Ariadne Oliver is playing games.
She has arranged a Murder Hunt
with Clues, Victim and Suspects
for a charity fête. Did we say
"victim?" Call in Poirot.

Elephants Can Remember

Lord Ravenscroft and his wife went for
a walk one day by the sea. That was over
twenty years ago. Now, Ariadne Oliver
tells Poirot, "What we've got to do is get
at the people who are like elephants."

AGATHA CHRISTIE'S LIFE

Torquay, not far from the eerie
Dartmoor, is where Dame
Agatha grew up, studied poison,
and took inspiration from the
Belgian refugees.

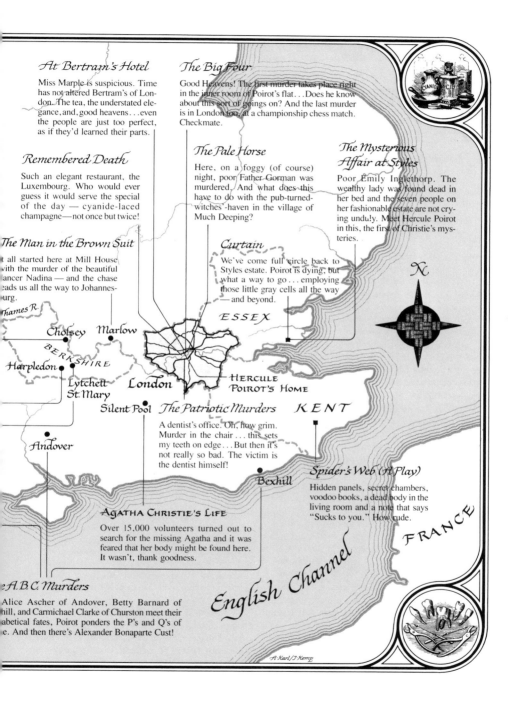

At Bertram's Hotel

Miss Marple is suspicious. Time has not altered Bertram's of London. The tea, the understated elegance, and, good heavens...even the people are just too perfect, as if they'd learned their parts.

Remembered Death

Such an elegant restaurant, the Luxembourg. Who would ever guess it would serve the special of the day — cyanide-laced champagne—not once but twice!

The Man in the Brown Suit

It all started here at Mill House with the murder of the beautiful dancer Nadina — and the chase leads us all the way to Johannesburg.

The Big Four

Good Heavens! The first murder takes place right in the inner room of Poirot's flat...Does he know about this sort of goings on? And the last murder is in London too, at a championship chess match. Checkmate.

The Pale Horse

Here, on a foggy (of course) night, poor Father Gorman was murdered. And what does this have to do with the pub-turned-witches'-haven in the village of Much Deeping?

Curtain

We've come full circle back to Styles estate. Poirot is dying, but what a way to go...employing those little gray cells all the way — and beyond.

The Mysterious Affair at Styles

Poor Emily Inglethorp. The wealthy lady was found dead in her bed and the seven people on her fashionable estate are not crying unduly. Meet Hercule Poirot in this, the first of Christie's mysteries.

The Patriotic Murders

A dentist's office. Oh, how grim. Murder in the chair...this sets my teeth on edge...But then it's not really so bad. The victim is the dentist himself!

Agatha Christie's Life

Over 15,000 volunteers turned out to search for the missing Agatha and it was feared that her body might be found here. It wasn't, thank goodness.

Spider's Web (A Play)

Hidden panels, secret chambers, voodoo books, a dead body in the living room and a note that says "Sucks to you." How rude.

The A.B.C. Murders

Alice Ascher of Andover, Betty Barnard of Bexhill, and Carmichael Clarke of Churston meet their alphabetical fates, Poirot ponders the P's and Q's of the case. And then there's Alexander Bonaparte Cust!

Thames R.

Cholsey   Marlow

BERKSHIRE

Harpledon

Lytchett St. Mary

London

Silent Pool

Andover

ESSEX

HERCULE POIROT'S HOME

KENT

Bexhill

English Channel

FRANCE

N

A. Karl / J. Kemp

DARTMOOR — THE DEADLY HEATH
by Pam McAllister

"The moor is a wonderful place."
— Emily in *Murder at Hazelmoor*.

It is little wonder that Agatha Christie, Queen of Mystery, herself lived so near and drew sustenance from one of the world's most mysterious, legend-haunted spots on earth — Dartmoor. Dartmoor is the beautiful but forsaken and untamed moor dominating 365 square miles of central Devonshire in southwestern England, through which the River Dart runs. Eerie granite tors (high craggy hills) and the rubble of Bronze Age huts dot the land, and in one corner of the expanse stands the infamous Princetown prison once described as "a great tomb of the living."

And it was to this spot that Dame Agatha went for the inspiration to write her first mystery, *The Mysterious Affair at Styles*. When, in 1916, Agatha's sister Madge pronounced her famous taunt, "I bet you can't write one in which I can't guess the ending," Agatha took the challenge to the Moorland Hotel at Hay Tor, on Dartmoor. There she holed up and in two weeks had almost finished her first novel.

"I used to write laboriously all morning till my hand ached. Then I would have lunch, reading a book. Afterwards I would go out for a good walk on the moor, perhaps for a couple of hours. I think I learned to love the moor in those days. I loved the tors and the heather and all the wild part of it away from the roads.... As I walked I muttered to myself, enacting the chapter that I was next going to write."

Dartmoor: the perfect place to create a sinister plot if ever there was one. Sir Arthur Conan Doyle had done it before her with his unforgettable *Hound of the Baskervilles*, set in the heart of the Dartmoor heath:

The longer one stays here the more does the spirit of the moor sink into one's soul, its vastness, and also its grim charm. When you are once out upon its bosom you have left all traces of modern England behind you, but on the other hand you are conscious everywhere of the homes and the work of the prehistoric people. On all sides of you as you walk are the houses of these forgotten folk, with their graves and the huge monoliths which are supposed to have marked their temples.

Miss Jane Marple knows about these prehistoric stones too, and she uses them to make a point in "The Thumb Mark of St. Peter" in *The Tuesday Club Murders*:

"There is a place on Dartmoor called Grey Wethers. If you were talking to a farmer there and mentioned Grey Wethers, he would probably conclude that you were speaking of these stone circles, yet it is possible that you might be speaking of the atmosphere; and in the same way, if you were meaning the stone circles, an outsider, hearing a fragment of the conversation, might think you meant the weather. So when we repeat a conversation, we don't as a rule, repeat the actual words; we put in some other words that seem to us to mean exactly the same thing."

What sort of place is this Dartmoor to make it so appealing to our prime mystery writers? In the book *Through a Dartmoor Window* by O.K. Parr, the author writes: "I maintain that things do not happen in other places as they happen here ...

Sudden deaths upon the moor or the highway are frequent, deaths with apparently insufficient cause."

Here modern-day suspicions mesh with the ancient legends to create new stories of moorland mystery. One such case involves a spot called the Coffin Stone. According to custom, a coffin would be borne on the shoulders of men in relays as they marched silently across the moor to the burial place. Once, however, as legend has it, a man died who had lived a fully wicked life. The coffin-bearers set out across the lonely moor and, after the long toil up Dartmeet Hill, they eased their burden by setting the coffin on the coffin stone provided. Suddenly, in the blue sky a small black cloud no bigger than a man's hand appeared over the coffin, and the voice of God echoed a warning that this evil man was to be an example to those to come after. In the next instant a thunderbolt struck the coffin and cleft the boulder in

two, forming the rough sign of a cross. It is still there today, a sign to us all.

Another haunted spot on the moor seems to be in the highlands at the foot of Hound Tor where a ridge of stones, the granite hounds, can be heard baying at twilight, warning that the shadow of death is hanging over some moorland dweller. These hounds were certainly the inspiration for *The Hound of the Baskervilles*.

"Halloa!" I cried. "What is that?"

A long, low moan, indescribably sad, swept over the moor. It filled the whole air, and yet it was impossible to say whence it came. From a dull murmur it swelled into a deep roar, and then sank back into a melancholy, throbbing murmur once again. Stapleton looked at me with a curious expression in his face.

"Queer place, the moor!" said he.

"But what is it?"

"The peasants say it is the Hound of the Bas-

DARTMOOR — THE DEADLY HEATH

kervilles calling for its prey. I've heard it once or twice before, but never quite so loud.

Aside from granite hounds, coffin stones, and lonely unmarked graves dotting the moor, there are invisible curiosities as well, such as the unusual terrestrial magnetism of certain moorland spots. Dartmoor, it is said, is "very electric"; certain places are consistently struck by lightning due to the presence of magnetic metal in the ground there. And it is because of this, it is said, that clocks and watches go absolutely mad on first arriving at Dartmoor.

To add just a bit more intrigue, there is a prison there, Princetown, with its own bit of legend. Built in 1806 to house French captives during the Napoleonic Wars, it was used during the War of 1812 for American prisoners and came to be known as a most brutal and inhumane place of confinement. The stories are absolutely gory. Between 1812 and 1816 some fifteen hundred American and French prisoners died there and were buried without funeral rites in a field beyond the prison walls. During one of the frequent epidemics, the medical officer had coffins stored in the infirmary within sight of the patients.

Little wonder that from this history would arise great legends of escape and attempted escape. One of the best real-life stories is of the prison Dramatic Society, which produced plays for the entertainment of the prisoners. One of the convict-playwrights wrote a three-act comedy called *La Capitaine Calonne et sa Dame*. Of course Officer Calonne and his wife were invited. Not only were they flattered to attend the performance but they even agreed to lend their dress and uniform for the first performance. The first act was marvelous. Since the actors impersonating the captain and his wife were not scheduled to appear again until the third act, no one noticed that the actors had taken a little stroll, still in their stage attire, right past the guards, bidding them good evening as they went.

An escaped prisoner would first try to obtain civilian clothes by breaking into a moorland dwelling. When the prison sounded the alarm, all the houses on the moor lit up in a signal to the fugitive that the owners were on the alert.

"Hark!" cried Charles suddenly.

He held up his hand. Then he went over to the window and opened it, and Emily too, heard the sound which had aroused his attention. It was the far-off booming of a great bell.

As they stood listening, Mrs. Curtis's voice called excitedly from below:

"D'you hear it? Plain as plain, isn't it? Well now, to think of that!"

"What is it?" asked Emily.

"It's the bell at Princetown, Miss, near to twelve mile away. It means that a convict's escaped. George, George, where is that man? D'you hear the bell? There's a convict loose."

— from *Murder at Hazelmoor*

Of course Dame Agatha managed to use this chilling scene with her own twist of humor:

"It's a pity that things happen all wrong," he said dispassionately. "If only this convict had escaped on Friday, why, there would be our murderer nicely accounted for. No farther to look. Hungry man, desperate criminal breaks in. Trevelyan defends his Englishman's castle — and desperate criminal biffs him one. All so simple."

"It would have been," said Emily with a sigh.

"Instead of which," said Charles, "he escapes three days too late. It's — it's hopelessly inartistic."

He shook his head sadly.

Escape over the rough moorland was almost impossibly difficult. This was in part due to the thick, white fog, which at first would seem an escaped convict's dream of the perfect cover, but was more likely to disorient the hunted man and leave him wandering in circles.

The Dartmoor prison was left unoccupied for

over thirty years until it was opened in 1850 as a civilian prison especially for prisoners with long sentences or those condemned to hard labor.

> Emily gave a faint shiver. The idea of the desperate hunted man impressed her powerfully. Mr. Rycroft was watching her and gave a little nod.
> "Yes," he said. "I feel the same myself. It's curious how one's instincts rebel at the thought of a man being hunted down, and yet, these men at Princetown are all dangerous and violent criminals, the kind of men whom probably you and I would do our utmost to put there in the first place."
> — *Murder at Hazelmoor*

And what of Dame Agatha in the midst of all this moorland fog and mystery? It suited her to a T. Not only did she go into the Dartmoor to write her first murderous mystery, but in 1939 she bought a secluded mansion called Greenway House on the river Dart above Dartmouth and enjoyed daytime trips to the moor as a favorite picnicking place.

But Dartmoor is the backdrop and not the stage in books like *Hazelmoor, Tuesday Club Murders,* and *Dead Man's Folly.* If she was in love with this haunted spot she certainly did not let herself get carried away with its more exotic possibilities. She kept Dartmoor at a distance. Why?

Nigel Dennis in a 1956 *Life* magazine article explained:

> But though rivers, trains and other forms of fluid motion are as dear as poison to Agatha Christie, she shows her liveliest, most characteristic form in orderly, settled surroundings. High-class advertisers have long known her rule of work: keep the background innocuous if you want your product to stand out.

And so she does. Though not quite ordinary, her backgrounds are at least simple and charming or cozy. The crime then is truly stunning ("like suddenly seeing Satan at a Sunday school retreat," one of her fans is reported to have explained). No one would be overly surprised to see Satan appear from the mists of the haunted moor as the granite hounds howl...but from the tea table at the vicarage?...

Oh, what a lovely moor!

"WHAT'S IN A NAME" WORD FIND (*page 91*)

Leftover Letters:

THE FOLLOWING ORIGINAL ANAGRAM: ITS
HER FIRSTLY FAMOUS. Y SEE
NEW
IATA

The last six words are an anagram of *The Mysterious Affair at Styles.*

Crooked House (1949)

Dead: One rich old man, Aristides Leonides, who had an unusual and generous attachment to his family.
Problem: None of the family really gained by his death. And no one was without an alibi.
Question: Why did someone put the poison in the hypo?

"I first came to know Sophia Leonides in Egypt towards the end of the war." So Charles Hayward begins his narrative of *Crooked House*. His love for Sophia brings him back to England, and step-by-step he finds himself embroiled in a perplexing mystery involving the close-knit Leonides family in their oddly gabled mansion.

Gazing at a portrait of Aristides in the front room, Hayward is struck by the vitality and intelligence revealed in the old man's face even through the painting. "My grandfather is something of a Person," Sophia had told him in Egypt. "He's over eighty, about four-foot ten, and everybody else looks dim beside him." And, Sophia added, she liked him "better than anyone in the world." So why had he been killed?

The family members hardly seem to notice Charles's presence. Sophia's father, Philip, ignores him, retreating coldly into his library to study his endless books. Her actress mother, Magda, uses Charles as an audience for exit lines. Aunt Clemency is hostile in a vague way. Against his expectations — and Sophia's preference — Charles finds himself sympathetic to the beautiful Brenda, Aristides's very young wife, whose fear communicates itself to him. She knows the family hates her, that they all believe, and want to believe, that she killed her husband. The tutor, Lawrence Brown, scuttles in and out, trembling at every encounter — his only friend is Brenda.

Why had old Aristides hired him, really?

As Inspector Taverner and Charles's father (coincidentally the Assistant Commissioner of Scotland Yard) investigate the case, all evidence does indeed point to Brenda and Lawrence. Too pat? Perhaps — but then, a conspiracy of murder might just be the answer. Sophia's young sister finds their love letters and then is discovered unconscious in the garden, nearly killed by a doorstop. At the accusation by the redoubtable Inspector, Brenda collapses, and Brown cannot defend himself.

But there is the odd comment that each denizen of the little crooked house makes to Charles upon the arrest — it sets uneasily — for the family each in turn had told Charles that Aristides's death was all right, "if the right one did the murder." Clearly, Brenda was the right one — she was *not* family, had never fit it. Some madness had captured their father's imagination; she was only a golddigger of poor station. She deserved to be accused.

But Dame Agatha seldom makes everything so easily resolved. *Did* they do it? Were the letters a deliberate plant? Could anyone really hate or fear Josephine, a mere child, enough to try to kill her? Or Nannie? Why should she fall victim? What was her secret, after thirty years with the Leonides household?

The figures of old Leonides looms over all the family's anguish. How could he have made an unsigned will, when everyone had been present at its formal announcement? We learn somewhat later that Sophia has known this — and she alone — from the beginning. Aristides had deceived the witnesses, had drawn up another will surreptitiously, leaving his entire estate to Sophia, his first

"Of my detective books, I think the two that satisfy me best are *Crooked House* and *Ordeal by Innocence*." —*An Autobiography*

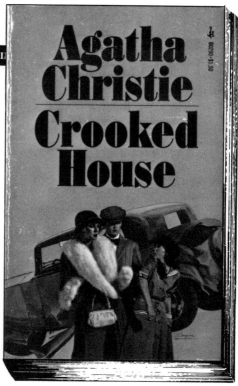

grandchild. Why? At the news, Philip is outraged, turns on his own daughter in a diatribe of anger and rejection. Magda pretends to beg for money, crooking her hand and plucking at Sophia's dress, a cockney voice letting out subtle venom. Suddenly Sophia is an outsider. She was the one to gain the most from the old man's demise, after all. But since the others had not known, did it matter?

It is to Josephine that Charles directs his attention, for she has a child's love of exploring. An ugly, gnomelike girl of eleven, somewhat ignored by her parents, she finds delight in keeping a clear record of events. Fascinated by "detecting," she listens at doors, follows people about—sees a great deal more than is healthy for her. Her intelligence compensates for her appearance, and Charles soon realizes he must protect her from enemies she may have unwittingly provoked.

Surely her own father would not harm her—yet, beneath his impersonal exterior, Philip Leonides seethes with passions unfulfilled. And Magda? She wants to send Josephine to a school in Switzerland, something Aristides forbade, desiring his family to be near him. But was it to keep the child safe, or to keep her from finding out anything more?

Roger and Clemency Leonides make an odd couple: Clemency in her spotless, uncluttered, white-walled apartment, Roger with his bearlike movements and bumbling ways. His father had given him total control of and profits from one of his corporations, and Roger's incompetence had resulted in the imminent collapse of Associated Caterers. Had his father refused to bail him out? Clemency defended him as a lioness would her cub.

Ruthless. That is the word Sophia uses to describe her family. Each in his or her own way has a streak of ruthlessness or unscrupulous inclination. Have these traits combined, perhaps, in the second child, Eustace, a frustrated, angry, fourteen-year-old boy, who had been crippled by

polio? Was it Eustace who had filled his grandfather's insulin bottle with eserine, driven by the dark shadows of memory when his grandfather insisted he be kept in solitude at the mansion?

And surely Aristides had made it easy for them all, when one evening they had gathered about him in his bedroom and he had described with particular detail what would happen if his medication were tampered with. The murderer had listened closely.

The hidden secrets of the Three Gables are manifold. Each member of the family has a private grief, an inner anguish. Yet, Aristides had kept his family around him out of love. In his lifetime he had continually increased his provisions to them. They stood to gain more if he continued to live than otherwise. Then why—why does it not ring true, really, to anyone, that Brenda and Lawrence were the perpetrators?

The tale ends on a cold, windswept autumn day at sunset, when, in simultaneous revelation, everyone realizes the truth.

REGINA SACKMARY

The Mousetrap and Other Stories (1950)

(Alternate title: *Three Blind Mice and Other Stories*)

For such a small and seemingly quiet village, St. Mary Mead is, by any cosmopolitan standards, generating a lot of business for the local police department. In this collection of nine Agatha Christie stories, St. Mary Mead and the inimitable Miss Marple get into the action four times. Hercule Poirot is given the opportunity to dazzle us with his peerless and gleaming intellect three times, and two stories in this collection are left to the resources of the minor Christie detective squad.

Though Marple and Poirot have gained a fame greater than any of the cases they have had to tackle, the title story of this collection has gained a name and reputation for itself, comparable to Miss Marple's, M. Poirot's, and even Dame Agatha's. This short story, "Three Blind Mice," was first presented under the title *The Mousetrap* on a London stage in 1952. And yet, this most impressive and popular mystery, this longest-playing show of all time, this masterpiece, was solved by the humble Inspector Tanner of Scotland Yard. Though immortalized by his place in *The Mousetrap*, Inspector Tanner remains a minor character in the Christie Hall of Fame.

Perhaps his lack of grandeur can be explained by the ease with which the "Three Blind Mice" unravels itself. With a customary late point of attack, the story begins at the moment of the first murder. We know nothing of the victim, Maureen Gregg, who was calling herself Mrs. Lyon, and we naturally know even less of her murderer. The police of Scotland Yard seem curiously distant, if not positively absent, from the scene of the crime. And then they seem slow to appear during the natural progression of events, which take the

story's focus from the anonymous London boarding-inghouse (the scene of the first murder) to Monkswell Manor, a small and very new guest house near a town called Harpleden in Berkshire County. "Three Blind Mice" is a departure from Christie's regular technique of web spinning in that we, the readers, appear on the scene at the payoff, so to speak, before anyone else. We know as much as, if not more than, the strangely power-less police force. Without Poirot or Marple to rival, confuse, or obscure our own sleuthing instincts, we readers are given the front seat on the roller coaster.

Giles and Molly Davis are the young proprietors of Monkswell Manor, which has opened just in time to receive its first four guests before being cut off from civilization by a record-breaking snowfall. Fortunately the phones do not go dead until after a representative from Scotland Yard appears, on snowshoes, to complete the party. It seems that on his way to the crime, the murderer of Maureen Gregg dropped a small notebook containing two vital clues concerning his homicidal intentions. One clue is the name of Monkswell Manor, and the second is simply the name of the nursery rhyme, "Three Blind Mice."

The stage is set, the system is closed. Monkswell Manor cannot be reached by telephone or by thoroughfare. And not long after he arrives, the snowshoes of the police inspector are stolen. The murderer must obviously be one of this painfully finite cast of six characters. Could it be the young, somewhat bohemian, architect, Christopher Wren? Or perhaps it is the austere and overbearing Mrs. Boyle. The foreign Mr. Paravicini seems to move with a vigor unusual for

"People are always asking me to what I attribute the success of *The Mousetrap*. Apart from replying with the obvious answer, "Luck!" — because it is luck, ninety per cent luck, at least, I should say — the only reason I can give is that there is a bit of something in it for almost everybody: people of different age groups and tastes can enjoy seeing it." —*An Autobiography*

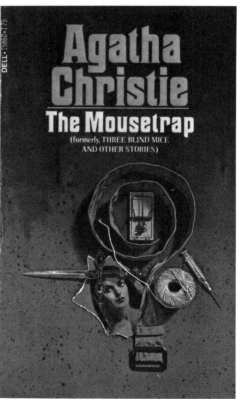

The Mousetrap and Other Stories (1950)

a man of his advanced years, and most suspiciously, he had made no reservation for his stay at Monkswell Manor. He simply appeared in the middle of the night, a supposed victim of the blizzard. Major Metcalf, the last member of the visiting party, always seems to be underfoot. He is up at the crack of dawn and is almost too anxious, as a paying guest, to be helpful with household chores. Yes, there is unanimous agreement among this group that the murderer must be one of them, but which one?

The suspicion escalates to the point where even the young lovers, the newlyweds, Molly and Giles Davis, begin to suspect one another of the heinous crime. Then, when it seems that the tension can mount no further, a second murder is committed, literally under the nose of the police inspector. So much for police protection.

But the most exquisite touch, the tour de force, occurs when our man from Scotland Yard decides to reenact the moments leading up to this second murder. Each member of the household is assigned to return, not to his or her own position at the moment of the murder, but, most paradoxically, to positions purportedly occupied by other individuals. There isn't an individual in this group whose heart does not pound at the prospect of being isolated in a strange position, in a strange house, with a murderer wandering about. But wait. There *is* one individual whose heart does not pound with terror. In this heart, the heart of the murderer, the simple melody of "Three Blind Mice" echoes.

The mousetrap snaps shut with a sudden jerk, and before our startled eyes we behold the criminal. But not a moment too soon, for on the very next page Agatha Christie immediately begins to embroil us in yet another unusual and intriguing yarn.

Among the stories included in this collection is "The Case of the Caretaker." In this saga we are able to observe Miss Marple in a totally uncharacteristic fit of depression. Bedridden because of a cold, Miss Marple is given a special remedy by Dr. Haydock in an effort to occupy her mind. The kindly Dr. Haydock has catalogued a series of events that actually occurred at Kingsdean House, an estate not far from St. Mary Mead.

The story: Harry Laxton, a poor lad and something of a rogue, leaves St. Mary Mead and years later returns, having married a wealthy woman named Louise. Harry is intent on remodeling and living in the Kingsdean House despite the fact that Mrs. Murgatroyd, the caretaker's widow, persists in cursing and frightening Louise. Louise is a lovely, small, blond woman, quiet and unpretentious. Why does Mrs. Murgatroyd hate her so? And why is Harry so determined to remain at Kingsdean House when it is so uncomfortable for his new wife? The doctor's prescription works, and Miss Marple solves the entire case from her sickbed.

As for Hercule Poirot himself, he tackles two murders and one kidnapping. At the close of "Four and Twenty Blackbirds," the fastidious Poirot remarks to the villain he has exposed: "A man who is upset about something *might* conceivably come down to dinner dressed in his pajamas—but they will be his *own* pajamas—not somebody else's." Definitely something to consider if one is contemplating a murder, *n'est-ce pas?*

DEBORAH J. POPE

A Murder Is Announced
(1950)

The place: Little Paddocks, a home on the outskirts of an English village called Chipping Cleghorn.

The time: A few years after the conclusion of World War II, when the English are readjusting to a peacetime life.

The events: An "accidental" killing, the climax of an unusually scheduled social gathering at the aforementioned Little Paddocks.

The mystery begins on a light, if somewhat macabre note, as the residents of this country hamlet gaze at their morning papers. Young and old turn to the "personal" notices of the Chipping Cleghorn *Gazette*. That column, like the personal notice listings of today's newspapers, tells the real news of their town. A listing for the "wedding gown—never used" or "brand new bedroom set, with only a little wear" tells the tale of a jilted bride or divorced couple. But on this autumn day in Chipping Cleghorn, the personal column lists a most unusual notice: "A murder is announced and will take place on Friday, October 29, at Little Paddocks, at 6:30 P.M. Friends please accept this, the only intimation."

The listing draws skeptical responses from the locals, who merely presume that Miss Letitia Blacklock, mistress of Little Paddock, is planning a social gathering and an innocent parlor game of mock murder. A few even attribute the advertisement to Miss Blacklock's young cousins, now residing with their older relative. But Chipping Cleghorn is a quiet community, and this unlikely announcement and invitation appeal to the curiosity of the acquaintants of Letitia Blacklock. A hearty attendance is guaranteed.

The "invited guests" expect the announced murder to be a simple act, with the lights turned off at 6:30 P.M. and one of them touched, perhaps on the shoulder, to signify victim status. So when their gathering is plunged into darkness at the appointed hour, there is no real panic. A man appears, announcing a holdup. He shines a flashlight from face to face when, suddenly, two shots ring out. Then a third, followed by screams in the kitchen.

When the lights come on, there is, indeed, a body to consider. A young man lies at the doorway, dead from an apparently self-inflicted wound. A smoking gun rests on the floor beside his body. Perhaps he tripped while attempting to escape. Maybe he decided, on this unlikely occasion, to take his own life. Could there be any other explanation?

Detective Inspector Dermot Craddock, however, is not satisfied with theories of accidental death or suicide. There's more to this untimely end, and he sets out to determine the real circumstances surrounding the bullet-accelerated departure of the young thief, now identified as Rudi Scherz.

After it is established that Scherz had, indeed, placed the personal ad announcing what turned out to be his own killing, there is still the question of why he chose Little Paddocks for his performance. There was no great supply of money on the premises. And why did he shoot his pistol only at Letitia Blacklock? He had aimed at her and fired twice. But how had he missed completely with one shot, and merely grazed her earlobe with the second? Or did he aim at the lady at all?

So many questions. And so confusing. Miss Blacklock had little money in the house at the

A Murder Is Announced (1950)

time, but she was due for a major inheritance within weeks. And with her new fortune, several of her guests might be motivated to dispose of the lady. Her own cousins — if indeed they really were her cousins — could have some stake in assisting their elderly relative into the afterlife.

And what of the housekeeper, a Middle Euro-

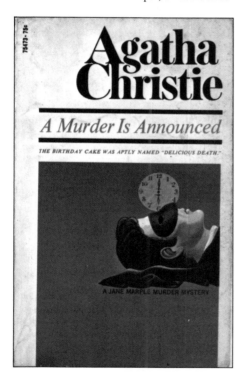

pean with high, shrill vocal cords, paranoiac fear of the authorities, and the only recipe for a dessert known as Delicious Death?

Did any of these contact Rudi Scherz, setting him up as the fall guy in the attempt on Miss Blacklock's life? And was it really Rudi Scherz who fired the gun? Perhaps he was, in fact, the intended victim of the murder that he had publicly announced in the Chipping Cleghorn *Gazette*. Could he have actually paid for his own death notice?

Miss Jane Marple, who just happens to be in the neighborhood, decides to pursue these questions. She is occasionally in league with Detective Craddock but more often is acting on her own, following hunches and the intuition developed over a lifetime of crime solving.

The initial list of suspects is lengthy, especially since several of the possible killers might be using false identities. If Miss Blacklock predeceases a certain elderly lady residing in northern England, the fortune would pass to a pair of twins, now in their late twenties. And there are several guests at Rudi Scherz's spontaneous funeral who could, possibly, be those notorious twins.

It's a case where appearances can be very deceiving, and each and every character's identity must be carefully scrutinized. How can the murderer be discovered when his (or her) identity — and motive — are just a little bit fuzzy?

But with Detective Craddock following the obvious clues and leads and Miss Marple focusing her attention on the not-so-obvious, our murderer can't breathe easy. It's only a matter of time until the murderer, too, is announced.

BRIAN HAUGH

They Came to Baghdad (1951)

An unidentified group of people, loosely bound together in an undescribed authoritarian political theology, has gathered together in an unidentified area of central Asia. In that area, construction of some otherwise unidentified and undescribed secret weapon is proceeding. A large number of persons with scientific, engineering, and management backgrounds have disappeared into the area.

At the same time, large quantities of the world's finest gemstones, as well as enormous sums of money, have disappeared.

Recently, confirmation of the nature of the fantastic secret weapon has been obtained by a British agent named Carmichael. Dakin, the chief British agent in Baghdad, knows that Carmichael is coming to Baghdad with proof of the tale.

Dakin has been told also that the "Great Powers" will meet in Baghdad to hear Carmichael's story and view his proofs. To fill out the meaning for the Great Powers' representatives, Sir Rupert Crofton Lee, famed British explorer, will be on hand to offer his expertise in topography, geography, and local customs. Anna Scheele, internationally renowned financial wizard, is also going to be in Baghdad to offer proof to the Great Powers' representatives of the nature of the financial transactions involved.

However, the Enemy is not asleep. *They know*. Six different individuals, all of whom fit Carmichael's general description, have been killed on one or another of the routes into Baghdad. Against such odds, can Carmichael reach the city?

Carmichael comes to Basrah and discovers that Dakin's organization has been penetrated. He saves himself only by a fluke, and passes a message to an old school chum, Richard Baker, out of desperation. Then he disappears again, after a second attempt is made on his life.

Others are coming to Baghdad besides the Great Powers. Victoria Jones is coming to be with her young man, Edward. Of course, she doesn't know Edward's last name, and Edward doesn't know that she is coming, but as Victoria reassures herself and us, "these details will work themselves out."

Edward's boss, Dr. Rathbone, is already in Baghdad. Benevolence, kindliness, and charm radiate from this distinguished elderly man. Yet the Olive Branch—the coffee shop, student activity house, youth hostel, and general meeting place that is run by Dr. Rathbone's organization — seems to be a hotbed of suspicion, ill feeling, jealousy, and hate. Victoria Jones felt the unpleasant atmosphere the moment she walked through the door. Why should this be? Victoria cannot understand.

Victoria understands even less when Carmichael appears in her room at a Baghdad hotel begging her to hide him from the police. But Carmichael dies in her arms, and Dakin appears to remove the body, and to explain what is going on to Victoria Jones.

Victoria tells Dakin of Carmichael's last words: "Lucifer — Basrah — LaFarge." Victoria is not altogether sure that she has heard the words correctly. The words themselves do not seem to help Dakin solve his puzzle. Where are the proofs Carmichael brought? Who killed Carmichael — and how? Who is the traitor in Dakin's organization? Who is the enemy? How can they be unmasked?

They Came to Baghdad (1951)

None of the major characters appear particularly suspect. Dr. Rathbone is much too kind. Catherine, Dr. Rathbone's Syrian assistant, doesn't like Victoria Jones, but that is just jealousy. Edward Goring, Dr. Rathbone's man Friday and Victoria's "young man," is too good-looking. It certainly is not his fault that women act a little silly and strange whenever he appears. Surely, just as Victoria reasons, that is not his fault.

Marcus Tio, hotelier, is much too charming to be suspect. Yet Carmichael was killed in his hotel. Richard Baker, old school chum, archaeologist, and Dr. Paunce Foot-Jones's assistant, had arrived just in time to save Carmichael's life in Basrah. What did he do with Carmichael's message to him?

Dr. Paunce Foot-Jones, archaeologist and absent-minded professor, is above suspicion, of course. His acceptance of Victoria Jones's credentials after only the most perfunctory inquiry is perfectly ordinary. Or is it?

But Victoria Jones will get her young man, and the Great Powers will assemble in Baghdad. The denouement and the Great Powers arrive together, and that should surprise no one.

EDWIN A. ROLLINS

AN OUTSTANDING STORY OF MURDER, INTRIGUE AND ESPIONAGE

THEY CAME TO BAGHDAD

"THE MOST SATISFYING NOVEL IN YEARS, FROM ONE OF THE MOST SATISFYING NOVELISTS!"
—The New York Times

AGATHA CHRISTIE

The Under Dog and Other Stories (1951)

THE UNDER DOG

Lilly Margrave has been sent to London by Lady Astwell, who wants the assistance of Hercule Poirot, renowned (and vain) Belgian detective. Lily dutifully carries out her ladyship's instructions, but the veteran sleuth senses that she is subtly trying to dissuade him from taking the case. Her guile merely heightens Poirot's interest, and he puts himself at Lady Astwell's service.

Thus begins "The Under Dog," title story in this volume of nine puzzlers. Agatha Christie wrote these stories in the 1920s, early in her career, and Christie devotees may recognize in some of them the germs of later, full-fledged novels.

"The Under Dog" is the most complex story in the volume. Sir Reuben Astwell has been murdered with some heavy instrument in the tower room (his "special sanctum") at his home, Mon Repos, near the village of Abbots Cross, whose attractions consist of "golf and nothing but golf." The manageress of a local hotel tells Poirot that her guests "don't go out after dinner because — well, there is nowhere to go, is there?"

All the evidence in the Astwell murder points to the guilt of Charles Leverson, the victim's nephew. But Lady Astwell *knows* that Owen Trefusis, her late husband's mild-mannered secretary, is really the killer. How does she know? "A woman's instinct, M. Poirot, never lies," she intones. The evidence proves that Trefusis *cannot* have killed Sir Reuben, but such trivia do not faze Lady Astwell in the least.

Is Charles guilty? Is Lady Astwell's intuition correct? Or is the murderer another person in the household? *Everyone* had quarrelled with Sir Reuben (a very ill-tempered codger, by all accounts) on the night of the murder — Charles, Trefusis, Lily, Victor (Reuben's equally volatile brother who has just returned from West Africa), and Lady Astwell herself.

But much of the mystery centers around the enigmatic and alluring Lily. Why did such an elegant and sophisticated young woman accept a position as a companion in this backwater village? And why was she so eager to be hired that she used false references? Needless to say, Poirot uncovers all the skeletons, literal and otherwise, in the Astwell closets, receiving valuable assistance from his friend Dr. Cazalet, a Harley Street hypnotist, and Georges, his impassive valet.

THE PLYMOUTH EXPRESS

When a young navy lieutenant boards a first-class compartment on the Plymouth express, he cannot get his suitcase under the seat opposite. The obstacle: the corpse of the Honorable Mrs. Rupert Carrington, stabbed through the heart. Mrs. Carrington, beautiful and rich, but with a penchant for irresponsible men, was the daughter of Ebenezer Halliday, the shrewd American steel magnate. Poirot has helped Halliday once before, and the millionaire enlists his aid again.

It seems that Mrs. Carrington, traveling with about $100,000 worth of jewelry, had been en route from London to a house party at the Duchess of Swansea's. She should have changed trains at Bristol. However, according to her maid, Jane Mason, she suddenly announced that she would be continuing on to Plymouth. The maid cannot explain this change of plans, but suggests that it might have something to do with

The Under Dog and Other Stories (1951)

the "tall, dark man" who was talking to Mrs. Carrington in her compartment. Could this man be the "utterly unscrupulous" husband? Or Count de la Rochefour, an equally roguish ex-beau? Or has Mrs. Carrington gotten herself mixed up with yet another bounder?

THE AFFAIR AT THE VICTORY BALL

Cocaine is but one villain in "The Affair at the Victory Ball," narrated by Poirot's good friend Captain Hastings. Lord Cronshaw ("twenty-five, rich, unmarried, and very fond of the theatrical world") is stabbed at a chic costume ball at the Colossus Hall. His rumored fiancée, the actress Coco Courtenay, dies of an overdose of cocaine the same night. The case is rather too glamorous for Inspector Japp of Scotland Yard, and he asks for Poirot's help. Japp seems to regret his request, however, when Poirot directs all of his attention to the china commedia dell'arte figurines from which the Cronshaw party's costumes were copied.

THE MARKET BASING MYSTERY

Poirot, Japp, and Hastings are enjoying a leisurely weekend in the country when they are confronted by murder. ("*Le crime, il est partout*," Poirot remarks ominously.) Mr. Protheroe, of Leigh Hall —a run-down old mansion—seems to have shot himself in the head. But the examining doctor is puzzled — the gun is in the corpse's right hand, fingers not closed over it, and the bullet entered the head behind the *left* ear. A clear case of murder disguised as suicide. At the house are Miss Clegg, Protheroe's housekeeper of long standing, and Mr. and Mrs. Parker, a shady couple who are definitely not out of the top drawer. (Hastings concedes that Mrs. Parker is attractive, "though in a coarse fashion.") Who are they, and what is the connection — if any — between their unexpected arrival at Leigh Hall and Protheroe's death?

THE LEMESURIER INHERITANCE

Many of us dream of receiving an inheritance, but the Lemesurier inheritance is one we would do anything to avoid. It is a curse, incurred during the Middle Ages, that prevents all firstborn Lemesurier sons from succeeding to the estate. The story opens at the Carlton, where Hastings and Poirot run into Vincent Lemesurier and his uncle Hugo. Vincent and Hastings had fought together in France during the war. Their conversation is interrupted by a cousin, Roger Lemesurier, who brings word of Vincent's father's accidental death. Later that evening, Vincent, Uncle Hugo, and Cousin Roger head north for the funeral, but Vincent falls from the train. Everyone assumes Vincent's fall is due to the news of his father's accident coming so soon after the shell shock he suffered in the war.

Two years later, a new series of accidents befalls male Lemesuriers, and Lord knows how many more tragedies might have occurred had not Mrs. Hugo Lemesurier (the American-born wife of Vincent's uncle) come to Poirot for help. Hugo has inherited the estate, and their elder son has had several narrow escapes from death. ("When Hugo met me," Mrs. Lemesurier recalls, "I thought his family curse was just too lovely for words...but when it comes to one's own children ...") Hugo believes the boy is doomed by the curse, but Mrs. Lemesurier is more down-to-earth. "Can a legend saw through an ivy stem?" she queries.

Convinced of foul play, Hastings and Poirot travel north where they meet the rest of the household — the two boys, the "nondescript" governess, and the handsome but "repellent" secretary. Does Poirot know enough to avert another "accident"?

THE CORNISH MYSTERY

"Many unlikely people came to consult Poirot," Hastings says in "The Cornish Mystery," but

Mrs. Pengelley "was the most unlikely of all." Why? ";She was so extraordinarily commonplace." Her problem, however, is *not* commonplace — she believes her husband is trying to poison her.

Her story intrigues Poirot sufficiently that he and Hastings travel to Polgarwith, a market town in Cornwall, to investigate further. They arrive too late — Mrs. Pengelley is dead. The doctor says it was gastritis, and her niece thinks it was the result of merely believing so strongly that she was being poisoned. Poirot knows it's murder, but he can't prove it — or who did it — just yet.

THE KING OF CLUBS

The South London suburb of Streatham is the setting for "The King of Clubs," a case that Hastings first encounters in the *Daily Newsmonger*. The "solid middle-class" Oglander family — father, mother, son, and daughter — are playing bridge in their drawing room when the French window to the garden bursts open and in staggers Valerie Saintclair, the dancer who is taking London by storm. (She is also the daughter of either an Irish charwoman or a Russian grand duchess, depending on which rumor you choose to believe.) Her gray satin frock is bloodstained, she utters one word, "Murder!" and promptly faints. The victim is Henry Reedburn, a lecherous impressario whose villa, Mon Desir, backs onto the garden at Daisymead, the Oglander home. Reedburn is found in his library, his head "cracked open like an eggshell."

Poirot is aware of these facts, of course, because Valerie's most serious suitor, Prince Paul of Maurania ("a strange-looking youth . . . with . . . the famous Mauranberg mouth" — whatever that is), has asked Poirot to clear up the mystery. The Prince is afraid that Valerie may have killed Reedburn because of some hold that he had over her. Poirot goes to Streatham to look into the matter. He does not look far enough — at first.

THE SUBMARINE PLANS

The submarine plans are missing, and Poirot and Hastings are urgently summoned to Sharples, the country house of Lord Alloway, the new Minister of Defense. Hastings recalls that the minister had once been implicated in an "ugly scandal . . . some jugglery with share," but has been completely exonerated. Was his reputation cleared prematurely, or is someone else in the house an enemy agent? His secretary, Fitzroy, was the last person to see the plans, and there are several weekend guests — Admiral Sir Harry Weardale (the First Sea Lord), his wife and son, and Mrs. Conrad, a London socialite whose French maid claims to have seen a ghost on the stairs. Obviously, there are strange goings-on, but the nation's security is at stake, and Poirot doesn't have much time.

THE ADVENTURE OF THE CLAPHAM COOK

"The Adventure of the Clapham Cook" rounds out the collection. Poirot is ready to spend a quiet day removing a grease spot from a new suit and trimming and pomading his famed mustache. These projects are forestalled, however, by the sudden appearance of Mrs. Todd, a stout matron from Clapham (another South London suburb), who wants Poirot to find her cook, Eliza Dunn. Poirot says he does not handle such cases, but his visitor will have none of it. "Only deal with Government secrets and Countesses' jewels?" she demands (not without reason, as we have seen). "A good cook's a good cook — and when you lose her, it's as much to you as her pearls are to some fine lady." Duly reprimanded, Poirot begins to investigate the affair, and then Mrs. Todd suddenly takes him off the case. But it is too late to stop Hercule Poirot. In the aftermath of the case, Poirot tells Hastings "never to despise the trivial," and as one closes this volume, one cannot help but agree.

JOHN STURMAN

The Mousetrap Double-Crostic

by Dale G. Copps

The Mousetrap, as everyone is tired of hearing by now, is the longest-running play in the history of the theater. This Double-Crostic is based on the story from which the play was adapted. The story originally had a different title, one which you will find in the grid quotation. And watch out for that quotation — it's tricky.

Directions: Answer as many of the clues as you can, transferring the answer letters to the corresponding numbered spaces in the quotation grid.

As words in the grid begin to form, you can guess at them and use the letters you fill in to complete the words to fill in the clues as well. The quotation is from the story. The first letters of the answers to the clues we call the clue line. They spell out a message as well. In this case, clue line is a particularly apt title, since the message is couched in terms familiar to anyone who has played that popular board game reminiscent of just this sort of Christie classic.

Grid:

Row 1: 1 U, 2 H, 3 R, 4 E, 5 I, ■, 6 T, 7 W, 8 J, 9 O, ■, 10 W

Row 2: ■, 11 W, 12 Y, 13 T, 14 E, ■, 15 W, 16 C, ■, 17 P, 18 W, 19 Z, 20 N, ■, 21 Z2, 22 R, 23 E

Row 3: 24 X, 25 R, ■, 26 S, 27 R, 28 Z, 29 H, 30 V, ■, 31 W, 32 K, ■, 33 K, 34 J, 35 R, ■, 36 W, 37 R

Row 4: 38 F, 39 Q, 40 S, ■, 41 Y, 42 I, ■, 43 M, 44 H, 45 Y, ■, 46 Z1, 47 U, 48 Q, 49 R, 50 J, ■, 51 Z

Row 5: 52 Z2, 53 U, 54 A, 55 I, ■, 56 A, 57 I, 58 Z, 59 T, ■, 60 A, 61 Z1, 62 U, 63 J, ■, 64 D, 65 Z, ■, 66 A, 67 W

Row 6: 68 L, ■, 69 O, 70 T, ■, 76 Z, 72 G, 73 S, 74 R, 75 A, 76 I, 77 U, ■, 78 L, 79 Q, ■, 80 A, 81 Z3, 82 G, 83 Z2

Row 7: 84 A, 85 C, 86 D, ■, 87 K, 88 L, 89 W, 90 J, ■, 91 V, 92 W, ■, 93 P, 94 W, 95 W, 96 Z1, ■, 97 Q, 98 M

Row 8: 99 B, 100 R, ■, 101 Z, 102 N, 103 M, 104 X, 105 A, 106 P, ■, 107 M, 108 W, 109 C, ■, 110 V, 111 Z, ■, 112 A, 113 X, 114 D

Row 9: 115 X, 116 B, 117 Z, 118 Z3, ■, 119 Z2, 120 A, 121 Z, 122 B, ■, 123 B, 124 A, 125 F, 126 Q, 127 J, ■, 128 Z3, ■, 129 F, 130 Q

Row 10: 131 A, ■, 132 C, 133 B, ■, 134 P, 135 Z3, 136 R, 137 Q, ■, 138 W, 139 R, 140 O, 141 E, ■, 142 V, 143 E, 144 R, 145 Y, 146 N

Row 11: 147 R, 148 Z2, 149 A, 150 G, ■, 151 Q, 152 N, 153 J, ■, 154 R, 155 P, 156 M, 157 N, 158 H, 159 S, ■, 160 R, ■, 161 H, 162 N

Row 12: 163 X, 164 U, 165 A, 166 Z1, ■, 167 G, 168 L, ■, 169 B, 170 W, 171 H, 172 U, 173 D, 174 Q, 175 O, ■, 176 Z, 177 Y, 178 S, 179 R

(Solution to puzzle on page 230.)

A The scene of the second crime: 2 wds ....

$\overline{56}$ $\overline{66}$ $\overline{54}$ $\overline{75}$ $\overline{80}$ $\overline{112}$ $\overline{120}$ $\overline{149}$ $\overline{165}$ $\overline{60}$ $\overline{84}$ $\overline{105}$ $\overline{124}$ $\overline{131}$

B The lyrics of our "signature tune," and others ....

$\overline{99}$ $\overline{116}$ $\overline{122}$ $\overline{123}$ $\overline{133}$ $\overline{169}$

C Without this, no one would have caught the drift ....

$\overline{109}$ $\overline{85}$ $\overline{16}$ $\overline{132}$

D Molly made them as fast as she could ....

$\overline{64}$ $\overline{173}$ $\overline{86}$ $\overline{114}$

E "Golden Boy" playwright ....

$\overline{143}$ $\overline{23}$ $\overline{141}$ $\overline{4}$ $\overline{14}$

F Molly's potatoes? ....

$\overline{179}$ $\overline{38}$ $\overline{125}$ $\overline{129}$

G Gregg was this — after Holloway ....

$\overline{150}$ $\overline{82}$ $\overline{167}$ $\overline{72}$

H Mrs. Boyle preferred bridge to this other tricky game

$\overline{29}$ $\overline{44}$ $\overline{161}$ $\overline{2}$ $\overline{171}$ $\overline{158}$

I "That is" in Latin ....

$\overline{57}$ $\overline{55}$ $\overline{76}$ $\overline{5}$ $\overline{42}$

J Giles went "across the county" for this, but returned
empty handed ....

$\overline{34}$ $\overline{50}$ $\overline{63}$ $\overline{90}$ $\overline{8}$ $\overline{127}$ $\overline{153}$

K A noted Mahal ....

$\overline{32}$ $\overline{33}$ $\overline{87}$

L Mrs. Boyle almost went off in one of these ....

$\overline{78}$ $\overline{88}$ $\overline{68}$ $\overline{168}$

M Aunt Katherine was this Miss to the solicitor ....

$\overline{98}$ $\overline{103}$ $\overline{43}$ $\overline{156}$ $\overline{107}$

N The scene of the first crime ....

$\overline{20}$ $\overline{102}$ $\overline{146}$ $\overline{157}$ $\overline{162}$ $\overline{152}$

O Commun- and capital-, for instance ....

$\overline{69}$ $\overline{175}$ $\overline{140}$ $\overline{9}$

P Montana town ....

$\overline{17}$ $\overline{155}$ $\overline{93}$ $\overline{106}$ $\overline{134}$

Q Called on again ....

$\overline{48}$ $\overline{79}$ $\overline{97}$ $\overline{130}$ $\overline{137}$ $\overline{151}$ $\overline{174}$ $\overline{126}$ $\overline{39}$

R Mr. Wren's sarcastic reply to Giles: 3 wds ....

$\overline{3}$ $\overline{100}$ $\overline{25}$ $\overline{27}$ $\overline{147}$ $\overline{37}$ $\overline{74}$ $\overline{139}$ $\overline{144}$ $\overline{154}$ $\overline{160}$ $\overline{22}$ $\overline{35}$ $\overline{49}$ $\overline{136}$

S The joints did this in the oven ....

$\overline{159}$ $\overline{73}$ $\overline{178}$ $\overline{40}$ $\overline{26}$

T Necessity for Molly's bread ....

$\overline{13}$ $\overline{59}$ $\overline{95}$ $\overline{70}$ $\overline{6}$

U Mrs. Casey and Joe both remarked on this vocal oddity

$\overline{1}$ $\overline{47}$ $\overline{53}$ $\overline{62}$ $\overline{164}$ $\overline{172}$ $\overline{77}$

V "When ___ a lad...": 2 wds ....

$\overline{110}$ $\overline{142}$ $\overline{91}$ $\overline{30}$

W The note so neatly pinned to the corpse: 4 wds .....

$\overline{170}$ $\overline{7}$ $\overline{10}$ $\overline{11}$ $\overline{18}$ $\overline{89}$ $\overline{92}$ $\overline{94}$ $\overline{108}$ $\overline{67}$ $\overline{31}$ $\overline{36}$ $\overline{138}$ $\overline{15}$

X Was Molly's cuisine this good? ....

$\overline{24}$ $\overline{113}$ $\overline{163}$ $\overline{115}$ $\overline{104}$

Y Attend upon; expect ....

$\overline{145}$ $\overline{177}$ $\overline{12}$ $\overline{41}$ $\overline{45}$

Z Paravicini's Santa Claus style?: 2 wds ....

$\overline{51}$ $\overline{19}$ $\overline{117}$ $\overline{58}$ $\overline{71}$ $\overline{101}$ $\overline{176}$ $\overline{121}$ $\overline{28}$ $\overline{65}$ $\overline{111}$

Z₁ Caesar's last query: 2 wds ....

$\overline{166}$ $\overline{46}$ $\overline{96}$ $\overline{61}$

Z₂ Washes ....

$\overline{52}$ $\overline{21}$ $\overline{119}$ $\overline{148}$ $\overline{83}$

Z₃ A fitting English farewell: Hyph ....

$\overline{118}$ $\overline{135}$ $\overline{128}$ $\overline{81}$

The Quotable Christie

On Writing

Function of Writing

"Writing is a great comfort to people like me, who are unsure of themselves and have trouble expressing themselves properly." (*McCalls,* February 1969)

Writing Schedules

"I must behave rather as dogs do when they retire with a bone; they depart in a secretive manner and you do not see them again for an odd half hour. They return self-consciously with mud on their noses. I do much the same." (*Agatha Christie: An Autobiography*)*

Getting Started

"There is no agony like it. You sit in a room, biting pencils, looking at a typewriter, walking about, or casting yourself down on a sofa, feeling you want to cry your head off."

Excuses

"One problem is that the interruptions are generally far more enjoyable than writing, and once you've stopped, it's exceedingly difficult to get started again." (*McCalls,* February 1969)

*Unless otherwise noted, all quotes are from *An Autobiograpy*.

Creating Characters

"I . . . decided once and for all that it is no good thinking about real people — you must create your characters for yourself. Someone you see in a tram or a train or a restaurant is a possible starting point, because you can make up something for yourself about them."

Organizing Plot Outlines

"I usually have about half a dozen [exercise books] on hand, and I used to make notes in them of ideas that had struck me. . . . Of course, if I kept all these things neatly sorted and filed and labelled it would save me a lot of trouble. However, it is a pleasure sometimes, when looking vaguely through a pile of old notebooks, to find something scribbled down . . . it often stimulates me, if not to write that identical plot at least to write something else."

Writer's Block

"It is rather like putting the ferrets in to bring out what you want at the end of the rabbit burrow. Until there has been a lot of subterranean disturbance, until you have spent long hours of utter boredom, you can never feel normal. You can't think of what you want to write, and if you pick up a book you find you are not reading it properly. If you try to do a crossword your mind isn't

"There is no agony like it. You sit in a room, biting pencils, looking at a typewriter, walking about, or casting yourself down on a sofa, feeling you want to cry your head off." —*An Autobiography*

on the clues; you are possessed by a feeling of paralyzed hopelessness."

Brevity
"There is no doubt that the effort involved in typing or writing does help me in keeping to the point…It is important to profit by the fact that a human being is naturally lazy and so won't write more than is absolutely necessary to convey his meaning."

Discussion Hinders Process
"I never mention my work till it's finished: I find the moment you've talked about a thing you're rather dissatisfied with it." (*The Writer*, August 1966)

Love in Mystery Stories
"I myself always found the love interest a terrible bore in detective stories. Love, I felt, belonged to romantic stories. To force a love motif into what should be a scientific process went much against the grain."

Ins and Outs of Mystery Writing
"One's always a little self-conscious over the murderer's first appearance. He must never come in too late; that's uninteresting for the reader. And the denouement has to be worked out frightfully carefully." (*Writer's Digest* reprint)

About Books Sold in Supermarkets
"I expect they'll feature them at the butcher's next." (*McCalls*, February 1969)

Book Jackets
"The Bodley Head were pleased with *Murder on the Links*, but I had a slight row with them over the jacket they had designed for it. Apart from being in ugly colours, it was badly drawn, and represented, as far as I could make out, a man in pyjamas on a golf links, dying of an epileptic fit.

Since the man who had been murdered had been fully dressed and stabbed with a dagger, I objected. A book jacket may have nothing to do with the plot, but if it does it must at least not represent a false plot."

ON CRIME AND CRIMINALS
On Murder
"Murder has no emotional connotation for me." (*McCalls*, February 1969)

Good and Evil
"Men can be evil — more evil than their animal brothers can ever be—but they can also rise to the heavens in the ecstasy of creation. The cathedrals of England stand as monuments to man's worship of what is above himself."

The Innocent
"It frightens me that nobody seems to care about the innocent …. Nobody seems to go through the agony of the victim—they are only full of pity for the young killer, because of his youth."

Judgment
"I am willing to believe that they [those who kill] are made that way, that they are born with a disability, for which, perhaps, one should pity them; but even then, I think, not spare them — because you cannot spare them any more than you could spare the man who staggers out from a plague-stricken village in the Middle Ages to mix with innocent and healthy children in a nearby village."

Apt Punishment
"Why should they not execute him? We have taken the lives of wolves, in this country; we didn't try to teach the wolf to lie down with the lamb — I doubt really if we could have …. The best answer we ever found, I suspect, was trans-

"One cannot pretend that differences in income do not separate people. It is not a question of snobbishness or social position. ... If they have a large income and you have a small one, things become embarrassing."
—*An Autobiography*

portation. A vast land of emptiness, peopled only with primitive human beings. . . . You might allow your criminal the choice between the cup of hemlock and offering himself for experimental research, for instance."

ON THE MOVIES
The Switching of Poirot to Marple in Some Films
"I get an unregenerate pleasure when I think they're not being a success."

The Use of a Non-Christie-penned Screenplay for the Film Murder Ahoy
"It got very bad reviews, I'm delighted to say."

Margaret Rutherford
"To me, she's always looked like a bloodhound."

ON LIFE

Philosophy of Life
". . . any moment before the end might be the important one. This I believe." (*New York Times,* October 27, 1966)

The Good Life
"When I re-read those first ones [mystery novels] I'm amazed at the number of servants drifting about. And nobody is really doing any work; they're always having tea on the lawn like in E.F. Benson. It gives one a great nostalgia for the past." (*The Writer,* August 1966)

On Humility
"I would say myself, from the ordinary observation of life, that where there is no humility the people perish."

Beauty
"An ugly voice repels me where an ugly face would not."

Class and Money
". . . one cannot pretend that differences in income do not separate people. It is not a question of snobbishness or social position, it is whether you can afford to follow the pursuits that your friends are following. If they have a large income and you have a small one, things become embarrassing."

Companionship
"Companionship is not a thing one needs every day—it is a thing that grows upon one, and sometimes as destroying as ivy growing round you."

On Ambition
"I have never been an ambitious person by nature."

God and the Human Race
"One does feel proud to belong to the human race when one sees the wonderful things human beings have fashioned with their hands. They have been creators — they must share a little the holiness of the Creator, who made the world and all that was in it, and saw that it was good. But He left more to be made."

On Aging
"I have enjoyed greatly the second blooming that comes when you finish the life of the emotions and of personal relation; and suddenly find — at the age of fifty, say — that a whole new life has opened before you, filled with things you can think about, study, or read about . . . It is as if a fresh sap of ideas and thoughts were rising in you. With it, of course, goes the penalty of increasing old age—the fact that your body is nearly always hurting somewhere . . . One's thankfulness for the gift of life is, I think, stronger and more vital during those years than it ever has been before. It has some of the reality and intensity of dreams—and I still enjoy dreaming enormously."

THE SELLING
OF CHRISTIE *by Michael Tennenbaum*

An example of the kind of sensational publicity created by Hollywood in the 1950s in an attempt to draw audiences away from their televisions and back into the movies. The action depicted has little resemblance to the content of the film. The famous Dietrich legs are featured, thanks to a scene written into the film just so they could embellish the poster.

METRO-GOLDWYN-MAYER
PRESENTS
ACADEMY AWARD WINNER*

MARGARET RUTHERFORD

(as Agatha Christie's Miss Marple)

New mischief amidst the mizzen-masts!

*Best Supporting Actress
M·G·M's "The V.I.P.s"

MURDER AHOY

CO-STARRING
LIONEL JEFFRIES · STRINGER DAVIS

SCREENPLAY BY
DAVID PURSALL and JACK SEDDON · LAWRENCE P. BACHMANN · GEORGE POLLOCK

PRODUCED BY

DIRECTED BY

THEATRE

Dame Margaret Rutherford
was blessed with a face and
body made for caricature as
evidenced in the poster opposite
for a Miss Marple film.
Hollywood later went art
deco in marketing Evil Under
the Sun, *with its all-star
cast, and tried again to
feature every big name in*
The Mirror Crack'd—*although
of course it was Elizabeth
Taylor's vehicle all the way.*

Richard Amsel is one of the most respected men in the field of movie poster art and his work is sought after by collectors in this relatively new field. Here are two examples of his best. His painting for Murder on the Orient Express so perfectly captured the combination of mystery and glamour achieved by director Sidney Lumet in the film that he was commissioned to do one for Death on the Nile. A bit more humor is evident in the latter, which can be seen if one looks closely at the figure of the Egyptian and the surrounding hieroglyphics.

IT'S NOT A PLAY, IT'S AN INSTITUTION: *THE MOUSETRAP*

by Elizabeth Leese

If there is one single thing which must be credited for keeping actors and actresses employed in London's West End, perhaps it is Agatha Christie's *The Mousetrap*, the world's longest-running play, which has been filling a theater since November 25, 1952.

More than 150 actors and actresses have appeared in it, following in the wake of Richard Attenborough and Sheila Sim, since it opened at the Ambassador Theatre.

But not only the cast has changed. The set, curtains, and furnishing have all had to be replaced (except for a leather armchair and a mantelpiece clock), and the play has even changed houses—to the larger St. Martin's Theatre — without any break in the run.

It has been translated into twenty-two languages and presented in forty-one countries (though it was staged in New York in 1952 and did not do well.) More than four and a half million people have seen it.

The play is presented by the impresario Peter Saunders, and in 1965 he formed the Mousetrap Club for theater people who have appeared in the production or who have been connected with it in some way. The club tie has a dark blue background with a little red mouse and a white *T*.

Saunders sold the film rights to *The Mousetrap* to Romulus Films back in 1956, with the usual condition that the film could not be released until six months after the end of the London stage run. Will the film ever be made? The play shows no sign of closing, but Romulus Films is apparently biding its time—Saunders has been unsuccessful in his attempts to buy the film rights back.

Mrs. McGinty's Dead (1952)

(Alternate title: *Blood Will Tell*)

Mrs. McGinty is dead and no one seems to care. No one, that is, except Superintendent Spence, who feels the investigation and conviction of James Bentley for the murder was tidy and neat. Too neat. Some intuitive sense brings him to London to the home of Hercule Poirot—an old friend from previous investigations. Somehow the facts of the murder and conviction do not sit right, and the Inspector would like to enlist the aid of Poirot in a surreptitious investigation.

Spence details the case for Poirot: Mrs. McGinty, a domestic, was discovered dead on the floor of her parlor. Her roomer, James Bentley, is found with blood on his cuff and yet claims not to have seen his landlady since the night before the murder. Her house has been ransacked, and thirty pounds that she had hidden under a bedroom floorboard had been removed but was later found hidden outside the cottage. The murder weapon had not been found, and there were no signs of forced entry.

When the case went to the jury, James Bentley was easily convicted of the crime and is awaiting the death penalty. Poirot agrees with Spence that the case was perhaps too pat.

Poirot agrees to go to Broadhinny, but not to open a quiet investigation. He will go as the great Hercule Poirot, who is not satisfied with the results of the trial. By openly advertising his objective, he hopes to bring forth reactions that will, should there be a murderer on the loose, start a new chain of events and reveal the truth.

In Broadhinny Poirot takes up residence in the only guest house in the immediate town. This disorderly disaster of a hostelry is owned and operated by a young couple, Maureen and Johnnie Summerhayes, whose attempts at organization crumble in defeat before sagging architecture, rambunctious animals, and ludicrous menus. Poirot flees as often as possible from this manic menage into the village and plants his intention to start a new investigation wherever possible.

He begins with an interview with Mrs. McGinty's only relative, a niece, Besie Burch, who seems to have grieved little for her auntie. He also meets the former employer of James Bentley, and along the way finds one sympathetic acquaintance of the convicted killer — a co-worker named Maude Williams, who seems to be the only friend the reclusively shy Bentley had acquired in Broadhinny.

In short order Poirot has found that he is investigating a murder in which the victim and the accused seem to have neither enemies nor animosities. The victim was in unusually bright spirits two days before her demise, and had bought a bottle of ink and clipped something from the *Sunday Companion* before her death. Upon checking that newspaper's files Poirot discovers that the story she had clipped was headlined, "Women Victims of Bygone Tragedies? Where Are These Women Now?" Were this clipping, the bottle of ink, and the elated spirits of the murdered Mrs. McGinty somehow related to the actual crime? Where *were* these women now?

Poirot now meets some of the other leading and colorful citizens of Broadhinny. There is Mrs. Laura Upward and her doting, artistic son, an upcoming playwright and genius of the popular theater; Mrs. Wetherby, who enjoys her ill health to the discomfort of her daughter Deirdre Henderson; Deirdre, whose discomfort is increased by the apparent dislike of her by her step-father, Roger Wetherby; Eva Carpenter, of doubtful background, and her social-climbing husband who is aiming at a political career; and the robust Ariadne Oliver. Mrs. Oliver, a friend of Poirot and a writer of mystery novels, appears on the scene to collaborate with young Robin Upward in the adaptation of one of her novels into a stage piece.

Perhaps all of these people are somehow connected with Mrs. McGinty's murder. She had worked for most of them at one time or another. Could the clipping in some way point a guilty finger, "Where are these women now?" Or was it simply, as the jury had decided, a simple case? Perhaps Hercule was at a dead end. But then, why would someone attempt to push Poirot in front of a train? Were too many questions being asked? Was more than just the murder weapon being hidden behind the walls of Broadhinny? "Where are these women now?" Or does it matter at all?

PAUL AND KADEY KIMPEL

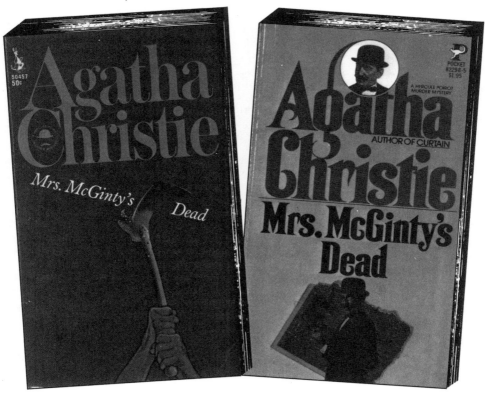

Murder with Mirrors (1952)

(Alternate title: *They Do It with Mirrors*)

Ruth Van Rydock has just returned from Stonygates, a gothic monstrosity in the village of Market Kimble in the south of England. She had been visiting her sister, Carrie Louise Serrocold, formerly Restarick, formerly Gulbrandsen (the internationally famous philanthropic family), and formerly, but not for many years, a maiden. "In distress?" you ask. Ruth thinks so, and Miss Jane Marple agrees. A look about seems in order. After all, they were all old school chums, and Carrie Louise has no nose for evil whatsoever.

> "You always believe the worst," said Ruth.
> Miss Marple's china blue eyes didn't even blink.
> "The worst is so often true," she said.

The old building had grown wings and outbuildings dedicated to various causes, to which Lewis Serrocold, Carrie's latest husband, has added his own: the reforming of delinquent boys. The place is stiff with therapists and psychiatrists like "Scoutmasters" enjoying themselves with their pets, the young misguided criminals. A philanthropic fad from some people's viewpoint, but not from Carrie's. She thrives on it, and Lewis is blissful in his work. He "always put causes before people," though devoted to his wife.

Carrie Louise has gathered around her the products of a lifetime of living in the clouds. Her prim and proper daughter Mildred Strete, the widow of some canon of the Church of England, fits her surroundings perfectly. No so with Gina Hudd, Carrie's granddaughter, descendant of her first adopted child, Pippa, now deceased, and her husband, some Italian marchese; Gina stands out, to her own delight, as the beauty of the castle. No love is lost between Aunt Mildred and niece Gina,

and a good old English snub is the lot of Gina's new American husband, Wally Hudd. The exG.I. never seemed to fit. He "didn't want a job feeding candy to gangster kids," and Gina just isn't the same girl he'd married back in the States.

Stephen Restarick, Carrie Louise's stepson — the product of her second husband Johnny Restarick's first marriage with some Russian dancer — runs the dramatics department of the reformatory, and he also runs after Gina. When his brother Alex comes to town, he does likewise. Even Lewis Serrocold's young and confused assistant, Edgar Lawson, drawn from the ranks of the "cases," hankers after her in his own weird way. Edgar is a story of his own. He has claimed to be Churchill's son, Lord Montgomery's, and, well, whoever suits his fancy. Lewis thinks the prognosis is hopeful.

Soap operas, thinks Jane Marple on first perusal, but nothing could harm Carrie Louise, "secure, remote at the heart of the whirlpool as she had been all her life...there was something a little wrong with Edgar Lawson...but surely that couldn't touch Carrie Louise."

Then, Christian Gulbrandsen arrives, a trustee of the fund and Carrie Louise's stepson, her first husband Eric's son, actually two years older than Carrie herself. A busy man. He can't stay very long. Some important matters to talk over with Lewis. Miss Marple overhears snippets from her window: "how to spare Carrie Louise the knowledge...," Gulbrandsen had said. "If it can be kept from her," said Lewis.

Everyone gathers in the great hall after dinner. Christian excuses himself, saying he has an important letter to write. Wally Hudd switches on a reading lamp and the fuse blows. He leaves.

The scene is in darkness with Stephen providing background at the keyboard. Enter Edgar triumphantly. "So, I have found you, O mine enemy" he says to Lewis. Lewis takes Edgar into the library to air his troubles. A great argument ensues. "Lies, all lies. You're my father . . . I ought to own this place." A shot is heard—it's outside. "You're going to die...to die," Edgar screams after a batch of unlisted profanities. Two shots— this time from behind the locked door. Miss Bellever, Carrie Louise's trusted handmaiden, returns with the keys. When had she left?

The lights come on. Wally Hudd returns. The keys don't work. Sobbing is heard from the library. The door opens from inside. Edgar Lawson, collapsed, sobbing at the desk. The revolver on the floor where it had dropped, and Lewis Serrocold—dead?

"Of course he missed me," snaps Lewis. There's no such thing as a bad boy, just maladjusted, just acting out his neurosis, not really dangerous. Carrie Louise's cloud is only mildly ruffled—she just couldn't believe Edgar would shoot Lewis. Everyone else is in shock. Wally Hudd wants to know how Edgar got his gun— and Christian Gulbrandsen has been murdered right in the middle of that very important letter.

Alex Restarick, proving his ability to be in the right place at the wrong time, coincidentally arrives for a visit only a few moments after the heinous event. His eyes immediately find Gina among the startled crew.

The terrace door was open all the time. Alex could've done it on the way in. Wally Hudd took his time at the fuse box, didn't he? Stephen's piano playing had ceased in ample time for him to go and come back. Even devoted old Miss Bellever was gone looking for the keys. She discovered the body. And consider, if you will, 200-odd maladjusted youngsters with a noted ability to diddle with the locks. ("Locks don't mean nothin' to me," one of them has said.)

"But why Gulbrandsen? The stranger within the gates," asks Inspector Curry of Scotland Yard. Christian Gulbrandsen knew something. He had spoken to Lewis about it. Something that would shake up the peaceful waters of Carrie Louise's life. Now Christian is dead. Lewis spills the beans to the inspector: someone, it seems, was slowly poisoning Carrie Louise. Christian had told him so. After their talk, Lewis had stopped Carrie from taking her tonic. This upset Miss Bellever. He had it examined. Arsenic. The letter (Lewis had removed it from the typewriter to keep the shocking news from reaching Carrie) had just gotten to this juicy part when Christian was forced to stop...everything...forever.

Why kill, slowly, a sweet rich old lady? Come now. Everyone would stand to benefit with dear old Carrie dead. The will showed that. But everyone adored her.

Of course, Wally didn't quite adore her and this would change things; a little quick money, and gone. Everyone hopes it was him, except Gina. She still has a soft spot for him.

Of course, the gun did turn up in the piano stool. An easy piece, huh, Stephen? Of course, Gina's real "blood" grandmother does turn out to be Katherine Ellsworth. "Wasn't that the woman who administered arsenic to her husband?" Of course, the box of poison chocolates was signed, "With love, Alex." The old double bluff? Carrie Louise just can't believe anyone would do that to her. Oh, and let's not forget Edgar. Certainly he hadn't killed Christian. He was busy trying to kill Lewis. Certainly he hadn't been poisoning Carrie Louise. He was too new in the house for that. He was, however, very open to suggestion and one wonders whom Lewis Serrocold's assistant was really assisting?

Things can get confused when a conjurer sets up the scene. So confused, you don't even know where to look. What looks like a lady sawn in half is a whole one again. Miss Marple knew the trick (Do you?) but she'll have to do it backwards before the crime is solved.

MARK FISCHWEICHER

A Pocket Full of Rye (1953)

Rex Fortescue, whom we only know through others, is already definitely dead on page seven. But even on page three, after a brief introduction to some of his employees, we know that it's all over for this shrewd businessman, who has been having problems with his two sons, with the unlikely names of Percival and Lancelot, and who has made the mistake of marrying a second time, this time with a former manicurist thirty years his junior.

There's a problem with getting any of his family informed about the tragedy. Percival, the elder son, is in northern England on business for the firm his father ran. Jennifer, Percival's wife (and a discontented wife at that), is in London for the day. The younger son, Lancelot, may be en route from Africa with Pat, his wife of less than a year. Daughter Elaine is out with the Brownies, and as for the present young Mrs. Adele Fortescue—she is playing "golf" with a Mr. Vivian Dubois.

After an interview with Miss Mary Dove, an attractive, efficient but cold young lady, Inspector Neele feels that anybody in the family or in the mansion, ridiculously named Yewtree Lodge, could have killed the man. But how?

Rex died in the office after being given a cup of tea (not even boiling hot) by a most efficient typist who had nothing to gain by such a dastardly deed. When an autopsy is made at St. Jude's Hospital we discover that the poison taxene was actually administered to him at breakfast via his marmalade. Although each member of his family and home staff is rattled by the murder, only the daughter cries.

Adele Fortescue is of course not playing golf but something else with Mr. Vivian Dubois.

When she hears about her husband's death she's upset. But she's certainly not devastated. Knowing that she's disliked by Percival, his wife, and probably by Elaine, she welcomes the charming Lancelot, the black sheep of the family who had been involved in bad checks years ago, and who was returning from East Africa to make amends with his father. Lancelot has recently married and seems genuinely in love with his wife, Pat. He refuses to let Pat come to the Lodge with him, preferring her to remain in a hotel away from the house that has no fond memories for him.

It certainly would seem that all fingers are pointing at Adele — until she too is found dead right after teatime. This time it's cyanide in her tea. And it's prim Miss Dove who finds her still lying on the couch.

All this upsets sympathetic Inspector Neele, who was trying not to be quick to point to Adele. It was all so simple. But the possible murderess had also become a victim.

In this somewhat unreal house with its unreal people and servants, occurs a third and most bizarre murder discovery. Gladys Martin, a not-too-bright, not-too-attractive parlormaid who had seemed very nervous at Inspector Neele's earlier questionings, is found in the laundry room strangled with nylon stockings. And a clothespin was put on her nose.

After this horrific news we're all comforted by meeting Miss Marple, who had known Gladys as a child and is determined to bring her elderly common sense to the strange case. Inspector Neele, quite perplexed and not without humanity, doesn't take umbrage at having this lady enter into the case.

He's really quite surprised, though, when Miss Marple, after a short discussion about the triple murder, begins to recite the Mother Goose nursery rhyme that begins with "Sing a song of six-pence, a pocketful of rye" and ends with "When there came a little dickey bird and nipped off her nose."

However, when Miss Marple, who knows all about the case through the sensational headlines in the London papers, points out the similarities between the rhyme and the action, he wonders if Miss Marple isn't on to something.

Rex, of course, means king. He's in the equivalent of a counting house. The queen in the library-parlor has left her bread and honey. And the murderer did put the clothespin on Glady's nose.

But where and why the blackbirds?

Needless to say all these activities upset the servants. Mr. and Mrs. Crump think they should leave. Ellen the housemaid enjoys the action. Miss Dove doesn't seem touched by the happenings at all.

Now is the time to introduce Miss Ramsbottom, who was Rex's sister-in-law via his first wife. She thinks the whole family is so odious she wonders why all this hadn't happened earlier. She's definitely against the sin and wickedness that this family seems to engage in. However, although Miss Marple isn't the same kind of Christian that she is, she seems to like her. But after all they're both eccentric old ladies!

The tension between the two brothers builds up too. Percival doesn't want Lance to have anything to do with the business. Lance almost seems serious about finally settling down. The inspector watches the brothers fight and hears them mention a Blackbird Mine which their father had owned and declared worthless years before.

Bits about the mine and a MacKenzie family are brought in at this point. Mr. MacKenzie and

Mr. Fortescue possibly owned the mine together. Did Mr. MacKenzie die of a fever? Was the mine worthless, as Rex declared? Who put dead blackbirds on Rex's desk two months before he was murdered? And what happened to the two MacKenzie children who had been raised to get revenge for their father's death? Are we to believe that the son, Donald, died at Dunkirk? And who and where is Ruby, the surviving sister who no longer visits Mrs. MacKenzie at the Pinewood Private Sanitorium?

There are the usual dealings with lawyers and wills. There are rivalries of the siblings and their spouses or intended spouses. Sister Elaine wants to open a school with a man named Gerald Wright, who's clearly marrying her for her money. Percival tries to stop her, but Lance tells her to do what she wishes.

Inspector Neele, after discovering that some of his prime suspects couldn't have done all three dastardly deeds, has another talk with Miss Marple. He rather reluctantly finds his suspect while Miss Marple goes home and we can all finally get to sleep.

ANITA GREENFIELD

Funerals Are Fatal (1953)

(Alternate title: *After the Funeral*)

To begin with, Richard Abernethie is dead. Dead as a doornail. Suddenly Richard's heart had stopped in the night, closing forever his chapter of family history and fortune building at the helm of Coral Cornplasters, Ltd.

As our book opens we find ourselves at Richard's country home, Enderby Hall. Erected by Richard's father, Cornelius, it is now almost a mausoleum. Parlors and halls once filled with family and music have lately heard only the slow step of the servants. This is the second time in six months that the door of the main house has been draped in black bunting. Only half a year ago Richard's sole surviving son, Mortimer, a keen and vigorous young man, was stricken with disease. Dead in a week. And now Richard. At sixty-eight, he had been as sharp as ever, though his life held few pleasures after the tragedy of his son's death.

After the funeral the dutiful, if dry-eyed, relatives return from the cemetery to Enderby Hall. They are greeted by Lanscombe, Richard's tottering Old-World servant. Lanscombe, well versed in "proper funeral procedure," supervises the serving of an excellent cold lunch. The gaggle of relatives is then led to the library for the main business of the day—the reading of the will.

Presiding over the gathering is Richard's astute — though now retired — barrister and lifelong friend, Mr. Entwhistle. The will itself is nothing extraordinary—the bulk of Richard's considerable fortune is divided equally among the heirs.

The will read, Entwhistle considers his duty done, though he does find Richard's death at sixty-eight a bit premature, since he himself is only seventy-two. His thoughts do not go beyond this point, until Richard's estranged sister Cora remarks: "It's been nicely hushed up, hasn't it? But he *was* murdered, wasn't he?"

It is smoothed over, of course, but no one in Enderby Hall can forget it. What does Cora, who has a disturbing habit of blurting out whatever is on her mind, know? Entwhistle decides to visit Cora in Berkshire as soon as possible.

But too late. For the very next afternoon the prim Miss Gilchrist, Cora's housekeeper and companion, returns from the public library to find her mistress dead in her bed. No question of the cause, either. During an afternoon nap Cora was bashed about the face and head eight times with a hatchet.

There is some evidence of an attempted robbery, but Entwhistle believes it is a purposely misleading clue. What he cannot figure out is who would profit from such a crime, unless her killer believed Cora knew too much — and, being Cora, would talk.

Under the guise of legal duties (a few papers to be signed) our barrister travels to visit each possible suspect and subtly snoop.

And what does he find?

Miss Gilchrist, the companion with the most opportunity to murder, appears to have no real cause. She is now out of a job, and has few prospects. Would you hire a companion whose last employer was mysteriously murdered?

Richard's brother Timothy, who felt entitled to the lazy lion's share of the estate, is a melodramatic invalid. After losing his own substantial inheritance he had asked Richard for money and been refused. But did Richard know how much he needed, how quickly, and how desperately?

Timothy is cared for by his devoted wife, Maude, a strong country woman who mothers and smothers. She apparently considers no sacrifice too great.

Mrs. Helen Abernethie, the widow of Richard's brother Leo, is a sensible, practical woman and trusted friend who would rather the investigation be closed. Her new income will come in quite handy in Capri, where she visits regularly. Odd she has never remarried.

And there is the younger generation. Sexy, hazel-eyed Susan Banks (Richard's niece) has an intuitive sense for business and the air of a woman who gets what she wants. Above all she wants protection for her husband, poor Gregory. Susan glows, while he is vacuous. Perhaps Richard knew about his past.

The other niece, the beautiful Rosamund Shane, has husband problems too. Her Michael has a charismatic style and tendency toward infidelity. Entwhistle thinks Rosamund herself to be a nitwit but one determined to find a way to hold her man.

And there is the nephew, George Crossfield, who had hoped to step into the shoes of Richard's dead son Mortimer. A broker, George has at least the appearance of having a profession. Yet the astute Entwhistle sees a warning glint in his eye.

Entwhistle, mystified, calls upon his dear friend, the now retired but still infallible Belgian detective, Hercule Poirot.

Poirot takes charge. The alibis of the suspects are checked. Lo and behold, each has one!

Meanwhile Susan travels to the cottage of her late aunt to pick Miss Gilchrist's memory for clues. Her mission is abruptly aborted when Miss Gilchrist is rushed to the hospital moaning pitifully. Arsenic in the cake. Though our housekeeper survives, the situation seems to be getting out of hand—three down and how many to go?

Accelerating the pace, the esteemed Poirot calls in the innocuous Mr. Goldby. He has the ability to send a hoard of unobtrusive persons into the streets. Disguised as fenceposts and postmen they will ferret out the secrets of any life—for a price. Alibis fall like blades of wheat before the scythe. Though each story has some truth, it would have been possible for any of our suspects to have slipped over and finished off Cora.

Mon dieu! We have not even narrowed the field. Our savvy Poirot perceives the methodology required: our murderer must be enticed into "self-revelation." He knows that most mortals cannot resist gloating, and in that moment of self-satisfaction the indispensable fragment of a clue may be revealed—if the observer is but keen enough to know it. A match of wits. To solve a crime, ask the criminal.

All the suspects are now enticed back to Enderby Hall for the second gathering. Here victim number four falls. Here Poirot, from behind the "flamboyant flourish" of his tailored moustache, forces the pieces of our puzzle into their proper places.   JOAN DANIELS

Spider's Web (1954)

The antique dealer, a Mr. Sellon, is dead. He fell down the stairs some months ago, if, indeed, he "fell." His house, musty furniture and all, is now rented to the Hailsham-Browns: Henry, a British diplomat of the bumbling variety; his young daughter Pippa; and his second wife, Clarissa, the dizzy heroine of the piece. They are joined, in this hilarious slapstick of a murder mystery, by three family friends, Sir Rowland "Roly" Delahaye, Hugo Birch, and the dashing Jeremy Warrender. And then, of course, there's the help.

Rumblings of the trouble to come begin quietly enough when Clarissa "fixes" a port-tasting contest among the three gentleman friends. Amidst fierce disagreement over which cup of wine contains the Dow '42 and which the Cockburn '27, Clarissa reveals that she's put nothing but humble grocery store port into each cup. The embarrassed gentlemen challenge Clarissa— if you were lying before why should we believe you now? "Nobody ever believes me when I'm telling the truth," Clarissa shrugs. "I suppose when you're making things up you get carried away and that makes it sound more convincing."

In fact, making things up is a favorite pastime of Clarissa's. She calls it supposing. "Supposing I had to choose between betraying my country and seeing Henry shot before my eyes." Or, more to the point as it turns out, "Suppose I found a dead body in the living room, what would I do?"

The above-mentioned living room boasts several interesting features even before a dead body is found in it. It's got a hidden panel disguised as bookshelves, which opens to a secret chamber between the living room and the library. It also has an antique desk that attracts a surprising amount of attention. Strangers drive up and offer huge sums of money for it and people who think no one is watching are forever rifling through it. It, too, has a secret compartment, discovered by Pippa, who dismisses the authentic autographs she finds within it ("Historical ones are rather moldy") and leaves her own secret message — "Sucks to you!"

Yes, Pippa is high spirited and happy...now. Not long ago she was miserable in the care of her real mother who was a drug addict and a meany as well. Miranda Hailsham-Brown finally left home and married the sleazy, drug-connected Oliver Costello. Pippa's dad also remarried more suitably, and with Clarissa as her new mother, Pippa is thriving.

Until Oliver Costello slinks up to the house that fateful evening in March, that is. Startled by Clarissa, he blurts out his intentions. He and his wife want custody of Pippa. Legal custody is still in Miranda's name though she had happily agreed to leave the child with her ex-husband. Now she wants her back, Costello says. Clarissa finds it hard to believe in this sudden resurgence of maternal feeling. You two don't want Pippa back, she accuses. You want blackmail. Well, we *are* a little short of cash, Costello acknowledges. At which point Miss Peake, the gumbooted Amazonian gardener, is called upon to show Mr. Costello the way out.

Unfortunately, Pippa has overheard the conversation and becomes hysterical. She is terrified of being sent back to her mother and the horrible man she married. "I'll kill him!" Pippa cries, "I'll cut my wrists!" Finally she begins to look on the bright side. "Perhaps he'll be struck by lightning."

"This was specially written for Margaret Lockwood .... She said at once that she didn't want to continue being sinister and melodramatic, that she had done a good many films lately in which she had been the 'wicked lady.' She wanted to play comedy." —*An Autobiography*

Meanwhile, on the international diplomacy front, Henry Hailsham-Brown has been given an important new assignment: his home is to be the site of a highly secret meeting between two heads of state due to arrive in a few hours. Everything must be quiet and perfect and, especially, discreet. He nervously explains all this to Clarissa who has just gotten Pippa off to bed. He's counting on her to see that it goes without a hitch; this is his big career break.

Henry heads for the airport as Clarissa runs around making sandwiches and being discreet. But how discreet can you be when you trip over something behind the living room couch and that "something" turns out to be a dead body? Not just any dead body, either. This is the dead body of Oliver Costello.

Well, it'll just have to wait. After the big meeting there'll be plenty of time to deal with this new development. As Clarissa, ever the efficient homemaker, drags the late Mr. Costello toward the secret panel, she wonders who perpetrated this not-unwelcome crime. "I didn't mean it, I didn't mean to," a horrified voice screams. Clarissa looks up. It's Pippa.

With this turn the drama takes on an urgency that doesn't stop till it becomes full-blown frenzy.

Sir Rowland, Hugo, and Jeremy try to shuffle the body off to a remote woods while Clarissa sets up a phony bridge game as an alibi and Henry, presumably, speeds from the airport with his VIPs. But when the doorbell rings it's not Henry, it's the police. Who invited them? Who, indeed?

Now we've got a body hastily hidden in the secret room, three pairs of gloves under a sofa cushion, an ace of spades where it's not supposed to be, a huge misunderstanding yet to be cleared up, and Clarissa being accused of murder no matter how many stories she tells, though some of them are even true.

But before you can cry "not guilty," that ubiquitous body, recently rediscovered, disappears. In its place is a note. "Sucks to you!" it says. This time it's Miss Peake who takes the credit (confidentially) in the interest of protecting Clarissa. "What I always say is stand by your own sex," she explains.

Things do work out eventually. Real murderers are caught just in the nick of time, voodoo books uncovered, invisible ink deciphered, world leaders lost and found, that sort of thing. But it is rather strenuous. As Clarissa says, "In a way, it's almost *too* much all in one evening."

JAN OXENBERG

HERCULE POIROT
The Man and the Myth
by Jerry Keucher

Neat where others were sloppy, organized where they were confused, sure of himself while they floundered, he cut a swath through England's murderers that left the police far behind.

Unimpressed by titles, unfazed by difficulties, untiring in his labors, Hercule Poirot stood as a bulwark protecting English society from legions of lady poisoners, gentlemen stranglers, and murderers of all sorts and persuasions who, without his efforts, would have escaped justice.

Though he occasionally berated himself for his few mistakes and miscalculations, he knew his own worth well enough. Spurning false modesty, he allowed as how his was "the greatest mind in Europe."

The "gray cells" of which he often boasted no doubt contributed to his remarkable longevity. It is incontestable that Poirot retired, full of honor, from the Belgian police force in 1904; we are told this in *The Mysterious Affair at Styles*, his first case in England. It is equally certain that his death did not occur until at least 1974, a year before the re-

lease of *Curtain*. We are never told his age, but it is difficult to imagine that he could have been less than sixty-five at the time of the Styles case in 1916. By all accounts the man lived at least one hundred and twenty years — how many miscreants he must have brought to justice! How well was justice served in that happy interlude!

On first finding Poirot—a refugee from his native country, exiled to the Essex countryside—Hastings informs us that

> Poirot was an extraordinary looking little man. He was hardly more than five feet, four inches, but carried himself with great dignity. His head was exactly the shape of an egg, and he always perched it a little on one side. His moustache was very stiff and military. The neatness of his attire was almost incredible. I believe a speck of dust would have caused him more pain than a bullet wound.

Over the years Poirot's appearance changed hardly at all, save for the inevitable effects of (extreme) age. He encouraged his black hair not to

Above: The famous "Sketch" portrait of Poirot by W. Smithson Broadhead; left: the versatile Charles Laughton, the first actor to portray Poirot, in Alibi *(1928), adapted from* The Murder of Roger Ackroyd.

"His head was exactly the shape of an egg, and he always perched it a little on one side. His moustache was very stiff and military. The neatness of his attire was almost incredible . . . . a speck of dust would have caused him more pain than a bullet wound."

turn gray by the use of "a tonic, not a dye"; his mustache, that unique creation, his pride and joy, was always waxed to furious points. His dress was formal, correct, and rigid: black jacket, striped pants, bow tie, and patent leather boots, topped by overcoat and muffler when the weather was anything but hot. It was indeed agony to him when any part of his ensemble was not perfectly arranged and clean, but being no mere dandy he would, in the interests of justice, tramp through mud in his patent leathers, venture out-of-doors in inclement weather, and even, as in *Death on the Nile*, brave tropical sand and heat.

His manner was as eccentric as his dress, and often as calculated. His fluency with the English language seemed like a radio he could turn off and on as it suited him. Complex thoughts always came easily to him in English, while he used French for the easy phrases. Through his speech there are scattered amusing transliterations from the French ("I demand of you a thousand pardons, monsieur. I am without defense"), and a certain charming hesitancy with common English idioms: e.g., "money for the *confiture*," "the side of the bed manner," and, for Americans, the doubly foreign "*portmanteau* call."

These problems with English were, one suspects, more feigned than real, for, as he knew, it was precisely his foreignness that was one of Poirot's greatest assets as a detective in England. He was shrewd in using the insularity of the English to his own advantage, as, for example, in questioning those present at a tragic Halloween party, when he hid his piercing appraisal "behind a foreign shield of flattering words and much-increased foreign mannerisms so that they should feel agreeably contemptuous of him." He knew that from lords to lackeys the English were unable to take foreigners seriously, especially one with such an "absurd" (that is, un-English) appearance; revealing one's secrets to a foreigner was not, therefore, as difficult a matter as it would have been had Poirot been a fellow Englishman. Over the course of his many cases, young and old came to him for advice and counsel, and he relished the roles of "Papa Poirot" and "father confessor" that his foreign birth and manner allowed him to play.

While language and mannerisms were, so to speak, tools of his trade, Poirot never had to hide the fact that his tastes and habits were most un-English. In a land where hunting, walks through the countryside, and gardening have for centuries been national pastimes, Poirot was noticeable for his love of the indoors. For him the country was generally like that around the Angkatell estate in *Murder after Hours*: "Best enjoyed from a car on a

HERCULE POIROT

fine afternoon. You exclaimed, *'Quel beau paysage!'* and drove back to a good hotel." English humor, English dress, and English eating habits were other facets of life that he found incomprehensible. How could it be, for example, that a sensible man like Inspector Spence would prefer a beer to a sweet liqueur, or bitter English tea to a cup of thick, sweet chocolate or chamomile?

As he indulged his love of exotic drinks, Poirot likewise gave free rein to his passion for symmetry. Most people choose a dwelling for its location, its view, or its size, but Poirot settled on his abode in Whitehaven Mansions because of the building's extreme symmetry. Of course the flat itself had "impeccable chromium fittings, square armchairs, and severely rectangular ornaments." No curves distracted from the stern horizontals and verticals. The books on his shelves were arranged strictly by height; when Hastings once put one in the wrong place, it was as if the poor man had slapped the detective in the face. It shouldn't be surprising to find that Poirot would have liked to extend his ideas of order into the world of nature. He found, as he once remarked to Inspector Japp, that it was "really insupportable that every hen lays an egg of a different size! What symmetry can there be on the breakfast table?"

His orderliness was useful to him in his work in two ways. On more than one occasion his automatic habit of straightening other people's mantelpieces and drawers led him to the murderer. But his love of symmetry around him was a cause as well as an effect of the precision of his thought processes and deductive method. At a critical moment in his first case he was to be found building cardhouses, for "with precision of the fingers goes precision of the brain."

It was this precision of the brain that was at the core of his investigative style. Not for him frantic sniffing after clues, though heaven knows no scrap of cloth or recently oiled door missed his notice. But the clue was of no use if the mind did not put it in its proper place in the sequence of events. The great mistake for the detective, as Poirot never tired of telling the wide-eyed Hastings, was to try to make the clues fit the interpretation. No, the mind of the detective must be sufficiently clear and orderly to arrive at the explanation that accounts for all the evidence. And though he was not above peeping at keyholes and reading others' mail ("Really, Poirot, that's the sort of thing that isn't done." "It is done by Hercule Poirot"), Poirot never betrayed his conviction that the physical evidence of a case is usually misleading without the proper understanding of its psychology. And for Poirot a

Poirot in some of his many incarnations: as Peter Ustinov (Death on the Nile), *Albert Finney* (Murder on the Orient Express), *James Coco* (Murder by Death), *and Francis L. Sullivan* (in the stage version of* Peril at End House*).

great part of detective work was sitting quietly and thinking, his eyes getting greener, and Hastings more fidgety, until the mind had reached that understanding.

A delicate balance must be struck, when the detective is of such caliber, to unfold the story in such a way that Poirot can be seen to be exercising his remarkable mind as soon as he comes into the picture without solving the case after the first tour of the scene of the crime. The pacing of the solution to the mystery often runs as follows: a "little idea" about some aspect of the situation, usually accompanied by a question so unexpected as to make those present doubt Poirot's sanity, is followed to the point when the idea proves correct, and Poirot is able to present the solution to a minor question while the central mystery remains veiled to us, and often to Poirot as well, until the end. Because he wins these minor victories throughout the book, he can bring us to the final scene ("Madame, I have your permission to hold a little *reunion* in the *salon*?" or, "I have been blind, *imbecile*. Quick, a taxi!") with his reputation intact, appearing to be anything but the "thirty-six times imbecile" to which he modestly, if hyperbolically, confesses.

Next to his prized mustache, it was his reputation as the greatest living detective that he valued most. Even before he reached England's shores, he enjoyed there a certain renown. Though at one point in the 1920s he sought anonymity in a gardenful of vegetable marrows, he found, as he told Dr. Sheppard, who narrated *The Murder of Roger Ackroyd*, that such leisure was not for him. Rather, he basked in being mentioned in the society columns, and took it for granted that his name was familiar to all. While making a famous journey on the Orient Express, the Countess Andrenyi asked whether he was investigating the

HERCULE POIROT

murder at hand, somewhat international in flavor, because he belonged to the League of Nations. "I belong to the world," was the assertive detective's reply. (It is not, after all, the mark of a self-effacing man to answer the telephone by saying with a certain grandeur of manner, "Hercule Poirot speaks.")

Unfortunately for his ego, there were many over the years who had not heard of him. Younger generations were always coming up who had not been made acquainted with his exploits. And there was the lamentable incident on the same train journey when a young American made the incredible confession that he had always thought the name was that of a women's dressmaker. Poirot was probably justified in his feeling that the younger generation was "singularly lacking in knowledge of notable celebrities."

As a celebrity he was fond of the good life. Luxury hotels, luxury flats, impeccable service, and above all, good food—one might say these were his avocations. He sometimes viewed the entire day as the building toward the climax of *Le Dîner*. "Alas," he was overheard to murmur to his mustache shortly before beginning the hunt for Mrs. McGinty's murderer, "that one can only eat three times a day...."

However, as we have seen with regard to his dress, his devotion to justice was such that in its quest he even tolerated the totally inadequate accommodations of Mrs. McGinty's Broadhinny.

The deepest part of his character can be expressed in the simplest words: Hercule Poirot did not approve of murder; those who perpetrated murder had to be brought to justice. Not for him the modern excuses of broken homes and negligent parents. He thought first of justice and was suspicious of mercy—misplaced mercy, that is. Not that he was inflexible in extraordinary situations. On more than one occasion he tempered strict justice at least with understanding. But his passion for truth and knowledge was such that

blind justice could have found no better seeing-eye dog than Hercule Poirot.

If he was not noted for his sympathy for murderers, he was far from insensitive to the minds and hearts of the innocent. He always did everything he could in the course of his investigations to save a marriage or to foster one. He was not above putting the Crown to the expense of the trial of an innocent man (evidence to support the acquittal was naturally forthcoming), if that's what it took to redeem a relationship. As he remarked in *The A.B.C. Murders*: "In the midst of death we are in life, Hastings.... Murder, I have often noticed, is a great matchmaker."

This is not meant to propose him for sainthood, however miraculous some of his deductions might appear. It is enough to accept him for what he knew himself to be—the greatest detective of his time. We can take comfort, as well as enjoyment and amusement, in the fact that, as he needed his investigations in order to display his mental skill, so he needed admirers like Hastings (and ourselves) to feed his ego. When Hastings was living in the Argentine, Poirot missed him, not only for the loyal and fine qualities that had always been so apparent in him, but also because "it is very necessary for a man of my abilities to admire himself—and for that one needs stimulation from outside. I cannot, truly I cannot, sit in a chair all day reflecting how truly admirable I am. One needs the human touch. One needs—as they say nowadays—the *stooge*."

Perhaps it was the admiration that helped extend his career, not to mention those of his loyal friend and chronicler, Hastings; Georges, his trusted manservant; and Inspector Japp of Scotland Yard. The pursuit of justice, perhaps, helped Poirot and associates find a special place here in this world, where age does not corrupt—at least not too quickly.

Alas, if only that brilliant career could have lasted longer.

POIROT AND I
A Hungarian-Born Fan Tells Why
He Identifies with Poirot
An Interview with Thomas Kertes,
lawyer and musician, New York City

EDITOR

Why do you think Agatha Christie captured your imagination?

KERTES

Well, first, I am a very big mystery fan. I always need new excitement and stimulation, and mysteries are the best kind of book for that. I want to be entertained, and no mysteries entertain me more than Christie's. I read every one of her books that I can find, which I can't say for any other author.

If a book doesn't capture me in the first thirty or forty pages I put it down. I don't give it that much of a chance. I have never put down an Agatha Christie book, except two that I couldn't get through. For some reason they didn't catch me, but they were the exceptions.

EDITOR

Agatha Christie stories are almost pure brainteasers. Other writers would get more into violence or sex.

KERTES

I don't find that vibrating excitement with any other writer that I find consistently with Christie. I always find it hard to get through five or six books by other mystery writers, but I had a very easy time getting through nearly eighty of hers. I get very depressed now when I go to a library and can't find a new book of hers. Unfortunately it's very tough to read her books more than once unless you read them years ago and don't remember what happened. In a mystery, the whole thing is who did it, and if you know, it's spoiled.

EDITOR

Do you remember how you came to read Agatha Christie?

KERTES

Ten Little Indians was the first Christie book I ever read. I probably read that while I was still in Hungary. It got me hooked from the beginning. I almost forgot about it because it was so long ago.

EDITOR

Who do you like better, Poirot or Marple?

KERTES

Poirot. No question. That's very easy to answer.

EDITOR

Why?

KERTES

The books that he is in are more exciting, more interesting than the Miss Marple ones. I love Miss Marple books too, but I like the Poirot stories better.

I think a lot of that can go back to their characters. Miss Marple is a lovable fussy little old English lady and she talks a lot. A lot of the time she just sits around and talks and describes things. I like action. Poirot's personality lends itself more to action.

Poirot is very believable to me. He's a foreigner, which I can really relate to, being one myself. And I love his mustache and the fact that he's a little skinny guy. I love that he is always being underrated. People think he's a weirdo. He's got more brains than all those people put together.

POIROT AND I

Maybe I relate to this. A lot of times I see myself as an underdog.

EDITOR
Do you like Tommy and Tuppence?

KERTES
One of the books that I couldn't get through was one of theirs, *Postern of Fate*. They blabber throughout the first two pages and nothing happens. I just couldn't make it. But then they are in one that is one of my top favorites, *N or M?*

EDITOR
Do you have a favorite book?

KERTES
One favorite? No, I have several. *N or M?*, *The Murder of Roger Ackroyd*, *Murder in Mesopotamia*, and *They Came to Baghdad*.

EDITOR
Have you seen the movies?

KERTES
Yes. I love them, *Death on the Nile, Murder on the Orient Express, Witness for the Prosecution*. I also saw the three Miss Marple English movies with Margaret Rutherford.

The only thing I have been amazed by is that they don't make more movies of her books. If I were a movie director I think I would. Her books lend themselves to movies. I think every one of them would be hits, if they were done well.

EDITOR
Why do you think so many people all over the world love Agatha Christie? She's been translated into more languages than Shakespeare.

KERTES
She's much more exciting than Shakespeare!

EDITOR
Why did she become so popular?

KERTES
First of all, she's the best. Her characters are wonderful. She had insight into human beings. She didn't deal with crazy, way-out people that people can't relate to. Her characters are very everyday kinds of people that a lot of readers probably recognize as like themselves.

She deals with little old ladies in English villages, and you can recognize your own grandmother. Other writers create mysterious lovers, but that is really like fantasy. In Christie's books I can see the people really walking around the street.

I particularly love the little prejudices she puts in against foreigners. That's something I think everybody has, whether they admit it or not. I love it, being a foreigner myself. I can really relate to that.

EDITOR
Some people would never pick up a Christie book and others are hooked. Why?

KERTES
Some people only read books to be educated. I know people like that. Those are the ones who won't pick up a Christie, the highbrows. I had a girl friend like that, an English teacher, and she would never read Agatha Christie. She thought it was beneath her. But if I had to choose between Agatha Christie and William Faulkner, I'd read Christie every time. When I read, it's to be entertained. Even that girl friend of mine, we saw all the Christie movies together and she loved them.

EDITOR
Do you think your reading Christie mysteries has influenced the way you think about people or your life?

KERTES

I think they've helped me develop analytical thinking. They really are puzzles you have to sit down and think about. But she wasn't a writer of that kind of heaviness that would affect somebody's way of thinking.

EDITOR

Your work as as lawyer and your mystery reading both involve analytical thinking.

KERTES

Yes, I was into mystery reading long before I became a lawyer. Agatha Christie and Perry Mason influenced me to go into law.

EDITOR

Were you conscious of this?

KERTES

Yes, and afterward I realized how dumb it was because, believe me, it really is nothing like that. Law work is not like Agatha Christie or Perry Mason. It's ninety-nine percent drudgery, sitting at a desk and doing paperwork. The exciting part, the investigation and the court work, is only one percent, but that's all I read about.

EDITOR

If I asked you to give a tribute to Agatha Christie, what could you say?

KERTES

She has been one of the biggest positive parts of my life. To me, happiness is putting a lot of good times together and if you have enough good times, you'll be happy. She has given me hours of good times.

Thomas Kertes

So Many Steps to Death (1954)

(Alternate title: *Destination Unknown*)

Scientists around the world are vanishing and Jessop, a crack British security agent, is determined to find out where and why. His bait? Thomas Betterton's wife, Olive. Dr. Betterton was the most recent scientific genius to disappear — at a conference in Paris. A mistress? Hardly, Jessop decides, assessing Olive, Betterton's bride of six months. Foul play? Perhaps, but if so, who, and why? And what is this business of Olive tripping off to Morocco to relieve her grief? Hardly appropriate for a bereaved wife.

> In his experience, women suffering from violent grief and anxiety did not neglect their make-up. Aware of the ravages grief made in their appearance, they did their best to repair those ravages. He wondered if Mrs. Betterton calculatingly abstained from make-up, the better to sustain the part of the distracted wife.

In Jessop's indefatigable pursuit of Betterton he persuades the suicidal Hilary Craven — beautiful, tall, and red-haired — to impersonate Olive Betterton (also lovely, tall, and auburn) when Olive is killed in a plane crash abroad. Hilary, divorced, her only child recently dead from meningitis, without friends or meaningful work, responds to Jessop's proddings. After all, doesn't every ardent reader of mysteries know that there is no better aid to mental health than high adventure and international intrigue? And that is exactly what Hilary, now Olive, encounters.

Her wit being as bright as her hair, she is equal to her task. But what to make of the brief encounter with the fabulously wealthy, aged, and eccentric Monsieur Aristides? Then she finds herself on a time-consuming journey complete with costume changes and transportation switches. It also includes peculiar fellow travelers — scientists from various countries who hold a variety of political convictions.

But Hilary gaily troops from connection to connection, and as her trail gets hotter, her connection with Jessop becomes more tenuous. Thank heavens for her pearl necklace — it's only costume jewelry—tacky but convenient for leaving a trail that Jessop can follow, one pearl at a time.

Olive-Hilary eventually finds herself in a sleek and secret multi-million dollar laboratory, peopled by scientists who have disappeared from all over the world. Some of them are hostile, some mysterious. And some are intriguingly attractive, like the friendly Andrew Peters.

Let no one say that Dame Agatha let time go by while her fiction ignored the changing world. This novel includes a number of references to life in the 1950s, among them anti-Communist hysteria in America. Christie rests her story on manifestations of the Cold War — bombs, germ warfare research, secret scientific advancements, defecting and kidnapped scientists. Much is made of the scientists' varying motivations — moral, material, and political.

Meanwhile, though, Hilary is still waiting in the secret lab. At this point she must decide for herself: Is this a true Utopia, dedicated to scientific advancement for all the world's good? Or is this an insidious dictatorship? Who does run the place? Will she see the tenacious Jessop again? What does all this have to do with Dr. Betterton? Does Hilary want to live after all? And what will become of her if her true identity is discovered?

MARCIA CLENDENEN

Hickory, Dickory, Death (1955)

(Alternate title: *Hickory, Dickory, Dock*)

When Felicity Lemon, Hercule Poirot's paragon of a secretary, makes three mistakes in one letter, something is gravely amiss. That something concerns Miss Lemon's widowed sister, Mrs. Hubbard, who is now a matron in a hostel for students at 26 Hickory Road.

Strange things have been happening on Hickory Road — the disappearance of items as disparate as a diamond ring and a pair of old flannel trousers; vandalism manifested by a cut-up silk scarf, a rucksack slashed to pieces, and important school notes destroyed by green ink.

Because M. Poirot has been a bit bored of late and can easily rationalize that a troubled Miss Lemon will annoy and inconvenience him by continued mistakes in his letters, he offers his help. Over a gracious tea Poirot meets Mrs. Hubbard and learns more about the inhabitants of 26 Hickory Road, as well as about the odd goings-on.

Our cast is indeed a motley group from all over the world. The principals among them are lovely Sally Finch, an American student on a Fulbright scholarship; Mr. Chandra Lal and Mr. Gopal Ram, students from India; Mr. Akibombo, a student from West Africa; Elizabeth Johnston, a brilliant law student from Jamaica whom the others call "Black Bess"; Nigel Chapman, a student of medieval history at London University who is generally disliked for his malicious tongue; Leonard Bateson, a medical student with a violent temper; Colin McNabb, a student of psychiatry; Patricia Lane, a serious archaeology student; Valerie Hobson, a cool and elegant lady who is involved in business; Celia Austin, a shy, rather dull young woman who dispenses drugs at St. Catherine's Hospital; and Jean Tomlinson, a rather sanctimonious young physiotherapist. We must not overlook Mrs. Nicoletis, the owner of the hostel, a Greek lady of fiery temperament and erratic moods.

Among the missing items are an evening shoe, a bracelet, a stethoscope, electric light bulbs, boracic acid, bath salts, and a cookbook. No rhyme or reason to any of it is the general conclusion. But Hercule Poirot, experienced detective that he is, knows better and is worried.

To arrange a visit that will not unduly alarm the occupants of the hostel, Poirot suggests to Mrs. Hubbard that he be invited to lecture on the theory and practice of successful detection. After his talk and some mingling with the boarders, clever Poirot advises calling in the police—assuming, no doubt, that this advice will act as a disturbing catalyst.

It does almost immediately. First Colin McNabb, the psychiatry student, deduces that because of a deprived, Cinderella-like childhood, a young girl has turned to kleptomania; it's evident that he suspects one particular girl. Poirot is quite aware of his uneasiness, and when moments later Celia Austin rushes in to confess that she has stolen a number of items, it's clear that the future psychiatrist already knows about psychology.

The revelation of Celia's appalling weakness attracts Colin more than she could ever have imagined—she has adored him for some time—and instead of shunning her, he says, "It's just a kind of illness you've had from not looking at things clearly. If you'll trust me, Celia, I'll soon be able to put you right."

Celia puts herself in his hands both literally and figuratively, and marriage seems in the offing.

It turns out, however, that Celia has been selec-

Hickory, Dickory, Death (1955)

tive in her kleptomania, and that not all the thefts can be traced to her. She swears that she has not touched the rucksack or the bulbs, stethoscope, boracic acid, or bath salts. Nor did she spill ink on Elizabeth's notes. But in her disclaimer, she admits to more than she intended. "I didn't mean... to be dishonest. It was only... I'm all mixed up."

Is she hiding something, Poirot wonders? Has somebody more clever than she—any number of people meet this criterion—put her up to this to arouse Colin's interest? And if so, who?

On the night that a blushing Colin announces their engagement, Celia dies — judging from a note she left, an apparent suicide. Suicide? When Poirot lurks nearby? Never! This is murder. Someone has slipped her a lethal dose of morphine tartrate, and she has died in her sleep.

On the evening of her death Celia is reported to have said, "There are some things I don't understand, like the electric bulbs the day the police came." Then this reputedly rather dull young woman went on to say, "I think someone forged a passport. I shall know more about it tomorrow." But for Celia, who unwittingly prompted her own murder, tomorrow never came.

As the mystery thickens and simmers, Inspector Sharpe interrogates the dark-haired, volatile owner of the hostel. Mrs. Nicoletis is hardly gracious or cooperative, but when she learns that the Inspector has a search warrant and intends to search even her sacrosanct room, she resorts to screams, curses, and threats. All to no avail. The locked cupboard in her room is broken open, and her secret is revealed. A frightened Mrs. Nicoletis mutters, "I did not want them to know. I am very uneasy. They may think...what will they think?"

Whatever "they" think, the landlady's fate is sealed. One evening as she sits sipping her double brandy, she meets the murderer, who once again

acts quickly. This time the morphia is slipped into the brandy, and later that evening, she is found by the police, "lying in a heap." Drunk is the first verdict. The final verdict, though, is murder.

While this has been going on, Poirot has hardly been idle. Unfortunately for the murderer, bits of seemingly unrelated information begin to appear. One of the boarders is a gambler; the father of one of the students is in a hospital for the insane; another has broken family ties and changed identity; there is evidence that a smuggler lurks among them; still another guest is a Communist. As these new clues, both real and false, keep cropping up, the master detective cleverly pieces together a most difficult puzzle.

Folk wisdom has perpetuated the concept of threes, and murder often generates murder. When Patricia Lane interferes with something that is obviously none of her business, she becomes the third victim, murdered by a marble paperweight slipped into a woolen sock.

Hercule Poirot knows that one member of the cast in this drama is the murderer. Could it be Len Bateson, the medical student who has a dark secret? Or brilliant Elizabeth Johnston, who has the ego of a Napoleon? Or Nigel Chapman, whose malice has won him many enemies? Or Colin McNabb, Celia's fiancé? Where did he go on the night she was murdered? Or Mr. Akibombo, from an exotic African culture where murder is not unknown? Or Sally Finch, the attractive American? Before Celia's ruse, Colin had been greatly attracted to her. Or Valerie Hobson, whose scarf Celia slashed to pieces? Or could it have been Mrs. Hubbard herself? Is she immune simply because she is Miss Lemon's sister? How often do unseasoned murderers follow in Raskolnikov's footsteps and lead the police directly to themselves?

Surely our illustrious detective with Dame Agatha's help will solve the three murders so that *hickory dickory* can once more be concluded with *dock* instead of *death*.   JEAN FIEDLER

Dead Man's Folly (1956)

The phone rings in the London office of our favorite Belgian detective, the dapper and mustachioed Hercule Poirot. At the other end of the line is his old friend Mrs. Ariadne Oliver, the successful mystery writer. She is calling from Devonshire where she is arranging a murder hunt, which is like a treasure hunt, with clues, victim, suspects, and prizes, for a charity fete. But something is "wrong" about the affair, she can tell that much even though she can't quite put her finger on what it is. She feels that she is being maneuvered somehow, but she isn't sure, and she doesn't know by whom, and she has no idea why, but would Poirot please come to help her figure out the situation?

To a regular reader of Christie murders, Poirot's response is uncharacteristic: he drops what he is doing and catches the next train. In fact, throughout *Dead Man's Folly*, Poirot engages in more physical activity than he does in four or five other books added together.

He arrives in the village of Nassecombe, 212 miles from London. While being driven to Nasse House, where Mrs. Oliver is staying, he meets two of the foreign travelers who are continually trespassing across the Nasse estate and through our story. These appearances are inevitably followed by revealing examples of upper-class British xenophobia. The region is popular with hikers; the river Helm runs through the area and Dartmoor is visible in the distance.

At Nasse House Mrs. Oliver confuses us by explaining what appears to be going on, and then clearly introduces many of the people who are helping to stage the benefit.

The hosts are Sir George and Lady Hattie Stubbs. Who are the Stubbses? "Nobody really. Just rich," says Mrs. Oliver. *Rich* is the word most often ascribed to Sir George, who is not really a sir at all, but as another character, Mrs. Masterton, explains, "the rich must be allowed their little snobberies." However, Sir George is highly acceptable to the community as much for his perfect portrayal of a country squire as for his wealth.

Sir George is charmingly devoted to his wife of a year, Hattie, who is generally conceded to be dim-witted and self-absorbed. She grew up in a wealthy family that owned sugar estates in the West Indies but was left destitute when the estates were destroyed in earthquakes. She then came under the guidance of Mrs. Folliat who brought her together with Sir George. (Back to Mrs. Folliat in a moment.) Hattie, whose exotic beauty is compared to an orchid, seems to spend her time reading *Vogue* magazine, longing for occasions that require smart clothes and jewelry, and peering into her large emerald ring. The high point of her existential inquiry is reached during an evening when people have gathered to work on the fete. She wonders, "What is the good of being rich if one has to do everything oneself?"

Hattie's mentor, Mrs. Folliat, is the former owner of Nasse House. Folliats had owned the estate since 1598 and built the present mansion in 1790. Several people note that there have always been Folliats at Nasse. Unfortunately for Mrs. Folliat, her husband and son managed to squander all the money and then conveniently die in World War II. Mrs. Folliat, left in cold financial straits, sold the estate to Sir George, and he was nice enough not only to rent her the gardener's cottage but also to marry her charge, Hattie. Mrs. Folliat seems content with her lot: everyone acts as if Nasse were still hers, Hattie is mindlessly

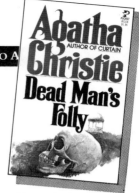

Dead Man's Folly (1956)

nearby, and she gets to putter around with the shrubs.

The estate itself is quite large—sixty-five acres with woods, garden, tennis courts, boathouse and dock on the Helm, and a Greek Folly. A Folly is a small white pilastered temple where people sit during the summer to look picturesque. Mrs. Oliver had originally planned that the victim of the murder hunt should be discovered in the Folly, but now the body will lie in the boathouse.

According to the scenario, the victim is the Yugoslavian first wife of the atom scientist and is dressed as a hiker. She is willingly played by an unattractive village adolescent named Marlene Tucker who thinks that meeting a sex maniac would be romantic. Her role consists of waiting in the boathouse until she hears clue-followers coming, and then she is to lie down and play dead. When Mrs. Oliver and Poirot arrive to see how she is getting on, they find a very real victim wearing a neck rope pulled tight.

Now Mrs. Oliver has imaginary motives for murdering imaginary Yugoslavs, but who would want to kill an overgrown fourteen-year-old without an enemy in the world?

The police are summoned, and they question the organizers of the event. Miss Brewis, Sir George's efficient secretary, claims to have taken a tea tray to the boathouse at 4:15 and Marlene was alive then. By 4:40, she was dead.

Outside, the fete continues. Then it is discovered that Lady Hattie has completely disappeared. And a man named Etienne De Sousa, who claims to be Hattie's West Indian cousin, arrives via a yacht, looking for Hattie.

On the morning of her disappearance, Hattie had received a letter from De Sousa apprising her of his arrival. She had told Poirot that she was afraid of De Sousa, that "he did bad things." De Sousa spends the rest of the investigation sitting on his yacht, watching the proceedings with amusement.

Days pass, but Hattie does not appear. Michael Weyman, Stubbs's architect who is working on the Folly, acts shaken up, but he may have been played with by Hattie. The redoubtable Miss Brewis isn't overly worried by Hattie's absence, but she loves Sir George and has plans for him.

The others?

There are Peggy and Alec Legge, whose marriage is dissolving in Peggy's growing ambitions and Alec's growing depression. Peggy was originally to have played the victim but switched instead to the role of fortuneteller, and she has a thin alibi for the crucial times. There is Mrs. Masterton, who has organized the whole show, helped by her lackey, "Captain" Jim Warburton.

Foreign hikers keep wandering about, particularly one young man in an obnoxiously loud shirt with turtles on it. He seems to have aroused at least Dame Christie's political suspicions, and she has offered him to us as her version of the Communist threat.

Mrs. Folliat believes Hattie to be dead. Poirot thinks she may be right, and returns to London to exercise his famous gray cells.

Then there is another death. Old Merdell, an ancient local man known for his garrulousness, is drowned one evening while trying to step from his boat to the quay. The authorities rule it an accident. Poirot had met the man at Nasse, and Old Merdell had intimated that he knew some secrets.

Poirot sits in London ruminating. But the pieces will not fit together and in another burst of alacrity he returns to Nassecombe. Once again he experiences that curious phenomenon he has noticed in other cases. The normally reticent Britisher will tell very private things to Poirot precisely because he is not one of "them" and therefore "safe." As he goes from house to house, *Dead Man's Folly* becomes one of Poirot's most energetic cases.   BETH SIMON

What Mrs. McGillicuddy Saw! (1957)

(Alternate titles: *4:50 from Paddington, Murder She Said*)

When trains run parallel at the same speed in the same direction the effect is to freeze motion; one can look into the compartment of the opposite train as if it were a stage. Elderly Elspeth McGillicuddy certainly didn't expect to get a free show of murder when she took the 4:54 to Brackhampton after doing her Christmas shopping in London. But murder—a tall dark man squeezing the life out of a purple-faced woman—is what she got. Well, try telling that to the ticket taker or the stationmaster! Good thing for Mrs. McGillicuddy, and for us, that she was on her way to see her old friend Jane Marple.

"The best thing, I think, my dear, is for you to go upstairs and take off your hat and have a wash. Then we will have supper..." That's the civilized Miss Marple, never one to overreact or, for that matter, miss the slightest nuance of a situation.

When the expected dead-woman-found-on-train item fails to appear in the morning paper, the two friends go to the police. Try as they may, though, the police just can't seem to locate a blonde female, 30–35, dead. No such person has even been reported missing. Perhaps Mrs. McGillicuddy saw something "less serious"? Well, Elspeth McGillicuddy knows what she saw, and she saw murder! But she has to go to Ceylon to see Roderick, so Miss Jane Marple, approaching her ninetieth birthday, is left to cope.

Now Jane Marple has the kind of subtle mind that doesn't need a decomposing body to tell her a murder has taken place. Self-important officials may snicker but Marple knows and trusts her friend. Since there *is* a body the only thing left to do is figure out where it *must be*. With the aid of maps, train schedules, and county histories Jane Marple does precisely that. Somewhere on the

grounds of Rutherford Hall, the overgrown Crackenthorpe estate along the curve in the railroad tracks, is a dead body.

What a nuisance that an 89-year-old can't go searching the grounds herself! But thankfully Miss Marple knows just the woman for the job, young Lucy Eyelesbarrow, who, after taking a First in mathematics at Oxford, is now pursuing a career as a domestic servant (she "has a taste for people"). Since Lucy is renowned as Britain's answer to the "you-just-can't-get-good-help" lament, she has no trouble securing a post at Rutherford Hall and the search is on.

Cantankerous old Luther Crackenthorpe and his kindly spinster daughter, Emma, don't seem too dangerous to Lucy—but one never knows. She pursues her goal surreptitiously, executing purposely lousy golf shots that land in the embankment she wants to explore or nosing around the pigsty under the guise of "finding a place to grow mushrooms." Of course Lucy has to do all this detective work in her spare time from preparing exquisite treacle tart, roast beef of Old England, and apple meringue, keeping every room of the large mansion in immaculate order, and ministering to the psychological needs of the Crackenthorpes. In other words, in the afternoons.

All that efficiency pays off. Lucy discovers the Long Barn, repository of a young Luther Crackenthorpe's follies in art collecting, and there, under the heavy lid of a hideous Greco-Roman sarcophagus, it is.

One might think that finding a body dead three and a half weeks would put Lucy off cooking for a few days, but it doesn't. It does, however, put Miss Jane Marple on to the theory that the train

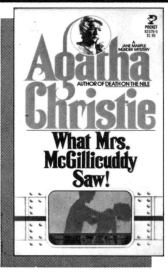

murder was cleverly premeditated by someone who is intimately acquainted with the grounds of Rutherford Hall.

Conveniently, most of the people who fit this description assemble for the inquest. There are the sons: Harold, the respectable London businessman whose financial problems can't be hidden much longer; Cedric, the eccentric painter living on an island off the coast of Spain; Alfred, connoisseur of shady deals; and Brian Eastley, son-in-law by marriage to the late daughter Edith, now a drifter. There is the professional help: Wimborne, the family lawyer, and Quimper, the doctor. And there is grandson Alexander and his school chum James who seem to do little except eat, but who occasionally come up with interesting clues. Officially observing the scene is Dermot Craddock, Detective Inspector, Scotland Yard. He's keeping to himself the knowledge that the murder was committed on a train.

But the murder of whom? No one admits to knowing the dead woman. Is she Martine, the woman whom the eldest son, Edmund, may or may not have married just before he got killed in the war and who may or may not have borne his

legitimate son and heir? Is she an imposter who was claiming to be Martine? Or is she a local girl who used the Long Barn as a "place of assignation" with her boyfriend — though why anyone would want to "assignate" among the grotesque Roman statues is a mystery in its own right.

There is no dearth of motives for murder among the Crackenthorpes. The huge family fortune will one day be divided among the offspring, one of whom will get the valuable land lusted after by developers of suburban Brackhampton. Unfortunately this is a motive for the murder of Luther Crackenthorpe, who is still alive and complaining. Even when two more members of the Crackenthorpe clan bite the dust, or shall we say, the arsenic, Luther isn't among them.

Will we find out who the dead woman was? Will the overconfident killer tip his hand? Will Lucy's "sick Aunt Jane" be unmasked as one of England's shrewdest detectives? Or will Lucy run out of gourmet recipes first and get fired?

The answers will have to wait for the return of Elspeth McGillicuddy from Ceylon—unless you are clever enough to figure out what Mrs. McGillicuddy saw.

JAN OXENBERG

The Unexpected Guest (1958)

Just when one thinks Agatha Christie cannot possibly come up with another unexpected ending, she comes up with *The Unexpected Guest*. Written in 1958, this play takes its cue from Laura Warwick's frightened memory of a childhood saying: "The door opens and the unexpected guest comes in." Indeed he does, bringing a stage full of unexpected consequences with him.

The guest is Michael Starkwedder, who comes out of a dense fog and into the study of Llongelert House in South Wales looking for help for his ditched car. Instead of help he finds the body of Richard Warwick and Richard's wife — er, widow—Laura, standing over him with a gun. It does not take Starkwedder (a "shrewd thinker") long to ask the inevitable question. When the inevitable "yes" comes back, Starkwedder wants to know why. "He drank. He was cruel. I've hated him for years," answers Laura.

Sufficient reasons for a murder in real life, perhaps, but in a Christie play? Beware. Starkwedder, however, apparently does not realize he's in a Christie play. He buys Laura's story completely and even goes her one better. He will make himself an accessory after the fact and help cover up the murder. But why? "For the simple reason, I suppose, that you're an attractive woman and I don't like to think of an attractive woman being shut up in prison for all the best years of her life." Ah, chivalry is not dead, even in South Wales.

Poor Richard is, however, and what to do about it? Surely he had his enemies? A big game hunter before a lion mauled and crippled him, he had taken recently to shooting at stray cats and dogs, with an occasional bird or rabbit thrown in

for luck. But there are no local SPCA fanatics to take the blame for his murder. What about that woman collecting subscriptions for the vicarage fete whom Richard had sent on her way amidst a hail of bullets? Or better still, the father of a child Richard had killed in a drunk-driving accident? The law had let him go scot-free, an infelicitous choice, since the father was a Scot who apparently did not share those exonerating tendencies. "A patient, dogged people, the Scots," says Richard's mother.

After piecing together words from a newspaper—"May 15, Paid In Full"—and leaving this incriminating piece of journalism on Richard's chest, Starkwedder sends Laura away while he reenacts the crime. Upon hearing the shot, she and rest of the family assemble to discover Richard's now very dead remains. The family members are: Benny, the housekeeper/secretary, a woman who thinks she knows what's best for everybody and is not afraid to act on her opinions; Angell, the male nurse, correct of manner, shifty of eye, not above a little blackmail to preserve his job; Mrs. Warwick, Richard's mother, near-deaf and near death and appreciating the "clarifying vision" such a state often affords; and Jan, Richard's half-brother, sweet, innocent — and retarded. Throw in a crippled sadist and a potential murderess and there you have it. Just your typical English household.

Into this wholesome home comes the local law: Inspector Thomas and Sergeant Cadwallader, the former dryly sarcastic, the latter Welshly poetic. The sergeant quotes Keats, the inspector questions caustically, and the evidence begins to mount up. It does, indeed, look as if MacGregor,

The Unexpected Guest (1958)

the bereft father, is the man—but wait a minute, that's impossible. The report from Scotland Yard has just come in: MacGregor's been dead for two years. So who killed Richard and left that note?

Surely not Major Julian Farrar, the handsome neighbor who is running for office and who was seen running from the house that night? Of course, everybody knew about him and Laura —except Richard, naturally, who was apparently too busy spotting rabbits to spot this. Jan, in that cute little way he has of remembering everything exactly, recalls Julian's prophecy to Richard one night: "One of these days, Richard, somebody'll put a bullet through your head." How sweet. But then, that's just sweet little re-

tarded Jan, going around brandishing Richard's pistols and saying "I'm the man of the house now!"

And how is our unexpected Mr. Starkwedder taking all this? He is suffering through what must be the Christie equivalent of Get The Guest. Everyone, it seems, comes to him and either confesses or points the finger at someone else. Finally, the sergeant captures and kills the murderer and the crime is solved. But wait another minute! We're still four pages from the end of the play. You mean that was just another misleading clue and we still don't know who did it? Of course. With Agatha Christie, always expect the unexpected.

GRANVILLE BURGESS

(The bottom portion of the page is printed upside-down, containing the answers to THE MOUSETRAP DOUBLE-CROSTIC (pages 198-99).)

THE MOUSETRAP DOUBLE-CROSTIC *(pages 198-99)*

Quotation: "'What's this?' I says to Bill. And he takes it and reads it out. '"Three blind mice."—must be off,' is, knocker,' he says—and just at that very moment—yes, it was that very moment, sir, we'ears some woman yelling, 'Murder!' a couple of streets away."

Clue Line: "Mrs. Boyle in the library with a belt."

Words:

A Monkswell
B Rhymes
C Snow
D Beds
E Odets
F Yams
G Lyon
H Euchre
I I'd est

J Netting
K Taj
L Huff
M Emory
N London
O Isms
P Butte
Q Revisited
R Aye Aye
S Roast

T Yeast
U Whisper
V I was
W This is the first
X Haute
Y Await
Z Black Market
Z1 Et tu
Z2 Leaves
Z3 Ta-ra
Commander

THEY GAVE THEIR LIVES FOR ART
A Study of the Christie Victims
by Janice Curry

We all remember that Hercule Poirot has a certain talent for the *mot juste* and that Jane Marple's eyes have, on occasion, twinkled. We remember the clues in their cases: for example, the monkey's paws in *Sleeping Murder*, or the burned piece of paper in *Murder on the Orient Express*. Without hesitation, we recall the murderers, usually with the footnote that we suspected them all along. Yet none of these would have any importance without the most crucial but most ignored characters in Christie's writings: the victims.

Dame Agatha, one of the last exponents of Victorian class values in a harsh modern world, was in one way, at least, a believer in equality. Rich man and poor man, viscount and charwoman, vicar's daughter and lady loanshark, all had something in common in Christie's world... all were victims of murder.

Who could be more different, one might ask, than wealthy Simeon Lee in *Murder for Christmas* and poor Henry Gascoigne in "Four and Twenty Blackbirds"? Or young aristocratic Viscount Cronshaw of *Poirot's Early Cases* and sixty-four-year-old widowed Mrs. McGinty, who was "in service" in *Mrs. McGinty's Dead*? Or Maggie Buckley, the unmarried daughter of a Yorkshire parson who succumbs in *Peril at End House*, and Marie Morisot, an elderly widow who is a moneylender to the upper class of England and France in *Death in the Air*? In Christie's books, riches (or poverty), title (or lack of one), station, position, employment, and connections present no barrier to the democratic bequest of her most questionable distinction, death by human agency rather than by natural cause.

Since her victims come from all walks of life, one would conclude that they would be recognizable and, therefore, memorable to the admirers of Christie's works. Not so. "Out of sight, out of mind" could serve as the epitaph for the entire group.

But not because their personalities are so shadowy that they fade before the page is turned. Linnet Ridgeway Doyle, one death in *Death on the Nile*, is not easily passed over. She's "a girl with golden hair and straight autocratic features — a girl with a lovely shape — a girl with millions." As her friend JoAnna Southwood says, "You've simply got *everything*. Here you are at twenty, your own mistress, with any amount of money, looks, superb health. You've even got *brains*!"

Miss Boyle, the second, "mouse" in "Three Blind Mice," is another victim with a strong personality. Being a "large, forbidding-looking woman with a resonant voice and a masterful manner," she bullies everyone with whom she happens to deal. At the moment, she is looking for a boardinghouse where there are "faded spinsters whom she could impress with her social position and connections, and to whom she could hint at the importance and secrecy of her war service" as a billeting officer. Although she snaps, ":I can look after myself," she makes a poor job of it. Still, a woman this aggressive is not easily overlooked.

Nor are the victims ignored because of their personal virtues. Both good and bad people are murdered in rather large numbers in Christie's books. Neither is especially well remembered. One could argue that oblivion is richly deserved

THEY GAVE THEIR LIVES FOR ART

by the rotters, bounders, and cads who populate some of the plots. No reader with anything that even approaches a rudimentary conscience can help but feel fulfilled when Oliver Costello of *Spider's Web* occupies an early grave. At twenty-seven he is already up to his neck in drug traffic. Neither does the demise of the wicked Mrs. Boynton of *Appointment with Death* suffocate the reader with sorrow. This wealthy American widow delights in cruelty for its own sake and has so terrorized her family that their main concern has become her care and feeding. Mr. Ratchett, an infamous American kidnapper, is a professional scoundrel and murderer. Six hours before he himself is murdered, he asks Poirot for protection. Astute Poirot sums up the case against him succinctly. "You do not understand, monsieur. If you will forgive me for being personal, I will not take your case because I do not like your face." Ratchett's death, which forms the central event of *Murder on the Orient Express*, certainly creates no shock waves of sympathy.

Not to be overlooked is that collection of scoundrels in hiding who form the corps of corpses in *Ten Little Indians*. General Macarthur, Philip Lombard, Vera Claythorne...all with little murders in their pasts. Anthony Marston, the first little Indian to meet retribution, looks like "a Hero God out of some Northern Saga" as he speeds around in his powerful car. He explains his transgressions by saying: "Must have been a couple of kids I ran over near Cambridge. Beastly bad luck ... Beastly nuisance." One can hardly mourn his passing.

Blackmailers in Christie are satisfying victims because they invariably have thrilling but short careers. Amberiotis, the sinister Greek of *The Patriotic Murders*, and Louise Bourget, the French maid of *Death on the Nile*, are rapidly dispatched, to no one's dismay.

Clearly, all these villainous victims deserve precisely what they get. Their murderers usher them into eternity and their readers dismiss them from their minds.

But consider the second and far larger group of victims. The worst that can be said about the men and women who fill this rank is that some are vacuous, silly, gullible, or shortsighted. Some, however, are sterling people brimful of virtue.

Of course, the victims cover a spectrum of humanity. To understand this, one would have to observe this spectrum as extending from Edna Brent in *The Clocks* to Elizabeth Margaret Temple in *Nemesis*. Brent is in her early twenties. She's plump, awkward, not bright but very well meaning, the incarnation of the poor fool caught in the cross fire. Temple, on the other hand, is tall, handsome, and athletic, a recently retired head-

mistress of an exclusive girls' school. She has a low, clear, incisive voice and is a sincere and intelligent person.

All manner of people fall between these two extremes. Rosemary Barton, who meets her Waterloo in *Remembered Death*, is a beautiful, vain, and wealthy socialite whose rather empty head solely anticipates approaching social occasions. George Barton, her husband, is a successful businessman whose main personality trait is that he doesn't have much of a personality. Yet, he's a kind man and deeply in love with his wife, which accounts for his willingness to follow her into death. Roger Ackroyd, of *The Murder of* fame, is

> an immensely successful manufacturer of wagon wheels. He is a man of nearly fifty years of age, rubicund of face and genial of manner. He is hand and glove with the vicar, subscribes liberally to parish funds (though rumor has it that he is extremely mean in personal expenditure), encourages cricket matches, Lads' Clubs, and Disabled Soldiers' Institutes. He is, in fact, the life and soul of the peaceful village of King's Abbot.

Sixtyish Sir Claud Amory, a respected scientist engaged in atomic research, forms the centerpiece of the play *Black Coffee*. Elderly Miss Emily French is "rich, eccentric, lives alone with one maid and owns no less than eight cats. She often speaks of being lonely and unhappy." However,

she is "a strong-willed old woman, willing to pay her price for what she wants." She pays dearly for companionship in *Witness for the Prosecution*. Rachel Argyle in *Ordeal by Innocence* is a middle-aged woman with inherited wealth who devotes herself to good causes, paticularly those having to do with children. Dr. John Christow, a successful Harley Street surgeon in *Murder after Hours*, is nearly forty, tall, blond, strikingly handsome. His vibrant, radiant air of vitality captivates all who meet him.

Granted, these victims might not have been paragons of humanity; still, by all standards, they are "good" people leading useful lives. They do not deserve execution. Why doesn't the irrationality of their deaths shock us into sympathy for them? Why are these poor folk so quickly forgotten as we readers rush to match wits with the sleuths?

Perhaps it is because we do not like to be reminded that we have no more guarantee of safety or sanity than they do. We, like Christie's victims, are all equal in our vulnerability. Rich or poor, well liked or hated, powerful or humble, good or bad, intelligent or foolish, young or old, male or female, no one is safe. Any given nasty fate lurks, if not under the bed, at least up the road about fifty feet or so.

It's no fun identifying with the losers.

The Miss Marple Double-Crostic

by Dale G. Copps

A Chair material .... $\overline{6}\ \overline{69}\ \overline{103}\ \overline{123}\ \overline{167}\ \overline{10}$

B Sir, in Ankara .... $\overline{23}\ \overline{106}\ \overline{160}\ \overline{37}\ \overline{98}\ \overline{138}\ \overline{43}$

C *Murder* ___. 3 wds .... $\overline{5}\ \overline{29}\ \overline{31}\ \overline{113}\ \overline{129}\ \overline{41}\ \overline{47}\ \overline{163}\ \overline{170}\ \overline{79}\ \overline{102}\ \overline{134}\ \overline{139}$

D Narrator of C: full name .... $\overline{56}\ \overline{76}\ \overline{85}\ \overline{125}\ \overline{143}\ \overline{179}\ \overline{187}\ \overline{192}\ \overline{196}\ \overline{25}$

E Ms. Protheroe of C .... $\overline{155}\ \overline{124}\ \overline{39}\ \overline{99}\ \overline{109}\ \overline{49}\ \overline{78}$

F Child's toy .... $\overline{2}\ \overline{120}\ \ \overline{7}\ \overline{145}$

G Festive occasion or a dire emergency .... $\overline{93}\ \overline{108}\ \overline{89}\ \overline{34}\ \overline{136}\ \overline{71}$

H Probable part of Miss Marple's walls .... $\overline{130}\ \overline{128}\ \overline{158}$

I Subject of D's last sermon .... $\overline{198}\ \overline{26}\ \overline{44}\ \overline{62}\ \overline{91}\ \overline{135}\ \overline{150}\ \overline{172}\ \overline{66}\ \overline{88}$

J Dress or an auto part .... $\overline{111}\ \overline{32}\ \overline{97}\ \overline{52}\ \overline{175}$

K "Cover her face; ___ dazzle...", from R: 2 wds ..... $\overline{1}\ \overline{54}\ \overline{48}\ \overline{21}\ \overline{35}\ \overline{80}\ \overline{116}\ \overline{95}$

L The grande dame, familiarly .... $\overline{13}\ \overline{171}\ \overline{28}\ \overline{181}\ \overline{176}\ \overline{74}$

M Young artist in C .... $\overline{110}\ \overline{122}\ \overline{20}\ \overline{197}\ \overline{40}\ \overline{162}\ \overline{58}$

N Brandy additive in R .... $\overline{117}\ \overline{183}\ \overline{174}\ \overline{151}\ \overline{90}\ \overline{169}$

O Rock; stone (Comb. form) .... $\overline{60}\ \overline{186}\ \overline{50}\ \overline{191}\ \overline{86}$

P It pervades the atmosphere of R .... $\overline{83}\ \overline{77}\ \overline{64}\ \overline{178}$

Q Immediately pending .... $\overline{127}\ \overline{72}\ \overline{101}\ \overline{149}\ \overline{133}\ \overline{188}\ \ \overline{19}\ \overline{166}$

R Miss M. said *"Let well alone"* in this novel: 2 wds. ... $\overline{24}\ \overline{55}\ \overline{63}\ \overline{73}\ \overline{148}\ \overline{168}\ \overline{180}\ \overline{11}\ \ \overline{12}\ \overline{17}\ \ \overline{70}\ \overline{121}\ \overline{132}\ \overline{193}$

S Take off .... $\overline{22}\ \overline{33}\ \overline{68}\ \overline{81}\ \overline{53}\ \overline{114}$

T Certify; demonstrate .... $\overline{156}\ \overline{126}\ \overline{144}\ \ \overline{4}\ \overline{118}\ \overline{152}$

U Castor, for one............................... $\overline{67}\ \overline{87}\ \overline{100}\ \overline{137}$

V Miss Marple's hobby in C: 2 wds .... $\overline{194}\ \ \overline{9}\ \ \overline{27}\ \overline{57}\ \ \overline{65}\ \overline{82}\ \overline{105}\ \overline{112}\ \overline{141}\ \overline{154}\ \overline{164}$

W Characteristic of a horse .... $\overline{59}\ \overline{140}\ \overline{161}\ \overline{61}\ \ \overline{14}\ \overline{42}$

X Cleft; break.................................. $\overline{115}\ \overline{117}\ \overline{184}\ \overline{96}$

Y Do ___ with .... $\overline{142}\ \overline{173}\ \overline{146}\ \overline{15}$

Z Medico in R .... $\overline{3}\ \ \overline{8}\ \ \overline{38}\ \overline{46}\ \ \overline{51}\ \overline{92}\ \ \overline{84}\ \overline{104}\ \overline{119}\ \overline{131}\ \overline{153}\ \overline{157}\ \overline{182}$

Z₁ Forthwith (Arch.) .... $\overline{30}\ \overline{107}\ \overline{36}\ \overline{45}\ \overline{94}\ \overline{16}\ \overline{190}$

Z₂ There's much of this (about *some*thing) in Christie ... $\overline{195}\ \overline{75}\ \overline{159}$

Z₃ Stir; drive out .... $\overline{165}\ \overline{189}\ \ \overline{18}\ \overline{147}\ \overline{185}$

1 K	2 F		3 Z	4 T	5 C	6 A									
7 F	8 Z	9 V	10 A	11 R		12 R	13 L	14 W							
15 Y	16 Z1	17 R		18 Z3	19 Q	20 M	21 K	22 S	23 B	24 R	25 D	26 I	27 V	28 L	29 C
30 Z1		31 C	32 J	33 S		34 G	35 K	36 Z1	37 B	38 Z	39 E	40 M	41 C	42 W	
43 B	44 I	45 Z1	46 Z	47 C	48 K	49 E	50 O		51 Z	52 J		53 S	54 K	55 R	56 D
57 V	58 M	59 W		60 O	61 W	62 I	63 R		64 P	65 V		66 I	67 U		68 S
69 A	70 R	71 G		72 Q	73 R	74 I	75 Z2		76 D	77 P	78 E	79 C	80 K		81 S
82 V	83 P		84 Z	85 D	86 O	87 U	88 I		89 G	90 N	91 I	92 Z		93 G	94 Z1
95 K	96 X		97 J	98 B	99 E	100 U	101 Q	102 C	103 A	104 Z		105 V	106 B	107 Z1	108 G
109 E	110 M	111 J		112 V	113 C	114 S	115 X	116 K		117 X	118 T		119 Z	120 F	
121 R	122 M	123 A	124 E	125 D	126 T	127 Q	128 H	129 C		130 H	131 Z		132 R	133 Q	134 C
135 I	136 G	137 U	138 B		139 G	140 W	141 V	142 Y	143 D		144 T	145 F		146 Y	
147 Z3	148 R	149 Q	150 I	151 N	152 T	153 Z	154 V		155 E	156 T	157 Z	158 H		159 Z2	160 B
	161 W	162 M	163 C	164 V	165 Z3	166 Q	167 A	168 R	169 N		170 C	171 L	172 I		173 Y
174 N	175 J	176 L		177 N	178 P	179 D	180 R	181 L	182 Z		183 N	184 X		185 Z3	186 O
187 D	188 Q		189 Z3	190 Z1		191 O	192 D	193 R		194 V	195 Z2	196 D	197 M	198 I	

(Solution to puzzle on page 308.)

Ordeal by Innocence (1958)

On the evening of November 9, 195–, between 7 and 7:30 P.M., Rachel Argyle was struck on the back of the head by a heavy iron poker in the study of her spacious home, Sunny Point. She was killed instantly. Shortly afterward her adopted son Jacko was arrested for the crime. He had come by earlier that evening, demanding money (which she refused) and vowing to get it "or else," according to other family members who had heard the row. The money, in marked bills, was in his pocket when he was picked up.

The trial was almost a formality. True, Jacko kept insisting that during the crucial half-hour he had been hitchhiking into nearby Drymouth, having been picked up just before seven by a dark car driven by a middle-aged man. Yet no trace of the man nor the car came to light, despite intensive publicity. It was, according to gossip, just another one of the lies Jacko'd been telling since childhood. Something in his genes, it was—God knows who his real parents were. The Argyles had given him everything, treated him like one of their own, forgiven him time and again, but in the end his bad blood had won out. Everyone knew Jacko was no good, violent, a liar, a thief. It wasn't hard to believe he was a murderer, too.

He received a life sentence but died in prison, of pneumonia, only six months later, which was poetic justice if anyone ever saw it. The rest of the Argyle family — husband Leo, and four other adopted children — tried to pick up the pieces of their lives. End of story.

Well, not quite. Dame Agatha was never one for the simple, straightforward tale. All of the foregoing — murder, trial, resolution — is prologue to the story that unfolds here, with its typical Christie twists and turns.

What more can happen to a crime already so strongly tied up? Only this: that two years after the fact, Dr. Arthur Calgary, just back from a trek to Antarctica, suddenly finds his memory returned after a period of partial amnesia — and what he remembers, as clearly as if it were yesterday, is giving young Jacko Argyle a ride into Drymouth that November 9, after having picked him up just before 7 P.M.

What a bombshell Calgary has dropped! Jacko, the scoundrel, is innocent after all! English Justice has condemned the wrong man!

A free pardon is duly issued by the home office — too late for Jacko, but at least his name is cleared. Calgary goes to Sunny Point to ease the guilt he cannot help but feel. He explains his failure to come forward in time: there was an accident, a concussion, days in the hospital, partial amnesia. Then slow recovery from the physical wounds, and finally departure with the scientific expedition to the South Pole. He had only just returned, and only then saw the picture in an old newspaper, the picture that brought it all flooding back.

Why are the Argyles so — shocked — at his news? They don't even seem glad to have the name cleared. In fact, they seem to wish he'd never come. Calgary is puzzled. He hadn't expected this.

It takes Hester, the second daughter, to point out the implications of Calgary's news: if Jacko is innocent, then one of the other members of the household is guilty. The front door was locked; whoever killed Rachel Argyle had been admitted by her, or entered with his own key. If it wasn't Jacko, then which one of them was it?

The local police reopen the case, though

"Of my detective books, I think the two that satisfy me best are *Crooked House* and *Ordeal by Innocence*." —*An Autobiography*

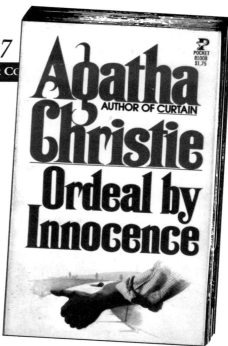

somewhat half-heartedly, but Calgary is obsessed and begins to investigate on his own. He *must* find the murderer, not so much to punish the guilty as to free the innocent, who are all now suffering under the terrible weight of suspicion that has fallen upon them all.

Rather ploddingly, Calgary digs in. His is hardly the inspired detection of a Hercule Poirot, nor the woolly sleuthing of a Jane Marple, but he makes progress in getting to know the family if nothing else. And one thing he discovers is that things are seldom what they appear to be, especially where murder is concerned.

The victim was rich, full of love, and generous to a fault. Rachel Argyle's main concern had always been children. She longed to have many herself, but when she couldn't she adopted five. Not blonde, blue-eyed babies, either, but older children, abandoned, mistreated, unwanted by anyone until she came along. Truly a selfless thing to do, and how she showered them with attention! She had fussed over every detail of their lives, always for their own good, of course — whether they liked it or not. She managed everyone that way.

But who would kill her? Would Mary, the oldest, who seemed so affectionate? When Mary's husband, Philip Durrant, became crippled by polio, Rachel insisted that they come to Sunny Point to live. But Mary wanted Philip to herself, and she had a habit of getting what she wanted....

Or Micky, who as a boy had cried so for the mother who had thrown him out? He never let Rachel know he hated her for taking him in; he could barely acknowledge it to himself. Micky wasn't even in the house on November 9; that is, he *said* he wasn't. He said he was out driving. Alone.

Tina is afraid. She loved her adopted mother, and she loves Micky too, but she thinks she heard him say something that night, and she wishes she hadn't. She hasn't even told the police she drove

over on November 9 — will they find out now? What other secrets will emerge?

Hester's world has collapsed. She knows her fiancé suspects her; he knows she had the opportunity. She hadn't really hated her mother, but it's hard to love someone who is always *right*! Can't parents realize that? Oh, why did Calgary have to come?

Leo Argyle has a different problem. He had respected his wife, but hadn't loved her for years. Her life, after all, was her children—nothing else. Now he is about to marry his long-time secretary, Gwenda Vaughan, but do they dare? Surely it will seem that they plotted to create their opportunity. The police, in fact, think it's the only real motive around.

Kirsten Lindstrom doesn't worry about motive. A loyal family retainer for eighteen years, she really brought the children up, and she loves the whole family — one of them, perhaps, too much. What does she know, and who is she protecting?

It isn't until still another murder has shattered the Argyle house that the terrible truth of Sunny Point emerges. It's a shame, in a way, that it has to be told. But it is the innocent, after all, who matter. Isn't it?

NORMA SIEBENHELLER

Verdict (1958)

Verdict is a rather serious drama from Agatha Christie and although it does hinge on murder there is nothing mysterious about the homicide. It is commited on stage, confessed to in the next scene, and the murderer is dead before you can refer to your playbill. It's what happens after that that is surprising.

But let's start at the beginning with books. Books? Yes, books all over the stage, overflowing from shelves onto chairs, rugs, couches, desks, and any other available surface in Professor Karl Hendryk's study. In fact it's a wonder that his invalid wife Anya manages to manuever her wheelchair through this dense terrain.

As the scene suggests, dedication to scholarship is Professor Hendryk's prime characteristic, though this is followed closely by sexual attractiveness to women. Both get him into trouble.

Rich, spoiled brat Helen Rollander wants nothing more than "private tutorials" with the learned professor and she's willing to have her Daddy pay whatever they cost. But Hendryk, sensing that Miss Rollander has something less than a calling for rigorous study, refuses. No amount of money can lure him from his principles; he'd rather give his time freely to a poor but true scholar.

When Rollander's protestations of earnestness get her nowhere she brings in the big guns. Sir William Rollander is the kind of fellow who thinks that "Every man has his price" is one of the Ten Commandments. And it may well be, for he has researched the resolute professor and indeed found out his price—the chance for his wife to be treated with a scarce new "miracle drug" that may cure her disseminated sclerosis.

So Helen Rollander gets a reading list and we are left wondering. Why would even an indul-gent father go to such lengths to satisfy his daughter's whim? Is his reason, "She's all I've got," really compelling enough?

Before we have a chance to ponder this, Helen is declaring her love for Professor Hendryk and her indifference to German grammar and syntax. He can't really be satisfied with his sick, deteriorating wife, can he? Hendryk tries to explain something about love and commitment but Helen is bored. Sensitivity is clearly not her strong suit.

Poor Professor Hendryk! All he's trying to do is lead a principled, intellectual life. Ideas are his supreme passion. Lisa Koletzky, the physicist hired by the Hendryks to take care of Anya (yes, that's right) paraphrases a quote from one of Hendryk's books to describe him. He believes, she says, that there *are* "fields of amaranth on this side of the grave" — amaranth being "an imaginary flower that never fades." Lisa, by the way, is also in love with him.

But Karl Hendryk's ideals also hurt the people around him. His decision to take in the family of a censured colleague caused him and his wife to be exiled from their native country. Anya remains bitter about this decision in which she had no part but which condemned her to a lonely life as an invalid far from friends, family, and comfort. She is severely depressed. She has no hope that the "miracle cure" will work on her; she even talks of suicide. As a precaution, her heart medication, which would be fatal if she took an overdose, is kept out of her reach.

When Anya Hendryk does die of an overdose of this medication it isn't suicide. It's the impetuous act of a thwarted Helen Rollander, clumsily made to look like suicide.

Miss Rollander has apparently never had occasion to notice that others may see things differently. She actually boasts to the grieving Hendryk that she murdered his wife so that now he can be "free" and their "love" can be consummated. She expects him to grasp her to his bosom in gratitude. He does indeed grasp her but it's around the throat and he stops just short of a second murder.

Still, he refuses to report Helen to the police, despite the urging of Lisa Koletzky and Anya's doctor, a family friend. It's a principle of his, mercy and compassion. Unfortunately the police don't share this principle. They arrest Lisa Koletzky for murder. All the circumstantial evidence in this case can be applied as easily to Lisa as to Helen. And there's one other thing. Mrs. Roper, the nosy housemaid, has overheard Hendryk declare his long-suppressed love for Lisa.

The Professor is incredulous. But this is *wrong*! Go ask Helen, I'm sure she'll tell you the truth. She has her faults but deep down . . . and so on. Very convenient story, say the police as they show Hendryk an item in his evening newspaper. "Sir William Rollander's only daughter, Helen Rollander, was the victim of a regrettable accident this morning. . . . She walked straight into the road without looking right or left and was killed instantly." Isn't that just like Helen!

And so the fate of Lisa Koletzky is left up to a jury of twelve men and women. What kind of people will they be? Will they only be interested in facts and principles or will they follow other dictates, of the heart perhaps? The verdict, on Lisa Koletzky and then on Karl Hendryk, is about to come in.

JAN OXENBERG

**"I still think it is the best play I have written, with the exception of *Witness for the Prosecution*. It failed, I think, because it was not a detective story or a thriller. It was a play that concerned murder, but its real background and point were that an idealist is always dangerous, a possible destroyer of those who love him — and poses the question of how far you can sacrifice, not yourself, but those you love, to what you believe in, even though they do not."
—An Autobiography

Cat among the Pigeons (1959)

Summer term at the Meadowbank School for girls, and a revolution in the Turkish city of Ramat—what do they have in common? Nothing, unless the connection is one conceived by Agatha Christie, who brings her familiar strategies as a master of suspense to *Cat among the Pigeons*. Twenty-seven characters combine in a sequence of events that involve a cache of precious gems, ill-timed blackmail, and someone with a predilection for murdering schoolmistresses. The intricacies of coincidence leave the reader, as usual, guessing at everyone for the villain.

Meadowbank is one of the finest schools in England, attended by royalty (including, of course, a young, precocious Turkish princess) and open to innovative educational techniques. Only recently, before the beginning of summer term, the distinctive Sports Pavilion had been completed. As opening day progresses, under the careful supervision of the school's articulate and capable founder, Miss Bulstrode, there is nothing to hint that death lies within the walls of that pavilion. Miss Bulstrode does experience a vague, undefined uneasiness, contrary to her usual decisive outlook. And there is the problem of Mademoiselle Blanche—not the most elegant of French teachers. There is Miss Springer, the tall, bony games mistress, who manages to annoy everyone with her blunt and aggressive behavior, and who is altogether too interested in the private lives of her colleagues. And Eileen Rich, the literature instructor, had taken a term of leave for illness, but actually was known to have spent her holiday in the Middle East.

Amidst the disciplined and dignified grounds of Meadowbank, there are intruders. We learn from the start that the young, attractive gardener, Adam Goodman, is a member of the CID. Miss Bulstrode's new secretary, Ann Shapland, has served in an executive capacity for government officials, but finds the atmosphere of the countryside interesting. Mrs. Upjohn, the impulsive mother of one of the students, is about to "take a bus through Anatolia," once her daughter is safely ensconced at the school. She chatters about her prospective trip to Miss Bulstrode on opening day, and happens to mention as well the excitement of her early intelligence work during the war. And suddenly, looking out the window of the headmistress's office, she exclaims in astonishment...

Meanwhile, in Ramat, a dedicated prince talks hurriedly to his old English school friend, Bob Rawlinson. Into Bob's hands the prince places a packet of jewels, the last legacy of a failed democracy. These, somehow, Rawlinson must get out of the country. The young man knows better than to walk around the beseiged city with a fortune in his possession. On impulse he visits his sister at her hotel, but she is not in. For twenty minutes Rawlinson stays in her room, unaware of the reflection in the closet mirror. He leaves, he thinks, unseen, placing the jewels somewhere in the belongings of Mrs. Sutcliffe and her daughter Jennifer. The two return to England for Jennifer's first day at Meadowbank, not realizing that a half-million pounds is at their fingertips.

To Mrs. Sutcliffe, it seems all too typical of modern life that thieves abound. Why, even the taxi driver looked too curiously at her luggage, and she was sure that man at the airport really did try to walk off with her green tote bag. The news that poor Bob has died in a plane crash in the Turkish mountains, in a vain effort to fly Prince Ali Yosuf out of Ramat, only confirms her belief that things just *aren't* what they used to be!

Back at Meadowbank's new sports pavilion, it is late, the beam of a flashlight appears on the walls, a shot rings out — and Miss Springer is murdered. Detective Inspector Kelsey has the distinct impression that almost anyone could have done it — certainly no one hesitates to tell him how unpopular the sportswoman had been. With due discretion, and a call to the home secretary by Miss Bulstrode, the affair is hushed up — the prestige of Meadowbank is secured. But later, at the same hour, in the same place, Miss Vansittart — likely successor to Miss Bulstrode — is found bludgeoned with a sandbag.

One student after another is removed from the school, Princess Shaista is kidnapped, and the prime suspect becomes the next victim!

Whodunit? The one relief comes from Julia Upjohn, whose mother is being pursued by intelligence officers while she tours Anatolia. Sharp-witted, it is Julia who discovers the jewels in a most extraordinary place, and who disappears from Meadowbank to head straight for London to seek the advice of the inimitable Hercule Poirot.

Even Monsieur Poirot is awe-struck as the child pours the flashing, multicolored stones before him. And it is Monsieur Poirot, twirling mustache, black patent shoes and all, who arrives at Meadowbank with the pertinent question: "And what about the knees of Mademoiselle Blanche?" From the beginning he knows exactly why Eileen Rich looks vaguely familiar to Jennifer Sutcliffe, only "not fat enough." Poirot ventures down to the village where a slightly mentally disturbed woman and her nurse greet him. They are the final clue. Except, that is, for Mrs. Upjohn, who must be found for the real killer to be identified efficiently.

Is it Miss Chadwick, for whom Meadowbank is a way of life, and whose affection for Miss Bulstrode is deep? Or could it be Miss Bulstrode herself, whose retirement is imminent? Perhaps it is the strange Mr. Robinson, who is definitely *not* English. And Miss Rich—they called her a little crazy. Is she? Or, among the 150 students, is there one twisted mind, some unpredictable and pathological source for the venom of the crimes committed? In *Cat among the Pigeons*, it is not only jewels that lead to murder.

REGINA SACKMARY

The Adventure of the Christmas Pudding (1960)

In the introduction to this short story collection, Agatha Christie wrote: "This book of Christmas fare may be described as 'The Chef's Selection.' I am the Chef!" She offers two "main courses" — "The Adventure of the Christmas Pudding" and "The Mystery of the Spanish Chest." The other four stories are a selection of appetizers. Of these six handpicked gems, five are Poirot's and one is Marple's.

The title story takes the cake, or should we say the pudding, for its re-creation of an old-fashioned English Christmas—snow and stuffing and logs crackling (merrily, of course) in the wide fireplace. But on Poirot's bed there's a sinister note: DON'T EAT NONE OF THE PLUM PUDDING ONE AS WISHES YOU WELL. What torture for Poirot, a gourmet to be reckoned with, when the pudding is brought in with glorious flames of blue and red rising around it. While the others cheer and ooh and ah, Poirot surveys his portion of pudding, baffled. How could his piece be any different from the others? He picks up his spoon and fork (brave Poirot) and gingerly takes a bite. Delicious! And another bite. And then he spies it—a foreign object in the pudding. He pries it out with his fork. It is a "bachelor's button," and this is just the traditional game of predictions.

"That means you're going to be a bachelor, Monsieur Poirot," explained Colin helpfully.
"That is to be expected," said Poirot gravely.

Soon after this, Diana finds a ring — predicting her early marriage; young Bridget gets the thimble — for a life as an old maid; and Colonel Lacy finds—good heavens, it is a bit of red glass, and it looks very much like a ruby. "How wizard it would be if it was *real*," says young Michael. How wizard indeed.

Poirot knows something only one (or two) of his fellow pudding eaters know: It seems that a young prince, soon to inherit the rule of his politically turbulent country, announced his betrothal to a proper, publicly approved woman of his same blood. With the wedding day set, he journeyed to England, ostensibly to have the royal ruby reset in appropriate modern settings by Cartier. But while on his last bachelor jaunt, he was most indiscreet and commited a few "follies of the pleasanter type." In a moment of weakness he was unwisely persuaded to allow a young lovely to wear his ruby for one evening. She got up to powder her nose and didn't come back. This was no time for scandal.

When Colonel Lacy picks the ruby out of his mouth during the Christmas dessert, Poirot takes a sharp look at the other guests.

The next morning Bridget, the fifteen-year-old, dark-haired cousin of Colin and Michael, is found in the snow in her scarlet pajamas, with a crimson stain on her white wrap. Poirot prys open the girl's stiff fingers and finds — the ruby. The family is stunned. They follow Poirot into the house for morning coffee, where Poirot reveals all.

The second story, "The Mystery of the Spanish Chest," is described by the author as a Hercule Poirot Special — the case he considers to be his best. Six long-time friends were to feast together at the home of well-to-do bachelor, Major Charles Rich: there would be a private buffet supper and dancing to records on the gramophone, good talk and good times, just like always. But at the last minute one of the six, a Mr. Clayton, was called to Scotland on urgent business. The disappointed Clayton rushed to Major Rich's home to explain why he'd be absent that evening, but Rich was not at home. Burgess, the manservant, granted Mr. Clayton permission to leave a note of apology in the living room.

The other five partied without Mr. Clayton that night and, as always, the party revolved around the magical Margharita Clayton, the young wife of the absent man. A good time was had by all.

However, when the manservant came to clean up the room the next morning, he made a gruesome discovery: a rusty, dark stain had grown on the light-colored rug by the old Spanish chest. He lifted the lid of the chest and was shocked to find the body of Mr. Clayton, who had been stabbed through the neck. Clayton was supposed to be in Scotland. What was he doing here in the Spanish chest?

It doesn't take long for the police to arrest Major Rich. He had apparently been in love with the enchanting Mrs. Clayton (as had most of the males in this circle of friends). He had probably come home on the afternoon before the party to find Mr. Clayton writing his note of apology. They had gotten into a quarrel; Rich had stabbed Clayton and stuffed him into the Spanish Chest and entertained his friends that evening. Simple. One thing bothers Poirot, however. He wonders how Major Rich could have slept so soundly that night without making at least an attempt to get rid of the body. Was Rich an imbecile, Poirot wonders?

The high-society partygoers are baffled too, including Margharita. Poirot visits her:

> She wore a close-fitting, high-necked gown of dull black that showed up the beauty of her body and the magnolia-whiteness of her skin.... There was about her a kind of medieval simplicity — a strange innocence that could be, Poirot thought, more devastating than any voluptuous sophistication.

Or, as fellow partyer Linda Spence explained:

> It was more than that. She had something. She would get men all het up — mad about her — and turn round and look at them with a sort of wide-eyed surprise that drove them barmy.

Finally, Christie serves her mystery gourmets the aged and seasoned wisdom of Miss Marple. When her visiting nephew, Raymond West, and a friend agree to witness the signing of a will at the old monster of a mansion known as "Greenshaw's Folly," Miss Marple gets worried. Old Miss Greenshaw has decided to leave everything to her housekeeper instead of to her nephew, the handsome actor Nat Fletcher. Just a few days later, in broad daylight, Miss Greenshaw screams, "He shot me...with an arrow." Sure enough, she is seen staggering away from the rockery where she'd been weeding, and an arrow is protruding from her breast. The witnesses find themselves locked into their respective rooms until the policeman frees them. Later, over the tea table, Miss Marple admonishes her nephew Raymond for joking about murder in general and this one in particular ... and goes on to explain, in accurate detail, the facts of the case.   PAM McALLISTER

Double Sin and Other Stories
(1961)

In this collection of eight fascinating short stories there are stolen gems, missing miniatures, a murder turned suicide—or was it vice versa?—and a strange doll with a will of its own. Among the crafty killers and evasive evil-doers, the incomparable Hercule Poirot, Christie's most suave sleuth, shares the spotlight with another of the grand gumshoes, Miss Jane Marple.

In "Sanctuary," Mrs. "Bunch" Harmon, the wife of the town vicar, enters the church in Chipping Cleghorn early one morning to find a shabby middle-aged man lying before the altar. Bunch soon realizes that the man has been shot.

As she checks his feeble and fluttering pulse, the stranger, in a quivering whisper, utters a single word, "sanctuary." A short while later he is dead.

The doctor and village sheriff are summoned, the man's belongings—meager as they are—are searched, but the mystery about who he was and what he was doing in the little church are still unresolved.

It's unresolved, at least, until Mrs. Harmon's godmother, the superb Miss Marple, is brought into the act. As easily as lighting a votive candle, Miss Marple learns the man's identity and discovers why sanctuary was of the utmost importance to him.

Still, in this series of Christie's shorter thrillers and mysteries, even the cool logic of Hercule Poirot or the detached brilliance of Jane Marple cannot unwind several of the Gordian knot-like plots.

In "The Dressmaker's Doll," for instance, the puppet doll, dressed in green velvet clothes with a painted mask of a face, sat sprawled upon a sofa in the fitting room of one of the finest *haute couture* shops in London.

Funny, several of the shop's rich clients remarked, how that doll looks almost alive. Funnier still was the fact that not one of the shop's employees, not even Alicia Coombe, the owner, could remember where the doll came from or how long it had been there. Stranger yet was that the little doll, made from scraps of velvet and silk, could almost always be found sitting in a different place each day.

No one, not a single customer or employee, would admit to changing its place. But each day would find the doll in a new spot: on the window seat, at the desk, on the couch. Even with all the doors locked and all the windows closed the doll would be moved.

Could this be someone's idea of a practical joke? Could the doll actually move by itself? Was it moved by a poltergeist? Were the absent-minded Alicia Coombe and her chief designer, Sybil Fox, going simultaneously mad?

Only the doll, and, as always, Agatha Christie, know for sure.

RICHARD REGIS

THE MARVELOUS MISS MARPLE
A Profile
by Norma Siebenheller

Her name is Jane Marple (Miss Marple, if you please) and she was born in 1928 at the age of seventy, give or take a few years. In the half-century since she has aged perhaps another twenty. She was—and she remains—very much the Victorial lady, "charming, very old-world," given to gossip and reminiscences as so many old ladies are, and appearing somewhat fussy, even fluffy, when viewed through younger eyes.

Physically she is a handsome woman—tall and straight ("I was taught to sit up"), very slim, with soft white hair neatly arranged in curls around her crinkled pink face. Her china-blue eyes are gentle and soft — "innocent," and yet sharply perceptive. "She has remarkable eyesight for her age," says one of the guests *At Bertram's Hotel*. "She sees everything."

Mostly, she sees evil wherever she looks. Beneath that placid exterior lies a deep-dyed cynic. "You always believe the worst," says Ruth van Rydock in *Murder with Mirrors*. "The worst is so often true," is Miss Marple's calm reply — as indeed she proved, in that case as in so many others she investigated.

Elsewhere she explains more fully: "People, I find, are apt to be far too trustful. I'm afraid I have a tendency always to believe the worst. Not a nice trait, but often justified by subsequent events."

But it takes more than a cynical mind to solve a murder, or every policeman would be an instant hero. "Believing the worst" is only the beginning

of Miss Marple's method. To understand the rest you must understand the little village of St. Mary Mead where she has spent all of her life.

St. Mary Mead is the quintessential English village. Far enough from London to be self-contained, it is small, intensely personal, yet it is home to a wide variety of people. All the ordinary tradesmen are represented, with their usual complement of shop assistants and delivery boys; there is a doctor—kindly, efficient, and always on call; there are assorted retired colonels and the like; and of course there is the vicar. All is as it should be in this best of all possible worlds.

It is a postcard scene, this little movie-set of a village. It is a quiet little backwater "where nothing ever happens," according to Miss Marple's worldly nephew Raymond West. Ah, but that is on the surface. Like Miss Marple herself, St. Mary Mead is sugar-coated with an outer shell of genteel respectability concealing a much more complex core. In the case of the little village, this core is downright iniquitous. Evil flourishes under the pastoral charm.

Being clear-sighted and realistic, Jane Marple doesn't miss a thing that goes on. She never has. "My hobby is studying people," she claims, "human nature, if you will." And human nature, she is quick to point out, is much the same the world over, whether in tiny St. Mary Mead or cosmopolitan London. Circumstances might be altered, externals may change, but people's reac-

THE MARVELOUS MISS MARPLE

tions will tend to be the same, given the same set of human passions.

And so for every event in her modern-day life, Miss Marple can find a village parallel—and it is this ability to draw analogies from one to the other that is the secret of her success.

"It's really what people call intuition," she explains to Griselda, the vicar's wife in *Murder at the Vicarage*. "Intuition is like reading a word without having to spell it out. A child can't do that, because it has had so little experience. But a grown-up person knows the word because he's seen it before. You catch my meaning?"

In other words, if a thing reminds you of something else, it is probably the same kind of thing. The only catch is in tracing the proper parallels, and in extracting the proper inferences from them once you have placed them side by side.

Jane Marple can do it all day. Eighty-plus years of gossip, decades of absorbing every action and reaction of the selfish, fearful, greedy, passionate, spiteful, fiery—i.e., normal—inhabitants of St. Mary Mead have given her a store of similes to draw on to the end of her days. Her well of information has never gone dry, and if she could live yet another fifty years she would still not deplete it.

Though basically she changes but little over the years, there are some differences between the Jane Marple of 1970's *Nemesis* (the last of her adventures to be written, though not the last published) and the Jane Marple of 1930's *Murder at the Vicarage*. These changes represent both the natural passage of time and the change in Christie's own perceptions of her popular heroine.

To begin with, the lady gets more likeable as she gets older. In her first appearance she is described as "the worst cat in the village"—a gossiping, meddling old busybody who spends most of her time wandering around with binoculars pretending to be looking at birds. She sees, instead, every last hitch and bump of the village

machinery; she hears every whistle and whine, and she remembers it all.

Though at the beginning she is new to murder, she already has a reputation among the locals of being perceptive and shrewd. "She's got an uncanny knack of being always right," declares the chief constable. And of course she is right, in the end, about the murder at the vicarage, and about all the other threads of the intricate web that has tightened around St. Mary Mead. All traceable to human nature—base, unchanging human nature.

In subsequent adventures, however, the nasty old cat retreats to the background and a more gently eccentric personality takes her place. People realize, as it were, that there is no malice in her, that though she always suspects the worst, she hopes for the best. In her heart she is truly fond of people (why else study human nature so intensively?) and wishes them well.

"People call her a scandalmonger, but she isn't really," says her friend Mrs. Bantry, in whose library a body was found—giving rise to *A Body in the Library* — "Jane Marple's really a remarkable woman."

Remarkable she is. While it is easy to dismiss her, as many new acquaintances do, as "that dithery old maid who is all caught up in her knitting," one cannot dismiss the fact that it is she, and not the local police, who sorts out the hidden identities and solves the baffling library crime. And all on the basis of a broken fingernail.

It is tempting to suspect that the knitting, that everpresent flurry of needles and wool, is a prop that Miss Marple uses to disguise her true personality. Not a bit of it. This *is* her true personality. She is straight out of the nineteenth century, spinsterish, proper, prim. She is a maiden lady, and a maiden lady of her day did certain things: she went to church (without necessarily being religious); she gossiped; she gardened; and she did needlework — embroidery or knitting.

Who ever wore all the fleecy scarves and sweaters that emanated from Miss Marple's needles, however, is a mystery that not even Agatha Christie cared to solve. There were always cousins and old school chums and nephews and, later, grand-nieces — not to mention all the various offspring of the kitchen maids and daily women who always managed to get paid, no matter how precarious the state of her finances might be.

Though there are a swarm of peripheral relatives, there is only one who really counts: Raymond West. He is the kind of nephew every elderly spinster ought to have. Generous and kind, genuinely fond of his "daffy Aunt Jane," he calls and visits with heartwarming regularity and even, in later years, sends the old girl off on several expensive holidays. He is miraculously unencumbered with parents or other hangers-on — there is only his painter-wife, Joan, who is as much of a gem as he is. He is also, thanks to some of his best-selling novels dealing with undisclosed but unpleasant subjects, impressively wealthy. Perhaps he is a bit stiff and lacking in humor, but one can't have everything. He does, admittedly, see his old aunt through a gauzy film of unreality — perpetually repeating, for example, that she is leading a dull and uneventful life in a dull and uneventful little town, even after all the murders and intrigues have been perpetrated and solved, book after book.

Her name and her unorthodox methods are quite well known in a dozen circles outside St. Mary Mead by the time she manages to get in on the scene in *A Murder Is Announced*. "A good deal older now" (it was, after all, 1950, some two decades after her first appearance) she manages to become "quite flustered, all incoherent with delight" when introduced to Detective Inspector Craddock. Again, as with the knitting, one might expect this to be a ploy, part of a caricature she is creating for herself, not a true reaction at all. But no; there is no artifice here. She is, remember,

very old, ancient, really; her world is fast disappearing, and her manners and mannerisms are relics of a distant day. She may understand the seamy side of life, but she blushes when introduced to a man. She is still, at times, that shy Victorian maiden she was so long ago. She may be out of date, but she is authentic.

Does the Inspector believe her to be "completely ga-ga?" No matter. He'll come around, when she unravels it all in the end, and she will have won another fan.

The passage of time is a problem when you start at age seventy. "I cannot remember ... what suggested to me that I should select a new character — Miss Marple — to act as the sleuth of the story *Murder at the Vicarage*," Dame Christie said in her *Autobiography*. "Certainly at the time I had no intention of continuing her for the rest of my life." If she had, she continued, she would have made her much younger, so that the aging process could have been a natural one.

Yet, on reflection, this would not have been possible. A different character would have emerged, of course, a young woman with fifty years of life ahead of her, and that woman could not have been Miss Marple. Miss Marple had to be old — age is a necessary part of her, not just an incidental fact.

Think a moment on her method — analogies between the present and the past, based on a long and thorough study of human nature. By its very nature this method would be ineffective in one who is young. There would be no rich past to draw upon, no ample store of incidents to pull out and examine. How can a young woman of twenty know the full range of village life? How can she draw parallels from experiences she has not had?

By 1959, in *What Mrs. McGillicuddy Saw!*, Jane Marple is "elderly and frail," forbidden by her doctor from working in her beloved garden. This restriction is very distressing to a woman who has

THE MARVELOUS MISS MARPLE

always been active. She really isn't content with "a little light pruning" but hasn't much choice. She keeps up her interest by following old Edwards about, making sure the sweet peas are properly trenched and the iris divided. Then comes a murder to solve, and she shows that whatever weakness has afflicted her body, it hasn't blunted her needle-sharp mind.

But she feels her age in still other ways. The post-war changes that come to every corner of the world come, too, to St. Mary Mead. The picturesque village remains, but beyond the vicarage gates, where once she saw cows at pasture, Miss Marple now sees the semi-attached, shuttered, fenced, and gated dwellings known to old-timers as the Development. And instead of familiar faces in the village shops there are strangers, people with no ties to the town. Even the shops themselves have changed. St. Mary Mead has a supermarket!

It is not what it once was—but then, what is? She ponders the question of where the blame lies, but having a clear line to reality she is quick to realize the truth: "What one really meant was the simple fact that one was growing old."

There may be a little of the voice of her creator in those lines as well. She, too, was growing old.

But neither is finished, not by a long shot. More crimes come Miss Marple's way, and when her computerlike mind alerts itself to a problem, the body finds a way of following.

So it is that she is able to visit Bertram's Hotel (nephew Raymond West paid for it, of course) and later take a trip to the Caribbean. It is even arranged—through a very mystifying bequest—that she journey to the Midlands on a chartered bus tour, incidentally uncovering murder and mayhem along the way. When it is over, she is £20,000 richer (the aforementioned bequest) and finally able to enjoy some special treats quite apart from the indulgences of nephew West. It must be

gratifying after all those years of penny pinching, and West, for all his kindness, must be rather glad for her too. Gifts are so much more enjoyable when one doesn't really *need* them.

A question that inevitably arises in any discussion of Christie and Marple is, were they one and the same? Was Miss Marple an autobiographical character in any way?

Not at all. Aside from the fact that they were both, in recent years, old ladies with white hair, there was no similarity. Miss Marple was always old, whereas Dame Agatha was quite in the prime of life when she created her heroine. Then, too, the author was no spinster: her two marriages spanned nearly her entire adult life.

Like most good fictional characters, Jane Marple is a blend of many things—bits and pieces of real people, with a large dollop of imagination thrown in. If there is any link at all it is with Christie's own grandmother, who "though a cheerful person, always expected the worst of everyone and everything and was, with almost frightening accuracy, usually proved right." Miss Marple is, however, "much more fussy and spinsterish than my grandmother ever was." She is in many ways a composite of all the Victorian ladies Christie may have known as a girl, though a little slimmer, no doubt, than most, and perhaps a tad more eccentric.

When finally Jane Marple's career comes to its close, the end, it should be emphasized, is very upbeat. Death does not overtake her as it does Poirot and even her frailty seems to evaporate. She *runs* up a flight of stairs to save the young wife in *Sleeping Murder*—this, after pulling some insistent bindweed from the perennial border, her first gardening effort in years.

Perhaps that £20,000 has rejuvenated her. In any case, she is clearly more agile and energetic than she has been for years—it seems unlikely, somehow, her long, illustrious career is over.

MARGARET RUTHERFORD
The Universal Aunt
by Michael Tennenbaum

There are two thoughts on the casting of Margaret Rutherford as Miss Marple that strike one immediately:

1. She is totally wrong for the role, and
2. She is perfect. As anything.

So perfect, in fact, as to induce some overzealous publicity person from MGM to produce bald-faced statements to the effect that Agatha Christie personally chose Miss Rutherford for the part and that the actress was the inspiration for the character in the first place, not Miss Christie's grandmother, as the author had always insisted. No doubt this well-intentioned soul had never picked up a Marple mystery or else he would certainly have noticed the author's description of the character as somewhat tall and thin, two qualities one does not usually associate with Margaret Rutherford, whom Brendall Gill once described as "plump, ramshackle, and yet quick-moving." Not exactly the same person. The mystery, then, is how this woman came to be associated with the famous fictional sleuth, and that story involves one of show business's most cherished legends, the Overnight Success.

Some overnights are longer than others. In Miss Rutherford's case, it took forty-six years. Born on May 11, 1892, her mother died when she was three and the child was sent to live with two aunts. These women were fascinated by the theater and satisfied this desire by writing and producing plays for children. Little Margaret enjoyed these theatricals immensely and for one role, the Bad Fairy, received her first rave review when a professional actress who had witnessed her performance remarked that "the child has great his-

trionic power." This comment should have solidified her desire to pursue a stage career, but it was not to be. Instead, Miss Rutherford went on to study music and became a piano teacher, travel-

MARGARET RUTHERFORD

ing on her bicycle from lesson to lesson. But in her heart, she still cherished the world of the theater. In her free time she acted with an amateur dramatic company, read poetry to servicemen during World War I, and studied elocution with an old Shakespearean actor. She became so accomplished in the speech arts that she was able to teach elocution as well as piano.

It was not until 1925 that she was able to pursue her true goal. Inheriting a small sum from one of her aunts allowed Miss Rutherford to give up teaching, at least for a while. She managed to get an introduction to Andrew Leigh, who was the director of the Old Vic School, one of the most famous acting academies in England. He arranged an audition with the founder of the Old Vic, the great Lillian Bayliss. The reading was not entirely successful and Miss Bayliss suggested that perhaps the young woman might try her hand at directing or producing.

But Miss Rutherford was not to be deterred; she pleaded for a chance and Bayliss agreed. Margaret Rutherford became a student at the Old Vic at the age of thirty-three. During this time she watched attentively and even had a number of small roles in the productions. But when her student term expired, no one offered her a contract.

It was back to piano lessons.

Two years later, she made the attempt again. Miss Rutherford began the familiar practice known to actors as making the rounds, which involves knocking on producers' doors and requesting an interview. One of these interviews went so badly (unsure of her looks, she had overdone her makeup and wound up looking like a tart) that she immediately wrote a note of apology and touched the heart of producer Nigel Playfair, who, true to his name, gave her another chance and then cast her as an understudy in the play *A Hundred Years Old*. This opportunity (the Big Break, as it's usually called) led to a number of other roles with other repertory companies and Miss Rutherford gained a reputation as a reliable

character actress. She was now well on her way.

Miss Rutherford made her debut in the West End, London's equivalent of Broadway, in 1933 when she was forty-one years old. Her performance as a cleaning woman in *Wild Justice* went unnoticed by the critics, but her next role in a production of Ibsen's *The Master Builder* gained some favorable mention. After a successful few months as a troublesome aunt in *Hervey House*, Miss Rutherford gained the public's attention in *Short Story*, written by Robert Morley (who was to be her co-star almost thirty years later in *Murder at the Gallop*). But it was not until 1938 that Miss Rutherford received the attention that qualifies one as a "star." The play was *Spring Meeting*, a comedy about impoverished gentlefolk in Ireland. Critic Ivor Brown described her performance as "astonishing." Then followed a three-year period during which Miss Rutherford played her most famous roles (besides Miss Marple, of course): Miss Prism in John Gielgud's production of *The Importance of Being Earnest* (1939), the grim Mrs. Danvers in *Rebecca* (1940), and the delightfully zany Madame Arcati in Noel Coward's *Blithe Spirit* (1941). When she repeated this last role for the movie in 1945, her success spread worldwide. Her place in the theatrical pantheon was secure.

Despite her stage work in several countries, Margaret Rutherford is best known outside the British Isles for her work in motion pictures. In March of 1960, Metro-Goldwyn-Mayer purchased for almost $3 million the rights to most of Agatha Christie's already-published works, the original intention being some kind of television series. But the studio controlled a motion picture facility in Borehamwood that employed contract technicians, and a series of low-budget theatrical features was planned instead. The first was to be *Meet Miss Marple*, an adaptation of *What Mrs. McGillicuddy Saw!* and the lead role was offered to Miss Rutherford, who turned it down. She had serious objections about the light-hearted treat-

ment of the subject matter. "Murder, you see, is not the sort of thing I could get close to," she said. But more realistic reasoning prevailed — Miss Rutherford was experiencing serious financial problems caused by England's lopsided tax structure—and she accepted the role. She grew to like her character and described her as "a dear spinster lady, very much like myself to look at. She is eccentric but her passion for justice is very real." The film, retitled *Murder She Said*, was released in 1961 as a standard second feature in England but was marketed as an art film in this country, which was experiencing an interest in British eccentricity. The series was under way.

The next two films were strange choices, as they were based on novels featuring Hercule Poirot. Both *Murder at the Gallop* (1963) and *Murder Most Foul* (1964) were well received by critics, but their public seemed to be dwindling. By *Murder Ahoy* (1964), an original screenplay by two writers who had adapted two of the earlier films, interest in the series had waned to the point where the fifth project, to be based on *The Body in the Library*, had to be abandoned. But the four completed Miss Marple films, buoyed considerably by the fact that Miss Rutherford won an Academy Award for her performance in *The VIPs* in 1963, were to be small treasures to her fans.

One hears that life on a movie set is rather dull, but this cannot be said of making a film with Margaret Rutherford. A spry seventy during the filming of *Murder Ahoy*, she would entertain the cast and crew during breaks by dancing the jig. When the script of *Murder at the Gallop* indicated Miss Marple doing a waltz at a club dance, she asked director George Pollock if she could substitute something a bit more modern and he consented; Miss Marple doing the Twist is something to see. For a fencing scene in *Murder Ahoy*, she again insisted on a touch of realism—her fencing abilities had to be convincing. Rupert Evans, who had taught the art of fencing to the

swashbuckling stars, was engaged to coach Miss Rutherford, who performed admirably.

Perhaps the most touching aspect of the filming of the Marple series was the presence of Stringer Davis in the role of Jim Stringer, Miss Marple's steadfast companion, a role created specifically for these films. Mr. Davis was Miss Rutherford's husband, best friend, and biggest fan. Every morning before shooting began he would rise early, prepare breakfast (tea), and then go wake his wife (who would usually sleep through the clock's alarm). Together they would rehearse the lines for the scenes to be shot that day, making cuts or breaking up speeches to make memorization easier. On the set he saw to it that she was always well supplied with her favorite ginger chocolates or peppermint creams. He made sure that her lunch—soup, cheese, and biscuits—was sent to her dressing room. Then he would spend some time personally answering her fan mail because it was his wife's opinion that those who cared enough to write deserved a reply. The magic of this special relationship is evident in their scenes together in the series. When Miss Marple turns down the marriage proposals of James Robertson Justice in *Murder She Said* or Robert Morley in *Murder at the Gallop*, we know why.

The last years of her life were a mixture of the good and the bad. In 1970 she was honored when Queen Elizabeth declared her Dame Margaret Rutherford. She was suffering in those years from a series of accidents and a long illness, during which she was visited on her deathbed by the prime minister of England. She passed away in 1972.

Perhaps we remember her best the way Leslie Halliwall describes her in *The Filmgoer's Companion:* "Inimitable, garrulous, shapeless, endearing British comedy character actress, who usually seemed to be playing somebody's slighty dotty spinster aunt." It mattered very little that she really didn't resemble Agatha Christie's grandmother; she *is* Miss Marple.

The Pale Horse (1961)

While walking down a dark street one foggy night, Father Gorman, a Catholic priest, was knocked on the noggin with a cosh. Who would kill a poor, well-liked priest, you say? The culprit, whoever it was, searched the priest inside out, even tearing his already ragged cassock. But the perpetrator did not check the poor father's shoes — therein lies the plot.

While London's Divisional Detective Inspector Lejeune sets out to find out why Father Gorman was nixed, our narrator-historian, Mark Easterbrook, and his sidekick, Ginger Corrigan, try to find out what's going on in that pub-turned-witches' haven, the Pale Horse, a house located in the village of Much Deeping. The two are positive that the three women who live there have something to do with some very unusual circumstances that might be connected with Father Gorman's death.

Mark Easterbrook is at a loss when he gets on the trail of a crime scheme too diabolical to mention here, and no one seems to take him seriously. He persuades Ginger to help him, and the two try to piece together the whys and the whos in this seemingly "perfect crime" operation. With Inspector Lejeune's brilliant mind and the determination of Mark and Ginger, the identity of the priest murderer and master criminal cannot be far behind.

We follow the three as they sift through clue after clue—and there aren't many: a list of names, a man following the father who couldn't have been following him, a witch who can will death,

and a description that seems to be too good to be true.

The cast of characters includes, in addition to Lejeune, Mark, and Ginger:

Hermia Redcliffe, the "damnably dull" intellectual of the bunch

Poppy Stirling, a semicomatose member of the Chelsea set — she knows more than she thinks she knows

Zachariah Osborne, a gentleman with a strong sense of civic duty

Rhoda and Colonel Despard, who'd like to know more than they're told

Rev. Caleb Dane Colthrop, who knows not

Mrs. Dane Colthrop, who knows more than she is telling her husband

James Corrigan, police surgeon

Mr. Venables, mystery man

C.R. Bradley, money man.

And the three Witches:

Thyrza Grey, who doesn't believe all she reads about witchcraft but practices it

Sybil Stamfordis, whose power puts her in another world

Bella, the cook who uses her crocks for something other than soup.

Is it possible that some fiendishly clever mind has found the ultimate murder weapon? Can it be that witchcraft has a hand in the goings-on at the Pale Horse? Or is it more likely that Father Gorman's murder occurred to give Inspector Lejeune's extraordinary deductive powers exercise?

RUTH FARMER

"Shortly afterwards I finished my instructional course; but I often wondered about Mr. P. afterwards. He struck me, in spite of his cherubic appearance, as possibly rather a dangerous man. His memory remained with me so long that it was still there waiting when I first conceived the idea of writing my book *The Pale Horse* — and that must have been, I suppose, nearly fifty years later."—*An Autobiography*

The Mirror Crack'd (1962)

(Alternate title: *The Mirror Crack'd from Side to Side*)

English literature buffs might recognize the obscure title, *The Mirror Crack'd*, right away. It is a phrase from a Tennyson poem:

> Out flew the web and floated wide;
>   The mirror crack'd from side to side;
> "The curse is come upon me," cried
>   The Lady of Shalott.

This poem really doesn't have anything to do with the story, though it is repeated at regular intervals throughout the book to describe Marina Gregg's face minutes before her murder occurs. Even the Chief Inspector uses this literary description unblushingly as if everyone in the community understands what the passage means. But then, St. Mary Mead is that sort of place.

It is the sort of place where Mrs. Bantry, the reliable, loving gossip, can find relief from the exasperating task of flower arranging in the visit of Chief Inspector Craddock to discuss murder.

It is also the sort of place where one's secretary can recognize the scent of cyanide (alas, a split second before she dies of the whiff). Nevertheless she does recognize it, something one does not expect of any but the most discriminating.

All of this is quite excusable because we are happy to be here. St. Mary Mead feels comfortable with its neat gardens, its afternoon teas, its small-town grapevine leading right to Miss Marple's door. And such an aesthetic murder it is . . .

Marina Gregg, an American beauty with high cheekbones, is remembered by her fans for her delicate and moving portrayal of Mary Queen of Scots. She and her director-husband, hideously ugly we are told, have just moved into a Victorian mansion in St. Mary Mead. One afternoon the glamorous Americans open their elaborately remodeled home for a town fund-raising event, and Marina and husband graciously invite a select group of guests "upstairs" for cocktails.

One of the guests is a jolly gusher named Heather Badcock, a conscientious and highly principled clubwoman who is, nevertheless, entirely thoughtless. When she is greeted by the gracious Marina at the top of the stairs, Mrs. Badcock blabbers on and on about having met Marina about eleven or twelve years earlier at another celebration where she had asked for and received Marina's autograph. Mrs. Badcock had gotten out of bed with . . . an illness . . . for that memorable event, a fact she proudly uses to convey her stoical devotion to the star.

At this moment in Mrs. Badcock's exuberant rambling, the gracious Marina suddenly stares beyond the fawning fan, her face frozen with the aforementioned literary look, like "the mirror crack'd from side to side."

But read carefully here. As the scene is being first described by Dame Agatha, Tennyson's line is *not* used. Instead the question is ever so cleverly phrased, "What on earth could she be seeing that gave her that basilisk look?"

Basilisk? The resourceful reader would here put down the book and run for a *Bulfinch's Mythology* to read that a basilisk is a legendary reptile whose look "caused an instant horror which was immediately followed by death."

Quite true, in this case. But back to the story. Marina, with the basilisk look, stares past Mrs. Babcock in the direction of the guests on the stairway who are still waiting to be received. Her line of vision also encompasses the copy of Bel-

lini's painting *Laughing Madonna*, a cheery, religious portrait of the Holy Mother holding up her Holy Child. Within moments, the once-again gracious Marina recovers her senses, calls for drinks, and goes on to greet the other guests.

The guests lined up on the stairway include Marina's first husband (whom she does not now recognize, though he is not disguised) and her adopted daughter, a famed society photographer (whom Marina also does not recognize). With such a memory one wonders how Marina ever learned her lines.

The gushy Mrs. Badcock proves to be a rather clumsy guest who disrupts the occasion when she spills her daiquiri (which her husband quaintly pronounces "dickery") all over herself and the movie star. Marina, ever gracious, immediately offers Mrs. Badcock her own untouched drink. Moments later Mrs. Badcock is dead of a lethal does of a rather common tranquilizer.

It does not take long for those investigating the murder to realize that Mrs. Badcock probably "got hers," we might say, by accident. She had been annoying but hardly significant enough in anyone's eyes to be the object of intended murder. Furthermore, Marina had passed her own drink to the clumsy woman, which would inevitably lead to the conclusion that the poisoned potable had obviously been intended for Marina's lips.

At this realization, the list of suspects grows. Could the murderer have been the steel-jawed secretary, Ella Zielinsky, who's madly in love with Marina's husband? Had she tried to poison Marina and, by a quirk of fate, wound up murdering an obnoxious but innocent woman?

Or was it Lola Brewster, whose husband left her to become Marina's third spouse? Lola had once promised, conveniently aloud, "I don't care how long I wait, years if need be, but I'll get even with her in the end." But, as Lola charmingly explained, "One's supposed to say things like that ... Oh, really, Inspector, I do think that you're being very, very silly."

Speaking of spouses, could it have been Mrs. Badcock's milktoast husband who — are you ready—turns out to be none other than Marina's first husband, the one she fails to recognize at the party?

And what of Marina's own apparently adoring husband? As Miss Marple says so convincingly, husbands are often the obvious suspects, and "the obvious is so often right."

But then there's the suspicious Margot Bence, the society photographer who, as it turns out, is one of Marina's long-neglected adopted children. She, too, speaks bitterly of Marina. "Why shouldn't I hate her? She did the worst thing to me that anyone can do to anyone else. Let them believe that they're loved and wanted and then show them it's all a sham."

Speaking of children, they pop up in the oddest ways. Marina can't bear the mention of them. It seems that after she adopted three of them, she got pregnant, as so often happens. Because she was a star, the media played up her approaching motherhood with a capital *M*. And then the child was born, as they say in St. Mary Mead, "batty," and Marina suffered a long emotional breakdown. That was eleven years ago.

Get the ... picture?

PAM McALLISTER

Rule of Three (1962)

In 1962 Agatha Christie presented three one-act plays in London—*The Rats, The Patient,* and *Afternoon at the Seaside* — under the comprehensive title *Rule of Three.* They contain the usual Christie ingredients: beautiful women, handsome men, jealous wives, dowdy spinsters, ambitious lovers, vengeful friends. But in this diminished dramatic form the dish is never quite as satisfying as in her longer, meatier meals. There is simply not the time to pile clue upon misleading clue so that now this character, now that becomes the Most Likely Suspect. These one-act plays are like tasty hors-d'oeuvres, exquisitely crafted, easily digested, and guaranteed to whet one's appetite for the main Christie oeuvre.

We begin with *The Rats,* which takes place in the Michael Torrances' flat in Hampstead. The Torrances are having a party and Sandra Grey, a smart thirty-year-old woman, "conscious of her own sensual attractions," is the first to arrive. "It's always so shaming to be early," she says to Jennifer Brice; especially weeks early. The Torrances, Miss Brice informs her, are not in. This would appear to be somewhat of an understatement, seeing as how the Torrances are, in fact, in the south of France. Miss Brice herself has just dropped in to feed the parakeet.

Jennifer Brice is one of those women who would rather feed gossip than birds, and she is dying to know whom Sandra is meeting today. Sandra is dying to know who invited her to one of the worst parties of the year. Then handsome and ambitious David Forrester shows up for the party as well. Sandra is surprised. David is surprised. Jennifer is not surprised. "Give my love to John, won't you?" she calls sweetly as she trots off.

Who's John? Sandra's husband, of course.

David and Sandra are not so surprised that they don't fall passionately into each other's arms once the coast is clear. But who has tricked them into coming here? Haven't they been careful? "Somebody always knows," says Sandra bitterly.

Perhaps it was Alec Hanbury who invited them. He shows up for the party as well, but then starts exhibiting some rather strange behavior. Of course he is, as they said in the sixties, "a pansy type," and that might explain it. But it is no secret he was very upset when Sandra's first husband died in that avalanche in Cornwall. He didn't seem to think it was an accident that befell his best friend. Got quite depressed, it seems. He's perfectly cheery today, however, remarking of the bare, cold flat: "What a horrible place to be shut up in if you couldn't get out!" Whereupon he promptly exits and locks the door behind him.

David and Sandra are now trapped—like rats, one might almost add. But why? Could it have anything to do with John's dead body lying inside that Damascus bride chest? (The Torrances were globe-trotters.) Or with the Kurdish knife that killed him hanging on the wall, the knife Alex entices them both to handle and then drops over the balcony?

We could tell you the answers here and not spoil a thing. Unlike any other Christie play, *The Rats* has no surprises, no dramatic twists at the end. So we could tell you. But we won't.

Much more satisfying dramatically is *The Patient,* where the murderer is not discovered until the last line of the play. And as usual, in the best Christie tradition, it is the least likely character of all.

We find ourselves this time not in the usual study or library, but in a hospital ward, where Jenny Wingfield lies paralyzed after falling from her balcony. It looks like a suicide attempt, but Inspector Cray is not satisfied, and he calls the family in for "a little experiment." Naturally, when a Christie family gathers in the same room, several closeted skeletons begine to rattle.

Helping shake those bones is Dr. Ginsberg, who has hooked Jenny up to a new electrical gadget. It seems she is not totally paralyzed, but has some slight movement in her right hand, just enough to press a rubber bulb which activates a little red light. One for yes, two for no, and away we go on a merry mystery ride.

The questions are asked, something like this: "You rested a little in your room after lunch, then you awoke and went out on the balcony?" One. "You lost your balance and fell?" Two. (Everybody gasps.) "Then what happened?—Let us go through the alphabet: *A* ... etc ... *P*—" One. "*P*? You mean, someone 'pushed' you?" One. (More gasps.) "Someone attempted to *M*—" One. "*U*." One. "*R*—" One. "To murder you?" One. (General confusion.) "And the name of this someone? *A* ... *B*—" One. "The name begins with *B*?" One. Then several lights in succession.

"Doctor, she's collapsed," notes the nurse.

"It's no good," Dr. Ginzberg replies, "I daren't go on." His admission relieves everyone, especially the murderer.

B. Well, that could stand for Jenny's husband, Bryan, quite a one for the ladies. "Bowled them over like ninepins" is the way Inspector Cray puts it. With the money Bryan would inherit from Jenny, he could become quite athletic. He's been intimate with his secretary already. "That was over ages ago," he swears, but then how can we trust her? Her name is Brenda.

Then there's Jenny's brother, William. He's a bit of a playboy, and you know how they are about always needing family funds. Big sister had

threatened to cut him off. "But she always called me William," he says smugly. Couldn't poor Jenny be forgiven for nicknaming, however, what with the whole alphabet to get through each time, and those two unparalyzed muscles in her right hand having to bear all the burden?

About the only safe one appears to be Jenny's sister, Emmeline. She's not the most popular of people. "It's women like you that write anonymous letters. Just because no man has ever looked at you," says Brenda. "How dare you!" replies Emmeline. "Oh, my God, women!" moans William. Then, too, she has always hated Jenny for taking Bryan away from her, and the feeling was apparently mutual. Perhaps Jenny was enlarging the scope of her vocabulary to include slang words.

Inspector Cray decides to forego the spelling bee, however, and leave Jenny alone for a moment. After all, the murderer can't afford to have the next letter spoken when Jenny is feeling better and the experiment can continue. Sure enough, the villain is caught red-handed trying to do in poor, paralyzed Jenny. Imagine the surprise when Jenny begins screaming "Help! Help, murder!"

Dame Agatha next takes us for an *Afternoon at the Seaside*. How pleasant it is, and how rare, to be in an outdoor setting with the grande dame of mystery making. There are bathing beauties to distract the eye, impossible old women to tickle the gizzard, and a nice little gentle twist of an ending that feels rather like the sunset on a delightful day at the beach.

The ocean breezes and warm sand seem to have affected our playwright. What, commit murder most foul here in the clean, open air of Little-Slypping-On-Sea?! No. The most she can bring herself to is a cat burglary of Lady Beckman's emerald necklace. Seems someone was seen prowling around one of the three little beach huts that decorate our set, and Inspector Foley is obliged to interrupt our pleasant little outing.

Rule of Three (1962)

When the curtain goes up, Noreen Somers is building a sand castle and flirting outrageously with Bob Wheeler, while her husband sits in a deck chair a few feet away, wearing an overcoat and scarf, with a heavy stick propped by him. If that's his idea of beach attire, no wonder she's displaying her charms elsewhere. Bob, moreover, is the kind of guy who's the life and soul of any gathering, which is great for Noreen, but not so thrilling for Mrs. Crum and Mrs. Gunner, who hadn't been expecting a "gathering" on *their* beach.

"Quite a different class of people nowadays," says Mrs. Crum, ducking a beach ball which this same young man keeps throwing back and forth.

"Those bikinis, as they call them. Didn't ought to be allowed," snorts Mrs. Gunner. "The Archbishop of Canterbury should preach against them."

If he did, you can bet your last tuppence that none of the men on our beach would have been there, for that bikini in question belongs on the body—well, at least on some of the body—of the Beauty. Such blatant titling augurs blatant drama-

tic use, and, sure enough, the Beauty's effect on men is devastating. George Crum can't take his eyes off her and keeps losing track of the conversation his wife insists on having with him. Bob Wheeler, noting her delicious French accent, strikes up a parley-vous, leaving pretty Noreen jogging solo. Percy Gunner, a shy young man smothered by mother, takes courage from the Beauty's warm smile and commits the unforgivable sin of leaving Mom to fend for herself. (Mrs. Crum, by the way, so epitomizes the hypochondriacal, jealous, domineering mother that one almost wishes there *had* been a murder in this play.) Even Mr. Somers abjures lameness for the pleasure of lighting Beauty's cigarette. And if they all only knew who she really is!

But what has happened to our crime? Oh, yes. The necklace is found in someone's pocket, and someone wins the thousand dollar reward and gets to take Beauty off to dinner. Then that nice little kicker of an ending. All in all, a great deal of fun. Just like an afternoon at the seaside.

GRANVILLE BURGESS

The Clocks (1963)

Rosemary stands for remembrance. But who needed to remember that Sheila Webb's real first name was Rosemary? Was the murder of a perfectly respectable middle-aged man, in a perfectly respectable neighborhood, in the home of a perfectly respectable blind woman, necessary as a simple reminder? What were those four clocks, frozen at 4:13, doing in the room of the crime, and why did one of them say "Rosemary" across its face? In fact, what do any of these facts have to do with one another?

Sheila Webb had never been to the blind Miss Pebmarsh's house before. The blind Miss Pebmarsh never called the Cavendish Secretarial and Typewriting Bureau to specifically request the services of the typist Sheila Webb. Neither Miss Webb nor Miss Pebmarsh had ever encountered the dead man found in Miss Pebmarsh's sitting room in his more vertical days. Indeed, the discovery of the dead body sent Shelia screaming into the street and into the arms of Colin Lamb, a young man who just happened to be passing by.

As Hercule Poirot remarks, as the haze of coincidence and irrelevant data cloud the less crystalline visions of Detective Inspector Dick Hardcastle of the Crowdean Police Department and Colin Lamb of the ubiquitous Secret Service, "One must concentrate on the essentials."

Poirot surveys the crime as an armchair exercise. He solves the riddle in the solitude and privacy of his own study in London, while allowing his young friend Colin Lamb to collect data and bother with the real-life details of ferreting out information concerning a crime that no one saw or heard happen, no one observed any preparation for, and indeed, in which no one, not even Scot-

land Yard, could identify the dead body.

But Poirot knows the solution to the puzzle. Unfortunately, or fortunately, according to how one looks at murder mysteries, Poirot does not share his information with his readers, and so the plot escalates on "the more the merrier" principle. No sooner are we utterly mystified and confused by the demise of "Mr. Curry" (the alias of the unidentified body) in the sitting room of blind Miss Millicent Pebmarsh than we are confronted with the strangulation, in a phone booth not far from Miss Pebmarsh's home, of poor Edna Brent. Edna in her happier days had been a typist, also at the Cavendish Secretarial and Typewriting Bureau. Who, and for that matter why, would anyone want to do in poor Edna, whose most salient personality traits were her affection for caramels and stylishly impossible shoes? Oh dear. It makes a body wonder, and there seem to be an ever-increasing number of bodies to wonder about.

Nineteen Wilbraham Crescent, the scene of the crime, the home of Miss Pebmarsh, is so situated as to abut five other homes also located on the crescent. Because the body of the victim remains unidentified, the motives for the murder remain unfocused, and so naturally the entire population in the immediate vicinity becomes suspect. But the personalities and life-styles of the neighborhood all bear the same sense of benign, characterless mystery that almost any home in the world might offer to a mildly curious spectator. After all, everyone has little secrets that never hurt anyone.

Take, for example, Mrs. Lawton, Sheila Webb's aunt. Mrs. Lawton never told her niece

The Clocks (1963)

that she (Sheila) had been born out of wedlock and deserted by her mother. It seemed so much simpler and less painful to tell the child that her parents had died together while she was still an infant. It was a small white lie, one that would never hurt anyone.

Or examine the history of Mrs. Bland, a neighbor of Miss Pebmarsh. Is her character type true to the description offered by her name and her dedication to a career of semi-invalidism? Why did Mrs. Bland's family in Canada so disapprove of her marriage to the truly innocuous Mr. Bland that they cut her off from the family fortune? Yes, almost anyone's life can appear harmless and mundane until a few crucial shutters are opened and doors unlocked. Then the complicating factors and intertwining histories multiply into a plethora of murder motives.

The first murder, having occurred in the home of Miss Pebmarsh, of course makes her a prime suspect. But she is blind. How could she stab a grown man without his evading her? *Is* Miss Pebmarsh really blind?

Why did Sheila Webb, the young typist with the cornflower blue eyes, the discoverer of the body, steal the "Rosemary" clock from the scene of the crime? It is frequently said that the individuals who discover dead bodies are not infrequently covering up for their participation in the crime. But Sheila has those big blue eyes. How could she murder anyone—and why should she want to if she could? Is it possible that Shelia is using her big blue eyes to distract the detective instincts of the admittedly romantic and susceptible Colin Lamb?

Then of course, there is the second murder to consider — poor Edna Brent. What did Edna Brent know about the first murder, and who needed to silence her so badly that they did it in a telephone booth? But wait—before we are able to properly adjust to two dead bodies, a third is veritably thrust upon us.

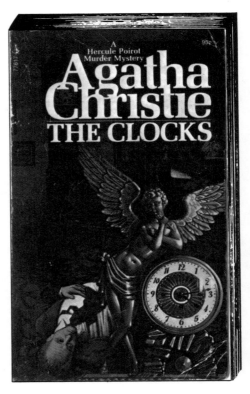

For Inspector Hardcastle, Colin Lamb, and perhaps quite a few readers, this case is proving a hard nut to crack. But Poirot sits in his study with a smug smile of understanding. If we didn't see so little of him, his superior knowledge might indeed become infuriating, and he himself might become victim number four in this ever-increasing chain of homicides.

All these questions—and the murderer is still at large. Time is just ticking right along, except for the time on those clocks found in Miss Pebmarsh's sitting room. They are frozen at 4:13.

DEBORAH J. POPE

THE WOMANLY ARTS
Gossip and Intuition as Detective Tools
by Jan Oxenberg

Jane Marple, commenting on a production of Macbeth, tells her nephew:

> "If I were producing this splendid play, I would make the three witches quite different. I would have them three ordinary, normal old women. Old Scottish women. They wouldn't dance or caper. They would look at each other rather slyly and you would feel a sort of menace just behind the ordinariness of them."
>
> *—from Nemesis*

Menace behind the ordinary is the essence of Agatha Christie; her ordinary women are a case in point. Employing the traditional women's avocations that are so often scorned or considered trivial, Jane Marple and her kind solve mysteries that leave the professionals (all men, or course) either completely baffled or in the midst of arresting the wrong person. Gossip, for example, is one much maligned "womanly" pastime. But it must forevermore hold an exalted place in the ranks of serious detection after Agatha Christie. In *Sleeping Murder*, Giles Reed, who has been doggedly pursuing a solution to the mystery himself, is incredulous at the amount of information Miss Marple has obtained, seemingly without effort.

> "How did you find all this out?"
> Miss Marple smiled apologetically. "I've been gossiping a little. In shops — and waiting for buses. Old ladies are supposed to be inquisitive. Yes, one can pick up quite a bit of local news."

One certainly can "pick up quite a bit" — by talking about the ailments of mutual friends or the best patterns for baby blankets or lost recipes for gingerbread — the point being that not everyone can successfully gossip. It's a fine art that requires real ties to a community or sensitivity to the manners and mores of a new setting. It's an "old girls network" and it works, even if the reasons for it working are sometimes unfortunate. In *The Pale Horse*, Ginger explains to Mark how she got information from a shop girl who wouldn't tell him a thing.

> "Girls together stuff. You wouldn't understand. The point is that if a girl tells things to another girl it doesn't really count. She doesn't think it matters."
> "All in the trade union so to speak?"
> "You could put it like that..."

Women who are acutely attentive to detail and to any divergence from the established way of doing things have been called tiresome or overbearing (in polite company). Yet it is just these traits that have helped Jane Marple solve many a puzzle. Woe be to the otherwise cunning gentleman who delivered the *wrong kind of rock* to her rock garden or the murderer whose female victim had suspiciously *inappropriate fingernails*! These are just the kind of things that the police might (and do) pass right by because they are not really clues in the traditional sense, they are little irritations that give the sensitive Jane Marple a "feeling" that something is not right.

This "feeling," or "woman's intuition" as it is sometimes called, is based on what Marple calls village parallels. Something about a case reminds her of a personality or situation from life in her village of St. Mary Mead. "Human nature being

what it is" (as she is fond of saying) the intuitive parallel is often helpful in setting her on a course of inquiry. This, says Miss Marple,

> "is really what people call intuition and make such a fuss about. Intuition is like reading a word without having to spell it out. A child can't do that because it has had so little experience. But a grown-up person knows the word because they've seen it often before. You catch my meaning, Vicar?"
>
> "Yes," I said slowly, "I think I do. You mean that if a thing reminds you of something else—well, it's probably the same kind of thing."
>
> "Exactly."
>
> —from *Murder at the Vicarage*

It's experience that nurtures intuition and who has more experience than the elderly? Jane Marple, values old people, especially old women. This puts her in the minority in a world that tends to consider old women "batty" when they make a fuss and non-existent when they don't. In *Nemesis*, Miss Marple is led to a group of strangers, one of whom may be the key to a mystery. She takes stock of her companions:

> "Miss Bentham and Miss Lumley? The old girls. Unlikely to be criminals but, being elderly, they might know plenty of gossip or have some information or might make some illuminating remark even if it happened to come about in connection with rheumatism, arthritis or patent medicine."
>
> —from *Nemesis*

And in *What Mrs. McGillicuddy Saw!* it is only Jane Marple's trust and belief in the admittedly fantastic story told by her elderly friend Elspeth McGillicuddy that insures a clever murder will not go undetected.

Elevating the conventional ways of women to new heights of significance is fine, but on the other side of the conventional ways of women is the conventional view of women. To be sure, Agatha Christie's stories abound with the jealous woman, the gold digger (though she certainly doesn't discriminate on the basis of sex when it comes to gold digging), the selfish and the silly woman. One woman is said to be "the kind of woman that could go on getting married again and again," because she is "a good listener" (*The Body in the Library*).

Jane Marple, of course, has never married. This in itself is a rather large offense against convention. What's more, Agatha Christie lets her get away with it; we encounter almost none of the

GARNER

snide or pitying remarks that spinsterhood so often provokes. Though certainly not opposed to marriage, Miss Marple does have a somewhat cynical view of this sacred institution. "So many men seem to murder their wives," she observes in *What Mrs. McGillicuddy Saw!* "It is so often a husband who is involved," she reflects in *Sleeping Murder*.

A character needn't have Marple's mind to see that male-female relationships can be exasperating. In *Sleeping Murder* Gwenda, just married to Giles Reed, goes ahead to England while he finishes business in New Zealand. Giles insists that she choose a house for them and get settled in it, without waiting for him, so that she won't have to "hang about in hotels." Gwenda sees right through this. "What you mean is, do all the work!"

Then there are the "men of the world" who have to be protected from their own ignorance of real life. When the body of a sexy young woman is found in Arthur Bantry's library (*The Body in the Library*) the staid ex-Colonel simply does not grasp the social consequences. Mrs. Bantry and her friend Jane Marple have to rush about to find the murderer before "dear old stupid" Arthur wakes up and realizes that people *will* talk and eventually snub him.

In fact they already are talking about Mrs. as well as Mr. Bantry. Miss Hartnell, a neighborhood do-gooder, gloats:

> "She thought too much about her garden and not enough about her husband. You've got to keep an eye on a man all the time—all the time," repeated Miss Hartnell fiercely.

Some women, however, are more interested in taking care of their own kind. In *Spider's Web* the "gum-booted" and "Amazonian" gardener, Miss Peake, heroically whisks a dead man's body away on her shoulders so that the mistress of the house won't be falsely accused of murder. "What I always say is stand by your own sex," she explains. Miss Marple herself might occasionally be accused of harboring similar sentiments:

> As usual Miss Marple said the word "gentlemen" in the way of someone describing a foreign species.
> —from *The Mirror Crack'd*

In fact, the sentiment quoted above is a slight refinement. In 1941 in *The Body in the Library*, Miss Marple uttered the word "gentlemen" in "the old maid's way of referring to the opposite sex as though it were a species of wild animal."

A Caribbean Mystery (1964)

Ah, the deep blue of the sea, the steadfast accompaniment of the steel band, the soft, sensuous Caribbean breezes, the plethora of planter's punches—who could ask for more? Not wishing in any way to appear ungrateful (for it is only at the generous insistence of her wealthy nephew Raymond that she has come to this Caribbean island at all), Miss Jane Marple, a woman of modest means (but most assuredly good taste), finds that living graciously among the idle rich in tropical paradise is just not all that it's been cracked up to be. "Lovely and warm, yes—and so good for her rheumatism — and beautiful scenery, though perhaps — a trifle monotonous? So many palm trees. Everything the same every day — never anything happening."

What Miss Marple yearns for, if the truth must be told, is a bit of "spice" befitting her exotic West Indies locale. After all, there are limits to the amount of polite interest even the abundantly gracious Miss M. can show in the "somewhat uninteresting recollections of a lifetime" recounted to her by Major Palgrave. The "regrettably unattractive" major's vicarious fascination with the infinite details of a multitude of murders provides little, if any, diversion for Miss Marple.

She prefers the homicides of everyday people, like those back home in St. Mary Mead, to the major's encyclopedic collection of headline-grabbing, untimely demises of the wealthy. After all, money is just so *basic* a murderous motivation. Certainly the vagaries of rural life are more interesting.

Nonetheless, Miss Marple is most appreciative of the idle rich when the sound of their idle chatter diverts the major from yet another tale—this one

a seemingly-normal-husband-kills-sweet-young-wife caper. In fact, the indefatigable major quite abruptly curtails his monologue when he notices the other Golden Palm Hotel guests approaching the veranda. Strange. Stranger still is the major's rather hasty attempt to conceal his cache of allegedly factual photographic evidence—after all, this is the age of audiovisual appreciation. To quote the ever-succinct Miss Jane Marple: "Interesting."

Interesting, indeed, but not apparently of much importance. After all, it's time for another evening of high spirits and good fun at the Golden Palm, where hosts Tim and Molly Kendal so diligently attend to the needs and desires of their varied clientele.

In addition to Miss Marple and the major, the guests at the Caribbean retreat include several others of, shall we say, considerably advanced age. There's old Mr. Rafiel, wealthiest of the wealthy, and oldest of the old; Dr. Graham, who tends to the real and imagined maladies of the island population; Joan Prescott, who has, to put it kindly, an eye for detail; and her brother, Canon Jeremy Prescott, "breather of geniality." When all gather for evening festivities, it is no wonder that "Miss Marple sighed for youth."

Fortunately, youthful enthusiasm can be detected in the energetic (if a bit middle-aged) foursome of Edward and Evelyn Hillingdon and Greg and Lucky Dyson. They pursue rare butterflies, exotic birds, and life in general, with gusto. In fact, this set of "mixed doubles" has on more than one occasion given pause to onlookers. (We're not talking tennis — but are we talking love?) Frankly, more than one Golden Palm guest has expressed confusion as to just who is married to whom.

Youth is also represented, chronologically speaking, by Tim and Molly Kendal, the aforementioned attractive hosts, and Arthur Jackson and Esther Walters, the brooding valet and younger-than-she-looks secretary, respectively, to Mr. Rafiel.

As usual at the Golden Palm, tonight's music is delightful (if you like steel bands), and the company's divine. Ah, the carefree Caribbean...Such joviality! What joie de vivre!

Who would have reason to suspect, on this clear evening, that by morning the merry group would be decreased by one? Major Palgrave—so ebullient, so effortlessly effervescent — deceased by daybreak? Sad, yet tragically true.

But, as astutely pointed out by so many in the Golden Palm community, the major was on in years, and suffered from high blood pressure (which caused his death). Miss Marple, however, is troubled by more than the gentleman's passing. Odd, isn't it, that the major never once, in so many hours of conversation, mentioned his health problem to his gracious listener, Miss Marple? Peculiar, doesn't it seem, that no reference was ever made to the medication the poor man was forced to rely upon?

Major Palgrave's death is also a particular cause of concern for Molly Kendal, who fears that word of the tragedy will spread and cause people to cancel their reservations at the Golden Palm. She and Tim have worked too hard to get to where they are today for their success to be spoiled by an old man's death. And Molly, who always appears carefree, does tend to worry. In fact, she is even subject, as Esther Walters explains to Miss Marple, to "these odd fits of depression." Molly, who also suffers frightening dreams, has gone so far as to confess to Evelyn Hillingdon her fear that someone is always watching, "spying on me. Somebody hates me. That's

what I keep feeling." Strange.

Nonetheless, both Molly and Tim keep their respective upper lips stiff and see that gracious living proceeds as usual at the Golden Palm...even when another cloud of death darkens their fair Caribbean sky.

This time it's the young hotel maid, Victoria Johnson. No victim of natural causes is she—unless, of course, one considers death by stabbing a natural cause. Victoria, who lived with "the man who, without benefit of ceremony, she considered her present husband," had also been disturbed by Major Palgrave's death. Was she, perhaps, a bit too inquisitive about the circumstances surrounding his demise?

How unfortunate to have this placid playground intruded upon by, as Esther Walters so aptly states, "reminders of mortality." Even the easygoing Dr. Graham, for so many years acquainted with the mystery and the magic of St. Honore, is mystified.

Miss Marple is concerned enough about the events to act the part of a doddering old fool in hopes of obtaining pertinent information from the doctor. Several days later our favorite sleuth, again out of character, must for a short time assume the role of the proverbial little old lady in tennis shoes (de rigeur for silent searching). To what ends the pursuit of justice!

To what ends, too, this terrible tale of tragedy in the tropics? Is there a plot to be unearthed, as Molly fears? A lusting lover (of any number of Golden Palm guests) run amok? What are we to conclude from the distressing discovery of yet another victim of foul play? Did the woman found dead in the creek know the answer to the most complex Caribbean mystery?

Perhaps the only thing we do know "is that one really doesn't know anything about anybody.... Not even the people who are closest to you."

Interesting.

ANN COHEN

At Bertram's Hotel (1965)

More than simply a hotel, Bertram's of London is an environment. After greeting the tall, punctilious Irish commissionaire, replete with gold braid and chestful of ribbons and medals, one follows him through the swinging doors and steps back seventy-five years. Happily, time has passed Bertram's by, allowing it to retain its mien of comfy Edwardian correctness.

Established in 1840, and renovated after the Blitz with painstaking attention to detail, the hotel attracts a clientele of old clergy, retired generals, admirals who could reminisce about past campaigns, and dowager ladies who Jane Marple refers to as "fluffy old pussies." It also attracts boarding school girls, whose parents know their daughters will be unmolested there, and American tourists (especially readers of Henry James) who find the understated elegance the epitome of everything English. It is one of the few places where tourists can still observe the venerable English tradition of afternoon tea, but at the same time find the amenities—still rare in Europe—of central heating and private toilets. The tea, served in the commodious lounge, is always the best Indian, Ceylon, Darjeeling, or Lapsang Souchong, dispensed by a squad of slim, well-uniformed youths under the direction of Henry, the quintessential butler.

Small writing rooms are available for those whose conversations are more private. But one had best check the two high-backed armchairs facing the fireplace first, as their position makes it impossible to see if they are occupied. And if they are, an indiscreet intimation might easily be overheard.

While a television room is maintained, it is closeted away so neatly that one would probably never notice its presence nor moan its absence. Breakfast is served in the rooms and consists of two fares: for the Americans there is cereal and chilled orange juice, while Britishers can opt for bacon and eggs, kippers, kidneys and bacon, cold grouse, or York ham. Of course the meal is served by a bright and comely chambermaid wearing a striped lavender print dress and a freshly laundered cap.

Everything is quite correct. All the employees are bewilderingly efficient. Not a detail forgotten nor a courtesy missed.

Indeed.

It is sentimentality that brings Miss Jane Marple to Bertram's. She was only fourteen when she first stayed there with an uncle and aunt, and she is at first delighted to find that the place has remained remarkably unchanged over the intervening decades. But what is it about the place that unnerves her now? Everything is just as she had remembered it, and like the rest of the clientele she can find nothing obviously untoward. All is perfect, simply perfect.

Yet something arouses her well-honed sense for evil. Yes, everything *is* perfect, too incredibly perfect. The help, for instance, know their parts too well, almost like well rehearsed actors. Beneath this veneer of Edwardian politesse Miss Jane Marple can sense something sinister.

The perfection of the place also disturbs Chief Inspector Fred Davy of Scotland Yard, but he has more tangible reasons to find the hotel suspect. A rash of spectacular holdups and thefts are plaguing England, and the arrest of the ringleaders would be a spendid way for "Father" Davy to cap an already commendable career. In at least two instances, thus far, suspects in the robberies were discovered to have been residing at Bertram's at the very time they were seen elsewhere committing their heinous acts.

Curious place, this Bertram's.

Miss Marple is sitting in the lounge knitting and chatting with her friend Lady Selina Hazy when she notices someone whose presence seems incongruous at Bertram's. Lady Bess Sedgwick is a celebrity, having regularly captured the headlines by performing one exploit always more daring or outrageous than the previous one. She had weathered several marriages, flown solo across the Atlantic, driven racing cars, and served a stint with the French Resistance during the war. Such a woman would be equally comfortable in the company of the Royal Family or aborigines. But what could Bertram's possibly have to offer her?

Then there is this gauche fellow in a black leather jacket Lady Bess has, er, been seen with. More than one guest is piqued by the presence of this race-car driver — Ladislaus Malinowski. Definitely improper company for a refined lady to be keeping.

One morning, as fate would have it, Miss Marple quite accidentally overhears a conversation between Lady Bess and Colonel Derek Luscombe. Luscombe, it seems, is the guardian of one Elvira Blake, the fruit of one of Lady Bess's several marriages. Though the meeting at Bertram's is purely coincidental, Bess insists that Luscombe take the seventeen-year old Elvira elsewhere. The only reason she offers for her insistence is that she considers herself to be dangerous. There has been no communication between mother and daughter since the girl was a baby, and Lady Bess intends to keep it that way.

Strange revelation.

The next conversation Bess has, through the window in the writing room, is with Michael Gorman, the handsome Irish commissionaire (the

bloody doorman!). Their dialogue is a little too relaxed and familiar, and there is the suggestion of their having had a romantic escapade some years back in Ballygowlan, Ireland. Lady Bess Sedgwick and a doorman? Hmm.

For one whose life has been filled wih intrigues, it seems inconceivable that Lady Bess would not have thought to check to see if the two high-backed chairs by the fireplace were occupied. While Jane Marple is only mildly curious about what she overhears, Elvira Blake is ashen.

Oddly moved by something in the conversation, Elvira pays a visit to the family barrister to

At Bertram's Hotel (1965)

check the details of her father's will as regards herself. This done, she mysteriously vanishes for a few days, leaving word with her intimate friend and confederate, Bridget, that she has something more to check and that she will be flying Aer Lingus to wherever it is she is going.

Canon Pennyfather, a doddering old scholar afflicted by mental vagueness, is scheduled to leave Bertram's for a few days to attend a theological colloquy in Lucerne. With his fondness for forgetting what he is doing in the midst of doing it, it is not surprising for him to find at the airport that he is a day late. What is remarkable is that upon returning to his room he should receive a blow to the head and wake up three days later in a town miles from London with no recollection of his adventure.

More than the fact that a mail train is robbed by a gang of criminals that same evening (a spectacular success for the thugs), it is the disappearance of the canon that seizes Chief Inspector Davy's attention. He now has an excuse to scrutinize Bertram's Hotel a little closer, and the evidence becomes compelling. The hotel is owned by the Hoffman brothers, heads of a crime syndicate on the Continent. A sports car of the same rare type as Ladislaus Malinowski's was seen at the site of the mail robbery, although the license number is off by two digits—similar coincidences have occurred during other robberies. But most curiously, it is Jane Marple who discovers that so many people in the hotel are other than they at first seem to be. Even the chambermaid turns out to be an actress.

One foggy London evening Davy is making further inquiries at the hotel when there is a shot outside followed by a scream and a second shot. Davy rushes to the street to find the commissionaire, Michael Gorman, dead on the street with a hysterical girl standing over him sobbing that Gorman had come between her and the person who was trying to shoot her. But who would want to kill young Elvira Blake?

First, the weapon found at the scene is revealed to belong to our friend Ladislaus Malinowski. Is it possible that Malinowski was having a liaison with daughter as well as mother? Then, if he were jilted by Elvira and saw her fortune slipping away, such a sleazy fellow as he might be tempted to take revenge.

Second, there is Lady Bess Sedgwick. A quick trip to Ireland confirms for Davy that she had once been married to the dead commissionaire. Maybe he was blackmailing her, threatening to reveal her as a bigamist. Or might he have been blackmailing her for being the head of a crime syndicate working out of Bertram's Hotel? A crime organization certainly could have used a person of her talents.

Third, there is young Elvira Blake. Just how sheltered has her life been up until now? Yes, her life had been threatened some years back by someone named Guido, but that could have been a schoolgirl's fantasy, a prank. Possibly her brief disappearance might be accounted for by a trip to Ballygowlan, where she made the same discovery about her mother as Chief Inspector Davy did. But how could her mother's bigamy present her with a motive for foul murder?

Curious place, this Bertram's.

Even more curious, the guests.

PETER J. FITZPATRICK

Third Girl (1966)

Third Girl is late Agatha Christie and late Hercule Poirot. M. Poirot, older now, does not like his routine upset. When his breakfast is interrupted by an unscheduled visit from a young, unknown girl, he is disturbed. When she informs Poirot that she "might have committed a murder," he is further disturbed. When she refuses to elaborate, because Poirot is "too old," and then flees in obvious dismay, his disturbance is total.

Ariadne Oliver, mystery writer and Poirot's friend, is quick to clear up one of the initial puzzles. The strange young girl is Norma Restarick. Norma lives with two other girls, Frances Cary and Claudia Reece-Holland, in a block of postwar flats in central London. Claudia Reece-Holland, a tall, dark, handsome girl, is employed as confidential secretary to Andrew Restarick, Norma's father. Frances Cary travels extensively in her work, arranging the sale and exhibition of paintings in galleries in Britian and on the Continent. She is arty, world-weary, and elegant. Norma herself is employed at an art gallery in Soho and looks, to Poirot, rather like "an Ophelia devoid of physical attraction." More alarmingly, she has now disappeared.

Poirot is worried. Norma Restarick is gone, but no one seems to care. Her roommates, Claudia and Frances, appear quite unconcerned. Her stepmother, Mary Restarick, thinks that Norma is in London. Andrew Restarick knows his daughter is missing, but does not want the police informed. David Baker, Norma's "young man," claims not to know where she has taken herself.

Poirot searches for Norma, and as his search widens, he uncovers more and more reason to wonder about Norma Restarick. Why does she hate her stepmother so violently? What was the mysterious illness that felled stepmother Mary Restarick at Crosshedges, the Restarick country house in Long Basing? Why did Mary recover so quickly when she was removed to a hospital? Why are the servants whispering about poison? How did the bottle of weed killer get into Norma's dresser at Crosshedges? How, also, did the bottle get half-emptied?

What did Norma Restarick mean when she said that she "might have committed a murder"? Where is the murder? There appears to be no murder that Norma could have done. True, Louise Charpentier, a fiftyish, single, drunken woman has committed suicide by throwing herself from her window. Miss Charpentier lived on the floor above Norma. But there seems to be no connection between the two.

There was blood in the alley behind the flats, or so the porter says. However, there is no body and Poirot can uncover no report of a body. Did the porter see a gun in Norma's hand? He says he did, but as Poirot's investigators make clear, the porter is not an altogether reliable witness. If murder has been done, where is the body? Poirot cannot rest; he warns Ariadne Oliver that there is danger.

Ariadne Oliver decides to take a hand. She succeeds, quite by chance, in locating Norma, who is sitting with her boy friend, David Baker, quietly having "elevenses" in a second-rate coffee shop in London. Miss Oliver calls Poirot and tells him of her discovery. In spite of Poirot's warning, Ariadne follows David Baker when he leaves the coffee shop. David leads her to an artist's loft, where she meets Frances Cary again and another artist friend. Shortly after she leaves the loft, Miss Oliver is coshed. She wakes up in the hospital.

Norma Restarick has disappeared — again. Poirot's investigations begin to bear fruit.

Third Girl (1966)

Norma's mother is dead. Her father Andrew, having returned to England to settle the estate of his only relative, the recently deceased Simon Restarick, is unhappy and restless in Britain and talks of returning to South Africa. Stepmother Mary Restarick is obviously uncomfortable about Norma and is visibly angry when she encounters David Baker at Crosshedges. She seems at a loss to understand Norma or Norma's hatred for her. At the same time, she seems quite content in her new home, England, and appears to be extremely busy house-hunting in London.

Poirot is confused by Andrew Restarick. Aggressive, assertive, he appears to be the complete businessman. Why then did he cut his ties fifteen years before and leave the business to his brother? Could it have been because of his infatuation with another woman? Could an affair that lasted barely a year have caused him to wander the world for fifteen years? And how strange it is that everything this wanderer puts his hands to seems to turn to gold.

Slowly, Poirot also learns more about the suicide of Miss Charpentier. Years before she and Claudia's father, now a member of Parliament, had an affair.

When Frances Cary returns home from Manchester to discover the body of David Baker in her living room, the stage is set for the denouement. Norma Restarick, bloody knife in her hand, quietly admits to the killing as she huddles in the corner of the room where David was killed. Surely Poirot has no more to do. Or does he?

Who killed David Baker? Why? Is Norma the murderer, or is she perhaps a victim?

Third Girl is late Christie, but Dame Agatha hadn't lost her touch. With so many girls in the story, Poirot is clever indeed to discover which is the third girl.

EDWIN A. ROLLINS

Endless Night (1967)

The series of sinister "accidents" that had taken place at Gypsy's Acre had convinced even the most cynical and down-to-earth residents of Kingston Bishop not to shrug off a gypsy's curse.

But Michael and Ellie Rogers, a young newly wed couple, who had "fallen in love at first sight," ignored the old fortuneteller's warning. They saw the abandoned and decaying country estate, with its beautiful view and wooded surroundings, as the perfect place to start their "happily ever afterward" marriage.

The couple, because they were from diverse backgrounds — he working-class, she a wealthy oil heiress — were secretly married after a whirlwind romance. After spending several weeks stealthily honeymooning around the Continent, they came back to England to check the progress of Rudolf Santonix, a well-known architect, who was hired to build their dreamhouse.

That dream would soon become a nightmare.

First, the village gypsy, Mrs. Esther Lee, warns the couple of a dangerous future if they choose to remain in the newly completed home.

It comes to pass.

Ellie's stepmother, two money-hungry uncles, and the family's lawyers arrive on the scene, quicky sizing up her "wrong-side-of-the-tracks" husband.

After passing several nasty comments, and upon settling several legal matters—most important of which is making sure that their allowances will not be stopped—all depart.

Several days later, though, while touring the estate, Ellie slips and falls, spraining her ankle. To be certain that someone will always be available to look after her, Ellie, over the protests made by Michael, sends for her governess and friend, Greta Andersen.

Greta's arrival caused quite a stir. Ellie, joyous and assured, welcomes the beautiful Nordic blonde into the household with open arms. Michael, on the other hand, dislikes and is somewhat jealous of this influential woman who has placed herself between his wife and himself.

After several weeks, this evident hatred comes to a head, with Michael and Greta having a loud and heated argument. However, Ellie again persuades him that Greta is needed, and he allows her to remain.

A new friend, Claudia Hardcastle, convinces the somewhat frail Ellie to take up horseback riding once again. But Ellie's pleasant rides through the beautiful, wooded countryside soon become a horror. Mrs. Lee, the gypsy hag, appears from behind trees, reiterating her dire threats and scaring Ellie out of her wits.

Is this really the gypsy's doing, or has someone, an irate family member perhaps, or a jealous neighbor, paid her to do so? The sheriff did mention that Mrs. Lee had come into some money.

Michael assures his wife that the old woman is a bit crazy. "Pay no attention to her," he says gruffly. "I think she's half off her head anyway. She just wants to frighten you off."

And so Ellie continues to gallop about the estate each day.

One day, the day she is to meet Michael for lunch in Market Chadwell, a nearby town, she asks his advice and goes out riding. She never returns.

Endless Night (1967)

Her crumpled body is found in the woods, apparently thrown by the horse that stands grazing by her on the grassy field.

Apparently, but...

Dr. Shaw, the elderly village physician, tells the coroner's inquest that "there was no specific injury to have caused death ... she had died from heart failure caused by shock."

That is the official verdict, at least. Others believe that it was the gypsy. Could old Mrs. Lee have taken her fortune-telling a step too far? And what about Michael? While he does seem to have an airtight alibi, he also had a vast fortune to gain, keeping him from returning to his working-class background forever.

Perhaps it was Greta? No real motive is apparent. Not greed anyway. Ellie had given her a large cash settlement after she and Michael were wed. Revenge for an old hurt? Maybe.

Could it have been Claudia Hardcastle? Hardly. Her body is found several days after Ellie's funeral, another victim of a riding "accident."

Perhaps the coroner's verdict is correct. Perhaps Ellie did die of natural causes.

Perhaps, but as all Agatha Christie readers know, not likely.

RICHARD REGIS

The Agatha Christie Title Crossword

ACROSS

1 Some judgments
5 African witchcraft form
10 Bubbly initials
14 Monty, of fame
15 She's "like a dream come true."
16 —— *facto*
17 Great lake
18 Personality feature
19 Crop; stomach
20 Christie title (1935)
23 Notices
24 Work units
25 Modern
28 Prefix meaning "over; above"
31 *Much* ——...
32 Italian trousers?
34 Cave: Poet.
38 Christie title (1945)
41 Ht.
42 "Singular" French town?
43 National Theatre of Europe: Abbr.
44 Happening
46 Rejoinder for "You are not!"
48 Hindu goddess of beauty
50 Theatre grp.
51 What "They" did, in a Christie title (1951)
57 Starchy root
58 Janson's *History* ——
59 Shortly
61 East African tribe
62 Swiftian being
63 Trio in a Christie title (1950)
64 Miss M.
65 Proust character
66 Actress Sommer

DOWN

1 Haggard heroine
2 Medicinal plant
3 What GW could not tell
4 "Information, ——"
5 Where the "Cards" were, in a Christie title (1936)
6 Karloff
7 Impetuosity, in Paris
8 Got down
9 Biblical word
10 Where Miss Marple first met murder, in a Christie title (1930)
11 Stripling, twig
12 Glacial ridges
13 Wham!
21 When you should know where your childen are
22 Poetic contraction
25 "O, —— Ben Jonson!"
26 Noble: Ger.
27 Lassie directive, homewise
28 Parade walk
29 Addict
30 The "4:50" was from here, in a Christie novel (1957)
33 Night light
35 Storm; carry on
36 Bismarck, to his pals
37 Kojak,'to *his* pals
39 Not at all what the raven said
40 Popular Christie title word
45 Contend (for)
47 Señora, in Nice
48 La ——
49 —— al-Rashid
50 Hank
52 "—— in the Attic"
53 Organization For Ailing Writers: Abbr.
54 —— California
55 Indigo dye
56 Word in a Christie title (1955) (Brit. version)
57 Word with Mahal
60 Born

(Solution to puzzle on page 325.)

ARIADNE OLIVER
Dame Agatha's Alter Ego

by Beth Simon

She may have been larger, more prepossessing, and certainly more preposterous. Her tone was unquestionably more acerbic, and her voice more booming. But there seems to be little doubt that Mrs. Ariadne Oliver, the fictional author of forty-six best sellers and creator of a famous vegetarian Finnish detective, was to some extent the alter ego of her own creator, Agatha Christie.

The parallels are certainly too obvious to ignore. Both Christie and Oliver liked comfortable shoes, well-cooked meals, Shakespearean names, and their privacy. They found themselves disgruntled at inappropriately dressed young women and long-haired young men. They were upset by scandal but willing to face it.

Both women entered middle age early on, and Mrs. Oliver remained meandering there at least until 1972 (*Elephants Can Remember*), when she wondered if it were safe for her to eat meringue while she was wearing dentures. Both women had thick grey hair and a tendency toward thickening about the middle.

Both enjoyed considerable commercial success with their tales of a foreign-born and eccentric sleuth. But their careers took different directions. Agatha Christie's murderous musings first took hold in a hospital dispensary and she confined her professional life to chronicling them. But we first meet Ariadne Oliver in 1934, when she is an employee of the detective Parker Pyne, although her fiction is already popular.

Pyne operates what is nominally a detective agency specializing in the fabrication of improbable romantic scenarios that it then foists on its bored and witless clients.

For example, "The Case of the Discontented Soldier" concerns a recently retired major who stumbles upon a "slightly anemic" blond young thing struggling bravely but ineffectively "in the grasp of two enormous Negroes." The major, after beating up the two, goes on to translate the anemic Miss Clegg's Swahili treasure map, which may lead them to a huge cache of tusks taken from illegally slaughtered elephants. He proposes marriage and a trip to East Africa for the honeymoon. Miss Clegg sighs "How exciting."

Who is the mastermind of this racist humbug? —Mrs. Ariadne Oliver, who sits in an office two flights up "at a table on which were a typewriter ...general confusion...and a large bag of apples." In her *Autobiography*, Christie claimed she worked in much the same conditions.

But Mrs. Oliver also had some differences. In *Cards On The Table* (1936), where she begins her thirty-six-year relationship with Hercule Poirot, she is presented as "handsome in a rather untidy fashion, with...substantial shoulders, and a large quantity of rebellious grey hair with which she was continually experimenting .... Mrs. Oliver would suddenly appear with Madonna loops, or ...untidy curls."

And while Agatha Christie spoke in a soft soprano, Mrs. Oliver's voice is variously described as bass, baritone, or tenor—and loud.

In each of the seven novels in which she appears, someone always takes the straight-man role, feeding her a line which allows her to assert a Christie policy or feeling. In *Cards*, when told by the breathless and admiring Rhoda that "it must be marvelous to write," Mrs. Oliver replies, "Why? One actually has to think, you know, and thinking is always a bore .... Some days I only keep going by repeating over and over ... the amount of money I might get for my next serial rights. That spurs you on...."

Mrs. Oliver proceeds to actively work as the colleague and competitor-detective with Poirot. While his work is directed by his logic-ridden lit-

Agatha Christie (or Ariadne Oliver?), the world-famous author, on her first visit to the Acropolis in 1958.

tle gray cells, hers is led by her "intuition." Within an hour of the Shaitana murder, she determines that Dr. Roberts is the killer; she knew "instinctively that there was something wrong with that man as soon as I saw him. My instincts never lie." Because Roberts is "hearty," and murderers are often hearty, she insists that Superintendent Battle of the Yard arrest the good doctor immediately.

She uses this same line of reasoning to conclude that the doctor also did it in *Mrs. McGinty's Dead* (1952). Poirot chances upon her in Broadhinny extracting herself from her tiny European car, apples flying in all directions. He is there to clear a man of murder, and she is there to collaborate on transforming one of her books into a stage play. She decides to help Poirot. She will, with her "woman's intuition," find the murderer, and all Poirot need do is to amass the evidence.

This situation allows Mrs. Oliver to rant about what had become two major issues. One was Christie's growing dissatisfaction with the results of others' efforts to turn her stories into plays and movies. Mrs. Oliver complains to Poirot that she doesn't know why she participates, that she makes enough money from her books — "that is to say the blood suckers take most of it, and if I made more, they'd take more, so I don't overstrain myself." She calls it "agony" to see her characters changed beyond recognition.

The agony-causing character in question is Mrs. Oliver's popular detective with the unpronouncable name, Sven Hjerson. She hates him. We know that in the mid-40s, Christie was so tired of Poirot that she wrote *Curtain* (which was not published until 1975). By 1952 she had perhaps had it to the eyeballs with him. Oliver, with Christie's approval, explodes into the following tirade. Try substituting "Belgian" for "Finn," and "mustaches" for "vegetable."

ARIADNE OLIVER

He's always been a vegetarian. He takes round a little machine for grating raw carrots. How do I know why I ever thought of the revolting man? I must have been mad. Why a Finn when I know nothing about Finland. Why a vegetarian? Why all those idiotic mannerisms he's got? These things just happen. You try something — and people seem to like it — and then you go on — and before you know where you are, you've got someone like that maddening Sven Hjerson tied to you for life. And people even write and say how fond you must be of him. Fond of him? If I ever met that bony, gangling vegetable eating Finn in real life, I'd do a better murder than any I've ever invented.

Mrs. Oliver next surfaces in 1956, in *Dead Man's Folly*. She has gone to Nasse House to arrange a Murder Hunt as an event for a charity fete. She feels that she is being somehow manipulated, and when her pretend murder victim turns up truly dead, she dissolves into hysteria and incoherency under police interrogation. Having served her literary purpose, she simply fades out.

But the shock effect remains. In *Pale Horse* (1961) she almost refuses to go sleuthing, her favorite activity, because it requires that she attend a charity fete.

Pale Horse is an interesting book for a number of reasons. Christie has named it as one of her five favorites. Regathered in it are several characters from previous Oliver-Poirot books, now older, married, or retired, all arrayed, of course, on the side of good. The only person missing is Poirot himself.

In this book, Christie again parodies herself at work through Mrs. Oliver. We intrude upon her, wrenching at her masses of hair as she prowls through her workroom, which is papered in tropical birds lurking in dark foliage. She creeps and mutters, designing the intricate plot twists of her next book, *The White Cockatoo*.

Mrs. Oliver expands on her theory of writing:

"It's safer, I think, to stick to what you know. People on cruises, and in hostels, and what goes on in hospitals, and on parish councils ... and music festivals, and girls in shops, and committees, and daily women, and young men and girls who hike round the world in the interests of science, and shop assistants —"

Mrs. Oliver is an important participant in each of the next three Poirot novels, and beginning with *Third Girl* (1966) she demonstrates definite personality development. Up to then, she is basically just a babbly, successful writer whose rantings lead readers and characters alike to blithely ignore her very sound intuitions about the moral fiber of the suspects. At times she resembles a hysterical bloodhound or an elephantine damsel-in-distress, and her vigorous efforts as a detective serve primarily to offset the perception and methods of Poirot.

In *Third Girl* she and Poirot have become old friends. She keeps his favorite cloying refreshments on hand; she stuffs him with billows of rich whip cream; she pours thick, effective oils on his wounded ego. And on the case itself, not only does she do most of the legwork and amass a great many of the clues; not only does she take her life in her hands and get herself nearly murdered for it; but, quite simply, Poirot could not have solved the case without her.

This novel presents Mrs. Oliver's peak performance, and within that, her most brilliant moment. After tailing a man she doesn't like to an area in London she doesn't know to find herself surrounded by people she doesn't trust, she admits to herself that she may be in danger. Isolated, trapped, but concerned that she may have misjudged these people, the ever-creative Mrs. Oliver buys some time by placidly reaching up and pulling out her hairpins. Rolls of false hair tumble to the floor, amazing everyone, while she prattles away, escaping down the stairs. Poirot never thought so fast.

Mrs. Oliver's role in *Hallowe'en Party* (1969) is reminiscent of that at the Nasse estate fete. This time she is helping to conduct a party at Apple House when the book opens, and she is on the premises during the party when a young girl is murdered.

Perhaps because advancing years rendered the crisp munchiness of apples less appealing, Christie arranges for the thirteen-year-old victim to be drowned in a apple-bobbing bucket. Mrs. Oliver is one of those who find the body, and in direct consequence she undergoes severe behavior modification. From that evening on, she can't stand the taste, the sight, even the thought of apples.

In her last book, *Elephants Can Remember* (1972), Poirot aids and guides her as she attempts to determine whether several years earlier, in an apparent double suicide involving an old friend, the wife shot the husband first or vice versa. As she goes the rounds of her old acquaintances — "elephants" who remember things — questioning them, the aging process becomes evident. Her friends have become deaf, or dotty, or arthritic, living under care or in nursing homes. Even Poirot seems slower, more impatient, or more easily bored. Mrs. Oliver, oddly enough, still bustles as energetically as ever, collecting information.

In *Elephants Can Remember* is the only reference to a *Mr.* Oliver. Agatha Christie's personal life, comments in her *Autobiography*, and her portrayal of couples in her books, suggest that she grew increasingly skeptical of marriage as a generally sound institution. Mrs. Oliver, who often mentions nephews and nieces and godchildren, admits to her own marriage only once, and that once is a by-the-way. Explaining to her goddaughter, Celia, how she lost track of Celia's mother, Mrs. Oliver says merely that "I married and went somewhere . . . ."

Children of her own are never even suggested, and we never find out what happened to the accommodating Mr. Oliver.

In any event, *Elephants* comes to a romantically satisfying conclusion. And we can assume that Mrs. Oliver returns to her workroom to first repaper it once again, and then have it out in peace and private with Sven Hjerson, "that idotic Finn."

While Oliver and Christie liked Shakespearean names, Christie also liked those from Greek myths. It is possible that she bestowed a similar career and first initial on her fictional stand-in so that the public could recognize her if it wanted to. But the name *Ariadne* has particular significance on its own.

In mythic times, on the island of Crete, trapped within what appeared to be an inescapable maze, lived the minotaur, a semirational but voracious beast. It was the hero-prince Theseus who had to defeat the minotaur, but it was Ariadne, daughter of King Minos, who tells the hero to unwind a thread as he moves through the maze and in this way he will be able to find his way out again.

Although one may have difficulty visualizing Hercule Poirot as the tall and handsome Theseus, the analogy between the two Ariadnes is obvious.

However Ariadne Oliver functions as a mouthpiece or as comic relief, she also serves a very important literary function. She provides us, and Poirot, with the clue of thread. All we need do is follow it.

Christie has Poirot, in *Hallowe'en Party*, realize this, and he is kind enough to admit it to Mrs. Oliver one day while he is resting his suffering feet, which he has insisted on keeping stuffed inside patent leather shoes:

> "Again and again you indicate to me the path, the how do you say, the *chemin* that I should take or that I should already have taken. You show me the way I should go. . . .I shall rely, as so often, on your intuition, madame."

OUT OF THE TOP DRAWER
Or, How They Dressed
by John Sturman

Oscar Wilde may have had tongue in cheek when he said, "It is only shallow people who do not judge by appearances," but this view was taken quite seriously by much of British society — despite some protestation to the contrary—until recently. Even today, in certain circles, dress may "give one away." And the ritual of dressing for dinner, though perhaps somewhat on the wane, is still far from rare.

In the 1920s, when Agatha Christie rose to prominence as a mystery writer, Britain was governed by a rather all-encompassing dress code. There was a prescribed outfit for virtually every possibilty—what to wear in town, in country, in the day, in the evening, to both formal and informal occasions. And one broke these rules at one's own peril.

H. Dennis Bradley outlined the basics of correct dress for men in *Etiquette for Gentlemen* in 1925. His essay "The Subtleties of Dress" explained that modernizing and democratizing influences were altering the face of men's fashion. Of the four styles of attire that he deemed required for the gentleman in town — lounge, morning, dinner, and full dress — two were falling into disuse. The morning coat (basically an updated frock coat) was still correct for political or purely formal social calls. But it had been replaced for more general daytime wear, such as business or informal calls, by the lounge suit — what we simply call a suit today.

For evening wear "in these days of informality [*sic*]," the dinner jacket was becoming increasingly popular. It was acceptable for informal engagements such as the theater, nightclub dances, or small dinner parties. Full evening dress — tail coat, white waistcoat, starched shirt, and white tie — was expected only at large, formal dinner parties.

In spite of this relative latitude, though, there were occasions that demanded quite specific attire. To weddings and the races at Ascot or Epsom, gentlemen would — and many still do — wear a morning coat, silk hat, and wing collar. Bradley warns, "If you should make the mistake of being seen at Ascot in a lounge suit, your social career will be blasted. It is conceivable that you might be forgiven a mistake at a wedding — because many mistakes have been made at weddings — but a mistake at Ascot is sacrilege." And tweed and brown boots, which were perfectly acceptable for tea at country houses, were not to be worn in town "unless you want the butlers and hall-porters to despise you."

Overdressing was as serious an offense as underdressing. Small wonder, then, that several Christie characters were dismissed witheringly as "not quite quite" simply because of their dress. Consider the example of Alfred Inglethorp in *The Mysterious Affair at Styles*, who committed the grievous social sin of wearing patent leather boots (expected only with evening dress) "in all weathers."

A gentleman also would own several kinds of sporting outfits. When golfing, for example, he wore "plus fours," which were baggy knickers. For tennis, he wore a thin white silk shirt and white trousers, skin-tight at the waist with a strap and buckle at each side seam. When hunting, he wore a red coat, white buckskin breeches, and a black silk hat. This traditional garb is still often worn for the hunt today.

The ins and outs of proper attire (from left): for a royal garden party at Buckingham Palace in the mid-1930s; a quiet New Year's Eve at home, from the same time; and another garden party at Buckingham Palace in the early 1920s.

Christie rarely describes men's clothing in detail. She notes that Norman Gale, the handsome young dentist in *Death in the Air*, wears a periwinkle blue pullover on the plane (casual attire was acceptable for traveling), and she sometimes mentions "stout country shoes" or an "old gray mackintosh" in passing. Some of her male victims — George Barton in *Remembered Death* and Richard Warwick in *The Unexpected Guest*, for instance — are killed in evening dress.

W. Somerset Maugham said, "The well-dressed man is he whose clothes you never notice," which might account for Christie's indifference. But a similar principle governed ladies' dress as well. The well-dressed lady, according to Bradley's *Etiquette for Ladies*, "never wears anything which would attract undue attention either to her appearance or her conduct." British ladies wore simple dresses, called frocks, for visiting or receiving guests during the day. Somewhat more elaborate creations — sometimes with a high neck — were worn for informal dinners or dances. Until around 1925, acceptable dress length was mid-calf. Hemlines then rose, and fell again in the '30s. Frocks were enhanced by neckwear and handkerchiefs; gloves were worn virtually always. In the country, but there only, as for the gentleman, tweeds were correct.

Evening gowns were reserved for formal occasions. Satin and chiffon were popular fabrics for evening wear, if one can trust Christie's fashion reportage. And only with evening dress were diamonds correct. Debutantes were not expected to wear — or own — much jewelry; jewels, like wrinkles, were to be acquired as a lady aged. With tweeds, even a strand of pearls appeared incongruous at best.

> In his way Tressilian was a connoisseur of ladies' dress. He always noted and criticized the gowns of the ladies as he circled around the table, decanter in hand.
>
> Mrs. Alfred, he noted, had got on her new flowered black and white taffeta. A bold design, very striking, but she could carry it off, though many ladies couldn't... Mrs. David now, a nice lady, but didn't have any idea of how to dress. For her figure, plain black velvet would have been the best. Figured velvet, and crimson at that, was a bad choice. Miss Peela, it didn't matter what she wore; with her figure and her hair she looked well in anything. A flimsy cheap little white gown it was, though.
>
> — *Murder for Christmas*

Christie is more specific about women's dress than men's, but she often leaves a good deal to the imagination. *Death in the Air* is oddly rich in sartorial detail. It contrasts the Honorable Venetia Kerr (a young "country society" type) and the Countess of Horbury (an upstart who had been a chorus girl until she snared an earl). At an inquest, Lady Horbury attracts the attention of the press because she is fashionably dressed in black, wearing "one of the new collegian hats and fox furs." Miss Kerr causes far less sensation; she is well-bred, so she knows better. Pale fox furs, by the way, were very chic in the 1920s and '30s.

Rosemary Barton in *Remembered Death* was murdered while wearing them. And the Honorable Mrs. Rupert Carrington in "The Plymouth Express" (a short story in *The Under Dog*) was last seen wearing a white fox fur toque (a fashionable hat of the period) with a white spotted veil and an electric blue coat and skirt.

Cigarette smoking became widely popular in the '20s and its ascendancy gave rise to accessories that no lady or gentleman went without. In *Death in the Air*, the authorities inventory the personal effects of the passengers on the plane. Apart from Lady Horbury's cocaine they find little, other than a great number of handkerchiefs (silk and linen) and silver cigarette cases. Rosemary Barton in *Remembered Death* owns one in platinum. Silver lighters were also *de rigueur*. For ladies, long cigarette holders were a must. Even horsey Miss Kerr carries two — one ivory and one jade.

A favorite aristocratic diversion was the costume ball. In Christie's lore, these parties invariably have tragic consequences, but one must assume that, on this point, her stories grossly exaggerate reality. In *The Mysterious Mr. Quin*, young Lord Charnley is killed while wearing brocaded dress and a powdered wig. In *Partners in Crime*, Lady Merivale is stabbed while dressed as the Queen of Hearts. Her assailant is disguised as the gentleman in *Through the Looking-Glass* who wore newspaper. And in "The Affair at the Victory Ball" (a short story in *The Under Dog*), Lord Cronshaw's ill-fated partygoers wear the costumes of the *commedia dell'arte* characters Pierrot and Pierrette, Harlequin and Columbine, and Punchinello and Pulcinella.

Of course, not everyone in society obeyed its conventions. And here, a bit of social history is in order. In Britain, as in the United States, the

An aristocratic young couple in riding costume, 1920s.

OUT OF THE TOP DRAWER

1920s were a decade of rebellion against established norms and values. In Britain, this revolt was largely the result of a general disillusionment brought about by the disastrous consequences of World War I. In the Battle of the Somme alone, the British lost about 500,000 men. The young generation who came of age in the years following the war held its elders responsible for this decimation and renounced all the old Victorian-Edwardian ideals of self-restraint and morality.

The leaders of this social insurrection became known as the Bright Young Things. Far from being revolutionaries in the accepted sense of the word, they were blatant posers whose flamboyant dress and makeup and wild parties flew in the face of etiquette. Their antics are captured in the novels of Evelyn Waugh, Aldous Huxley, and Nancy Mitford. In an episode of Waugh's *Vile Bodies*, which is replete with simultaneously — and deliberately — jaded and childish chatter ("too, too divine, darling" or "too, too sickmaking," they yawn), the irrepressible Agatha Runcible is turned away from several respectable country hotels and inns because she is wearing trousers. Trousers, of course, were *quite* unheard of for ladies, except in riding habit. (One of Christie's victims, Ellie Rogers in *Endless Night*, is in riding habit when she "accidentally" falls from her horse.)

The male counterparts to the Agatha Runcibles were dandies. In his semiautobiographical *Brideshead Revisited*, Waugh describes Sebastian Flyte, an aristocratic Oxford undergraduate who always carries a teddy bear and wears, on his first appearance, "dove-grey flannel, white crepe-de-chine, a Charvet tie."

Christie very occasionally does introduce — with obvious suspicion — a Bright Young Thing into her books. One example is Theresa Arundell in *Poirot Loses a Client*. Theresa is described as belonging to a "young, bright, go-ahead set — a set that had freak parties and occasionally ended up in

the London police courts." Her clothes are expensive but "slightly bizarre." (One should note that they are not bizarre to her dowdy cousin Bella, who desperately tries to copy them.)

Agatha Christie came of age shortly before World War I, and her fashion sense — and values in general — is that of the older generation. Even though she was not much older than many of the Bright Young Things, she seems terribly prim and middle-aged in comparison. The genteel elderly ladies who dot her books are bemused by the young, and these characters seem to reflect Christie's viewpoint. Even her younger characters are basically traditionalists. Her favorite young men seem to be charming, well-bred bounders, and anything but dandies. Her favorite young heroines are sophisticated and often outspoken, but wearing trousers or heavy makeup would simply never occur to them. Much later in her career, in *The Pale Horse,* Christie does describe a young woman, Ginger Corrigan, who wears "skintight trousers." But Ginger is an artist and wears "London artistic livery," which apparently exempts her from conventional norms of dress.

A not-inconsequential number of Christie's women live well beyond convention altogether. These are her *dérangées*, who are amusedly tolerated as "eccentric," rather than damned as "improper." Salome Otterbourne, the writer of graphic romances in *Death on the Nile*, wears a turban and "floating batik." Lady Vanda Chevenix-Gore in "Dead Man's Mirror" (in the anthology of the same name) is a self-professed reincarnation of an Egyptian queen and dresses in oriental robes. And the psychic Sybil Stamfordis in *The Pale Horse* wears a green sari ("which did nothing to enhance her appearance"). But although she admitted occasional variations, Christie — and a great many of her contemporaries — were happiest when everyone had a place, knew it, kept it, and dressed accordingly.

By the Pricking of My Thumbs (1968)

Tommy and Tuppence Beresford are gray and getting "elderly." Tuppence, however, is still intuitive and impulsive. Her instinct for a mystery and her persistence in following her interest lead her to seek answers where others might admit defeat.

Tommy and Tuppence decide it is time to visit his Aunt Ada in her nursing home at Sunny Ridge, even though Aunt Ada is a starchy old soul. Tommy is welcomed by Aunt Ada, but she rejects Tuppence as an unsuitable companion. "No good her pretending she's your wife. I know better. Shouldn't bring that type of woman in here."

While she waits for Tommy's visit to end, Tuppence meets a couple of residents of the nursing home who have something on their minds. Mrs. Moody is sure she hasn't had her cocoa yet today, and Mrs. Lancaster inquires dolefully, "Was it your child?" which rather startles Tuppence as the beginning of a conversation.

Shortly after their visit, Aunt Ada dies in her sleep, and the Beresfords return to Sunny Ridge to dispose of her effects. They choose to keep a desk, a worktable, and a charming painting of an attractive house beside a bridge over a canal. Tuppence thinks she recognizes the house as the same one she has seen not too long ago from a train window. The signature of the artist begins with a *B* but is otherwise illegible. The only information Miss Packard, the head of the nursing home, can give them about the painting is that Mrs. Lancaster gave it to Aunt Ada. And Mrs. Lancaster has been taken away by a relative, Mrs. Johnson.

Tuppence doesn't believe they should keep the painting without permission from Mrs. Lancas-

ter; and she sets out in her own indomitable fashion to find her. Her letter to the Cleveland Hotel, the last-known address the nursing home had, is returned with "Not known at this address." When she calls the hotel, she is informed that neither Mrs. Lancaster nor Mrs. Johnson stayed there. She calls Miss Packard and gets the name of the lawyers who made all the arrangements for Mrs. Lancaster while Mrs. Johnson was in Africa. Tuppence insists that Tommy call the attorney, Mr. Eccles, because "They just think women are silly and don't pay attention—"

Grumbling, Tommy makes the call and obtains the name of a bank. Tuppence mails a letter to the bank but never receives a reply. Tuppence is sure that Mrs. Lancaster has been "spirited away." She determines to find her somehow and hopes she will be in time — Tuppence senses danger.

Tommy has to attend a tiresome conference on the Continent, and Tuppence takes his absence as her opportunity to track down the scene of the painting, since her efforts at directly tracing Mrs. Lancaster have been to no avail. She has been able to probe her memory to reveal the train trip on which she had seen the house and knows the general area to explore.

After motoring through many narrow lanes, she does find the house, and Alice and Amos Perry, who inhabit the back half of it. Alice looks like a good witch and enjoys inventing romances. Amos seems somewhat slow-witted and frightening, perhaps because of his size and perhaps because of something else. A pleasant tea with the Perrys is followed by the plaintive sounds of a bird which has fallen in the chimney in the closed-off front half of the house. Tuppence goes with the Perrys to rescue the bird and finds a doll in the fireplace debris. Could it have something to do with the fanciful tale Alice was telling her of the sometime inhabitant of the house, an actress who came only occasionally and had an unhappy love affair? Alice and Tuppence thoroughly enjoy their flights of fancy about the mysteries of the house, and Tuppence is determined to find out more.

She takes a room at Mrs. Copleigh's in the nearby village of Sutton Chancellor and has lovely chats with the vicar in the church graveyard, with Nellie Bligh over tea, and with Mrs. Copleigh at dinner. Mrs. Copleigh has more romantic tales than Alice Perry and much gossip about the people in the neighborhood as well. She knows who painted the picture; his name was Boscowan, and besides being a colorful person, he had an eye for the women. He was even suspected for a time of being the person who did away with several children in the neighborhood.

No one, however, knows Mrs. Lancaster. The house agents are downright discouraging. Tuppence's search seems doomed to lead her only into blind alleys.

The vicar enlists Tuppence in the search in the graveyard for the tombstone of a Major Waters's problematic daughter who might have died as a small child. As Tuppence uncovers a gravestone with a somewhat cryptic marking, darkness descends on her mind.

Tommy is disturbed when he returns from his meeting to be told by Albert, their "domestic mainstay," that Tuppence had expected to return in time for dinner and is not home yet. She doesn't show up the next day either.

Tommy goes to London to see Mr. Eccles, the attorney, for further information about Mrs. Lancaster, in hope of finding where Tuppence might be. Mr. Eccles is no help. And Dr. Murray arrives with a disturbing tale of Mrs. Moody's (the one who wanted cocoa) morphine poisoning at the nursing home. The doctor is also full of·

speculation about past cases of murderers who killed groups of people. There seem to be more questions every moment, and no answers in sight. Ivor Smith of Intelligence, whose man has been following Eccles, thinks he has some ideas. Dr. Murray may have others. Tommy's friend Robert puts him in touch with Mrs. Boscowan, who wonders why someone has added something to her husband's picture.

But the burning question is where is Tuppence —and no one seems to know the answer until the Beresfords' married daughter in Invergashly calls and inquires about a newspaper account of an accident to one Prudence Cowley. That's Tuppence's maiden name!

Albert, the Beresford's servant, reveals unprecedented knowledge of the inner workings of furniture, and a hidden belated message from Aunt Ada sends Tommy in a tremendous rush to Tuppence's side. Naturally, the explanation for her silence is the blow on the head followed by a small bout of amnesia.

The doll from the chimney reveals unexpected inner strength. Tuppence and Tommy attend a party at the vicarage in Sutton Chancellor, where Tuppence finally meets the impressive Mrs. Boscowan and Sir Philip Starke, the local landowner, botanist, and industrialist who is, sadly, a childless widower.

The next day Tuppence, impetuous and intuitive as ever, continues to check every little clue, including the inscription on the gravestone, which leads her to need a Bible. Following an unexpected confrontation, she calls on Alice Perry and is happily received by an unexpected person who helps her understand all the pieces of the puzzle. Unfortunately, she also finds herself again in danger and is soon breaking a window and screaming for help. Readers will be happy to know that help arrives in the nick of time, and all is made clear.

GAILA PERKINS

Hallowe'en Party (1969)

Mrs. Ariadne Oliver, famed mystery-story writer and notorious apple addict, is visiting her friend Judith Butler in Woodleigh Common, a small town thirty or forty miles from London. During her visit she attends a Hallowe'en party given by the local society leader, Mrs. Rowena Drake, for the entertainment of the "eleven-plus" students, ages ten to seventeen, who are leaving the local school, the Elms, and going on to other schools.

On the afternoon preceding the party one of the students helping with the preparations, Joyce Reynolds, claims to have seen a murder committed "years ago," but says she didn't know it was a murder when she saw it, until "something that somebody said only about a month or two ago made me think, 'Of course, that was a murder I saw.'"

Mrs. Oliver, however, accepts the opinion of everyone else that Joyce is a boastful child who will say anything to attract attention.

On the evening following the party, Hercule Poirot receives a surprise visit from Mrs. Oliver at his London flat. Nearly hysterical, Ariadne tells him that Joyce had been found after the party, drowned in a galvanized bucket of water, her head pushed down among the bobbing apples. "I hate apples...I never want to see an apple again." Unfortunately, the dear lady cannot escape from her favorite fruit that easily. After all, the murder has been committed at a house called Apple Trees.

Assuming that the child was killed because of her pre-party statement, Poirot feels that he must tackle two major problems. First, whose murder did Joyce witness? Second, was Joyce killed by the same person who killed the first victim, or by someone attempting to protect the original murderer?

The first move Poirot makes is to visit his old friend Superintendent Spence who has retired — surprise! — to Woodleigh Common. Spence and Poirot had been associated years before in the investigation of another death.

Spence provides Poirot with a list of people who have been murdered, or *possibly* murdered, near Woodleigh Common over the past few years. This includes the following people:

— Mrs. Llewellyn-Smythe, a wealthy widow, who apparently died of natural causes. The aunt of Rowena Drake's deceased husband, she left a will to which was appended a codicil leaving the bulk of her estate to an *au pair* girl, Olga Seminoff, who had attended Mrs. Llewellyn-Smythe during her last year. The codicil proved to be a forgery, and the *au pair* girl ran away, never to be seen again.

—Charlotte Benfield, a sixteen-year-old shop assistant, found dead in the Quarry Wood. She was savagely beaten. Two subjects were questioned, but they both had alibis.

—Lesley Ferrier, a lawyer's clerk, twenty-eight, found near the Green Swan Pub, stabbed in the back. He may have been having an affair with the wife of the pub's landlord, but nobody ever proved that the affair was the motive for his murder.

— Janet White, a schoolteacher strangled on a footpath leading from the schoolhouse to her home. She was said to have been afraid of an ex-lover, but no one ever found out who he was.

Which one of these people might have been the victim of the murder little Joyce had witnessed? Perhaps none of them have anything to do with the present murder, though Poirot thinks that one of them may. He places a checkmark next to the name "Janet White" as the most likely victim to have been observed and recognized by Joyce.

His next move is to question each person who was present at Rowena Drake's home during the party preparations.

Judith Butler, pretty and blonde, reminds Mrs. Oliver and Poirot of a sea nymph or water sprite, placid and serene; "she could have been a Rhine maiden."

Ann Reynolds, sixteen, the dead girl's elder sister; she is not much liked, because she tries to impress everyone with her superior intelligence.

Leopold Reynolds, Joyce's eleven-year-old brother, may be a mathematical genius, but he "listens at doors," and is considered by his peers to be rather sneaky. Lately, he has been spending more money than his parents can afford.

Rowena Drake was present, of course. She is a "tall, handsome woman of forty-odd," with graying blonde hair and blue eyes. She seems to run Woodleigh Common. Late in the narrative she tells Poirot that she saw Leopold Reynolds step out of the murder room and slip back in again at just about the time that the murder took place. Unfortunately, her evidence comes too late to help anyone, particularly Leopold.

Perhaps the most interesting guest at the party, although not present during the preparations, was Mrs. Goodbody, a cleaning woman who doubles as the local witch. She talks to Poirot about evil, not black magic—"that's nonsense, that is. That's for people who like to dress up and do a lot of tomfoolery." She'd rather talk about the true evil that comes from people who are touched by the devil's hand.

Two other people who were not at the party capture the interest of Poirot. One is Michael Garfield, a young landscape artist. Several years ago, employed by Mrs. Llewellyn-Smythe, he created a sunken garden in the old stone quarry on her property. After finishing this work, he settled in Woodleigh Common in a cottage bequeathed to him by his employer. Poirot describes him as a "beautiful young man," not merely good-looking, but beautiful, with a passion for beauty that equals Poirot's passion for truth.

The garden that Michael has created is a place of magic, where fauns and nymphs might frolic, a place that might have been made by fairies. It is here that Poirot meets Miranda, Judith Butler's twelve-year-old daughter, and Joyce Reynolds's closest friend. She is called by both Mrs. Oliver and Poirot a wood-nymph, innocent and wise. She tells Poirot that she and Joyce told each other everything. How much does Miranda know?

What finally happens at Woodleigh Common? Well, Poirot triumphs, naturally. Mrs. Oliver gives up apples, at least temporarily. And we finally learn whether or not Joyce Reynolds's statement was an innocently coincidental falsehood or a fatal truth.

ALBERT NORTON

Passenger to Frankfurt (1970)

The transit passenger lounge at Frankfurt is crowded as Sir Stafford Nye, an unambitious British diplomat, slips off his crimson-lined cloak and sips his beer. Traveling from Malaya to London, Nye had not expected the sudden two-hour delay in Germany. He did not expect to meet the woman sitting across from him either.

Described as "twenty-five or six," with "a delicate high-bridged aquiline nose, a black heavy bush of hair reaching to her shoulders," the woman tells Nye that someone is trying to kill her. She proposes a plan: Nye will allow her to steal his cloak, wallet, and passport, and knowingly drink a beer spiked with knockout drops to make it look like an actual robbery. She will cut her hair, wear his cloak, and pass through customs as Nye.

The adventurous Nye agrees, and is thrown into a world of intrigue and death.

Upon arriving home many hours later—after a rather uncomfortable nap in the passenger lounge—Nye finds Henry Horsham, the stalwart government security man, waiting for him. Horsham, who seems to know most of the answers, grills Nye about his journey and his slight delay.

After Horsham leaves, Nye learns that someone—a man posing as a messenger from the dry cleaners—has rummaged through his room. Several days later, while walking through Green Park along Birdcage Walk, Nye is nearly run over by a car. The next day, another car—an old-fashioned Daimler limousine—tries again.

His interest piqued, Nye places an advertisement aimed at the woman in Frankfurt in the personal column of a newspaper. After seven days of scanning the tiny type, he receives a reply. He is to meet the woman from the airport — Daphne

Theodofanous, alias Mary Ann—at the Festival Hall during a Wagnerian opera. The encounter is brief. No words are spoken.

Finally, at a dinner party several nights later at the American Embassy, quite by chance—or is it?—Nye again meets the woman from Frankfurt. Introduced this time as the Countess Renata Zerkowski, Nye finds that she is quite at home in the social-diplomatic world. Afterward, she asks if he needs a ride home. Sir Stafford Nye accepts.

They proceed to a house near Godalming, where Nye and Mary Ann-Daphne-Renata meet with Henry Horsham; Lord Altamount, a British hero; Sir James Kleek, his trusted companion; and the mysterious Mr. Robinson. These men wish to know—wish Nye to investigate—just who is behind the young, violent dissidents who have staged riots around the globe. They want to know just who wants to take over the world.

Nye agrees, and he and Mary Ann begin their search in Germany. After two nights of modern music at the Festival Youth Theater, Nye and Mary Ann travel to a castle near Berchtesgaden. Known as Hitler's country, it is the perfect setting for "World Take-Over Central."

While there, as the guests of the Grafin Charlotte von Waldsausen, "a whale of a woman" whose hunger for food is the only thing greater than her hunger for power, they meet Franz Joseph, a member of the super race of Aryan youth, a holdover of the Nazi vision of total world domination.

They soon leave the schloss and head for "a stronghold in the Dolomites" where they attend a mass gathering of youth in an amphitheater in the mountains. It is like a marathon of madness. The clowns have definitely taken over the circus, and Franz Joseph, or Young Siegfried as he is known, is the ringmaster.

Meanwhile back in Paris, with the youths' violent insurrection against the Establishment fully under way, five men, representatives of various governments, discuss a way to halt the destruction.

In London, too, Prime Minister Cedric Lazenby and his cabinet wrestle with the same problem. Just who is behind all this, they ask? Who controls the armaments, the drugs, the finances, and the scientific technology needed to run a global revolution? Just who is Juanita, the missing piece of the puzzle? Is Franz Joseph really the illegitimate son of Adolph Hitler?

As they speak, organized bands of young people — clean-cut and power-crazed — escalate their assault. The "Golden Youth" is "properly drilled, properly armed, properly commanded, armed with planes, bombs and handguns."

France, Italy, Egypt, Russia, Jerusalem, and Syria have already fallen, and the United States and England are just beginning to feel the devastation. The world's leaders decide it is time for drastic action.

Perhaps Admiral Blunt has the right idea. Resurrect Project Benvo, an irreversible means of turning the world benevolent. But does Professor Robert Shoreham, the creator of Project Benvo, remember the formula? Has the research scientist, now a helpless paralytic, really destroyed all his notes? What will a world of pacifists be like?

Will Nye survive? What is to become of Mary Ann? Not to mention the world?

RICHARD REGIS

The Golden Ball and Other Stories (1971)

In *The Golden Ball and Other Stories*, Christie, who sometimes minimizes romance—an aspect of life which tends to be a bit more complicated than a well-done homicide — gives us George and Elizabeth, Edward and Maud, Jane and the artist, a middle-aged matron and a nobleman, Dorothy and Edward, George and Mary, James and Grace, Dickie and Esther, Macfarlane and Rachel, Arthur and Phyllis, Richard and Theodora and Vincent and Theodora, and lastly Joyce and Terry. Jewels disappear and reappear, sometimes in the hands of those who don't even want them. Ghosts, clairvoyants, and religious mystics also put in appearances.

In "The Listerdale Mystery," Mrs. St. Vincent, once a comfortably well-off woman and now a member of the genteel poor, finds a lovely, well-kept house for rent at a "purely nominal" sum. While her daughter, Barbara, is able to accept the family's incredible good fortune, her young son, Rupert, declares that there is something "decidedly fishy" about the house. And when Rupert discovers that the house in question is the residence from which Lord Listerdale mysteriously disappeared, he becomes convinced that the lord has been murdered and that his body will be found under the floorboards. Rupert believes this in spite of the story currently being circulated that Listerdale "disappeared" to East Africa.

Of course there's Colonel Carfax, Listerdale's cousin, to consider; he's been invested with power of attorney in order to be able to conduct Listerdale's affairs in his absence. Listerdale was reputed to have quite a bit of money, not to mention a number of real-estate holdings. And then there's Quentin, the butler, who, when asked about his master, replies "Lord Listerdale *was* a very selfish gentleman, Madam; with no consideration for others." A very strange statement indeed. Can we believe that Lord Listerdale is actually in East Africa, as the story goes, or are his mortal remains reposing under the floorboards?

In another story young George Rowland, just fired by his uncle for arriving at work late after a night on the town, decides to take a train trip and seek his fortune elsewhere. Just as George has settled himself in the first-class carriage, a young woman jumps in, exclaiming, "Oh! Hide me—Oh! Please hide me." George, the true gentleman, stows her beneath his seat just as an angry face appears at the window, bellowing, "My niece! You have her here. I want my niece." And so commences "The Girl in the Train." Our fair maiden deposits a small, wrapped parcel with George, along with instructions to follow a bearded stranger, and disappears. George, true to his word, clings to the package, and while following the stranger encounters another bearded stranger, "a grey-haired, pompous gentleman who speaks excellent English," and "a tall, somewhat pimply young man with a blond Teutonic cast of countenance." The latter two appear on the scene to inquire as to the whereabouts of Grand Duchess Anastasia Sophia Alexandra Marie Helena Olga Elizabeth of Catonia, as they are convinced that George knows something of her. From here events progress at a dizzying pace, with the parcel vanishing and reappearing, a stranger in a mood to wrestle bounding

AGATHA CHRISTIE | EL MISTERIO DE LISTERDALE

Selecciones de Biblioteca Oro

out of a closet, and a final explanation provided by the beauteous damsel in distress.

Miss Dorothy Pratt and Mr. Edward Palgrove, out on a Sunday afternoon drive, stop to buy a basketful of cherries from a roadside stand in "Fruitful Sunday." The situation becomes complicated when Dorothy discovers a ruby necklace whose description just happens to match exactly that of a recently stolen necklace worth £50,000. Now Edward and Dorothy face a crisis. Should they go to the police with the jewels, or keep them?

In "The Golden Ball," the title piece, yet another George, this time George Dundee, is fired by his uncle for taking a day off without asking leave. Our unemployed friend stands on the curb contemplating his future, when famed society girl Mary Montresor, whom he recognizes from the illustrated papers, appears, extending an invitation to George to come driving with her. As he had always been admonished by his aforementioned uncle to grasp "the golden ball of opportunity," George graciously accepts, but is just slightly startled when Miss Montresor asks, "How would you like to marry me?" as they are taking a wild sweep round a corner. Anxious to continue the game, George replies in the affirmative, and Miss Montresor suggests that they go off into the English countryside to find a house to live in. She quickly spots one to her fancy, and concocting a story about a fictitious Mrs. Pardonstenger, she drags George along to inspect the dwelling. They are greeted by a real Mrs. Bella Pardonstenger and a rather unpleasant brute waving a large revolver who sneers, "Thought you were mighty clever, didn't you? Coming here like this and playing the innocents. You've made a mistake this time—a bad mistake. In fact, I very much doubt whether your friends and relations will ever see you again."

For those who have an interest in the supernatural and the inexplicable, Christie proffers a number of selections. "The Hound of Death" concerns a nun, Sister Marie Angelique, who was involved in the supposedly spontaneous explosion of a convent under attack by the Germans. She is thought to go into trances, have hallucinations, and be mentally unstable. She imagines a new religion, a Brotherhood of the Crystal, and thinks that she possesses the power of death in her hands, a belief that is ridiculed by others until some very odd "coincidences" take place.

"The Gypsy" is about a beautiful young woman who has psychic powers and "The Lamp" is the story of a haunted house where the ghost of a lonely child walks. "The Strange Case of Sir Andrew Carmichael" involves the concept of the metamorphosis into animals, and "The Call of Wings" gives us a millionaire, happy with the comfort and luxury of money, who dreams of the sights of another world.

This collection of short stories, fifteen in all, shows Christie's lighter side. Told with a deft touch, they contain plot twists and surprise endings. In fact, as we peruse this volume, we get the distinct impression that dear Dame Agatha may just have been pulling our leg.

CATHERINE DeLOUGHRY

HE AND SHE
Two Fans Tell How They Turned Each Other On to Christie

An interview with Elinor Greenberg, psychoanalyst, and Alan Zimmerman, accountant, New York City

EDITOR

Which one of you was hooked first on Agatha Christie?

ELINOR

I was.

EDITOR

Do you remember what got you started?

ELINOR

When I was a child I read three or four books a day. I was reading Mickey Spillane, and then I started looking in the mystery section for other things to read and came across the Christies. I tried one — it might have been *The Man in the Brown Suit* — and it was very, very different from Mickey Spillane.

EDITOR

Were you hooked right away?

ELINOR

Yes, I was hooked immediately. I started reading them one right after the other. One thing that pleased me was that they were in the public library. They seemed to be considered extremely wholesome, so I could get them anywhere.

EDITOR

Alan, were you influenced by Elinor?

ALAN

Yes. Ellie suggested I read Christie. I read the first one about a year and a half ago, and then I read several within a couple weeks.

ELINOR

Alan likes large series of things.

EDITOR

Well, you had plenty to work with.

ALAN

That's one of the really good things about the Christie series. There are a lot. It gives you something to look forward to and get caught up in. If you enjoyed one, you know there will be another thirty or forty more to follow.

ELINOR

Alan's style of being involved in it is very different than mine. I'm very haphazard. I preferred not to know exactly how many books there were. I could just continue and feel like they were endless. Alan immediaely catalogued them.

ALAN

I tried to read them in order, because there were certain character developments. I went through them all that way.

EDITOR

What's it like to reread a Christie book when you already know the way it turns out?

ELINOR

I became a gestalt therapist because of the emphasis on the present. I have a very bad memory for the past. (laugh) I'll be reading one and think, "Hmm, this is a familiar plot" and I won't remember how it turns out even on the third reading.

*Elinor Greenberg
and Alan Zimmerman*

ALAN

Some of the plots are used more than once, so this allows you to go back.

EDITOR

How does a person know when they're a fan and not just a reader?

ELINOR

For me, it's when I go into a bookstore and look for an Agatha Christie rather than just any good book. I consciously search them out.

ALAN

Well, when I gave the bookstore a list of the Christie books I was missing, I knew I was a fan.

EDITOR

Do you talk about the mysteries with each other?

ELINOR

No, we never discuss the books.

ALAN

There are a lot of the books and they're very enjoyable, but as soon as I finish reading one I want to forget about it.

EDITOR

When you're halfway through and you think you know who did it, you don't go running down the street shouting "Eureka!"? I did.

ELINOR

Reading Agatha Christie is a solitary pleasure. It's a way of getting away from the world.

EDITOR

Why do you read Agatha Christie?

ELINOR

I like the main characters. Miss Marple is my favorite. I didn't like Tommy and Tuppence. I didn't like their names. They sound like the Bobbsey twins. But I like Jane Marple a great deal. It is really neat to read books where an older person is a respected heroine rather than this pitiful old creature going to a nursing home or being taken care of by relatives. I like that she's an old woman and very sharp, and she keeps on referring everything back to the village. She solves things by the continuity of character traits. She believes that if people run in a certain pattern they're likely to behave similarly to other people who run in the same patterns. I like the way she figures things out.

Miss Marple is always saying that so-and-so

HE AND SHE

reminds her of just this character in her village, and that would end up being the deciding factor —because so-and-so would actually act in the end just like the character in the village. The character in the village was sneaky and would run away with the ten dollars from the pharmacy, and this other person also turns out to be sneaky—only on a larger scale.

ALAN

Also, she's sedentary, so you get a panoramic view of the story. The story unfolds much more slowly, with more depth to it. In a village you have a continuity of characters who have known each other for many years, and that lends itself toward character development.

ELINOR

I wish she'd written more Harley Quins. He was a mystical character. I mean, Poirot is very solid; he's a Belgian detective. Marple is a little old lady. But it's never clear what Harley Quin is. It's suggested that he's some kind of phantasmic aura. He's not quite real. Nobody ever sees him except the old man he's always helping. His presence is always signified by colored lights, or something that brings him to mind. That was an interesting twist.

My favorite thing is the happy endings. I can tell from the happy ending that it's an Agatha Christie, and that's really what I want.

ALAN

Good triumphing over evil.

ELINOR

Yes! Continuously! I don't want it to end on a sour note.

EDITOR

How about the ending of *Curtain*? I thought that was sad when Poirot died.

ELINOR

I would have preferred it to have been left open, with me assuming that Poirot was in a little old-age home for happy detectives.

EDITOR

What do you think people who love Christie have in common? Is there a typical profile of a person who loves this kind of book?

ALAN

You have to be obsessive, simply because there are so many books, probably more of a solid series than any other writer has.

ELINOR

Christie readers would have to be idealistic, even if they were cynical on the surface, because good always triumphs over evil and everything usually ends up well for the good characters. If someone doesn't share that belief, it must be boring to always see it happen.

EDITOR

Then who would dislike these stories?

ELINOR

I would say people who are very much involved with the tragedy of life, with lack of fulfillment, who are identifying themselves with the outlaws of society.

EDITOR

Do you ever feel apologetic about reading mystery stories? A lot of people just say, "Well I wouldn't read that sort of thing." Do you ever feel like you can't admit this?

ALAN

Not at all. We're both involved in fairly intellectual occupations, so we can be relaxed with something that doesn't require an overly involved thought process.

ELINOR

Yes, I always thought that kind of intellectual snobbery was kind of silly. People prefer what they prefer.

EDITOR

Do you have a favorite period in Christie's works? Do you prefer her early books as opposed to her later?

ELINOR

I prefer her early ones, because I like prewar England.

ALAN

I felt the early ones were done a little bit better. She may have gotten a bit tired of such things after a while. The later ones were less thorough than the early novels, which were clearer and more controlled. *Postern of Fate* was one of her later books and probably one of her worst.

EDITOR

Christie always said that her worst book was *The Mystery of the Blue Train*.

ALAN

I enjoyed that one.

EDITOR

Maybe she said that before she wrote *Postern of Fate*.

ALAN

Well, if her writing diminished with age, I don't think she'd recognize that.

EDITOR

Do you think it did?

ALAN

The two I didn't like particularly were the last two

she wrote. She was getting older. She had written a lot of books. It was probably harder for her by then.

ELINOR

In her early books nobody was a grand criminal type. There were murders of passion, murders for money. Typical kinds of village murders. And then she started getting influenced by books that other people were writing, in which there were great international plots, James Bond plots, and it didn't come off. It was not her type of thing.

ALAN

She didn't do conspiracies well. When she tried it, she didn't have the experience with it. It's really a very different type of book from the kind she usually wrote.

EDITOR

Do you see your mystery reading interacting with your real life at all?

ALAN

I enjoy the character developments in the books — the sort of problems I don't always get involved with in real life.

ELINOR

For me it's the opposite. Alan works with numbers all day. For him these character developments are very involved. For me they're shallow. Mysteries are very relaxing to me. When I used to read Mickey Spillane as a kid, they were not relaxing. My adrenaline was going; my heart was pumping. I wanted to go out and throw ash cans at people's heads. That's not the effect with Christie. Christies are like doing needlepoint.

EDITOR

Christie has been read worldwide, translated into

HE AND SHE

more languages than Shakespeare, and that means places that are not at all like England, like the Orient and Africa. Why? What accounts for her popularity?

ALAN

She wrote very good classic mystery stories. And she wrote a lot of them.

ELINOR

They're very simple stories. Good triumphs over evil. That is appreciated in every country.

ALAN

And she played fair. She didn't write herself into a corner and have to resort to a trick ending. You have the feeling that you have a chance at guessing the ending. Some other mystery writers pull the rug out at the end.

ELINOR

The themes are very elemental. They're love, hate, murder, passion, all the things that motivate people everywhere. They're simple, moralistic stories. And they're wholesome.

EDITOR

Back to wholesome!

ELINOR

That's important. We are fairly lax here in that we'll let pretty much anything be read and be on the shelves at the library. And many countries have strong censorship rules or have strong religious prohibitions against explicit sex or against adultery or whatever. The Christie books have always been, not prudish, but sex is a separate issue in the books. So it's not offensive to somebody whose values may prefer less explicit sex.

ALAN

I guess she doesn't offend anybody. People aren't reading her books for sex or any other such things. By not including it she doesn't offend anyone.

EDITOR

If you were asked to give a tribute to Agatha Christie, what could you say?

ELINOR

I wish I had another Agatha Christie to look forward to reading.

ALAN

That says it. It would be nice if there were more.

Rx: Dr. Freud

"[Ernest] Jones was disheartened to hear from Anna Freud of Freud's great love for detective stories, especially following operations; Agatha Christie and Dorothy Sayers were special favorites."—Paul Roazen, *Freud and His Followers* (New York: Alfred A. Knopf, 1974)

"HOW DO YOU FEEL ABOUT THAT, JANE?"
If I Were Miss Marple's Shrink — A Fantasy
by Ro King with Pam McAllister

Psychotherapy notes and case history summary: Miss Jane Marple

First Impression: A very sharp-witted old woman. I could never determine her exact age but her mass of fluffy white hair, pink crinkled face and references to historical events place her apparently in her early nineties. She has china blue eyes and generally wears fleecy wool clothes with a Shetland shawl. Her basic kind, grandmotherly image conflicts strongly with a pessimistic view of human nature.

Unusual behavior: Patient insisted on knitting during the sessions. Peculiarly, although the garments all had the same fluffy, fleecy appearance, upon close examination a new and different project was well under way at each session.

Treatment plan: Short-term therapy geared to presenting problem. See selected transcripts of sessions below:

Miss Marple shifted in her seat. Her hand raised in a fluttery motion almost covering her mouth but returned almost immediately to the knitting needle in her lap. She sighed, then sat upright, increasing the pace of her knitting vigorously.

". . . .so she had a large following, as it were; a number of different people quite enjoyed their visits with her."

"Yes, Jane, but how do you feel about that?" I said.

"Well, I'm about to tell you. Mrs. Poole, the carpenter's wife, could hold her tongue. People came from villages very far away just so they could talk to her. It always seemed to ease their troubles. And she served good tea as well. I myself, of course, never confided in her. She was from my own village and I didn't feel it would be the right thing."

"I see—other people enjoyed confiding in her but you never felt that you could."

"Yes, that's right. It was too close to home, you know. That's where the vicar's wife's niece's friend comes in. Her friend's second husband's sister happened to know a friend who had recently met with her older sister. Well, that sister spoke very highly of you."

"Are you concerned about your personal information getting around your very intricate social network?"

Miss Marple nodded without slowing the rhythm of her knitting.

"I don't want anyone to know what I'm about to tell you. This, this—eh—is confidential—is it not?"

"Yes. What would you like to tell me?"

After a moment of silence she continued. "You see, although I've never been official, I've had a bit of a career solving murders."

"How do you feel about that, Jane?"

"Well, you know, murder is a very serious thing, not a joking matter. Nothing trivial about it. But to tell the truth I rather enjoy them. Oh, not the murders themselves. Dreadful, awful things people do to each other. But I do enjoy the puzzle of it all, and of course I get my reward from helping people who need the help, like poor Gwenda Reed in my last case, *Sleeping Murder.*"

"It pleased you to help Gwenda?"

"HOW DO YOU FEEL ABOUT THAT, JANE?"

"Yes, and Giles Reed too, though of course I didn't do anything extraordinary at all. But I do think I have a definite knack for solving murders."

"You are pleased with this skill?" I prodded.

"Yes. Yes, and my nephew Raymond West, the writer, brags about me, but ... Well, I'm sure he's proud. He's always telling friends..."

"*But* what? Can you finish that sentence?"

"Well, he *is* proud of me and quite amazed at the way I handle the big cases, but ... he does joke a bit about me too, as though he didn't really think it was a skill but one of an old lady's silly eccentricities. You know, daffy old Aunt Jane — 'disconnected' as the youngsters say nowadays."

"I see. You don't feel that your nephew really appreciates your accomplishments?"

"Oh, heavens, it's not just my nephew at all. They all laugh. You don't think I'm blind and deaf enough to miss the police inspectors who think I'm just meddling or who think I've lost my train of thought when I am reminded of a parallel situation from St. Mary Mead? But this technique so often works. People are pretty much the same, you know, and when I remember these things I'm inevitably on the right track, but they smirk and point to their heads in a sign that I'm a daffy, senile old woman."

"You seem angry now."

"Well—angry...I wouldn't go that far...perturbed. I'm a bit perturbed."

"Let's look at that perturbed feeling ... just stay right with it, don't talk, just feel it. Let that feeling speak to you."

Miss Marple leaned back in her chair.

"Close your eyes," I said, "and ask yourself gently: What's so perturbing? Don't answer right away, wait until the feeling speaks to you."

She was silent for a moment.

"I think I'm jealous." Miss Marple sat up and began to knit again.

"Jealous?"

"Yes, I believe I am. Jealousy, you know, is a strong feeling, often the motivation for murder, I must say. It is not an easy emotion to handle."

"Who are you jealous of, Jane?"

Miss Marple suddenly looked aghast.

"Oh, drat! I've lost a stitch." She seemed preoccupied for several moments while she struggled, not only to regain the lost stitch, but her composure.

"You seem to be upset now, Jane."

"Oh, it's very silly, really. I know I'm Agatha's favorite, after all. She has stated that quite openly in her interviews and even in her *Autobiography*, you know. She said she was bored with Poirot herself."

"You are jealous of Poirot? Hercule?"

Miss Marple's already pink cheeks turned a shade pinker at this.

"Agatha even admitted she wished she could have killed him off and would have, but the public wouldn't let her ... Oh, my, what am I saying? Really you must forgive me. I didn't mean ..."

"You don't need to apologize for these feelings, Jane. The feelings cannot harm anyone, but they are unpleasant feelings to have. Try to talk about this a little more."

Reassured, Miss Marple put down her knitting to find a handkerchief in the bottom of her purse. Her eyes had clouded over with tears.

"Go with the feelings, Jane. It's all right to cry in here."

"I feel so silly. I'm usually so level-headed, even in the worst circumstances when others are barking up the wrong trees and being all flustered, I'm usually not. And that's the point. I have solved crime after crime and still they look at me as though I'm daffy. Each time, I get the same resistance to my M. O. I remember the time old Miss Greenshaw in "Greenshaw's Folly" was murdered. Everyone was so impatient with me for dwelling on Mr. Naysmith, who had nothing to do with the Greenshaw case at all except that it reminded me very much of the way he had of giving people false impressions just for fun . . . and sure enough I was glad I was reminded of Naysmith because the Greenshaw case turned out the very same way. You see?"

I nodded. "Go on."

"Yes. Well, I'm not daffy. I put two and two together, but so often the others don't see the same two and two that I see."

"Is this true of Monsieur Poirot?" I asked.

Miss Marple started at the mention of his name.

"Oh, yes, I did get off the track. He's a very good detective, there is no doubt about that. I respect the work he has done. Very clever. He doesn't have the knack for gossip and making community contacts that I have, of course, because he's a gentleman and a foreigner too. I can so easily go into the stores and start up old memories among the shopkeepers and learn so much that way."

"Go on." I encouraged her. Miss Marple's breathing became slightly faster now and her knitting needles clicked in time with the new pace.

"He's just so arrogant. He hates the country and the fresh air and acts as though nothing exciting ever happens in the villages. But I could tell him a thing or two about that. As I always say to my nephew Raymond, there is a great deal of wickedness in village life. But Hercule thinks he has a corner on all the big murder cases.

"And another thing — though I'm Agatha's favorite, it's Hercule that gets all the glory. There was a painting of him done for *The Sketch* and a full obit in *The New York Times*. He's been rated one of the most recognizable detective characters of all time. He's even on a postage stamp in Nicaragua. And me? No."

"You seem very upset now, Jane."

"Upset? Well look at me. I'm tall and thin. Do you know that most people think I'm short and plump? They think I'm just a fussy little pink and white Margaret Rutherford. Well, I'm not." Miss Marple threw down her knitting needles in a rage. "I'm not Margaret Rutherford," she shouted.

"Say that again, louder," I encouraged.

"I'm not Margaret Rutherford. I'm not Margaret Rutherford." Miss Marple fell back into her chair suddenly exhausted.

When Jane opened her china blue eyes they were red-rimmed but steady. For the first time in the session her hands lay still on the arms of the chair, the knitting needles no longer needed as an outlet for nervous energy.

"You've done very good work today, Jane. You've broken through to some very deep feelings. These feelings shouldn't stay buried. How do you feel?"

Nemesis (1971)

When you're pushing eighty and live in the tiny village of St. Mary Mead, the highlight of your day is reading the local obituary column. This 1971 Marple mystery opens with the saintly spinster pondering the list. Alloway — Barton — Olegg — Omerod — Rafiel — Rafiel? Hm-m-m. Sounds familiar. "It will come to me," says Miss Marple, turning to the crossword. Eventually she remembers Jason Rafiel as that rich and disagreeable invalid she met on her Caribbean vacation last year. She spends the day walking through the garden thinking about the late Mr. Rafiel.

The following week a letter arrives from Rafiel's solicitors. Complying with their request, Miss Marple appears at their London office to learn that she stands to inherit twenty thousand pounds if she agrees to investigate and "properly elucidate" a "certain crime." In a letter written before his death, Rafiel praises Miss Marple's natural flair for crime detection, adding, "Our code word, my dear lady, is NEMESIS." Though she has not a single clue to the nature of the crime she is to investigate, Miss Marple announces that she will spend her legacy on partridge dinners, boxes of *marrons glacés*, and visits to the opera.

A month passes. Miss Marple is getting worried. How can she "properly elucidate" when she has no idea what crime Rafiel wanted properly elucidated? At last a missive from the late financial genius arrives, urging her to accept a proposal she will soon receive by mail. Right on cue, a letter from the London Travel Bureau appears in the post, informing Miss Marple that she has been booked for the Famous House & Gardens Tour, courtesy of the late Jason Rafiel.

Jane Marple can take a hint. Packing her knitting, she joins her fellow passengers on the luxurious coach headed northwest out of London. The old dear chats with each tourist, one by one, hoping to stumble upon that "certain crime." Why, this may be more fun than reading the obituary column — this is like "a crossword puzzle with no clues given," she says to herself.

There is the tall dark foreigner moving restlessly in his seat — possibly a dangerous character. And the student, Emlyn Price, with his mop of undisciplined hair — a dedicated anarchist perhaps? Or Elizabeth Temple, just radiating integrity—conceivably the type to commit murder for some noble cause? Shifting focus from potential murderer to possible victim, Miss Marple considers the rich, disagreeable Mrs. Riseley-Porter and then her niece Joanna Crawford. But of course—Joanna would most likely inherit everything. But then, what would be the connection to Jason Rafiel?

Redoubling her efforts, Miss Marple tosses out the name of the late Rafiel. Only Elizabeth Temple, retired headmistress of the exclusive Fallowfield Girls' School, has even heard of him. She tells Miss Marple that Rafiel's son Michael had been engaged to one of her favorite pupils. Before they could marry, however, the girl died. "Why did she die?" Miss Marple asks. "Love!" comes the answer. "One of the most frightening words there is...Love..."

The third day of the tour finds the group lodged at the Golden Boar in the village of Jocelyn St. Mary. Miss Marple is approached by a plump, pleasant woman who introduces herself as a friend of the late Mr. Rafiel. She explains that, before his death, Rafiel had written to suggest that Miss Marple be invited to the family home for a night or two, as this part of the tour is too strenu-

ous for such an elderly person. Why question Fate? Miss Marple accepts the invitation.

The Old Manor House is occupied by three sisters. Miss Clotilde Bradbury-Scott, the oldest, is tall, handsome, and well educated. The good-natured Lavinia Glynne, a widow, tends to the domestic affairs of the home. Anthea Bradbury-Scott, at fifty, is the youngest of the sisters. She reminds Miss Marple of "a mature Ophelia," with her wraithlike appearance and bizarre behavior. After lunch Anthea takes the elderly guest on a tour of the garden, which, like the house, has been sadly neglected. Her eyelid twitching, Anthea confides her desire to repair the decayed greenhouse now covered over with white flowering creepers. Frankly, the woman herself gives Miss Marple the creeps.

It is the maid who finally supplies the vital clue Miss Marple has been seeking. According to the servant, the girl engaged to Rafiel's son had once lived in the Old Manor House and was like a daughter to the oldest sister, Clotilde. Six months after her sudden disappearance ten years ago, the girl's brutally beaten body was found buried in a ditch several miles from the village. Clotilde had to go with the constable to identify the body, and Michael Rafiel was subsequently convicted of murder.

Before Miss Marple can properly elucidate this crime, word arrives that Elizabeth Temple has been seriously injured by a falling boulder while hiking up a nearby hillside. Returning to the Golden Boar, Miss Marple is informed by Professor Wanstead that he is on the tour at the request of the late Jason Rafiel, who had asked that he "keep an eye on" Miss Marple. The professor explains that the prison governor and Rafiel were both convinced of Michael's innocence. After listening to Miss Marple's review of the past several days, Wanstead agrees that her mission is undoubtedly to find the true killer. Now, with Miss Temple on her deathbed, the professor suggests that there may be another murderer on the loose, for Joanna

Crawford and Emlyn Price had reported seeing a person trying to dislodge a boulder just before the accident.

Elizabeth Temple sends for Miss Marple, to whom she confides her dying words: "Verity. Find out about Verity. Truth. Another name for truth, Verity." A bit repetitious, perhaps, but why be critical at a time like this? Miss Marple returns to the Old Manor House and, as little old ladies will, lets one word carelessly slip out of her reverie: "Verity." Knitting needles drop to the floor! Tears flow! And Anthea starts chattering wildly. "Verity? Verity did you say? Is it Verity Hunt you mean? They found her body in a ditch."

Armed only with her knitting bag, Miss Marple hobbles about the town in search of a murderer. Who would want to kill the lovely Verity Hunt? Why didn't she show up for the secret wedding she'd arranged with Michael? What happened to Nora Broad, the wild and pregnant girl who left town just about the time Verity was murdered? Could Elizabeth Temple's death have been an accident, or was she deliberately murdered? What was in the strange parcel Anthea took to the post office?

"One of my names," Miss Marple warns, "is Nemesis. Nemesis is long delayed sometimes, but it comes in the end." And in the end, of course, Nemesis does come, and, with the crime properly elucidated, Miss Jane Marple returns to St. Mary Mead to enjoy a partridge dinner as she ponders the local obituary columns.

ANITA McALLISTER

Elephants Can Remember
(1972)

Mrs. Ariadne Oliver, writer of mystery novels, attends a literary luncheon where a nasty and overbearing woman accosts her with questions about a double suicide over twenty years ago. The victims were parents of a goddaughter of Mrs. Oliver, Celia Ravenscroft, and the accosting woman—Mrs. Burton-Cox—must know, "Did her mother kill her father or was it the father who killed the mother?"

Unfortunately, unlike the elephants of the title, Mrs. Oliver cannot even remember her own goddaughter, let alone the particulars of the mysterious deaths. She manages to escape the disagreeable woman and the boring luncheon, but the seeds of mystery have been planted in her mind. Mrs. Oliver now cannot rest until she has found her goddaughter and learned the details of the deaths.

She calls upon her good friend Hercule Poirot, who advises her to forget the project — no one will remember the details of these deaths of twenty years ago. But of course mystery writers and detectives cannot resist intrigues of this sort and soon Mrs. Oliver and Poirot are plotting strategies for uncovering the particulars of these mysterious deaths. "What we've got to do," says Mrs. Oliver, "is get at the people who are like elephants. Because elephants, so they say, don't forget."

While Poirot digs through police records of the incident, Mrs. Oliver reestablishes contact with her goddaughter. Celia is engaged to the son of Mrs. Burton-Cox, and the concern about who shot whom seems to have some bearing on the genetic desirability of having Celia as a daughter-in-law.

Celia admits to Mrs. Oliver that she detests Mrs. Burton-Cox but that the circumstances surrounding the deaths of her parents have become something of an obsession for her and that she would like Mrs. Oliver to find out what she can. Celia was only twelve at the time the bodies were found on a lonely cliff on the family estate at Cornwall. Lord Ravenscroft had retired from service in India some years before and had brought his family to live by the sea. On one seemingly ordinary day he and his wife, with the family dog in tow, went out for a walk. Later that day both of them were found dead from shots fired from Lord Ravenscroft's revolver. The police termed the deaths a double suicide, but no plausible motive was ever agreed upon. The couple had no financial problems, seemed to get along quite well, had no enemies. Celia was in school in Switzerland and the only persons in the house at the time of the suicide were an elderly housekeeper, a former governess, and Celia's aunt, none of whom had any apparent motive to kill Lord and Lady Ravenscroft.

Mrs. Oliver searches her memory. Celia's mother had been Molly Preston-Grey, a friend from long ago, who had married Major Alistair Ravenscroft, later promoted to general. The Ravenscrofts had been a most ordinary couple — not at all the type given to murder and suicide. Mrs. Oliver digs out her old address books to go in pursuit of elephants — persons from the past who might have memories of the Ravenscrofts.

From the elephants, Mrs. Oliver puts together a seemingly unrelated series of facts about Celia's parents: the general was slightly deaf, Lady Ravenscroft had four wigs, rumors of the general involved with a younger woman, rumors that Lady Ravenscroft's sister had been involved in the murder of a child, Lord Ravenscroft's having received a mysterious blow on the head while abroad, a gardener caught stealing, a nephew in trouble with the police, a handsome young tutor of whom Lady Ravenscroft was particularly fond.

Exasperated, Mrs. Oliver returns to compare notes with Poirot. She tells him her hypotheses: Lady Ravenscroft was involved with the tutor, or the general was involved with his secretary, or mental illness in the famly, or trouble over a child adopted in India, or...Poirot tells her to stop, that all the theories are plausible. They must go back even further into the past and find someone who knows something that hasn't been mentioned yet. Mrs. Oliver tells Poirot that now it is his turn to look for elephants.

The following day, Desmond Burton-Cox, Celia's fiance, comes to call on Poirot. Now he, too, is obsessed with these deaths of over twenty years ago. Celia won't marry him if there is some kind of mental deficiency in her family. He tells Poirot that Lady Ravenscroft spent many years in an asylum and that the Ravenscrofts had two French maids, both now living on the Continent, who might be able to offer some information.

Poirot is still at a loss as to a motive for the deaths, although he is suspicious of the interest of Mrs. Burton-Cox in this case. All theories aside, what are the facts? On one day that seemed like all the rest, General and Lady Ravenscroft were found dead on a cliff. The shots were from the general's handgun. The police had said double suicide, but if so, why had Lady Ravenscroft bothered to put on one of her wigs before committing suicide? And why had they taken the dog along when they went out? Poirot finds these two facts particularly disturbing and suspicious.

Mental illness in the family, the mysterious deaths of children, four wigs — Poirot goes over the facts of the case again and again. The elephants can only remember parts of the story. He must make them into a coherent whole. Poirot asks for assistance from an associate, Mr. Goby, who is known as a purveyor of information. Mr. Goby has found out that Desmond is the illegitimate son of his father's mistress and was adopted by Mrs. Burton-Cox. With this bit of information Poirot begins to see some light. The facts of the case finally begin to make some sense to him, and when Mrs. Oliver telephones later that day, he questions her about the dog that went walking with the Ravenscrofts on the day of their deaths.

Now certain of the facts of the case, Poirot leaves for the Continent to confirm his theory through one of the French governesses. Mademoiselle Zélie, who, we hope, was in the house at the time of the tragedy, will be the greatest elephant of all.   ROBERT SMITHER

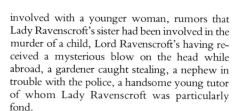

Akhnaton (1973)

While Agatha Christie found twentieth-century Western Europe, and in particular southern England, the most fertile site for her stories, occasionally she wandered farther afield, both in space and time.

Murder in Mesopotamia, for instance, was just that: murder in a modern-day archaeologists' compound in the Middle East. *Death Comes as the End* took us back to pre-Christian Egypt, as did the play *Akhnaton*, based on the life of the pharaoh of the same name who tried to turn polytheistic Egypt to the worship of one deity — Aton, the sun god. Published in 1973 but written much earlier, the play is Christie's version of the reign of Amenhotep IV, who ruled Egypt from 1375 B.C. to 1358 B.C.

Amenhotep IV changed his name to Akhnaton (son of Aton) to indicate his devotion to the sun god. He ruled the Egyptian empire with anything but an iron hand, according to Christie.

We first see him in the play through the eyes of Meriptah, high priest of the god Amon, at the time the most powerful sect in Egypt.

> The young prince is sickly. He dreams dreams and sees visions. He is the beloved of Ra Haratke who is the Lord of Visions. I fear that the Prince will dream and not rule.

How true that turns out to be — in a way. For Akhnaton dreams of "A kingdom where men dwell in peace and brotherhood, foreign countries given back to rule themselves, fewer priests, fewer sacrifices."

It hardly seems to be the stuff of which young pharaohs are made. At the time, the Egyptian empire stretched into Syria and beyond, and the Egyptians, if we are to believe Christie and her characters, enforce a kind of *Pax Egyptiana* over the region as far as the Euphrates River.

Nor do they decline to shoulder the contemporary version of the white man's burden. The sturdy Horemheb, early in the play, asks the high priest if it is worth Egypt's trouble to try to tame the local barbarians since "Even the native princes who have been educated in Egypt soon relapse into native customs when they get back... One wonders sometimes if it's much use trying to civilize them."

In an answer that would have made a Victorian proud the high priest responds: "It is our aim to improve all the subject peoples under our care."

Akhnaton, though, foresees a realm of tranquility, where justice and reason prevail, even over the wild tribes at the empire's edges. In the meantime, during breaks from dictating memos about the power of Truth to his people, Akhnaton devotes himself to Beauty in the person of his queen, Nefertiti, and the city he has founded in honor of Aton, the City of the Horizon.

Ah, but the generals grumble. Things are not what they might be. Egypt's neighbors see as weakness Akhnaton's reluctance to send in the marines at the first sign of trouble. The power of Truth is lost on them, apparently. The adherents of Amon, especially his priests, grumble too. For their temples have been taken over, their lands seized, their treasury emptied. Even the people grumble. Their old gods are gone, their pharaoh is flirting with moral turpitude (having himself portrayed in statues actually *kissing* his wife — not like the good old days) and the price of food has gone up, because the local administration is as corrupt as ever, if not more so.

Aton alone knows what would be happening if it weren't for the faithful Horemheb, governor of part of the country, who runs things with a just, if not very merciful, hand. He wants to punish evildoers by having their noses and hands cut off. Tough? Perhaps so, but the people revere him.

They certainly don't feel that way for Akhnaton, nor for Nefertiti ("dressing in that gauzy stuff and showing herself here, there and everywhere …"). There is still a reservoir of affection for Akhnaton's mother, the old queen Tyi, but Nefertiti's sister Nezzemut draws no raves, running around with that Ethiopian dwarf Para, who is known to have much skill with poisons.

Nezzemut is a woman with ambitions. She wouldn't mind at all being queen of Egypt, and she's got her eye set on Horemheb, who may be devoted to the king, but who can't be blind to what's happening to his country.

Meanwhile let's not forget that bright young lad Tutankaton, Akhnaton's son-in-law. He shows a lot of promise, that boy. But his name works against him. Now suppose we were to change it to Tutankhamun? That's got a certain ring to it, don't you think? That's a real pharaoh's name.

DICK RILEY

The Hercule Poirot Double-Crostic

by Dale G. Copps

This trickly little acrostic is inspired by a number of Poirot tales. Clues C, K, M, R, S, and X are all titles, or parts of titles, of Poirot mysteries. The quotation is from the Belgian master himself. The clue line (the first letter of all the clue answers) explains the significance of the quotation.

1 A	2 M	3 I	4 K	5 H	6 E	7 C	■	8 R	9 I	10 K	11 J			
■	12 K	13 J	14 N	■	15 R	■	16 X	17 E	18 M	19 J				
20 F	21 Q	22 Y	23 M	24 K	■	25 O	26 Q	27 U	■	28 G	29 K	30 W	31 C	■ 32 E
33 I	34 N	35 M	36 K	37 R	38 C	■	39 U	40 X	41 C	42 Q	43 S	44 K	45 E	46 L
47 H	48 X	49 L	50 K	■	51 N	52 O	53 H	54 F	■	55 F	56 P	57 U	58 E	59 M	60 O
■	61 H	62 P	■	63 L	64 P	65 E	■	66 W	■	67 V	68 E	69 X	70 P	71 G	72 Q
■	73 Z1	74 M	■	75 N	76 X	77 D	78 B	79 O	■	80 Q	81 N	82 M	83 J	84 F	85 I
86 Y	87 K	■	88 U	89 D	90 M	■	91 C	92 L	93 S	94 Q	95 K	■	96 M	97 T
98 X	99 B	100 V	■	101 N	102 O	103 R	■	104 S	105 X	106 V	107 A	■	108 Y	109 S
110 X	111 Z1	112 C	113 T	114 D	■	115 C	116 Z	117 A	■	118 O	119 S	120 X	121 G	
122 C	123 F	124 N	125 D	126 Z1	127 I	128 B	129 P	■	130 P	131 G	132 B	133 F	134 S	■ 135 L
136 N	■	137 M	138 S	139 Z	140 D	141 P	142 J	■	143 Z	144 R	145 D	■	146 K	147 Q	148 R
149 C	150 S	■	151 S	152 Z	153 N	154 T	■	155 U	156 T	157 V	■	158 N	159 P	160 Y	161 S
■	162 U	163 E	164 M	■	165 K	166 Z1	167 U	■	168 K	169 O	170 S	171 H	■	172 W	173 T
174 M	175 P	■	176 H	177 P	178 Z1	179 D	■	180 I	181 T	182 W	183 U	■	184 W	185 M	186 I
187 F	■	188 F	189 T	190 Z	■	191 M	192 U	193 Y	194 J	■	195 M	196 R	197 D	198 B
199 Q	200 G	201 Y	202 I	■	203 D	204 I	205 V	206 W	■	207 Z	208 U	209 J	210 F	

THE BEDSIDE, BATHTUB & ARMCHAIR COMPANION TO AGATHA CHRISTIE

A A war, o' sorts . . . .
$\overline{117}\,\overline{107}\quad\overline{1}$

B "__ Ho!" as in clue A . . . .
$\overline{99}\,\overline{128}\;\overline{132}\;\overline{78}\;\overline{198}$

C __ Can Remember (1972) . . . .
$\overline{7}\;\overline{31}\;\overline{38}\;\overline{41}\;\overline{91}\,\overline{112}\,\overline{115}\,\overline{122}\,\overline{149}$

D What Archimedes sought, to move the world . . . .
$\overline{114}\,\overline{125}\,\overline{197}\,\overline{140}\;\overline{145}\;\overline{77}\,\overline{203}\,\overline{179}$

E Count on the Calais Coach . . . .
$\overline{17}\,\overline{163}\;\overline{65}\;\overline{68}\;\overline{45}\;\overline{32}\;\overline{6}\;\overline{58}$

F A rose for love or a dove for peace . . . .
$\overline{187}\,\overline{188}\;\overline{20}\;\overline{55}\,\overline{123}\;\overline{84}\,\overline{133}\,\overline{210}\;\overline{54}$

G "__ of Anxiety": 2 wds . . . .
$\overline{121}\;\overline{89}\;\overline{71}\;\overline{28}\,\overline{131}\,\overline{200}$

H Australian burrower . . . .
$\overline{176}\;\overline{53}\;\overline{61}\;\overline{5}\;\overline{47}\,\overline{171}$

I "Walks o'er the dew __ eastern hill": Hamlet, I, i, 3 wds
$\overline{3}\;\overline{85}\,\overline{186}\,\overline{204}\;\overline{202}\,\overline{127}\;\overline{33}\,\overline{180}\;\overline{9}$

J Nostrum . . . .
$\overline{11}\;\overline{83}\;\overline{13}\;\overline{19}\,\overline{142}\,\overline{209}$

K 1956 opus: 3 wds . . . .
$\overline{4}\;\overline{10}\;\overline{12}\;\overline{24}\;\overline{29}\;\overline{36}\;\overline{87}\;\overline{95}\,\overline{146}\,\overline{165}\,\overline{168}\;\overline{44}\;\overline{50}$

L Latin step . . . .
$\overline{46}\;\overline{49}\,\overline{135}\;\overline{63}\;\overline{92}$

M 1940 opus (alternate title, with An): 3 wds . . . .
$\overline{2}\;\overline{18}\;\overline{23}\;\overline{35}\;\overline{59}\;\overline{74}\;\overline{82}\;\overline{90}\;\overline{96}\,\overline{137}\,\overline{164}\,\overline{174}\,\overline{185}\,\overline{191}\,\overline{195}$

N Ephemeral, suspiciously temporary: 3 wds . . . .
$\overline{51}\;\overline{75}\;\overline{81}\,\overline{101}\,\overline{136}\,\overline{153}\;\overline{14}\,\overline{124}\,\overline{158}\;\overline{34}$

O Gat; rod . . . .
$\overline{118}\;\overline{79}\,\overline{169}\;\overline{25}\;\overline{60}\;\overline{52}$

P Motive, in many a Christie, for murder: 4 wds . . . . . .
$\overline{56}\;\overline{62}\;\overline{64}\;\overline{70}\,\overline{102}\,\overline{129}\,\overline{130}\,\overline{141}\,\overline{159}\,\overline{175}\,\overline{177}$

Q Certain parallelogram . . . .
$\overline{72}\;\overline{26}\;\overline{21}\;\overline{80}\,\overline{199}\;\overline{42}\,\overline{147}\;\overline{94}$

R Source of the Quotation . . . .
$\overline{8}\,\overline{144}\;\overline{148}\;\overline{37}\,\overline{196}\;\overline{15}\,\overline{103}$

S Where the Evil was (1941): 3 wds . . . .
$\overline{43}\;\overline{93}\,\overline{104}\,\overline{109}\,\overline{138}\,\overline{150}\;\overline{151}\,\overline{161}\;\overline{170}\,\overline{119}\,\overline{134}$

T Words with "the land" or "The Last Minstrel": 3 wds.
$\overline{113}\,\overline{156}\;\overline{194}\,\overline{181}\;\overline{97}\,\overline{154}\,\overline{173}\,\overline{189}$

U S.J. Perelman title (1977): 2 wds . . . .
$\overline{27}\;\overline{39}\;\overline{57}\;\overline{88}\;\overline{155}\,\overline{162}\,\overline{167}\,\overline{183}\,\overline{192}\,\overline{208}$

V Staid; sober; influential: Fr . . . .
$\overline{67}\,\overline{205}\;\overline{157}\,\overline{100}\,\overline{106}$

W Quirk; curiosity . . . .
$\overline{182}\,\overline{184}\;\overline{206}\;\overline{66}\,\overline{172}\;\overline{30}$

X Where the Murder was (1937): 3 wds . . . .
$\overline{105}\,\overline{120}\;\overline{98}\;\overline{16}\;\overline{69}\;\overline{40}\;\overline{76}\;\overline{48}\,\overline{110}$

Y Kerr or Barnes forte . . . .
$\overline{160}\,\overline{193}\;\overline{22}\;\overline{86}\,\overline{201}\,\overline{108}$

Z Hateful; vile . . . .
$\overline{116}\,\overline{207}\;\overline{139}\,\overline{143}\;\overline{152}\,\overline{190}$

Z1 Our Belgian friend's eternal goal . . . .
$\overline{73}\,\overline{178}\;\overline{166}\,\overline{126}\;\overline{111}$

(Solution to puzzle on page 310.)

Postern of Fate (1974)

The list of clues that Tuppence carefully assembled read:

Black Arrow
Alexander Parkinson
Mary Jordon did not die naturally
    Oxford and Cambridge porcelain Victorian seats
    Grin-hen-Lo
KK
Mathilde's stomach
Cain and Abel
Truelove
To which we might add:
The Monkey Puzzle
China menu cards
Dodo
The census
Crab apple jelly
Swallow's nest
Peter Pan

But then again, in *Postern of Fate* everything sounds suspicious, everything sounds like a potential clue. This is not a single, one-track mystery of the whodunit school. There is, to be sure, the basic question of who was Mary Jordan and how and why did she die. But the same could be asked about Alexander Parkinson, and even old Isaac. And who are Tommy and Tuppence, our "detectives"? Was the crime and its related complications all completed sixty years before the time of this story? It initially seems so, and yet the characters are inclined to say immensely helpful things such as

Ah, *you've* heard rumors, have you? Ah well, don't think about them any more. They're not supposed to be known much. Don't think I'm

going to rebuff you for coming here asking me questions. I probably can answer some of the things you want to know. If I said there was something that happened years ago that might result in something being known that would be — possibly — interesting nowadays, something that would give one a bit of information about things that might be going on nowadays, that might be true enough. I wouldn't put it past anyone or anything. I don't know what to suggest to you though.

The book opens when Tuppence and Tommy Beresford, apparently a simple retired couple, start to settle into the Laurels, their recently acquired house in the small English village of Hollowquay. They have with them only Hannibal, a Manchester terrier with a most inquisitive and protective personality who will play no small part in the unfolding mystery, and Albert, their "devoted henchman."

There's a lot of dealing with plumbers and electricians who leave jobs undone and holes in the floor in unlikely places. "They came, they showed efficiency, they made optimistic remarks, they went away to fetch something. They didn't come back. One rang up numbers on the telephone, but they always seemed to be the wrong numbers. If they were the right numbers, the right man was not working at this particular branch of the trade, whatever it was."

But Tuppence becomes fascinated by going through the old children's books left in the house, remembering her own childhood favorites. In one, she finds a "curious phenomenon." Over the course of four pages, various words are underlined in red. Copied out, they make no sense. Then Tuppence notices that it is only particular letters in each word that have the red marks.

The big new bestseller from the Queen of Crime
First time in paperback

Agatha Christie

Postern of Fate

Three sentences appear, with a meaning all too clear.

> "Look here, Tuppence," said Tommy, "you're not going to get a thing about this, are you?"
> "What do you mean, a thing, about this?"
> "Well, I mean working up a sort of mystery."
> "Well, it's a mystery to me," said Tuppence. "*Mary Jordan did not die naturally. It was one of us. I think I know which one.* Oh Tommy, you must say that it is very intriguing."

Tuppence begins to make inquiries around the village, casual inquiries such as would be natural for a newcomer curious about the history of her new house and town. People keep saying "It was before my time," but gradually a story, or rather, many versions of a story, begin to emerge. Yes, there was some kind of "trouble" ("the disgrace," says Mrs. Griffin) in the village during the First World War. And Mary Jordan was somehow involved. She was a German nursemaid, a "frow-line," for the Parkinsons, who lived at the Laurels. On her days off she made mysterious trips to London and was thought by many to be a spy. But her death was accidental, a "silly mistake" on the part of the cook when someone erroneously picked floxglove leaves and mixed them in with the lettuce from the garden. At the inquest it was said, "It was a mistake that *anyone* could make." But was Mary Jordan the only one to eat dinner that night? And is there enough digitalis in a few foxglove leaves to kill someone?

Tuppence's husband, Tommy, has feigned a lack of interest in her research, but he comes back from a day trip to London saying that he has "put certain things in motion." When Tuppence

Postern of Fate (1974)

presses him for details, he's as infuriatingly unspecific as everyone else in the book:

> I mean, there are things that you can find out. Things that you could obtain information from. Not just by riding old toys and asking old ladies to remember things and cross-questioning an old gardener who probably will tell you everything quite wrong or going round to the post office and upsetting the staff by asking the girls there to tell their memories of what their great-great-aunts once said.... You must remember, Tuppence, that occasionally in my life I have been in connection with people who do know how to go about these sorts of things. You know, there are people you pay a certain sum to and they do the research for you from the proper quarters so that what you get is quite authentic.

So now another level of mystery has been added. It seems that this is not the first time our couple has been involved in solving a mystery. They occasionally drop references to "the time when we were investigating the Jane Finn business" or "N or M and goosey goosey gander."

Tommy has an interview with a Colonel Atkinson, who is very interested that the Beresfords are now living in Hollowquay and who seems to feel that they've moved to the Laurels on some sort of official business. "Perhaps you've been sent down there to have a look around, eh, my boy?" he says. Tommy also contacts various other official types who seem to know him from the past and who drop hints about not only Mary Jordan, but Tommy and Tuppence themselves.

Then the gardener who is working for the Beresfords and who may or may not have been around at the time of Mary Jordan is "coshed on the head," fatally. In a moment of astute observation Tuppence says, "I've got an uneasy feeling that there's something—something wrong with it all here. Something left over from the past." Tommy tells her not to get worked up, advice which hardly seems to fit the situation and which he himself does not even pretend to follow, especially when Tuppence is grazed by a bullet while doing a little more sleuthing in their own back yard.

From that point, I would like to say that the plot moves swiftly to its denouement, with a complete clarification of all the mysteries, a knitting in of the many loose ends. Perhaps. To speak in the language of the characters in this book, certain facts become known. Certain dramatic actions are taken. Several identities are revealed, and the past is linked to the present. And Hannibal takes the action into his own hands, or more correctly, paws—action that leads to the event in the last few lines of this book:

"I hearby create you a Count of this Realm."

"Count Hannibal. Isn't that lovely?" said Tuppence. "What a proud dog you ought to be."

When you enter in through the postern of fate, even a dog may find a strange reward.

CYNTHIA A. READ

THE MISS MARPLE DOUBLE-CROSTIC (*pages 234-35*)

Clue Line: "Really Miss Marple is rather a dear." (*Murder at the Vicarage*)

Quotation: "My dear young man, you underestimate the detective instinct of village life. In St. Mary Mead every one knows your most intimate affairs. There is no detective in England equal to a spinster lady of uncertain age with plenty of time on her hands." (*Murder at the Vicarage*)

Words:

A Rattan
B Effendi
C At the Vicarage
D Len Clement
E Lettice
F Yoyo
G May Day
H Ivy
I Sinfulness
J Shift
K Mine eyes
L Agatha
M Redding
N Poison
O Litho
P Evil
Q Imminent
R Sleeping
S Remove
T Attest
U Twin
V Human nature
W Equine
X Rift
Y Away
Z Doctor
Z1 Kennedy
Z2 Elfsoon
Z3 Roust

Poirot's Early Cases (1974)

Forgetfulness leads to the discovery of a body, a nursery rhyme provides the clue to a poisoner, and politics and chocolate mix in these early cases by the redoubtable Poirot.

In "The Third Floor Flat," four young people — Pat, Mildred, Jimmy, and Donavan — realize they are locked out of Pat's apartment one evening. Tiresome indeed. But suddenly Pat remembers that the coal lift opens into the kitchen — and she's sure she hasn't bolted the door.

Both men, who obviously admire the keyless Pat, brave the darkness of the coal lift and make their way into the kitchen, Donavan going first. He rattles around, bumping into things in the darkness, until Jimmy follows and turns on the light.

It is obvious they are in the wrong apartment.

Well, no harm done. They get back into the lift and try again, this time making it into Pat's kitchen, and let the girls into the apartment. But — what a pity — Donavan has hurt his hand — there's blood on it. He washes the blood away but strangely enough can find no cut or scrape.

Let it not be said that young English men and women cannot see the obvious. They return forthwith to the flat below, and this time take a serious look around. The kitchen is still empty, but in another room, sticking out from behind a heavy curtain, is a woman's shoe. As one might expect, there is a foot in it, a foot attached to the body of a dead woman.

Donavan returns to Pat's apartment, where they discuss the case and decide to call the police. But as they talk in the doorway of the apartment, the renowned eavesdropper, Hercule Poirot, makes his presence known.

He had heard them earlier trying to figure out how to get into the apartment and had thought of offering to pick the lock for them. Since he did not do that, courtesy alone would now compel him to solve the mystery for them.

Which he does.

Amelia Barrowby, the newspaper obituary read, was seventy-three when she died — certainly an age when death cannot be unexpected. But even so, Poirot is curious, thus beginning the case in "How Does Your Garden Grow?"

Not long before, he had received a letter from Amelia in which she intimated that strange things were going on around her and that she would welcome a visit from the illustrious detective. He had told his secretary to send Amelia Barrowby a reply, saying that he would confer with her whenever she was available. There was no answer to his note, and now, of course, he realizes why.

Just to keep the pot boiling, he sends another note to the now-dead lady, telling her that although she has not answered his note to her, he will meet with her on a Friday. Who will reply, he wonders?

The answer is not long in coming. Mary Dela-Fontaine, niece of Amelia Barrowby, lets him know that since her beloved aunt is dead there is no point in Poirot making the trip to Chalmers Green.

Anything but deterred, Poirot journeys to the scene of what he suspects is a crime. The garden around the house meets with his approval. He finds daffodils, tulips, hyacinths, and shells, bringing to mind the nursery rhyme:

Poirot's Early Cases (1974)

Mistress Mary, quite contrary,
How does your garden grow?
With cockle shells, and silver bells,
And pretty maids all in a row.

It is a pretty maid, ironically, who opens the door for him, but he is more taken with a small, sallow girl with suspicious eyes. Not one to beat about the bush, she tells Poirot that the money is hers and that she intends to keep it.

Motive enough for murder? Perhaps. One must include the sullen girl among the suspects. But let's not forget the niece, Mary DelaFontaine, and her tall, grizzled husband — if murder, indeed, is what we are dealing with.

Inspector Sims leaves no doubt. Death by strychnine poisoning, the autoposy has revealed. Logic certainly points the finger of guilt at the girl. But Poirot has his own methods, which include close attention to nursery rhymes.

A cup of hot chocolate reminds Poirot one evening of one of his few failures — the case of "The Chocolate Box." The case began one night when a very anti-Catholic Frenchman died just before he was about to assume an important post with his government.

Poirot was on vacation at the time, but was persuaded to look into the matter by a heavily veiled young woman. The young woman, it develops, was a poor cousin of the Frenchman's wife. That wife had died two years before her husband, perishing after a bad fall down a flight of stairs.

His curiosity piqued, Poirot agrees to look into the case. Poisoning is the obvious means, if indeed murder took place. Poirot recapitulates the dead man's entire meal, and begins to feel that the suspicion that the man died of anything but natural causes is groundless.

But Poirot's eyes must take in every detail. He finds a chocolate box, a pink box whose lid is blue — very strange. François, an old servant in the house, tells Poirot that his master enjoyed having sweets after his meal. François even manages to rescue from the trash the last box of chocolates, and this one is blue — with a pink lid.

Chocolate, Poirot discovers, can contain poison. Dinner on the fatal night, he also discovers, included two guests — an Englishman who suffered from angina and a French religious fanatic. Poirot's suspicions tend strongly in one direction — but the murderer turns out to be someone he didn't suspect at all.

ANITA GREENFIELD

THE HERCULE POIROT DOUBLE-CROSTIC (*pages 304–5*)

Clue Line: The last words of Hercule Poirot.

Quotation: "Good-bye, *cher ami*. I have moved the amyl nitrate ampoules away from beside my bed. I prefer to leave myself in the hands of the *bon Dieu* . . . We shall not hunt together again, my friend. Our first hunt was here — and our last . . . They were good days. Yes, they have been good days . . . . "

Words:

A Tug
B Heave
C Elephants
D Leverage
E Andrenyi
F Symbolism
G The Age
H Wombat
I Of yon high
J Remedy
K Dead Man's
L Samba
M Overdose of
N Fly by night
O Heater
P Eye for an eye
Q Rhomboid
R Curtain
S Under the Sun
T Lay of the
U Eastward Ha!
V Posec
W Oddity
X In the Mews
Y Review
Z Odious
Z1 Truth

Curtain (1975)

"Who is there who has not felt a sudden startled pang at reliving an old experience or feeling an old emotion? *'I have done this before . . .'*"

Arthur Hastings asks us this question at the opening of *Curtain* as we journey once again to Styles Court in Essex, where he has been summoned by his dear friend, detective Hercule Poirot. We have come full circle. It was at Styles Court during World War I (*The Mysterious Affair at Styles*) that Hastings first met Hercule Poirot, who would "mold my life." Several times during Poirot's extraordinarily long and successful career Hastings has aided him, and now, one last time, they will "hunt together again." After that, Poirot says to him, you may "Ring down the curtain."

Styles Court itself has changed with the times and the economy. It is being operated as a genteel guest house, and has been "modernized" in the worst ways. The grounds are ill-kept, the rooms partitioned and full of plywood furniture, the coffee and food unpalatable. But the paying guests at Styles resemble people from other Christie books. Again, an odd assortment of deceptive and disgruntled people have gathered, this time for the purpose of vacationing and getting on each other's nerves. They proceed to speak and act in the most suspicious ways possible.

Poirot has called Hastings to Styles for work on what Poirot knows will be his last case. He has Hastings read the summary of what appears to be five totally unrelated open-and-shut murder cases, and mentions that the only point they seem to have in common is that for each murder there was only one obvious and probable murderer. But there is one other connection — a person, labeled X by Poirot, who not only knew each of

these victims, but also was nearby each time the death occurred. In short, this X is quite likely to be the true murderer.

Thus far, X's crimes have been undetected by all but Poirot, and executed so as to be outside the bounds of the law. And now, X is known to be at Styles.

Poirot plans to prevent the next death, and Hastings's assignment is to figure out which guest X has picked for death. Hastings agrees, but asks who X is. Poirot refuses to tell him. Too dangerous, he says.

Hastings is sure that Poirot will succeed in stopping X. We may not be so sure. For one thing, this is not the dapper, animated Poirot of old. He has greatly aged. He suffers from a weakened heart which "may go — phut — any moment." He is thin, wrinkled, and his hair and luxuriant mustache, once his pride, is now pathetically dyed black. His gray cells are still excellent, but he is so afflicted with arthritis that he is confined to a wheelchair. He is old. He mentions young girls once a chapter.

There may be another obstacle — Hastings himself, a well-meaning man who plays Dr. Watson to Poirot's Holmes. But it takes time for Hastings to see the obvious, and he has trouble even seeing much more than that. The problem is compounded at Styles because Hastings is obsessed with two ideas. One, he decides *he* must discover the identity of X. Two, he is driven to distraction by the notion that his brilliant, beautiful daughter Judith is about to be debauched by Major Allerton, who is known to be a "notorious womanizer."

Major Allerton, whom Hastings "instinctively dislikes," is a man of salaciously bad reputation

who spends his time telling locker-room stories and pursuing Judith. Allerton knew one of the victims in Poirot's files. Hastings determines that Allerton is X, and begins to lose his perspective.

We, however, should not. Everyone at Styles looks equally like a candidate for X and the next victim.

Colonel and Daisy Luttrell own and run Styles, and Daisy gushes about, trying to make it pay. The colonel shoots pigeons. While in the army he made "subalterns shake in their shoes," but now he has been reduced to a mustache-pulling yes-man by his wife, who verbally humiliates him in public and beats the pants off him at bridge. All the guests agree that nobody would blame old Toby if he shot Daisy. One afternoon, with two guests in earshot, she mortifies him, and then goes out to prune. Goaded by a guest's story of an Irish batman who shot his brother, Luttrell claims to see a rabbit nibbling a tree, but Daisy is wounded instead.

Is the colonel X, and Daisy the victim? Why isn't Hastings paying attention?

Hastings is preoccupied. Having overheard Allerton planning a delicious London rendezvous, he is taking steps to end Allerton's escapades, permanently.

Is Hastings X, and Allerton the victim?

Another guest is Dr. Franklin, a dedicated, brusque biochemist who has rigged up a laboratory where he spends almost all his time doing experiments on the physostigmine alkaloids derived from the Calabar bean — an "ordeal" bean used by West African tribes to determine guilt

and innocence. Some of Dr. Franklin's solutions are quite toxic. He has let everyone know that he believes "about eighty per cent of the human race ought to be eliminated."

Franklin employs Hasting's daughter Judith as a research assistant. Her father's clumsy attempts to interfere in her life exasperate and enrage her. Like Franklin, she is passionately dedicated to the dispassionate pursuit of scientific knowledge. She announces as loudly and more often than he that "useless lives ... should be got out of the way." Dr. Franklin's nervous wife, Barbara, fits Judith's definition of "useless" to a *T*.

Barbara Franklin, who suffers from something constant and vague, lies all day, wan and beautiful, on a chaise lounge bemoaning her health and commanding attention from anyone in earshot. Her activities vary from open flirtation with Sir Boyd Carrington, a rich, widowed admirer, to saintly insistences that she is standing in the way of her husband's career, to bathetic considerations of suicide.

Sir William Boyd Carrington is staying at Styles while his baronial manor is being remodeled. He has known Barbara for many years, once almost proposed to her, and has always regretted not doing so. He is the only one openly sympathetic to her, but he is not above having his palm read by Barbara's "young and vigorous" Nurse Craven.

Although Nurse Craven does admit that Mrs. Franklin suffers from depression, she adds that "she certainly enjoys bad health." The nurse's work is primarily fetching and carrying for Barbara.

One evening Barbara Franklin invites all the guests to her room for coffee. The following morning she dies, from a solution of physostigmine alkaloids added to her coffee. Her death is ruled suicide.

Now who is X?

Is it Elizabeth Cole, another guest whom Hast-

Curtain (1975)

ings finds more and more attractive? She reveals to him that her real name is Litchfield. Hastings knows that her father's murder case is included in Poirot's files. To Hastings, she describes herself as "one of the maimed."

She is usually found with the mild, little gray-haired Stephen Norton, a bird watcher. Norton, who becomes sick at the sight of blood, is a true bird aficionado and is always wandering near strategic locations with an excellent pair of binoculars.

Following the inquest of Mrs. Franklin's death, the sorrowing Boyd Carrington decides to move back home. Hastings accuses him of leaving because of the abominable food. Franklin and Judith blithely announce that since the obstacle has been removed, they are leaving for Africa to do research together. And Norton begins muttering tantalizing, unfinished sentences.

One morning Norton does not appear. They break down his door and find him on his bed, with a bullet hole in his forehead.

Where is Poirot, of the indomitable gray cells? Poirot, who in *Curtain* states, "It is my work in life to save the innocent," seems to have been beaten, at least by his heart condition if not by X. Just hours after Norton is found, Poirot dies, succumbing to a heart attack. The ampules of amyl nitrite that he uses to alleviate his condition are not by his bed.

The grieving Hastings is left to forage among the ashes of clues by himself. But Poirot gives Hastings every chance to figure out what is indeed one of Poirot's most intriguing, yet logical, cases. He tells him "I had been curious...to see if your well-known flair for the obvious would work."

Hastings blows it, of course. But there is the astounding "Postscript."

BETH SIMON

Famous Last Words: Dying Declarations

"Henrietta."
— Dr. John Christow, *Murder after Hours*

"Alfred...Alfred..."
— Emily Inglethorp,
    The Mysterious Affair at Styles

"The destroyer."
— Mayerling, *The Big Four*

"Bingo did it."
— Lady Merivale, *Partners in Crime*

"Don't...leave..."
"Mr....Brown..."
— Marguerite Vandemeyer,
    The Secret Adversary

"Elinor...Mr. Seddon...Mary...provision."
— Laura Welman, *Sad Cypress*

"Why didn't they ask Evans?"
— Alan Carstairs, *The Boomerang Clue*

"The taste of that coffee is still in my...mouth."
— Sir Claud Amory, *Black Coffee*

"Find out about verity. Truth. Another name for truth, verity. Good-bye. Do your best."
— Margaret Temple, *Nemesis*

"I can't go on."
— Mona Symmington, *The Moving Finger*

Sleeping Murder (1976)

Young Gwenda Reed, born in India but raised in New Zealand, arrives in England for the first time. Her husband, soon to be arriving, has told her to find a house anywhere in southern England. So Gwenda wanders aimlessly about the countryside for a few days until she comes to the remote little village of Dillmouth and finds a house that "feels just right."

As soon as she's bought the house she sets about making the necessary renovations. At once she has a very strong inclination to build porch stairs where the bushes are now, so she hires a man to do this. Oddly, the builder discovers old steps, planted over and covered up, right in that very spot.

Gwenda develops an embarrassing problem. She consistently walks into the wall of one room as though there were a doorway there. There isn't, but she feels there should be. She orders a doorway connecting the drawing room to the dining room and again, the workman discovers that there had once been a door there, long since plastered over.

And when Gwenda asks the workman to open the painted-over doors of an old cupboard, she finds inside it the room's original wallpaper — a design she had clearly imagined she would like to use in that room.

The coincidences give her the creeps, an appropriate reaction we must admit. Fearing for her sanity, she flees to London for a little rest. There her hosts introduce her to Miss Jane Marple, of course, and they all go off to the theater to see *The Dutchess of Malfi*.

Let us pause here to consider that poor Gwenda is under terrible strain. Her hosts have put themselves out to take her mind off her problems. And out of all the London theaters they could attend that night, from the endless choice of drama at their disposal, they choose this one... *The Dutchess of Malfi*, the play that contains the key phrase to the mystery. If they had gone to see *All's Well That Ends Well* instead, for example, Gwenda would never have been reminded of the murder she had witnessed at the age of three. But no, they go to see *The Dutchess of Malfi*, and when the actor speaks his line, "Cover her face; mine eyes dazzle; she died young," Gwenda runs out of the theater in hysterics. She now recalls that she once heard those very lines spoken as she witnessed the strangulation and murder of ... Helen. Helen? Your guess is as good as Gwenda's. She doesn't remember anyone named Helen.

But Miss Marple, our Queen of Coincidence, pieces all of this together in seconds without so much as puckering her eyebrows. The "most natural explanation", she suggests calmly, is that Gwenda had lived in the very same Dillmouth house once before, which would explain her uncanny sense of where everything belonged, and that there she had witnessed the murder of a woman named Helen. Of course.

Marple helps whittle down the family tree to find the murderer. As one character warns, "I don't really think I should dwell too much on the past. All this ancestor worship — it's a mistake." Even Miss Marple senses that they should let "sleeping murder" lie... but anyone who has gotten family tree fever knows how obsessive it can be, especially with an unsolved murder lying dormant for eighteen years.

And so the past is confronted. Gwenda and the

now-present Giles Reed gradually discover that Gwenda had been born in India but had moved to England when she was two or three with her father shortly after her mother's death. On the boat to England her bereaved father met and immediately married the beautiful, young Helen Kennedy. Then they all went to Dillmouth and settled into, yes, the very same house Gwenda had so randomly picked. But this happy scene ended abruptly a year later when Helen ran off with another man. Gwenda's father was admitted to a mental institution, obsessed and eventually driven to suicide, by the delusion that he'd actually strangled his young wife, and Gwenda was sent to New Zealand to be raised by relatives.

And if you believe all this, you're as gullible as Gwenda.

Jane Marple makes her slow, steady pace through the town, casually chatting about old times with the natives, and eventually the old housekeepers and cooks and maids begin to talk. It seems one of them had seen something from a window and she'd told Lily, the high-spirited parlormaid.

Lily, now married to a rather Neanderthal type and living miles from Dillmouth, reads one of Gwenda's information-wanted-about-Helen Kennedy-ads in the paper. Lily doesn't want to get mixed up with the police but her curiousity gets the best of her. To be on the safe side, she writes not to these strangers, Gwen and Giles, nor to the police, but to the old doctor whom she remembers was Helen's devoted brother. She agrees to meet him and discuss all she remembers, which in turn he will share with his friends Gwen and Giles. (The doctor remembers tiny "Gwennie" of eighteen years ago and is grateful that she's taken up the search for Helen. He had thought it odd that Helen had only written him two letters since her abrupt disappearance so long ago.)

But on the day Lily is expected to meet the doctor for tea, she fails to show up... for a very good reason. She's been murdered only minutes after she stepped off the train.

Lily must have known something someone else didn't want revealed. And it must have been murder after all. But who murdered poor Helen all those years ago? And why did he say "Cover her face; mine eyes dazzle; she died young?"

Was it Walter Fane, a nondescript, mediocre sort of fellow, now a lawyer, who lives a little too quietly with his mother? He was once jilted by young Helen with whom he was madly in love.

Could it have been Captain Richard Erskine, a handsome man who had a passionate love affair with Helen on board ship but who is kept in an iron grip by his jealous, deep-voiced wife?

Or could it have been J.J. Afflick, flashy operator of Daffodil Coaches? He'd been Helen's first steady, but Helen's brother had successfuly broken up the match because J.J. was downright seedy.

Of course there's still the possibility that Gwenda's father was right: that he had, in fact, strangled Helen after he'd found her note saying she was going off with another man. (She had taken a suitcase full of the strangest clothes ... a silver evening gown with gold shoes. Very poor taste!) On the other hand he could have been drugged and later convinced that he'd committed the crime.

One never knows when digging up the family tree. Perhaps it is best to let sleeping murder lie.

PAM McALLISTER

CHRISTIEMOVIE II
And Then
There Were More
by Michael Tennenbaum

THE MIRROR CRACK'D

EMI, 1980. Directed by Guy Hamilton, featuring Angela Lansbury, Elizabeth Taylor, Rock Hudson, Kim Novak, Tony Curtis, Edward Fox, Geraldine Chaplin, Wendy Morgan, Charles Gray. Based on the 1962 novel.

When a local busybody dies after drinking a poisoned daiquiri presumably meant for a visiting movie star, Jane Marple enters the glamorous world of moviemaking to solve the mystery. However, Jane and the entire plot take a back seat to the real point of the film—the back-biting bitchiness of Taylor and Novak as fading, feuding movie queens in town to outdo each other in an unlikely remake of *Mary, Queen of Scots*. In an interesting attempt to establish a sense of time and style (1950s British drawing-room mystery) the movie opens with a scene from *Murder at Midnight*, a supposed film from that period. Unfortunately, some reviewers found this clever pastiche more interesting than the actual film that followed. Never mind. Angela Lansbury's clever and charming portrayal of Miss Marple no doubt led indirectly to the notion that she would be wonderful in a Christie-style television series, which became the highly successful *Murder, She Wrote*.

(An interesting footnote: Some conjecture that the solution to the mystery of *The Mirror Crack'd* was actually based on the real-life tragedy of former movie star Gene Tierney.)

Top: Kim Novak, Rock Hudson, Elizabeth Taylor, and Tony Curtis play suspects in The Mirror Crack'd. *Left: Angela Lansbury is the watchful Miss Marple.*

THE BEDSIDE, BATHTUB & ARMCHAIR COMPANION TO AGATHA CHRISTIE

EVIL UNDER THE SUN

Universal, 1982. Directed by Guy Hamilton, featuring Peter Ustinov, Diana Rigg, Maggie Smith, James Mason, Roddy McDowall, Sylvia Miles. Based on the 1941 novel.

A promiscuous actress is murdered at an otherwise pleasant resort hotel, thereby interrupting Hercule Poirot's vacation, much in the same way the real actors' pleasant sojourn in sunny Majorca was occasionally interrupted by the fact that they were to make a movie. James Mason recalled this time as the most relaxed experience of his long career. His laid-back attitude seems to have infected the entire production and the critics were unanimous in mentioning the garish period costumes and Cole Porter sound track over the slow-moving plot and direction. This was, after all, Hollywood's third attempt to duplicate the success of *Murder on the Orient Express* by weighing down a Christie novel with an all-star cast to insure box-office appeal.

WITNESS FOR THE PROSECUTION

Hallmark Hall of Fame Productions, 1982. Directed by Alan Gibson, with Sir Ralph Richardson, Diana Rigg, Deborah Kerr, Wendy Hiller, Donald Pleasence, Beau Bridges.

This high-quality remake of the stage and screen success was especially notable for the classy performances of Richardson and Kerr in the roles made famous by Charles Laughton and Elsa Lanchester. But Beau Bridges seemed strangely miscast as leader character Leonard Vole, especially when paired with the wonderful Diana Rigg in the tricky title role.

Clockwise: In Evil Under the Sun, *Peter Ustinov as Poirot points at suspect before taking an ocean dip. Below: Suspects galore! (See cast list.)*

Left: Ustinov questions Colin Blakely.

MURDER IS EASY

Warner Brothers Television, 1982. Directed by Claude Whatham, with Helen Hayes, Olivia de Havilland, Bill Bixby, Lesley-Anne Down.

In November 1980 Warner Brothers Television announced the formation of a deal with Agatha Christie, Ltd. to produce five novels as two-hour television movies under the umbrella title *The Agatha Christie Mystery Theater*. In its press release, Warner Brothers declared that this marked the first time Christie works would be allowed to be produced directly for American television. Lost somewhere in television's "Golden Age," however, there had already been *four* adaptations broadcast live between 1950 and 1959: *The Case of the Missing Lady* (with Ronald Reagan and Cloris Leachman as Tommy and Tuppence Beresford), *Witness for the Prosecution, A Murder Is Announced*, and *Ten Little Indians*. Nevertheless, capitalizing on Dame Agatha's well publicized aversion to television, Warners stated these would be big-budget productions, patterned once again on the multistar formula of *Murder on the Orient Express*, but updated to attract a younger audience. The proposed five titles were *Murder Is Easy, They Came to Baghdad, The Man in the Brown Suit, Destination Unknown*, and *The Secret of Chimneys*.

CHRISTIEMOVIE II

A CARIBBEAN MYSTERY

Warner Brothers Television, 1983. Directed by Robert Lewis, with Helen Hayes, Maurice Evans. Based on the 1964 novel.

Miss Marple's dull vacation at a Caribbean resort is livened somewhat by the unexpected demise of a retired British Major.

SPARKLING CYANIDE

Warner Brothers Television, 1983. Directed by Robert Lewis, featuring Anthony Andrews, Deborah Raffin, Harry Morgan. From the 1945 novel, a.k.a. *Remembered Death*.

A glass of poisoned champagne is the murder method used in this tale of life among the idle rich in contemporary Southern California. A strong Anglo-American cast of television actors included Anthony Andrews, best known to American audiences as young Sebastian Flyte, the tragic hero of that orgy for Anglophiles on PBS—*Brideshead Revisited*.

MURDER WITH MIRRORS

Warner Brothers Television, 1985. Directed by Dick Lowry, featuring Helen Hayes, Bette Davis, John Mills, Leo McKern, Dorothy Tutin. Based on the 1952 novel.

The inspired casting of Helen Hayes and Bette Davis as old school chums was somewhat diminished by the obvious frailness of Miss Davis who was recovering from the effects of a recent stroke. Still, with Miss Hayes once again as Jane Marple, and a topnotch British supporting cast, this tale of murder on an estate-turned-rehabilitation center for juvenile delinquents is among the best of the current series.

Starting left, counterclockwise: Helen Hayes as Miss Marple and Maurice Evans drink a toast in A Caribbean Mystery; *later, the irrepressible Miss Marple dresses for an Island costume party; Christine Belford, Pamela Bellwood, and June Chadwick in* Sparkling Cyanide; *ad for* Murder with Mirrors; *Helen Hayes as Miss Marple, John Mills, and Bette Davis in* Murder with Mirrors; *Bette Davis in part of Carrie Louise in same picture.*

CHRISTIEMOVIE II

THIRTEEN AT DINNER	DEAD MAN'S FOLLY
Warner Brothers Television, 1985. Directed by Lou Antonio, featuring Peter Ustinov, Faye Dunaway, Lee Horsely, Amanda Pays, David Suchet, and David Frost as himself.	Warner Brothers Television, 1986. Directed by Clive Donner, with Peter Ustinov, Jean Stapleton, Tim Piggot-Smith, Constance Cummings, Susan Wooldridge. From the 1956 novel.
Ustinov returned to the role of Hercule Poirot in this story, which had been previously filmed in 1934 as *Lord Edgware Dies*. In this modern version, Poirot encounters a famous actress (maybe) while appearing on a talk show hosted by David Frost. An invitation to the dinner of the film's title leads to a murder, some incredible duplicity, and a showcase for the talents of co-star Faye Dunaway, on temporary leave from her series of portrayals of nonfictional characters (Joan Crawford, Eva Peron, Queen Isabella, etc.).	Finally, audiences are introduced to Ariadne Oliver, the one Christie character who most closely resembles the author. As portrayed by Jean Stapleton, the American version of Ariadne may remind viewers more of the middle-aged mystery writer from the Christie-inspired series *Murder, She Wrote*, a role Miss Stapleton says she was offered, but declined. Teamed with Ustinov's fourth Poirot, they investigate a game of murder that has turned into the real thing.

Left: Ad for Thirteen at Dinner. *Below: Faye Dunaway in dual role of actress and clever impersonator.*

Left: Peter Ustinov as Poirot and Jean Stapleton as Ariadne Oliver examine clue in Dead Man's Folly.

Right: Susan Woolbridge, standing, is secretary to Nicolette Sheridan's rich and philandering husband.

TOMMY AND TUPPENCE
Partners in "The Great Game"
by Bruce Cassiday

Spies? Cloaks and daggers? Cryptic messages? Forces of the Evil Empire stalking English streets? In Agatha Christie?

Oh, yes! You'd better believe it. Like all good mystery novelists, Dame Agatha turned her hand to espionage, dubbed so unforgettably by Mahbub Ali in Kipling's *Kim* "The Great Game."

But, and typically Christie-like, she did it with a flair: instead of one spy, she created a *pair*—almost as if she recognized the seemingly contradictory traits that characterize the best spies: caution and imprudence, logic and intuition, imagination and common sense.

Although she called her spies Tommy and Tuppence—names more on the level of a nursery rhyme than international espionage—she selected them carefully for their Englishness and their symbolic values.

On his initial appearance, "Tommy" had just been demobilized from the British Army after World War I; the name Tommy then stood for Tommy Atkins, the prototype of the British soldier. And "Tommy," whose family name was Beresford, was essentially an embodiment of all good British qualities of character: reserve, stolidity, tenaciousness, reason, and common sense.

"Tuppence"—the English word for "twopence," then a familiar small British coin—was petite, but sharp and bright as a penny, and that was the way her author conceived her. In addition, Tuppence always seemed to be eager to get in her "two cents' worth."

Mr. Thomas Beresford's background is somewhat obscure, although he was born sometime in 1894 in Suffolk in east England. No father is ever mentioned. Yet there is a strong hint that some shadow hovered over his birth. His uncle, Sir William Beresford, disowned him after engaging in a bitter argument with Tommy's mother. The argument apparently stemmed from Sir William's desire to adopt the boy and remove him from his mother's influence; stubbornly, and most Tommy-like, young Beresford resisted and opted to stay with her. And there he remained until her death. Eventually, and happily, Sir William became reunited with his nephew, and Tommy was once again in the family's good graces, as we learn at the close of *The Secret Adversary*, the first Tommy and Tuppence adventure.

Physically, Tommy is typically British: his red hair is "exquisitely slicked-back," height and weight are inconsequential, his face is "pleasantly ugly—nondescript, but unmistakably the face of a gentleman and a sportsman." "Nondescript" is the operative word —the most important element, as any good spy buff knows, in the makeup of a successful agent.

Miss Tuppence Cowley's background is a trifle more detailed, but essentially obscure as well. She is the fifth daughter of Archdeacon Cowley of Little Missendell, Suffolk. The date of her birth is never specified, yet since she has "grown up" with Tommy down in Suffolk, it is obvious their ages are similar.

Like Tommy, Tuppence is also typically British: "Tuppence had no claim to beauty, but there was character and charm in the elfin

TOMMY AND TUPPENCE

lines of her little face, with its determined chin and large, wide-apart grey eyes that looked mistily out from under straight, black brows."

Although Tuppence has at least four sisters, none of them is ever mentioned by name, nor do we ever meet one of them during any of her adventures. This, in spite of the fact that several of Tuppence's aunts *do* appear from time to time. She exists on her generation level as alone as Tommy.

Miss Cowley's first name is "Prudence," but no one ever calls her that. Indeed there is nothing *in the world* prudent about this Prudence. She is the soul of *imprudence*. If Tommy is steadfast, if he thinks out his moves with logic, if he reasons carefully before acting, Tuppence is volatile, rushing into any danger with characteristic impetuosity and verve.

It is the conflicting opposites that make the pair work. Perverseness gets them into trouble and out of it time and again. Their conflicting attitudes help them solve problems encountered.

A man known to them only as "Mr. Carter"—actually head of the British Secret Service and the man who hires them to help solve a difficult espionage problem in *The Secret Adversary*—sums up the two of them in a brief meeting with the Prime Minister:

"Outwardly, he's an ordinary clean-limbed, rather block-headed young Englishman. Slow in his mental processes. On the other hand, it's quite impossible to lead him astray through his imagination. He hasn't got any—so he's difficult to deceive. He worries things out slowly, and once he's got hold of anything he doesn't let go. The little lady's quite different. More intuition and less common sense. They make a pretty pair working together. Pace and stamina."

It is Tuppence's pace—her impetuous-

ness—that propels her into trouble, and yet she tends to rely on her slow-witted partner "more than she realizes."

Why? The author explains. "There was something so eminently sober and clear-headed about him, his common sense and soundness of vision so unvarying, that without him Tuppence felt much like a rudderless ship."

And, "He might be slow, but he was very sure." Stamina!

It is Tuppence's intuition to skirt the rules of convention as well as the rules of propriety. When Tommy is called on to perform a Secret Service mission during World War II in *N or M?*, long after they are husband and wife, Tuppence is not above engineering a fake telephone call so that she can eavesdrop on the private conversation between her husband and his Intelligence contact.

Later, Tommy recalls this breach of decency with outrage. "You got inside a wardrobe next door to the room where I was being interviewed in a very interesting manner, so you knew exactly where I was being sent and what I meant to do, and you managed to get their first. Eavesdropping. Neither more nor less. Most dishonorable."

"With very satisfactory results," Tuppence responds breezily.

During the 1920s in *Partners in Crime*, when the pair take over a detective agency vacated by the arrest of its operator in order to intercept secret messages from the Germans, Tuppence fabricates a phoney jewel theft so the agency can solve the crime in record time, thus publicizing its ability to break a mystery in twenty-four hours!

Tuppence is devious; Tommy is direct. When he pulls a fast one, it is essentially open and aboveboard. Usually his ploys involve escape from the clutches of, and he is frequently in the clutches of.

In one tight spot in *The Secret Adversary*, Tommy is locked up in an obscure room of a house, and it takes the help of a wily young woman (not Tuppence) to fabricate a diversion in order to distract his captors to effect his escape. The ruse works, largely because no one can conceive of Tommy's ability to operate in such a crafty fashion!

In another memorable instance in *N or M?*, sequestered and unseen and bound and gagged, Tommy "snores" out a plea for help in Morse code to Albert, his "man"—dit-dit-dit, dah-dah-dah, dit-dit-dit (S.O.S.)—and it works!

Albert, like Peter Wimsey's Bunter, serves as the Beresfords' body servant. Originally a hotel pageboy encountered during their first adventure, Albert became their assistant at their "detective agency" when he was a teenager. Later he joined the household. He married in 1934 and opened The Duck and Dog pub in South London, but later rejoined their service.

Somewhere along the line, incidentally, Tuppence bore a pair of twins, Deborah and Derek. The Beresfords were married sometime after the end of the postwar era and by 1940 Deborah was old enough to be a member of the Secret Service and Derek a lieutenant in the Royal Air Force. During World War II, the Beresfords adopted a child named Betty who figured in their adventure in *N or M?* Betty later took up government work in South Africa.

"I'm always full of hope," Tuppence once tells Tommy, contrasting their attitudes about life.

"I know you are," Tommy replies ruefully. "I've often regretted it." Tommy shrugs it all off. "I'm like the tortoise, I suppose." Tuppence, he opines, resembles the mongoose.

Her flashes of intuition continue to lead her

not only into danger, but out of it as well. She "feels" things about people, functions on instinct and often says things like, "I felt suddenly that I—well, that I wouldn't like to get on the wrong side of him—or meet him in a dark road at night."

For all his pose of common sense and blockheadedness, Tommy has his own instincts: "But all the same," he thinks in *By the Pricking of My Thumbs*, "I don't like Mr. Eccles." Or as Tommy puts it: "He sounds all right. He looks all right, he speaks all right, but all the same—"

Beginning their adventures in their early twenties—"their united ages would certainly not have totalled forty-five"—the Beresfords solve espionage problems and mysteries of one sort or another long enough to become grandparents when their final adventure befalls them in *Postern of Fate*, ironically enough one involving a mystery dating back in time to the early years of their lives. There they are in the 1960s, the bouncing Beresfords, still pinballing into and out of jeopardy *in their seventies!*

A long, long time to be involved in The Great Game—but certainly Great Players to be so engaged!

James Warwick and Francesca Annis as Tommy and Tuppence during the 1920s in "Agatha Christie's Partners in Crime" on the PBS Mobil-funded series Mystery!

WASTE NO WORDS
The Short Fiction

by Edward D. Hoch

Just in time for Christmas of 1984, Agatha Christie's lifelong American publisher, Dodd, Mead & Company, brought out *Hercule Poirot's Casebook*, the first collection of all fifty Poirot short stories and novelettes. It was followed late in 1985 by *Miss Marple, the Complete Short Stories*, which collected all twenty of the Marple tales and signaled a new interest in the author's shorter works. Agatha Christie's two most famous characters were probably more at home in full-length novels, but there are some high spots among their shorter cases as well—and in the non-series short stories that she frequently wrote.

What, then, is the very best Agatha Christie short story of them all? Opinions may differ, but I would join several critics in casting my vote for "The Witness for the Prosecution," her deft, surprising tale of a trial for murder. Leonard Vole's predicament following the murder of his elderly friend still involves us in the mounting suspense of his trial preparations, the trial itself, and the startling aftermath. Most amazing of all, Christie wrote this story for *Munsey's Magazine* in 1924, two years before *The Murder of Roger Ackroyd*. Its later success on stage and in films (with an added twist at the end) has somewhat eclipsed the original story, but it can still be read with great pleasure. Without giving away too much of an extremely clever plot, I'd mention the early use here of disguise, a factor that plays a large part in the solution of some later Christie novels.

Those fortunate enough to own a copy of *Witness for the Prosecution and Other Stories* also possess two additional Christie masterpieces in the short form—"Accident" and "Philomel Cottage." Both are stories of poisoning, and concern murders past and present, but no two stories could be more different in their plots or their outcomes. It should come as no surprise that some of Christie's best short stories concern poisonings, since it was the favorite murder weapon in her novels as well. There are said to be eighty-three cases of poisoning in her works.

Not in the same league with these three stories but still deserving a mention is Christie's novelette "Three Blind Mice," which has since become the longest-running play in theatrical history, *The Mousetrap*. Readers and audiences love to be fooled, and Christie fools them quite nicely in "Three Blind Mice." The shifting suspicion among the guests and residents of a snowbound guest house is admirably handled, and the final unmasking of the psychopathic killer still manages to surprise one in an old-fashioned way. Because of the continued popularity of the play in London, "Three Blind Mice" has never been published in England, although an earlier version was broadcast there in 1947 as a radio play.

The remainder of Agatha Christie's non-series stories are fairly routine mystery, crime, or supernatural tales. For other high-spots in her career as a short-story writer we must turn to the series sleuths, beginning with Hercule Poirot. My own favorite among Poirot's shorter cases is probably the novelette "Dead Man's Mirror," included in the collection of the same title. The puzzle here, involving a murder in a locked study, a shattered mirror, and the sound of a gong, could easily have been expanded to novel length, yet it works perfectly as published, with Poirot unmasking a well-hidden killer. (A shorter and somewhat different version has been published as "The Second Gong," but the story works best as "Dead Man's Mirror.")

Poirot fans will also want to read "The Chocolate Box," the final story in Christie's first collection, *Poirot Investigates*, for an account of the master sleuth's only failure. For some of his more dazzling successes, the reader is directed to "The Third-Floor Flat" in *Three Blind Mice*, "Murder in the Mews," another novelette in *Dead Man's Mirror*, and "Yellow Iris" in *The Regatta Mystery*. This last story was later expanded into the novel *Remembered Death* (British title: *Sparkling Cyanide*), but with Colonel Race solving the mystery instead of Poirot.

The best all-around Poirot collection is without doubt *The Labors of Hercules*, in which he undertakes to solve twelve mysteries which parallel the mythological labors of Hercules in modern life. "The Nemean Lion" might be reduced to a Pekinese dog for purposes of the scheme, but the stories still work remarkably well—especially in the case of "The Lernean Hydra."

Thirteen of the twenty stories about Miss Marple can be found in *The Tuesday Club Murders* (British title: *Thirteen Problems*), including three of the best: "The Tuesday Night Club," "Motive v. Opportunity," and "The Affair at the Bungalow." It's interesting to remember that their magazine publication predated the first Miss Marple novel. The spinster sleuth had her origins in the short-story form.

In addition to Poirot and Miss Marple, Agatha Christie penned three volumes and a few individual stories about a trio of other series detectives. Tommy and Tuppence appear in *Partners in Crime*, a good-natured spoof of other mystery writers. Parker Pyne solves a dozen cases in *Mr. Parker Pyne, Detective*, notably "The House at Shiraz," and reappears for two further adventures in *The Regatta Mystery*. Harley Quin helps unravel twelve cases in *The Mysterious Mr. Quin*, and returns for another story in *Three Blind Mice*.

Strange as it might seem, there exists a final Harley Quin short story that has never appeared in any of the Christie's American or British collections. Titled "The Harlequin Tea Set," it is probably the last short story she ever wrote, and first appeared in the British anthology *Winter's Crimes 3* in 1971, edited by George Hardinge and published by Macmillan London. It was reprinted in America in *Ellery Queen's Mystery Magazine* (June 1973) and later in an anthology, *Ellery Queen's Murdercade* (1975). A detective story complete with ghost, "The Harlequin Tea Set" has been overlooked in most listings of Christie's published work. It deserves inclusion in a future edition of *The Mysterious Mr. Quin*.

Agatha Christie published 150 short stories in her lifetime, in addition to 66 mystery novels, some romances, and nonfiction. If the short stories often are not the equal of the best of her novels, they still sparkle on occasion with her vitality and ingenuity, reminding us anew of the pleasures of a well-crafted tale.

AGATHA
The Movie That Almost Wasn't
by Michael Tennenbaum

Here's the part we know: At 9:45 P.M. on the evening of December 4, 1926, Agatha Christie left her home in Sunningdale, outside London, drove off in her car—and disappeared. Just a few months earlier the young author had become a literary sensation delighting critics and lovers of murder mysteries with her creation of the dapper detective Hercule Poirot. Yet this newfound fame only added to the pressures on the shy Mrs. Christie. The recent death of her mother and the slow but obvious dissolution of her marriage to the flamboyant World War I flying ace Colonel Archibald Christie may all have been contributing factors that led to her flight that evening. Her car was found abandoned in a wooded glen early the next morning.

For the next week and a half, news of Mrs. Christie's disappearance filled the newspapers. Armies of searchers combed the countryside near her home. Tabloids printed lurid tales of murder, kidnap, and intrigue, and *The London Daily News* offered a staggering reward for information leading to the discovery of the whereabouts of the author —"if alive."

Eleven days from the night of her disappearance she was discovered at Harrogate, a posh health spa in Yorkshire, registered as Mrs. Neele, the name of her husband's mistress! When asked by reporters why she had kept her whereabouts a secret, she had no answer. Her husband offered a convenient response—she had amnesia. It was this explanation that became the official story.

After Mrs. Christie's death in 1976, Kath-leen Tynan, an ex-reporter for *Newsweek Magazine*, began to speculate on the possible truths behind the disappearance and, through detective work in the press library of the British Museum, pieced together a mixture of facts and conjecture that became the novel, *Agatha*.

Ms. Tynan offers the following hypothetical situation: What if Mrs. Christie, stunned by her husband's request for divorce, imagined herself as diabolical as one of her fictional characters and created this ruse as part of a complex scheme to dispose of her rival? And, what if an American journalist, obsessed with Mrs. Christie and her work, discovered her at the spa and became more involved in the plot than he had bargained for? What indeed . . . ?

It was this intriguing blend of fact and fancy that attracted the attention of the movie industry. The original owners of the property, The Rank Organization, dropped the project after serious objections about the fictional aspects of the story were received from Dame Agatha's estate. "Agatha Christie, Ltd.", the corporation that controls all rights to the author's work and likeness, reminded the producers that Colonel Christie was a longtime member of Rank's board of directors, and to show him in such a bad light would do neither the organization nor the estate much good. The project was shelved.

In October 1977 First Artists, a fledgling studio, announced its intention to produce *Agatha*, starring Vanessa Redgrave as Mrs. Christie, Dustin Hoffman as the American journalist, and Julie Christie as Nancy Neele, the other woman. Once again, Agatha Christie, Ltd. jumped into the breach, filing for an injunction to halt production and throwing in a multi-million dollar suit for defamation of character, claiming again that the entire story was based on conjecture, not fact. This lawsuit, however, seemed to vanish in the light of the battle of egos and artistic temperament that almost succeeded in sinking the project from the very start.

First Artists started its life as the idealistic vision of five American superstars (Paul Newman, Steve McQueen, Sidney Poitier, Barbra Streisand, and Dustin Hoffman) in an attempt to wrestle some of the power away from the major studios and acquire for themselves a degree of artistic freedom previously unheard of in the industry. And while they would pick the scripts and make the movies, Phil Feldman was hired to oversee the company and keep them all in business. Feldman considered *Agatha* a bad property from the start. He warned Hoffman that the role of the journalist was obviously overshadowed by the presence of Agatha Christie who *was*, after all, the title character. Hoffman, however, saw another story, and he *was*, after all, the executive producer.

The screenplay was originally prepared by Ms. Tynan and screenwriter Arthur Hopcraft. Now they were joined by Hoffman and his close friend, writer Murray Schisgal, who saw in the character of Wally Stanton, the American journalist, more than just a plot device to reveal Mrs. Christie's motives. Soon the journalist's importance threatened to throw the film off balance and Vanessa Redgrave joined these script meetings to serve as a constant reminder of the film's title. After almost a month of thrashing about, Hoffman asked for three more weeks of script preparation time. Feldman said no. Already behind schedule on other First Artists projects, the

company needed more product on the nation's movie screens in order to remain a viable entity. *Agatha* had to go into production immediately, despite the collaborators' protests that the script was now an unfathomable mess. In November 1977, its screenplay incomplete, filming began on *Agatha*. Dustin Hoffman's well-deserved reputation as a perfectionist can be a double-edged sword. In film after film he creates characters that can live on their own, and he never considers his "image" (in Hollywood terms) when he takes on a role. But this emphasis on aesthetic truth has been known to cause production-delaying arguments that can push a tight shooting schedule far overtime. Phil Feldman knew his job. When *Agatha* had run 15 percent over budget, and all the script revisions and explorations of character and plot had pushed the film twenty-three days beyond its forty-nine-

AGATHA

day schedule, Feldman called an end to shooting. Hoffman argued that one key scene was still to be shot—the scene that would explain his character's motivation for the entire plot. He even offered to use his own money to finance this additional sequence. But Feldman was adamant. In January 1978 First Artists took over complete control of the film, denying Hoffman his right to the final edit. Furious, the actor sued First Artists and Warner Brothers (the parent company) for $65,000,000 in an attempt to regain control of the property. But legal battles did not deter Feldman from the postproduction process. Editing went on without Hoffman, and in a last-stand effort to stall the film's completion, the actor steadfastly refused to report to the studio for "looping," the process wherein dialogue is re-recorded for clarity or correction of flubbed lines. In the months that followed, the stand-off between Hoffman and First Artists was well-publicized. In a lengthy interview in *Variety*, the actor told his side of the story in an eloquent plea for the artistic freedom of the artist up against the cold materialistic demands of the big studio. Finally, a year after losing control of the film, responding to director Michael Apted's entreaties, Hoffman did the final dubbing on his scenes. (Feldman had decided to release the film with or without their leading man's cooperation anyway.)

When the film was released in February 1979 critics were somewhat surprised to discover that this was not the spine-tingling thriller First Artists promised in its advertising, but rather a charming and intriguing film about obsession and romance. Again, Hoffman's instincts were right, and the unlikely pairing between him and Redgrave worked to give the film what *Newsweek Magazine* called an "incongruous but disarming chemistry." Who can say what minor film classic could have resulted had Hoffman been able to exercise the full creative control he later held on such successes as *Tootsie* or *Death of a Salesman*? Perhaps the bitter experience of losing artistic control of *Agatha* led to those later triumphs of personal will and public acclaim.

The original design for this film's advertising featured a wide-eyed Vanessa Redgrave up front, and Dustin Hoffman in the background, full-size but partially obscured. Redgrave was, after all, the title character. The final version finds the more marketable face of Hoffman prominently in the foreground, with a troubled Agatha staring in fear over his shoulder.

I WAS MURDERED AT AN AGATHA CHRISTIE MYSTERY WEEKEND

by Bruce Cassiday

The voice on the phone is persuasive, low-keyed, professional. A salesman? A fund-raiser? A broker?

Well, actually—none of the above.

There is to be a Mystery Weekend at the Hotel Stamford Plaza in Connecticut, with an Agatha Christie-type country-house gathering and with built-in murders for the guests to solve. My name has been mentioned as a mystery writer. Will I participate as a member of the cast?

But I'm a writer, not an actor, I remind my caller.

"You'll be great! You die the first night."

I can't help but recall the old vaudeville wheeze as the agent tells the actor: "I've got you a great part in a Broadway play. You're killed before the curtain goes up!"

"You're the Reverend Bentley Humberstone," the voice goes on. "A full-fledged vicar."

Never in my wildest dreams. . . . A vicar?

Well, why not? Mystery Weekends have become the rage—at hotels, on railroad trains, at summer resorts, on cruises, or anywhere participation can be regulated. All part of the American quest for vicarious adventure via gamesmanship—from Trivial Pursuit to the Wheel of Fortune. I suspect that a psychologist could have a field day at a mystery weekend, watching murder buffs trying to turn fantasy into reality without destroying the suspense and excitement.

Not being a great one for games, I have never yet been involved. Yet as a writer of mystery stories, it seems incumbent on me to

live out at least one mystery weekend, to see how far fantasy merges into reality inside a strictly confined game plan.

And so I agree and within a week a bundle of single-spaced pages arrives by mail. It comes from Chris Warren, my telephone correspondent and producer/director/author of the Mystery Weekend. Outlined in the packet are character profiles, plot twists, and the main story idea:

In the reign of King Charles a family curse has been settled on the Humberstone family of Devon. The Mystery Weekend itself is a family reunion taking place at Humberstone Hollow in 1929, at which the troubles commence. The date of the reunion allows participants *and* cast to dress up in the garb of the flapper era, to take part not only in a mystery contest, but in a costume contest as well.

As at any Agatha Christie weekend, the family reunion sets all the various family tensions resonating against one another. The catalyst, in this case, is the remarriage of the widowed Humberstone patriarch to a noted London spiritualist. In turn, this causes a re-alignment of family loyalties, setting off confrontations and squabbles that are bound to generate—but of course!—*murder*.

This Humberstone clan is a big family. Bentley has more than a handful of siblings. Surprisingly, at only thirty-two, he's become one of the youngest vicars in English history—in fact, he's the Vicar of Wakefield!

Phone call. Chris Warren. "Can you dance the Charleston?"

Absolutely not. You never said I had to—

I WAS MURDERED AT AN AGATHA CHRISTIE

"In the synopsis you'll see that the Indian doctor hypnotizes guests during the first evening. You submit and are questioned about your feelings toward your father's remarriage. Then you are given post-hypnotic suggestion. Later you leap up and dance a Charleston."

Even under *real* hypnosis, I can't *do* it.

"We need an act for you."

But I am supposed to be dead Friday night!

"Didn't work out. What *can* you do—1920s-like?"

I used to play the piano—

"Jazz! Ragtime! Great!"

Mostly piano rolls, but look—I'm *not* thirty-two. It's not even *close*.

"No problem! Let me handle it."

Ahah! The magic of makeup! I ask when my script will arrive so I can learn my lines.

"There aren't any lines. It's an improvisation."

So. A little commedia dell'arte—1980s-style.

Two weeks before the event we rehearse at the hotel. Chris Warren gets his first look at me, pales, and puts on a brave happy face. "Great casting! I *love* it!"

Around a long conference table we meet to discuss character and cast relationships. The plot calls for me to be engaged to an attractive young lady in her early twenties. There is no makeup in the world—magic or non-magic—that can make me look thirty-two. Thus—

"Bentley has been sent on missionary duty to some remote outpost," Warren ad libs, pacing. "Uprisings, dengue, leeches, perhaps a debilitating mental problem—"

In Africa, I suggest.

"Of course! Missionary work has prematurely aged you, but in spite of it, your fiancée anxiously awaits marriage!"

Apparently everyone goes with the flow

and the "premature aging" ploy is adapted in the scenario.

On opening night we all arrive fully costumed, and I am surprised at how colorful the members of the cast appear. The Indian doctor is dressed in traditional exotic garb complete with turban. The military Humberstone son is in regimentals. The Egyptologist married to a Humberstone daughter wears typical "digs" dress. I am myself in clerical garb. The women are wearing obviously flapper-era costumes, some quite striking.

The reception line provides cross-fertilization between cast and guests. Chatting individually with all two hundred people takes time and energy, but the feeling of "belonging" is essential to the success of the game.

My fiancée and I indulge in small talk as the guests come by to say hello and look us over. Naturally, we speak of things that are "occurring" in 1929, to give a sense of reality to the fakery. We discuss Al Capone and the notorious St. Valentine's Day Massacre in Chicago some eight months ago. We talk about Lucky Lindy and his round-the-world honeymoon by air, with the Lone Eagle no longer alone now that he is married to the former Anne Morrow. We even mention English mystery novelist Agatha Christie, who has just announced her engagement to noted archeologist Max Mallowan, who will be her second husband.

With the guests finally out of the reception line and in their seats, the program begins with Lord Hubert, the Humberstone patriarch, welcoming the family members and the assembled guests. I am invited to give the invocation, which I do, hoping for a friendly and convivial family reunion on this festive occasion.

Almost immediately simmering antagonisms surface, and my brother Brandon and his wife Patricia engage in a shouting match

MYSTERY WEEKEND

over his earlier sexual escapade with Babette, a—how should I put it?—physically *endowed* Humberstone housemaid. I intervene and the furor subsides.

But within minutes a loud confrontation takes place between the irrepressible Brandon and my stepmother Daphne. Brandon calls her a "phoney" spiritualist and challenges her to prove her abilities. And Daphne does so, reading the minds of three people—one cast member and two Mystery Weekend guests. The mind-reading act goes over with a bang, because now everyone is involved in the action.

But peace is not restored among the battling Humberstones. An ugly scene quickly erupts between Dr. Petal, the Indian doctor, and Major Byron Humberstone, who has soldiered in India and hates Mahatma Gandhi, Indians, *and* Indian independence. Challenged by Byron, Dr. Petal agrees to demonstrate his spiritual abilities by hypnotizing—me!

Under hypnosis I am questioned about my feelings for my father's new wife. I believe in the sanctity of marriage; I have no animosity toward Lady Daphne, etc. The hypnotist then plants a post-hypnotic suggestion, instructing me to play the piano when my fiancée says a certain number. It has already been established that I have a tin ear and do not know how to play *any* musical instrument.

Shortly thereafter my fiancée plays a flute solo. Tempers then flare between Prudence Humberstone and her husband, the Egyptologist. Prudence has been drinking heavily, and almost drowns her husband Arthur when she throws a drink in his face. He goes to his room to change.

Commanded to play the piano by my fiancée's inadvertent use of the magic number, I do a ricky-ticky rendition of an old 1920s tune called "It Had to Be You." This amuses the guests, but Arthur returns to in-

form us that he has been attacked in his room by, he believes, the estate manager, Quentin Partridge.

When Quentin is summoned, he and Arthur have a fist fight, Quentin drawing blood by a blow to the mouth. But this is only *part* of the action. In the other corner of the room Brandon screams and collapses, bleeding at the throat. He has been dispatched by a poisoned dart shot from a blowpipe that I have brought back from Africa and presented to my father for his weapons collection. Brandon is the first victim of the Humberstone "curse."

Since I am new to these weekend games I am absolutely stunned at the excitement and muted hysteria aroused by the first murder. Almost half of the two hundred people in the room leave their seats and run across the room to rubberneck the dying man's last throes. The fake blood looks very, very real! Immediately the members of the cast form a ring around the corpse and haul Brandon away. I am one of the carriers. Man, is Brandon ever heavy! As soon as we get the corpse out into the corridor, someone grumbles: "Why can't we kill off some *little* light guy?"

Body removal, incidentally, is one element of reality that tends to be ignored in the Golden Age mystery novel. The physical presence of death, of a corpse, demands removal as quickly as possible—usually by survivors in the story!

Upon Brandon's death, and with the evening's "program" at a close, a "challenge" is presented to the guests to solve the murder.

And so to bed.

Penelope Humberstone, a kind of 1920s women's liberationist and Member of Parliament, is selected to look after Brandon's widow Patricia, sedated by Dr. Petal. Penelope sleeps in Patricia's room, yet in the morning she is found stabbed to death by a dagger apparently stolen from her brother Major Byron.

A seance is planned later on Saturday morning to call up the spirit of Penelope for possible information about her murder. However, before the seance can begin, Major Byron announces that he has found a poisonous snake—a krait—in his bed! Obviously he too has been marked for murder.

Now an argument begins between Dr. Petal and Major Byron, during which Petal has a heart seizure. He calls for his black bag and injects himself with digitoxin, a poisonous medicant used to control heart conditions.

When finally the seance takes place, the spirit of Penelope appears in the darkness and urges Patricia to reveal the killer's name. And, sure enough, Patricia suddenly leaps out of her seat and screeches, "I know who killed Penelope! I know! I know!"

Fat lot of good that does, for instantly there is a loud pistol shot, and Patricia falls down dead, a bullet in her throat. On the floor lies a pistol that is eventually traced to the estate manager who claims it was stolen from its holster the night before.

And now comes the crucial part of the participatory segment of the Mystery Weekend: the interrogation of the suspects by the guests who have been divided into ten "teams." All cast members are paired off to be questioned together. I accompany my fiancée.

"Father Bentley," someone asks, "have you ever been in a mental institution?"

Not to my knowledge, I assure my questioner. And I remind her that my title is "minister," not "father," since I am, Agatha Christie–like, a member of the Anglican church.

In real life I have worn a wedding ring for thirty-six years; actually I could not get it off with a blow torch. But someone now spots

the ring—ahah!

"Have you been married before, Father?"

A good question, indeed! I think fast and shrug it off with a smile. It's an old family heirloom given to me by my mother, I ad lib. I always wear it.

A tea break is scheduled for Saturday afternoon along with a 1920s Dance Demonstration staged by a professional group. I am not there. Instead, I am being made up for my big scene. Ironically enough, the only makeup I get is to make me look older, not younger. And when the makeup artist is through, I am a mess—green, blue, black, with heavy lines and shadows. A walking dead man.

I wait for a complicated series of signals and finally appear in the glass elevator cage at the top of the open shaft located in the center of the hotel lobby. There I am visible to the guests and cast at the tea and dance demo. I peer out through the glass, making feeble efforts to attract attention.

Somebody has turned on the gas jets while I'm napping, and I'm lucky to get out with my life.

The doctor calls for his medicine bag while my fiancée comforts me. I've escaped death—but for how long?

At the main floor I am assisted out of the elevator by Dr. Petal. I gasp out the fact the someone has turned on the gas jets to try to kill me. At my side, my faithful fiancée is vainly trying to minister to me.

My brother Major Byron hands me his brandy, which Petal helps me drink to get me back on my feet again—but—

Wouldn't you know? The drink has been poisoned by a dose of the doctor's digitoxin medicine. I die.

Petal examines me. "This man is dead." The men in the cast dutifully haul my corpse off into the back rooms of the hotel—conceivably pretty well stacked with bodies by now.

"*None* of these guys is really light!" grouses one of the carriers. "There is no such thing as a light corpse!"

I have to keep a straight face through all this. As of that moment, I am through. I go home.

On Sunday morning I am back again. The ten teams present pantomime versions of the way the murders occurred—shades of Hamlet's players!—and there are a lot of good laughs. Then the original cast demonstrates what *really* happened.

I am interested to discover that I have been murdered by accident. The poison in my brother Byron's brandy was meant for him. *Two* people wanted to kill him—one using the krait in his bed and the other using poison in his drink. Only one wanted to kill me, using illuminating gas, but I wound up dying in Byron's place. He, who had the double whammy on him—survived!

Talk about Christie irony.

AGATHA IN THE EIGHTIES
by Pam McAllister

Whoever said you can't judge a book by its cover didn't live in the eighties when packaging is everything.

Packaging wasn't *everything* to Dame Agatha, still, after one bad experience, even she took a personal interest in the jackets that clothed her stories. She was, in her words, "really furious" about the original cover of her third book—*Murder on the Links*. She thought the colors were ugly and the drawing not only of poor quality but misleading as well. After "a good deal of bad feeling over this," the Bodley Head (her publishers) agreed to secure Agatha's approval of subsequent jackets before publication.

Action is in and prices are up and both trends are reflected on the current covers of Agatha Christie mysteries. Gone are the sinister, murky colors and ponderous clutter of clues traditionally used on mystery covers. Series covers are popular—making the "Marples" easily distinguishable from the "Poirots" in a glance at the airport book rack. And if you can't judge a book by its cover, you can certainly be induced to buy one if it has the right stuff.

For Pocket Books, the right stuff in the eighties has been the uncluttered attention to detail achieved through the crisp silhouette cover art of David FeBland. A bold experiment, Pocket has for some time been departing from the dark and dreary, streamlining to primary contrast—black on white or cream. In the 1970s Pocket covers had pared away the clutter of clues, highlighting the author's name and book title above a simple image, most often of the flesh-and-blood variety—the face of a detective, a suspect or a victim—instead of a weapon or clue. In the eighties, Pocket covers go even further—opting for action over intrigue.

FeBland's striking covers are freeze frames on the moment of murder. *A Pocket Full of Rye* catches shrewd businessman Rex Fortescue violently spilling his poisoned tea, tea bag flying, spoon falling, tongue protruding, left hand clutching abdomen.

On the cover of *Third Girl*, a high-heeled woman is falling to her death from a window several floors above survivable level.

A woman is about to bash another on the head on the cover of *By the Pricking of My Thumbs* and on the cover of *Evil Under the Sun* the beautiful Arlena is sunning herself on the beach and looking sexy, unaware that she is about to be strangled by the hands *we* see.

The Pale Horse has always lent itself to creative, fancifully macabre cover art. FeBland's silhouette is creatively realistic rather than fanciful, the horse is where it belongs—on the tavern sign of the Pale Horse Pub beneath which poor Father Gorman is forever frozen at the moment of his murder, being clobbered on the head with a cosh, mouth open, hands in the air, rosary and cross flying helter-skelter.

Cora is caught napping, out like a light. But wait—a hand holding a hatchet is just milliseconds away. Blessedly we are spared, but just barely, a cover depiction of the bloody crime in *Funerals Are Fatal*.

The FeBland/Pocket covers don't always depict a murder in progress; some let us be first on the scene. A dead man sprawls in the

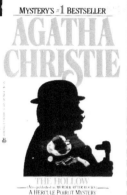

gutter on the cover of *At Bertram's Hotel* where a woman is screaming and a bobby is running toward us.

A bloody knife, still warm, has been placed beside the elegant, prone body featured in *Murder on the Orient Express*, the cover of which has finally graduated from the "major motion picture"—related art of the mid-seventies.

Over at Berkley, silhouettes are also in, but these are used to frame a small collection of clues. On *The Hollow*, the mustached silhouette tells us it's a Poirot mystery and inside the silhouette are a tea cup, a pocket watch, and a lovely pearl-handled pistol.

Miss Marple's silhouette graces the cover of *The Moving Finger* and serves as a window to a few essential items featured in the story including a sinister note composed of printed words and cut-out letters pasted onto pink letter paper, and this resting on a lace doiley. How sweet.

The cover of *Double Sin and Other Stories* combines the silhouettes of the two great detectives, back to back, and frames a votive candle and a doll dressed in green velvet. Hmmmm.

From the traditional conglomerations of clues to the action-packed come-ons of the eighties, Dame Agatha's larger-than-life name on the covers is the real magic ingredient. It is magic that makes readers take for granted the back cover promo "Over 500 Million in Print!" Yeah? Well, of course! Agatha in the eighties—Agatha forever.

INSIDE THE DETECTION CLUB

by Ann Romeo

The shy, reclusive Agatha Christie chose to avoid the limelight and habitually deferred to others when called upon to make speeches or presentations. She did not relish public scrutiny, preferring to keep her life private and to let her work speak for itself. On the other hand, Mrs. Christie was eager to associate with other writers of the genre. Early in her mystery-writing career she became one of the founding members, (and later president), of an organization created by and for the writers of the mystery—the Detection Club.

Founded in London in the late 1920s, the Detection Club remains today the oldest continuous organization for the writer of detective fiction in the world. A partial list of the founding members reads like a who's who of the greatest writers of the prewar mystery: Dorothy L. Sayers, G. K. Chesterton, Anthony Berkeley, Henry Wade, A. E. W. Mason, E. C. Bentley, John Rhode, Monsignor Ronald A. Knox, R. Austin Freeman, Freeman Wills Crofts, Hugh Walpole, and, of course, Agatha Christie. Former presidents of the club represent even today some of the best practitioners of the British mystery: Chesterton, Sayers, Christie, and presently, Julian Symons—distinguished writers all.

Unfortunately for both literary scholars and fans of the Golden Age detective novel, few early documents detailing the activities of the Detection Club have survived World War II and none of the original members of the club are alive today to answer any of our questions. Today the organization is a supper club, meeting three times a year to hear speeches, talk shop, and initiate new members into the club. Guest lectures are given by esteemed intellectuals who are avid fans of the mystery without having attempted to write any themselves. Twice a year the Detection Club convenes at the Garrick Club, London, for dinner and conversation. The third meeting is at the Café Royal where the annual initiation rites are held for those few writers invited to join.

Reflecting the subtle changes in detective fiction, qualifications for membership of this exclusive club have changed over the years. In an introduction to one of the club's early literary ventures, Dorothy L. Sayers explained that Detection Club membership "is confined to those who have written genuine detective stories (not adventure tales or thrillers) and election to the club is secured by a vote of the club on recommendation by two or more members." These rules were useful during the Golden Age of the mystery; however after World War II membership was gradually expanded to include authors of all types of detective fiction, including the modern spy novel (John le Carré, Len Deighton), thrillers (Geoffrey Household, Francis Clifford), psychological novels (Patricia Highsmith, Ruth Rendell), adventures (Dick Francis, Desmond Bagley), as well as the traditional writer of mysteries (P. D. James, Christianna Brand, Michael Innes, and H. R. F. Keating). Though it is still an exclusive organization the size of the group has more than doubled and its affairs are less secretive and its tone less stuffy.

The rituals of the club have also undergone some change over the course of time. As documented by Mr. Symons in an essay in the *New York Times Book Review*, the present initiation rites involve all the trappings of the traditional Gothic mystery: a scarlet and black cloak, candles, a darkened room, daggers and revolvers (empty, we hope!), and Eric the Skull who emits ghostly light from gaping jaw and eye sockets. The nominee must also participate in a fanciful oath, pledging to uphold the purity of the mystery in any of its special forms and to refuse to reveal the exact rites of the club to outsiders.

Before World War II the Detection Club kept regular rooms in Central London. In order to pay for the upkeep a novel idea was proposed: why not get the club's members to write a mystery, then sell it to the public, using the proceeds to finance the group's digs? The idea was quickly adopted and throughout the 1930s mysteries composed by the Detection Club were broadcast by air or sold in limited editions to the public. What makes these works special is their construction. As Mrs. Sayers explained in her introduction to one of the club's projects, *The Floating Admiral*:

> Each contributor tackled the mystery presented to him in the preceding chapters without having the slightest idea what solution or solutions the previous authors had in mind. Two rules only were imposed. Each writer must construct his instalment with a definite solution in view—that is, he must not introduce new complications merely "to make it more difficult." He must be ready, if called upon, to explain his own clues coherently and plausibly.

This is not to say that the authors of these communal efforts did not try to stump the succeeding contributor; one cannot help but feel sympathetic for the poor soul selected to tie the whole thing up and write the final solution. Indeed, part of the fun of reading these works is to see how these different writers were able to add new meaning to events that on the surface seem to be obvious.

Several collectively written mysteries were published by the Detection Club in the years before the war.

Mrs. Christie's contributions to these three works are short, concise chapters, usually appearing early in the story and dominated by an interview between the hero investigator and an eccentric personality. The character she created for *The Floating Admiral* (a gossiping lady innkeeper) is one of the most memorable in the book, and typifies what we enjoy best about Dame Agatha's writing: the humor, the lovable characters, and the subtle presentation of pertinent information.

The first of the Detection Club projects was *Behind the Screen*, a radio script that was broadcast by various authors and then published in a local weekly, *The Listener*. This proved to be so successful that it was soon followed by *The Scoop*, *The Floating Admiral*, and other works, most of which are now lost and forgotten.

Although not an exceptionally well-written story, *Behind the Screen* is remarkable for being a forerunner of the now-popular "contest mystery," where the writers leave off a solution and the general public competes to identify the motive and identity of the murderer. In the story, a young medical intern has a premonition of doom as he calls on the family of his fiancée, Amy Ellis. His fears soon prove to be well founded. While in the family drawing room he discovers, hidden behind the Japanese screen, the corpse of the family's infamous tenant, Mr. Dudden (who also had designs on Amy). The police are called in and it is soon revealed that almost

INSIDE THE DETECTION CLUB

everyone having anything to do with the Ellis family had motive to kill Mr. D., including all the members of the household and the tradespeople who visited it on that fateful evening. At this point the reading public was invited to send in solutions to the crime, complete with reasons as to who was guilty. The interesting construction of this story led to much confusion—indeed, the final announced solution seems fair but quite far-fetched.

The next literary effort of the Detection Club was *The Scoop*, a work much better organized. A cub reporter, Mr. Johnston, is sent by the *Morning Star*, a bastion of free press and public scandal, to investigate the murder of one Geraldine Tracey, reputed to have been a kept woman and estranged from her mysterious husband. Mr. J. calls his paper with the news that he is returning to the office with new evidence about the crime, certain to scoop the competition. However, he is mysteriously stabbed in the telephone box at Victoria Station before he is able to tell all he knows.

Whodunit? Enter the *Morning Star*'s ace reporter, Mr. Oliver, who doggedly tracks down every lead. Who was the secret lover of Mrs. Tracey? Where was her husband all this time? What clue could Mr. J. have found so important that the murderer felt obliged to strike again? The plot of *The Scoop* is well paced and evolves smoothly to its unexpected conclusion.

Longer, more ambitious, and more complex than either of the two works described above, *The Floating Admiral* possesses all the good qualities of the British Golden Age mystery novel. The result is a story that is tighter, better organized, and better paced than anything the club had done so far.

The body of Admiral Penistone is found floating in a boat on the River Whyn near his estate. Although he had served his country with distinction during the war and was well liked by the men who served under him, the admiral had been forced to resign his commission in his youth due to a scandal that occurred while he was in the navy serving in the Orient. Could the admiral's mysterious past have something to do with his murder?

He was also the guardian of his wealthy niece, the homely Elma Fitzgerald, engaged to marry the handsome and shady drifter, Arthur Holland. It was known that the admiral was not happy about the engagement. And then, what are the police to make of the fact that within twenty-four hours of the murder, Elma and Arthur marry! There are also rumors of bad blood between the admiral and the other luminary of the region, Sir Wilfrid Denny, a retired civil servant, who had spent some time in the Orient. Could he have something to do with the murder?

The local vicar, Mr. Mount, was one of the last people to see the admiral alive—and he, too, has a scandalous past. And what's this about a sighting of Elma's long-lost (presumed dead) brother? Could he have killed the admiral to get at Elma's money? And finally, what is one to make of the local eccentric fisherman, Neddy Ware, the man who discovered the body and knew the river like no one else? Didn't he, too, serve in Her Majesty's Navy in the Orient?

This story of blackmail, mistaken identity, and recovery of a man's honor makes an excellent mystery, complete with a second murder, complex train schedules, changing tides, and a wonderful surprise ending. It represents the best of the Detection Club's works so far uncovered and republished for our reading pleasure.

CHRISTIE ON THE BBC

by Michael Tennenbaum

"My grandmother did not care much for television," said Matthew Prichard, referring to the famous mystery writer whose estate he now controls as Chairman of the Board of Agatha Christie, Ltd. She considered it a "great gobbler of material," and while she allowed dozens of adaptations for radio and motion pictures, she never permitted British television to showcase any of her work. Enter Pat Sandys.

Miss Sandys, in an interview in *The New York Times*, said, "Lots of people had asked for the rights before, but nobody had done the homework. I did the homework." First, there was a written statement of her analysis and intent. Then, to further the comparison with a major academic project, came the meeting with the board of trustees, which Miss Sandys likened to an oral examination. The board, some fifteen people in all, included the heirs, their lawyers, financial advisors, and literary experts.

"But evidently I passed and we got permission first to do *Why Didn't They Ask Evans?* (*The Boomerang Clue*) and then *The Seven Dials Mystery*." Miss Sandys, working at the time with London Weekend Television, stayed with the project as writer-producer. The shows were first presented on British television in the spring and winter of 1980. They were shown the following year on American television on The Mobil Showcase Network.

Although both projects were treated rather harshly by the critics, the programs drew huge audiences and Miss Sandys felt encour-

aged to seek approval for more material. She chose a number of the lesser-known short stories and found the going much easier. "Trust had been established," she said—obviously because the trustees opened the vault of short stories and let her pick and choose. In all, ten stories were produced under the umbrella title of *The Agatha Christie Hour* and the programs drew large audiences despite the fact that they featured none of Dame Agatha's well-known characters. Here, instead, were interesting romantic pieces, with a touch of mystery thrown in. These included "The Red Signal," "The Manhood of Edward Robinson," "Magnolia Blossom," and "The Girl in the Train"—four episodes that were eventually purchased by Mobil for *Mystery!* on PBS.

Now the flood-gates were opened. Agatha Christie, Ltd. became more and more receptive to offers from British television producers. London Weekend Television obtained the rights to a collection of Tommy and Tuppence Beresford stories and came up with a ten-part series of adaptations called *Partners in Crime*, featuring Francesca Annis and James Warwick as the stylish sleuths. And, most recently, the BBC has scored with multi-episode versions of *The Body in the Library* and *The Moving Finger* that feature Joan Hickson in what critics feel is the "definitive" interpretation of Miss Marple, much closer physically and emotionally to the character as written by Mrs. Christie than any other film and TV actresses who have portrayed her.

And so, hopefully, it will go on. Thank you, Pat Sandys, for opening the door.

JESSICA FLETCHER
A Liberated Miss Marple?
by Emma Lathen

At long last Agatha Christie has a successor. Jessica Fletcher, the writer-detective on CBS's *Murder, She Wrote*, is right up there with all those gray-haired spinsters who take one look at a corpse and then faultlessly solve the crime. We are never told what kind of mysteries Mrs. Fletcher writes, but it's a safe bet that she's a lot closer to Dame Agatha than to Mickey Spillane. One thing is clear. She is no Miss Marple, placidly knitting while murder stalks the village. Jessica is all energy from sparkling eyes to dimpled elbows. Sitting still isn't her style.

Now most energetic American detectives use guns, fists, and high-powered cars. This distinction was established many years ago during the Golden Age of the mystery. English murders, as we all know, took place during house parties at country mansions and featured a body in the library together with a suspicious butler. American thrillers were markedly different, possibly because so few of us are in a position to invite a dozen people for a weekend and butlers have never exactly been a dime a dozen. No, our detectives were not gentlemen inspectors from Scotland Yard. Instead they wore fedoras, drank Prohibition booze and were immortalized by Humphrey Bogart in *The Maltese Falcon*.

Not surprisingly, the authors differed as much as the books. Over here, it was usually the men who were writing about those dark city streets and bone-breaking encounters. In England, many of the great names belonged to women, probably because they found the domestic environment congenial. Some, indeed, went one step further and replaced the Scotland Yard man with an amateur spinster. Christie's Miss Marple was famous with readers long before Margaret Rutherford and Helen Hayes brought her to life on the screen. These spinsters all share several characteristics. They are ladies of the old school, noteworthy for their rock-ribbed rectitude, their genteel manners, and their knowledge of human nature.

Of course, America had its honorable exceptions to the blood-and-guts school. There were male detectives who preferred to solve crimes with their little gray cells. Nero Wolfe might move his tonnage to indulge his passion for gourmet cooking, but, when he was working, he was sitting in a chair. Perry Mason started thinking deeply in law school and never stopped. Even my own banker-detective, John Thatcher, avoids throwing punches while he reasons his way to the spot where the money is hidden.

But Jessica Fletcher has only one prime-time hour (less commercials) for her weekly operation. She cannot painstakingly assemble a patchwork of clues. So how does she nail the villain? She does it the same way they do it on *60 Minutes*. Angela Lansbury may ask fewer questions, but they are just as probing. Give her a small discrepancy, and she is onto it faster than you can say Mike Wallace.

And that's where she has an edge over all those knitting spinsters. In the first place, there is the simple consideration of money. When Agatha Christie had to send Miss Marple to far-off Caribbean islands, we were told these jaunts were due to the generosity of a nephew—who just happened to be a best-

selling author. In *Murder, She Wrote* it is Jessica, herself, who is the best-selling author. And while Miss Marple and her sisters lurked modestly in the background whenever they ventured into the great world, Jessica Fletcher is there by right. When she asks questions, she gets answers.

What's more, her horizons are unlimited. Miss Marple and Mrs. Fletcher are both born detectives because of their powers of observation and their interest in their fellow human beings. Miss Marple, however, is much stronger on personal relationships than on the material facts of life as it is lived anywhere outside her country village of St. Mary Mead. Take, for instance, this episode last season of *Murder, She Wrote.* The killer, after strangling his victim, waits twenty minutes and then stabs the corpse in the back. When questioned, he admits the stabbing, confident that the autopsy will establish another cause of death. It goes without saying that either of our ladies would be equal to this challenge. But Jessica does not have to wait for medical examiners: she sees at a glance that there has not been enough blood. Then, at a rapid clip, she notes that a sailor has tied a landlubber's knot, that a battered mystery novel is a valuable first edition, and, finally, that the murderer's grease-stained hands have rested in the wrong place. All of these are physical clues that have nothing to do with the personalities of the suspects.

Miss Marple would have proceeded very differently. She would have fastened on the tension between the married couple, she would have detected in the supposed widower a life-long bachelor, and then, in climax, she would have sensed the similarity between the culprit and someone in St. Mary Mead who always tried to cover a mistake with too much ingenuity. But different roads often lead to the same place. Both our detec-

Right: Angela Lansbury as Jessica Fletcher tries to help an injured man (Don Stroud) in a Murder, She Wrote *episode, while Tom Bosley and Miles Watson look on.*

tives would conclude that the confession was an elaborate ploy. The man who did the stabbing also did the strangling.

Does this mean that television is really trying to sell us a heroine who is all head and no heart? By no means. As played by Angela Lansbury, Jessica manages to have the best of both worlds. She has all of Miss Marple's virtues. She is everybody's favorite aunt—understanding, sympathetic, upright. And it is no accident that, far from being a spinster, she is a widow. Jessica has not been spending her time baking apple pies in the kitchen. It is no surprise to her to learn that young people are living together, that girls are hellbent on careers, that middle-aged men hanker after forbidden fruit. A lot of things may not be her style, but she is all too familiar with them. She can spot the tiny discrepancy, doubt the perfect alibi, resist the easy charmer. You could sum it all up by saying that Jessica Fletcher is a liberated Miss Marple.

In fact, from a mystery writer's point of view, the character of Jessica Fletcher suffers only one fatal flaw.

When in the world does she find time to write all those books?

THE IMPACT OF GENDER ON AGATHA AND HER CRAFT

by Pam McAllister

"Alas! a woman that attempts the pen, Such a presumptuous creature is esteemed, The fault can by no virture be redeemed." So said Lady Winchilsea, a poet and noblewoman born in 1661.

But surely things had changed on planet earth by the time Agatha took up her pen in the early twentieth century, no? Well, not so much as one might have hoped. Women writers were still fighting the image of being "presumptuous creatures," and worried about being taken seriously.

Agatha was tempted to hide behind a male pseudonym in order to be taken seriously at first. She especially liked the sound of something like "Martin West." "I had the idea that a woman's name would prejudice people against my work, especially in detective stories; that Martin West would be more manly and forthright."

In her forties, with more than ten books published and her fame international, Agatha wanted nothing of being a creature as "presumptuous" as a woman *writer.*

> I wrote things—yes—books and stories. . . . But never, when I was filling in a form and came to the line asking for occupation, would it have occurred to me to fill it in with anything but the time-honoured "married woman."

This statement echoed an earlier sentiment held by the eleven-year-old Agatha on the occasion of her first published work, a poem about trams.

I was elated at seeing myself in print, but I cannot say that it led me to contemplate a literary career.

In fact I only contemplated one thing—a happy marriage. About that I had complete self-assurance—as all my friends did.

After writing her first three books, Agatha was tempted to consider herself a writer, but even this thought was couched in appropriately feminine self-depreciation. She wrote in her autobiography, "It was by now just beginning to dawn on me that perhaps I *might* be a writer by profession. I was not sure of it yet. I still had an idea that writing books was only the natural successor to embroidering sofa cushions."

In her famed 1929 essay, "A Room of One's Own," feminist author Virginia Woolf prescribed the special requirements needed to encourage women writers: "a woman must have money and a room of her own if she is to write fiction." We might assume that Agatha Christie always had the money and the room, if not a number of them, but she claimed at one point not to need a room of her own at all. Indeed, if Agatha had written Virginia Woolf's brave essay, she might have titled it "A *Table* of One's Own."

> I never had a definite place which was *my* room or where I retired specially to write. . . . All I needed was a steady table and a typewriter. . . . A marble-topped bedroom washstand table made a good place to write; the dining-room table between meals was also suitable.

Agatha did have to fight for a table of her own at least once. Accompanying her second husband, Max Mallowan, on an archeological expedition to Nineveh, she encountered Dr. Campbell-Thompson who, it seems from the following account, might well have considered Agatha a "presumptuous creature."

> All I wanted was to buy myself a table in the bazaar. . . . What I *had* to have, if I was going to do my own work, was a solid table at which I could typewrite, and under which I could get my knees. . . . C.T. . . . looked down on me for being willing to spend money on something not absolutely necessary. . . .
>
> Writing books, I pointed out, was my work, and I had to have certain tools for it: a typewriter, a pencil, and a table at which I could sit. So C.T. gave way, but he was sad about it.

Eventually, Agatha did want a *room* of her own while on another expedition, this one at Nimrud where she wrote her autobiography. "I petitioned to be allowed to have a small room added on of my own. This I would pay for myself. So, for fifty pounds, I built on a small, square, mud-brick room, and it was there that I began writing this book."

She had come a long way in accepting her identity as a writer by the time she got that room. But don't be fooled. Agatha never rejected the lessons she had learned as a girl, nor rejected the tradition of playing the game talented, spirited women of her day had to play in this man's world. The game allowed for certain idiosyncrasies—even, in Agatha's case, a fancy for playing the boy's part in youthful theater productions. "We went through the Sleeping Beauty, Cinderella, Beauty and the Beast and so forth. I was fondest of the part of principal boy."

Such playacting, however, never slipped over into Agatha's idea of how women's lives were meant to be shaped. "*You didn't know what was going to happen to you.* That was what made being a woman so exciting. No worry about what you should be or do—Biology would decide. You were waiting for The Man, and when the man came, he would change your life!"

Cherishing this point of view, Agatha lamented the changes that were redefining the traditionally strict gender roles.

> The position of women, over the years, has definitely changed for the worse. . . . We have clamoured to be allowed to work as men work. . . .
>
> It seems sad that having established ourselves so cleverly as the "weaker sex," we should now be broadly on a par with the women of primitive tribes who toil in the fields all day.

Indeed, she applauded the ways women had been taught to manipulate men to get their way.

> You've got to hand it to Victorian women, they got their menfolk where they wanted them. They established their frailty, delicacy, sensibility—their constant need of being protected and cherished. . . . All my grandmother's friends seem to me in retrospect singularly resilient and almost invariably successful in getting their own way. They were tough, self-willed, and remarkably well read and well informed.

Lest we have any doubt that Agatha really meant what she said about the woman's sphere, she stated emphatically (with capital letters and italics no less!): "In one respect man was paramount. He was the Head of the House. A woman, when she married, accepted as her destiny *his* place in the world and *his* way of life. That seems to me sound sense and the foundation of happiness."

THE IMPACT OF GENDER ON AGATHA AND HER CRAFT

It was Agatha's good fortune to have a childhood filled with clever, strong women for models. And she had great admiration for them. Her mother was "an enigmatic and arresting personality—more forceful than my father." Her beloved Nursie was described as "the outstanding figure in my early life" and "the rock of stability."

There was Marie, Agatha's agreeable French governess and Jane, the cook, "who ruled the kitchen with the calm superiority of a queen." And there were family friends. "My mother's nicest friend was Pussy Richards, who often came to stay. She had short hair that curled all over her head, wore manly coats and white shirts, and she was heaven to play with. . . . She led a very adventurous life . . . taking all sorts of different jobs."

Another friend was Lilian Pirie, described by Agatha as "one of the most outstanding personalities I have ever known. . . . There was something faintly awe-inspiring in her . . . and I knew her up to the age of eighty-odd when she died. All that time my admiration and respect for her increased."

The men in Agatha's life were less consistently inspiring. Archie Christie, for example, was sometimes supportive. Of him she wrote, "He always took it for granted that I could do things about which I myself had a good deal of doubt. 'Of course you can do it,' he would say." He taught Agatha to drive, which delighted her no end. "Oh, the joy that car was to me! . . . To be able to go anywhere you chose; to places beyond the reach of your legs: it widened your whole horizon."

Archie was less than helpful, however, when it came to Agatha's writing. In fact he was downright harmful.

> Occasionally I felt the urge to outline to him some idea I had for a new story, or the plot

of a new book. When I had described it haltingly, it sounded, even to my ears, extraordinarily banal, futile, and a great many other adjectives which I will not particularize. . . . "Do you think it will be all right?"
> "Well, I suppose it might be," said Archie, in a completely damping manner. "It doesn't seem to have much *story* to it, does it?" . . . That plot thereupon fell dead, slain forever.

Max Mallowan was more consistently supportive and encouraging, though he could not bring himself to read his wife's books, which must at least have *felt* like a lack of appreciation. Nevertheless, Agatha insisted that, as she was a "lowbrow" and Max a "highbrow," they complemented each other nicely.

Such support from her husband notwithstanding, Agatha definitely drew strength from the women in her life—including some imaginary female friends, created in childhood, who stayed with her always. Deprived of attending school, she had populated a make-believe classroom with these friends —clever Ethel Smith with a great mane of hair; Annie Gray, pale, shy, and nervous; beautiful but "worldly" Isabella Sullivan whom Agatha actually disliked; Irish Elsie Green who was poor and wore Isabel's castoff clothes; conscientious, dull Ella White with the bushy hair; and Sue de Verte who Agatha supposed was really herself.

With remarkable candor, Agatha, at age seventy-five, wrote:

> Even now, sometimes, as I put away a dress in a cupboard, I say to myself: "Yes, that would do well for Elsie, green was always her colour." . . . It makes me laugh when I do it, but there "the girls" *are* still, though, unlike me, they have not grown old.

AGATHA CHRISTIE MADE ME DO IT!

"It's a cross between 'Laugh-In' and 'Perry Mason.'" That's how one reviewer described *Agatha Christie Made Me Do It*, a mystery comedy by Houston playwright Eddie Cope.

The curtain opens on Police Officer Hootspah, a middle-aged "dese-dose-and-dem" man, hard at work at a typewriter. He's obviously a two-finger operator. When he spots the audience he comes downstage to explain that he's ready to retire from the force and get rich and famous by writing mystery plays. He's been studying a book (hypothetical) titled *How to Write a Moider Play*. It analyzes the techniques used by our mistress of mayhem and master storyteller—Agatha Christie. Why not learn from the best? After all, Hootspah tells the audience (sounding more than a little like Archie Bunker), Christie wrote lots of stuff—like *Moider on the Shankhigh Express* and . . . uh . . . *Witness for the Prostitution*.

After hitting upon the idea that his play "will start with the first act," (a good idea, don't you think?) the bumbling officer proceeds to cook up a mystery before our very eyes, adding plenty of suspense, at least a barrel of laughs and mixing it all together with a dash of poetic license. Only once in a while do his characters get out of hand. The result is a merry spoof in three acts that has played dinner theaters since 1975 and delighted audiences at college, rep, community, and high school theaters in nearly every state in the USA as well as in Australia, Canada, and Panama.

The not-so-bumbling author, Eddie Cope, is a prominent member of the Houston theater scene. The play is published and promoted by I. E. Clark, Inc., St. John's Road, Schulenburg, TX 78956.

PAM McALLISTER

HAD ENOUGH YET?

For those who want more, here's a selected bibliography of recently published books and articles about Agatha Christie:

BOOKS

Bargainner, Earl F. *The Gentle Art of Murder: The Detective Fiction of Agatha Christie.* Bowling Green, Ohio: Bowling Green University Popular Press, 1981.

Barnard, Robert A. *A Talent to Deceive: An Appreciation of Agatha Christie.* New York: Dodd, Mead, 1980.

Maida, Patricia D. and Nicholas B. Spornick. *Murder She Wrote: A Study of Agatha Christie's Detective Fiction.* Bowling Green, Ohio: Bowling Green University Popular Press, 1981.

Morgan, Janet. *Agatha Christie: A Biography.* New York: Alfred Knopf, 1985.

Morselt, Ben. *An A to Z of the Novels and Short Stories of Agatha Christie.* New York: Phoenix Publishing, 1986.

Osborne, Charles. *The Life and Crimes of Agatha Christie.* New York: Random House, 1983.

Sanders, Dennis and Len Lovallo. *The Agatha Christie Companion: The Complete Guide to Agatha Christie's Life and Work.* New York; Delacorte Press, 1984.

ARTICLES

Culhane, John. "The Woman with a Knack for Murder." *Reader's Digest* (October 1985), p. 92.

Fryxell, D. A. "All about Agatha." *Horizon* (November 1984) p. 42.

James, P. D. "Agatha Christie." *TV Guide* (May 16, 1981) p. 34.

———. "One Clue at a Time." *The Writer* (February 1984) p. 9.

"Using the 'Little Grey Cells'." *English Journal* (September 1983) p. 37.

CHRISTIE ON VIDEO

CBS/Fox Home Video

Witness for the Prosecution	(1957)	$49.95

Pacific Arts

(Agatha Christie's *Partners in Crime* Series)

The Ambassador's Boots	(1985)	$24.95
The Clergyman's Daughter	(1985)	$24.95
The Crackler	(1985)	$24.95
Finessing the King	(1985)	$24.95
The Sunnydale Mystery	(1985)	$24.95

Paramount Home Video

Murder on the Orient Express	(1974)	$69.95

Thorn/EMI–HBO Home Video

Death on the Nile	(1978)	$79.95
Endless Night	(1971)	$59.95
Evil Under the Sun	(1982)	$79.95
The Mirror Crack'd	(1980)	$79.95

VCI

And Then There Were None	(1945)	$39.95

Warner Home Video

Agatha	(1979)	$69.95
Ordeal by Innocence (Details not available)		

THE UNREAD CHRISTIE

by Norma Siebenheller

I caught the bug at twenty-six
By thirty was quite bitten
You might say I was in a fix
You might say I was smitten

It was Miss Marple snared me first
(As could have been predicted)
And soon, for better or for worse,
I was indeed addicted

Hercule Poirot, the Beresfords too
Became my favorite friends
I followed all their exploits through
To neatly tied-up ends

I learned to look for subtle hints
Clues dropped among the knitting
Murderers painted in innocent tints
And victims all unwitting

From Styles to old St. Mary Mead
From Egypt to the Isthmus
'Twas great adventure, each new read
'Twas the Night-Before-Agatha-Christmas

I know I failed to face the fact
It all would end some day
What I would do then, how I'd act
I just refused to say

I kept on jumping round about
'Twixt murder, crime, and mystery
Lost in a web of suspicion and doubt
Engulfed in Agatha Christery

But now the unread stock did shrink
New ones were hard to find
I panicked — couldn't even think —
I feared I'd lose my mind

There weren't too many left, I knew
No more would join the list
All that remained for me to do
Was find the few I'd missed

I marked them off, then, one by one
Three left, then two — one — NO!
I couldn't let the thing be done
I put the book down — so —

I have it still, and still unread
Unopened, in my drawer
It lives, where all the rest are dead
Mysterious no more

I treasure it, like something rare
And muse about it wistfully
What devious puzzles hide in there?
All woven so Agatha Christfully?

The title, now — what might it mean?
Who will the villain be?
What house will figure in the scene?
Will everyone have tea?

Will I see the light before the end?
Will I even see a flicker?
Can I guess whodunit? No, my friend —
I just know it's not the vicar

Should I read — and cease to speculate —
My dreams would be diminished
It's more fun to anticipate
Than partake, and then be finished

The book's a symbol now, a token
Like an eagle, or a thistle,
Gleaming and bright, intact, unbroken
My jewel! My Agatha Crystal!

Agatha Christie Editions Currently in Print

Agatha Christie's first six books were published in England by The Bodley Head, the balance by William Collins Sons & Co., Ltd. In the United States the major Christie publisher for hardcover editions is Dodd, Mead & Company, New York.

Key:
H = Hardcover edition
PB = Paperback edition
LT = Large-type edition*
n.d. = No available publication date

NOVELS

The A.B.C. Murders. New York: Dodd, Mead, 1978 (H); New York: Pocket Books, 1979 (PB).

And Then There Were None (Ten Little Indians). New York: Washington Square Press, 1975 (PB)

After the Funeral (Funerals Are Fatal). Leicester, Eng.: Ulverscroft, 1978 (LT).

Appointment with Death. New York: Dell, 1978 (PB); Leicester, Eng.: Ulverscroft, 1975 (LT).

At Bertram's Hotel. New York: Dodd, Mead, reprint ed., 1965 (H); New York: Pocket Books, 1977 (PB); Leicester, Eng.: Ulverscroft, 1968 (LT).

The Big Four. New York: Dell, 1978 (PB); Leicester, Eng.: Ulverscroft, 1974 (LT).

The Body in the Library. New York: Pocket Books, 1975 (PB); Leicester, Eng.: Ulverscroft, 1972 (LT).

The Boomerang Clue. New York: Dell, 1978 (PB).

By the Pricking of My Thumbs. New York: Pocket Books, 1977 (PB).

Cards on the Table. New York: Dodd, Mead, reprint ed., 1968 (H); New York: Dell, 1974 (PB); Leicester, Eng.: Ulverscroft, 1969 (LT).

A Caribbean Mystery. New York: Pocket Books, 1977 (PB); Leicester, Eng.: Ulverscroft, 1967 (LT).

Cat among the Pigeons. New York: Pocket Books, 1978 (PB).

The Clocks. New York: Pocket Books, 1965 (PB); Leicester, Eng.: Ulverscroft, 1969 (LT).

*Agatha Christie's *The Pale Horse* inaugurated large-type editions when it was published in 1964 by Ulverscroft Large-Print Books, Leicester, England.

Crooked House. New York: Dodd, Mead, reprint ed., 1967 (H); New York: Pocket Books, 1978 (PB); Leicester, Eng.: Ulverscroft, (LT).

Curtain. New York: Dodd, Mead, 1975; New York: Pocket Books, 1976; Leicester, Eng.: Ulverscroft, 1976 (LT).

Dead Man's Folly. New York: Pocket Books, 1977 (PB).

Death Comes As the End. New York: Pocket Books, 1977 (PB).

Death in the Air. New York: Popular Library, 1975 (PB).

Death in the Clouds (including N or M?, Hercule Poirot's Christmas, Towards Zero). New York: Dodd, Mead, 1974 (H).

Death on the Nile. New York: Dodd, Mead, reprint ed., 1969 (H); Leicester, Eng.: Ulverscroft, 1971 (LT).

Destination Unknown (So Many Steps to Death). New York: Dodd, Mead, 1978 (H); Leicester, Eng.: Ulverscroft, 1968 (LT).

Dumb Witness (Poirot Loses a Client). Leicester, Eng.: Ulverscroft, 1973 (LT).

Easy to Kill. New York: Pocket Books, 1976 (PB).

Elephants Can Remember. New York: Dodd, Mead, 1972 (H); New York: Dell, 1976, (PB); Boston: G.K. Hall, 1973 (LT).

Endless Night. New York: Pocket Books, 1977 (PB); Leicester, Eng.: Ulverscroft, 1972 (LT).

Evil Under the Sun. New York: Pocket Books, 1976 (PB); Leicester, Eng.: Ulverscroft, 1971 (LT).

4:50 from Paddington (What Mrs. McGillicuddy Saw!). Leicester, Eng.: Ulverscroft, 1965 (LT).

Funerals Are Fatal. New York: Pocket Books, 1976 (PB).

Hallowe'en Party. New York: Pocket Books, 1976 (PB).

Hercule Poirot's Christmas (Murder for Christmas). New York: Dodd, Mead, reprint ed., 1974 (H).

Hickory, Dickory, Death. New York: Pocket Books, 1976 (PB).

A Holiday for Murder (Murder for Christmas). New York: Bantam, 1975 (PB).

The Hollow (Murder after Hours). Leicester, Eng.: Ulverscroft, 1974 (LT).

Agatha Christie Editions Currently in Print

Lord Edgware Dies (Thirteen at Dinner). New York: Dodd, Mead, 1969 (H); Leicester, Eng.: Ulverscroft, 1970 (LT).

The Man in the Brown Suit. New York: Dell, 1977 (PB).

Masterpieces of Murder (including *The Murder of Roger Ackroyd, And Then There Were None, Witness for the Prosecution, Death on the Nile*). New York: Dodd, Mead, 1977 (H).

The Mirror Crack'd. New York: Pocket Books, 1977 (PB).

The Mirror Crack'd from Side to Side. Leicester, Eng.: Ulverscroft, 1966 (LT).

The Mousetrap (Three Blind Mice and Other Stories). New York: Dell, 1978 (PB).

The Moving Finger. New York: Dodd, Mead, reprint ed., n.d. (H); Leicester, Eng.: Ulverscroft, 1970 (LT).

Mr. Parker Pyne, Detective. New York: Dell, 1971 (PB).

Mrs. McGinty's Dead. New York: Pocket Books, 1976 (PB).

Murder after Hours. New York: Dell, 1976 (PB).

Murder at the Vicarage. New York: Dodd, Mead, 1978 (H).

Murder in Mesopotamia. Leicester, Eng.: Ulverscroft, 1969 (LT).

Murder in Retrospect. New York: Dell, 1974 (PB).

Murder in the Calais Coach (Murder on the Orient Express). New York: Pocket Books, 1974 (PB).

Murder in Three Acts. New York: Popular Library, 1977 (PB).

A Murder Is Announced. New York: Dodd, Mead, reprint ed., 1967 (H); New York: Pocket Books, 1976 (PB); Leicester, Eng.: Ulverscroft, 1965 (LT).

The Murder of Roger Ackroyd. New York: Dodd, Mead, reprint ed., 1954 (H); New York: Garland Publishing, reprint ed., 1975 (H); New York: Pocket Books, 1975 (PB); Leicester, Eng.: Ulverscroft, 1972 (LT).

Murder on Board (including *The Mystery of the Blue Train, What Mrs. McGillicuddy Saw!, Death in the Air*). New York: Dodd, Mead, 1974 (H).

Murder on the Links. New York: Dell, 1977 (PB); Leicester, Eng.: Ulverscroft, 1977 (LT).

Murder on the Orient Express. New York: Dodd, Mead, reprint ed., n.d., (H); Leicester, Eng.: Ulverscroft, 1965 (LT).

Murder with Mirrors. New York: Pocket Books, 1977 (PB).

The Mysterious Affair at Styles: New York: Dodd, Mead, 1975 (H); New York: Bantam, 1975 (PB); Boston: G.K. Hall, 1976 (LT).

The Mystery of the Blue Train. New York: Dodd, Mead, reprint ed., n.d. (H); New York: Pocket Books, 1977 (PB); Leicester, Eng.: Ulverscroft, 1976 (LT).

Nemesis. New York: Dodd, Mead, 1971 (H); New York: Pocket Books, 1977 (PB); Leicester, Eng.: Ulverscroft, 1976 (LT).

N or M? New York: Dodd, Mead, reprint ed., n.d., (H); New York: Dell, 1977 (PB).

One, Two, Buckle My Shoe (The Patriotic Murders). Leicester, Eng.: Ulverscroft, 1958 (LT).

Ordeal by Innocence. New York: Pocket Books, 1977 (PB); Leicester, Eng.: Ulverscroft, 1958 (LT).

An Overdose of Death (The Patriotic Murders). New York: Dell, 1978 (PB).

The Pale Horse. New York: Pocket Books, 1977 (PB).

Parker Pyne Investigates (Mr. Parker Pyne, Detective). Leicester, Eng.: Ulverscroft, 1978 (LT).

Passenger to Frankfurt. New York: Dodd, Mead, 1970 (H); New York: Pocket Books, 1977 (PB).

Peril at End House. New York: Pocket Books, 1976; New York: Washington Square Press, 1976 (PB); Leicester, Eng.: Ulverscroft, 1978 (LT).

A Pocket Full of Rye. New York: Pocket Books, 1977 (PB).

Poirot's Early Cases. New York: Dodd, Mead, 1974 (H).

Postern of Fate. New York: Dodd, Mead, 1973 (H); New York: Bantam, 1974 (PB); Boston: G. K. Hall, 1974 (LT).

Remembered Death. New York: Pocket Books, 1976 (PB).

Sad Cypress. Leicester, Eng.: Ulverscroft, 1965 (LT).

The Secret Adversary. New York: Bantam, 1975 (PB).

The Secret of Chimneys. New York: Dell, 1978 (PB).

The Seven Dials Mystery. New York: Bantam, 1976 (PB).

Sleeping Murder. New York: Dodd, Mead, 1976 (H); New York: Bantam, 1977 (PB); Leicester, Eng.: Ulverscroft, 1976 (LT).

So Many Steps to Death. New York: Pocket Books, 1976 (PB).

Sparkling Cyanide (Remembered Death). Leicester, Eng.: Ulverscroft, 1978 (LT).

Starring Miss Marple (including *A Murder is Announced, The Body in the Library, Murder with Mirrors*). New York: Dodd, Mead, 1977 (H).

Taken at the Flood (There Is a Tide). Leicester, Eng.: Ulverscroft, 1971 (LT).

Ten Little Indians. New York: Dodd, Mead, 1978 (H).

There Is a Tide. New York: Dell, 1977 (PB).

They Came to Baghdad. New York: Dodd, Mead, reprint ed., 1969 (H); New York: Dell, 1976 (PB); Leicester, Eng.: Ulverscroft, 1965 (LT).

They Do It with Mirrors. New York: Dodd, Mead, reprint ed., 1969 (H).

Third Girl. New York: Pocket Books, 1976 (PB); Leicester, Eng.: Ulverscroft, 1968 (LT).

Thirteen at Dinner. New York: Dell, 1976 (PB).

Three-Act Tragedy (Murder in Three Acts). New York: Dodd, Mead, reprint ed., n.d. (H); Leicester, Eng.: Ulverscroft, 1975 (LT).

Towards Zero. New York: Dodd, Mead, 1972 (H); New York: Pocket Books, 1975 (PB); Leicester, Eng.: Ulverscroft, 1972 (LT).

What Mrs. McGillicuddy Saw!. New York: Pocket Books, 1977 (PB).

Why Didn't They Ask Evans? (The Boomerang Clue). New York: Dodd, Mead, 1968 (H); Leicester, Eng.: Ulverscroft, 1974 (LT).

PLAYS

Akhnaton: A Play in Three Acts. New York: Dodd, Mead, 1973 (H).

The Mousetrap and Other Plays. New York: Dodd, Mead, 1978 (H).

POETRY

Poems. New York: Dodd, Mead, 1973 (H).

SHORT STORY COLLECTIONS

Dead Man's Mirror. New York: Dell, 1978 (PB).

Double Sin & Other Stories. New York: Dell, 1977 (PB).

The Golden Ball and Other Stories. New York: Dodd, Mead, 1971 (H); Dell, 1979 (PB).

The Hound of Death. Leicester, Eng.: Ulverscroft, 1968 (LT).

The Labors of Hercules. New York: Dodd, Mead, reprint ed., 1967 (H); New York: Dell, 1978 (PB); Leicester, Eng.: Ulverscroft, 1978 (LT).

The Mysterious Mr. Quin. New York: Dell, 1976 (PB); Leicester, Eng.: Ulverscroft, 1977 (LT).

Partners in Crime. New York: Dell, 1978 (PB).

Poirot Investigates. New York: Bantam, 1978 (PB).

Regatta Mystery. New York: Dell, 1973 (PB).

Surprise! Surprise! Bond, Raymond T., ed. New York: Dodd, Mead, 1965 (H).

Thirteen for Luck. Bond, Raymond T., ed. New York: Dodd, Mead, 1961 (H); New York: Dell, 1977 (PB).

The Thirteen Problems (The Tuesday Club Murders). New York: Dodd, Mead, reprint ed., n.d. (H); Leicester, Eng.: Ulverscroft, 1968 (LT).

The Under Dog and Other Stories. New York: Dell, 1978 (PB).

WRITTEN UNDER PSEUDONYM

As Agatha Christie Mallowan:

Come Tell Me How You Live. New York: Dodd, Mead, 1976 (H); Pocket Books, 1977 (PB).

Star over Bethlehem. New York: Dodd, Mead, 1965 (H).

As Mary Westmacott:

Absent in the Spring. New York: Arbor House, 1971 (H); New York: Dell, 1972 (PB); Leicester, Eng.: Ulverscroft, 1978 (LT).

The Burden. New York: Arbor House, 1973 (H); New York: Dell, 1976 (PB); Leicester, Eng.: Ulverscroft, 1979 (LT).

A Daughter's a Daughter. New York: Arbor House, 1972; New York: Dell, 1976 (PB); Leicester, Eng.: Ulverscroft, 1978 (LT).

Giant's Bread. New York: Arbor House, 1973 (H); New York: Dell, 1975 (PB).

The Rose & the Yew Tree. New York: Arbor House, 1971 (H); New York: Dell, 1972 (PB); Leicester, Eng.: Ulverscroft, 1978 (LT).

Unfinished Portrait. New York: Arbor House, 1972 (H); New York: Dell, 1977 (PB).

Christie Books Arranged by Detective Featured

HERCULE POIROT

The Mysterious Affair at Styles (1920)
Murder on the Links (1923)
Poirot Investigates (1924)
The Murder of Roger Ackroyd (1926)
The Big Four (1927)
The Mystery of the Blue Train (1928)
Peril at End House (1932)
Thirteen at Dinner (1933)
Murder on the Orient Express (1934)
Murder in Three Acts (1935)
Death in the Air (1935)
The A.B.C. Murders (1935)
Murder in Mesopotamia (1936)
Cards on the Table (1936; with Oliver)
Poirot Loses a Client (1937)
Death on the Nile (1937)
Dead Man's Mirror (1937)
Appointment with Death (1938)
Murder for Christmas (1938)
The Regatta Mystery (some Poirot; 1939)
Sad Cypress (1940)
The Patriotic Murders (1940)
Evil Under the Sun (1941)
Murder in Retrospect (1943)
Murder after Hours (1946)
The Labors of Hercules (1947)
There Is a Tide (1948)
Witness for the Prosecution and Other Stories (one Poirot; 1948)
The Mousetrap and Other Stories (three Poirots; 1950)
The Under Dog and Other Stories (1951)
Mrs. McGinty's Dead (1952; with Oliver)
Funerals Are Fatal (1953)
Hickory, Dickory, Death (1955)
Dead Man's Folly (1956; with Oliver)
Cat among the Pigeons (1959)
The Adventure of the Christmas Pudding (five Poirots; 1960)
Double Sin and Other Stories (four Poirots; 1961)
The Clocks (1963)
Third Girl (1966; with Oliver)

Hallowe'en Party (1969; with Oliver)
Elephants Can Remember (1972; with Oliver)
Curtain (1975)

JANE MARPLE

Murder at the Vicarage (1930)
The Tuesday Club Murders (1932)
The Regatta Mystery (some Marple; 1939)
The Body in the Library (1942)
The Moving Finger (1942)
The Mousetrap and Other Stories (four Marples; 1950)
A Murder Is Announced (1950)
Murder with Mirrors (1952)
A Pocket Full of Rye (1953)
What Mrs. McGillicuddy Saw! (1957)
The Adventure of the Christmas Pudding (six Marples; 1960)
Double Sin and Other Stories (two Marples; 1961)
The Mirror Crack'd (1962)
A Caribbean Mystery (1964)
At Bertram's Hotel (1965)
Nemesis (1971)
Sleeping Murder (1976)

ARIADNE OLIVER

Mr. Parker Pyne, Detective (1934)
Cards on the Table (1936; with Poirot)
Mrs. McGinty's Dead (1952; with Poirot)
Dead Man's Folly (1956; with Poirot)
The Pale Horse (1961)
Third Girl (1966; with Poirot)
Hallowe'en Party (1969; with Poirot)
Elephants Can Remember (1972; with Poirot)

TOMMY AND TUPPENCE BERESFORD

The Secret Adversary (1922)
Partners in Crime (1929)
N or M? (1941)
By the Pricking of My Thumbs (1968)
Postern of Fate (1974)

SUPERINTENDENT BATTLE

The Secret of Chimneys (1925)
Towards Zero (1944)

Plays and Short Story Collections

Alibi (1928), dramatized by Michael Morton from the novel *The Murder of Roger Ackroyd.*

Akhnaton (1973), an original play.

Appointment with Death (1945), dramatized by Agatha Christie from the novel.

Black Coffee (1934), an original play.

Go Back for Murder (1960), dramatized by Agatha Christie from the novel *Murder in Retrospect.*

The Hollow (1951), dramatized by Agatha Christie from the novel *Murder after Hours.*

Love from a Stranger (1936), dramatized by Agatha Christie and Frank Vosper from the short story "Philomel Cottage."

The Mousetrap (1952), dramatized by Agatha Christie from the short story "Three Blind Mice."

The Mousetrap and Other Plays: 8 Great Stage and Screen Mysteries (1978, 1981)
Ten Little Indians, Appointment with Death, The Hollow, The Mousetrap, Witness for the Prosecution, Towards Zero, Verdict, Go Back for Murder.

Murder at the Vicarage (1950), dramatized by Moie Charles and Barbara Toy from the novel.

Murder on the Nile (1946), dramatized by Agatha Christie from the novel *Death on the Nile.*

Peril at End House (1940), dramatized by Arnold Ridley from the novel.

Rule of Three (1962), three original one-act plays: *Afternoon at the Seaside, Patient, Rats.*

Spider's Web (1954), an original play.

Ten Little Indians (1945), dramatized by Agatha Christie from the novel.

Towards Zero (1956), dramatized by Agatha Christie and Gerald Verner from the novel.

Unexpected Guest (1958), an original play.

Verdict (1958), an original play.

Witness for the Prosecution (1935), dramatized by Agatha Christie from the short story.

SHORT STORY COLLECTIONS

Adventure of the Christmas Pudding (1960)
"Adventure of the Christmas Pudding" (expansion of "The Theft of the Royal Ruby"), "Mystery of the Spanish Chest" (expansion of "The Mystery of the Baghdad Chest"), "The Under Dog," "Four and Twenty Blackbirds," "The Dream," "Greenshaw's Folly"

Dead Man's Mirror (1937)
"Dead Man's Mirror" ('Expansion of "Second

Gong"), "Murder in the Mews," "Triangle at Rhodes"

Double Sin and Other Stories (1961)
"Double Sin," "Wasps' Nest," "Theft of the Royal Ruby," "Dressmaker's Doll," "Greenshaw's Folly," "Double Clue," "Last Séance," "Sanctuary"

Golden Ball and Other Stories, The (1971)
"The Listerdale Mystery," "The Girl in the Train," "The Manhood of Edward Robinson," "Jane in Search of a Job," "A Fruitful Sunday," "The Golden Ball," "Rajah's Emerald," "Swan Song," "The Hound of Death," "The Gipsy," "Lamp," "The Strange Case of Sir Arthur Carmichael," "Call of Wings," "Magnolia Blossom," "Next to a Dog"

Hound of Death (1933)
"The Hound of Death," "Red Signal," "Fourth Man," "The Gypsy," "Lamp," "Wireless," "Witness for the Prosecution," "Mystery of the Blue Jay," "The Strange Case of Sir Arthur Carmichael," "Call of Wings," "Last Séance," "SOS"

Labors of Hercules (1947)
"How It All Came About" (Foreword) "The Nemean Lion," "The Lernean Hydra," "The Arcadian Deer," "The Erymanthian Boar," "The Augean Stables," "The Stymphalean Birds," "The Cretan Bull," "Horses of Diomedes," "The Girdle of Hippolyta," "The Flock of Geryon," "Apples of the Hesperides," "The Capture of Cerberus"

The Listerdale Mystery (1934)
"The Listerdale Mystery," "Philomel Cottage," "The Girl in the Train," "Sing a Song of Sixpence," "The Manhood of Edward Robinson," "The Accident," "Jane in Search of a Job," "A Fruitful Sunday," "Mr. Eastwood's Adventure" (also called "The Mystery of the Spanish Shawl"), "The Golden Ball," "Rajah's Emerald," "Swan Song"

Murder in the Mews (1937)
"Murder in the Mews," "Incredible Theft," "Dead Man's Mirror," "Triangle at Rhodes"

Mysterious Mr. Quin, The (1930)
"Coming of Mr. Quin," "The Shadow on the Glass," "At the Bells and Morley," "The Sign in the Sky," "Soul of the Croupier," "World's End," "Voice in the Dark," "The Face of Hel-

Plays and Short Story Collections

en," "Dead Harlequin," "The Bird with the Broken Wing," "Man from the Sea," "Harlequin's Lane"

Mr. Parker Pyne, Detective (1934)
"The Case of the Middle-Aged Wife," "The Case of the Discontented Soldier," "The Case of the Distressed Lady," "The Case of the Discontented Husband," "The Case of the City Clerk," "The Case of the Rich Woman," "Have You Got Everything You Want?", "The Gate of Baghdad," "The House at Shiraz," "The Pearl of Price," "Death on the Nile" (no relation to novel), "Oracle at Delphi"

Partners in Crime (1929)
"A Fairy in the Flat," "A Pot of Tea," "The Affair of the Pink Pearl," "The Affair of the Sinister Stranger," "Finessing the King," "The Gentleman Dressed in Newspaper," "The Case of the Missing Lady," "Blindman's Buff," "The Man in the Mist," "The Crackler," "The Sunningdale Mystery," "The House of the Lurking Death," "The Unbreakable Alibi," "The Clergyman's Daughter," "The Red House," "The Ambassador's Boots," "The Man Who Was Number 16"

Poirot Investigates (1924)
"Adventure of the Western Star," "The Tragedy at Marsdon Manor," "The Adventure of the Cheap Flat," "The Mystery of Hunter's Lodge," "The Million Dollar (Bond) Bank Robbery," "The Adventure of the Egyptian Tomb," "The Jewel Robbery at the Grand Metropolitan," "The Kidnapped Prime Minister," "The Disappearance of Mr. Davenheim," "The Adventure of the Italian Nobleman," "The Case of the Missing Will," "The Veiled Lady," "The Lost Mine," "The Chocolate Box"

The Regatta Mystery (1939)
"The Regatta Mystery," "The Mystery of the

Baghdad Chest," "How Does Your Garden Grow?", "The Problem at Pollensa Bay," "Yellow Iris" (Expanded into *Remembered Death*), "Miss Marple Tells a Story," "The Dream," "In a Glass Darkly," "Problem at Sea"

Surprise! Surprise! (1965) (no new material)

13 Clues for Miss Marple (1966) (no new material)

13 for Luck (1961) (no new material)

The Tuesday Club Murders (1932) (Also called *The Thirteen Problems*)
"Tuesday Night Club," "The Idol House of Astarte," "Ingots of Gold," "The Bloodstained Pavement," "Motive versus Opportunity," "Thumb Mark of St. Peter," "The Blue Geranium," "The Companion," "Four Suspects," "Christmas Tragedy," "Herb of Death," "The Affair at the Bungalow," "Death by Drowning"

The Mousetrap and Other Stories (1950) (Also called *Three Blind Mice and Other Stories*)
"Three Blind Mice," "Strange Jest," "The Tape-Measure Murder," "The Case of the Perfect Maid," "The Case of the Caretaker," "The Third Floor Flat," "Adventure of Johnny Waverly," "Four and Twenty Blackbirds," "Love Detectives"

The Under Dog and Other Stories (1952)
"The Under Dog," "Plymouth Express," "Affair at the Victory Ball," "The Market Basing Mystery," "The Lemesurier Inheritance," "Cornish Mystery," "The King of Clubs," "Submarine Plans," "The Adventure of the Clapham Cook"

Witness for the Prosecution and Other Stories (1948)
"Witness for the Prosecution," "Red Signal," "Fourth Man," "SOS," "Where There's a Will" (also "Wireless"), "The Mystery of the Blue Jar," "Philomel Cottage," "Accident," "The Second Gong," "Sing a Song of Sixpence"

Illustration Credits

Note: For the covers reproduced in this volume, edition and printing details from the copyright pages are given below. Edition date, where available, appears within parentheses. Information such as 10 pr/1969 designates tenth printing, 1969.

Page *Credit*

1 Dell (1971); Italian ed.: Arnoldo Mondadori Editore; Hungarian ed.: Palladis Rt. Kiadasa; Dell (1967); Pocket Books (1947) 16 pr/1971; Spanish ed.: Editorial Molino (1975); French ed.: Librairie des Champs-Elysées (1978)

7 Avon; Bantam (1961) 10 pr/1969; New Bantam ed. (1970) 16 pr/1978; Italian ed.: Arnoldo Mondadori Editore (1975) 3 pr/1978

10 Spanish ed.: Editorial Molino (1975)

14 Spanish ed.: Editorial Molino (1975)

17 New Bantam ed. (1970) 6 pr/1978

18 National Gallery, London

19 New York Public Library Picture Collection

20 New York Public Library Picture Collection

21 New York Public Library Picture Collection; New York Public Library Picture Collection

22 New York Public Library Picture Collection

23 The Mansel Collection, London

25 Dell (1967); Dell (1968); Dell (1971)

28 Pocket Books (1939) 30 pr/1975

31 Dell 2 pr/1969

34 Pocket Books (1940) 34 pr/1974

37 Bantam (1964) 2 pr/1971

41 Dell (1967)

42 Spanish ed.: Editorial Molino (1960)

43 British ed.: Fontana; Japanese ed.: Hayakawa Publishing; Dell (1966); French ed.: Librairie des Champs-Elysées (1978)

45 The Raymond Mander & Joe Mitchenson Theatre Collection, London

47 Dell (1968) 4 pr/1969; Dell (1972)

49 Dell (1966); British ed.: Fontana (1961) 10 pr/1978

51 Pocket Books (1942) 31 pr/1976

53 Alexander Wilensky

54 S. Zaffarano/A. Allutto/D. Sarsfield

55 Lane D'Amore

57 Lane D'Amore

60 Dell (1975); British ed.: Pan (1977) 2 pr/1978

64 Spanish ed.: Editorial Molino; Dell (1976)

67 Dell (1978)

71 Alexander Wilensky

72 New York Public Library Picture Collection

79 Pocket Books (1940) 37 pr/1975; Japanese ed.: Hayakawa Publishing (1960)

82 Dell (1971)

85 Spanish ed.; Editorial Molino (1975)

87 Popular Library (1975)

88 Paramount Pictures

89 Paramount Pictures

93 Pocket Books (1941) 26 pr/1970; Pocket Books (1941) 27 pr/1971; Pocket Books (1941) 36 pr/1976

95 Dell (1961)

97 French ed.: Librairie des Champs-Elysées (1978); Dell (1975)

99 Dell 2 pr/1969

101 The Raymond Mander & Joe Mitchenson Theatre Collection, London; Twickenham, courtesy of National Film Archive/Stills Library, London

102 Real Art, courtesy of National Film Archive/Stills Library, London; Real Art, courtesy of National Film Archive/Stills Library, London

103 Trafalgar Productions, courtesy of National Film Archive/Stills Library, London; The Rank Organization, courtesy of National Film Archive/Stills Library, London

104 United Artists Corporation; United Artists Corporation; United Artists Corporation; United Artists Corporation, courtesy of National Film Archive/Stills Library, London

105 Metro-Goldwyn-Mayer Inc.; Metro-Goldwyn-Mayer Inc.

106 Metro-Goldwyn-Mayer Inc., courtesy of National Film Archive/Stills Library, London; Seven Arts Pictures

106-7 Metro-Goldwyn-Mayer Inc.

107 The L.B. Foster Co./Avco Embassy Pictures; EMI Films Ltd.

109 Radio Times Hulton Picture Library, London

112 New Bantam ed. (October, 1978)

113 EMI Films Ltd.

117 Dell (1975)

Illustration Credits

118 Spanish ed.: Editorial Molino (1965)
121 Bantam (1962) 15 pr/1973; Bantam (1962) 22 pr/1978; British ed.: Fontana (1957) 15 pr/1978
123 Pocket Books (1945) 26 pr; Spanish ed.: Editorial Molino (1958)
125 Wide World Pictures
126 EMI Films Ltd.
127 EMI Films Ltd.
128 EMI Films Ltd.; EMI Films Ltd.
131 Pocket Books (1944) 48 pr/1976; Pocket Books (1944) 32 pr/1973; Pocket Books (1944) 50 pr/1977; Pocket Books (1944) 19 pr/1966
133 Dell (1968) 6 pr/1971; Dell (1973)
134 Dell (1976)
137 Dell (1967)
141 The Raymond Mander & Joe Mitchenson Theatre Collection, London
142 The Raymond Mander & Joe Mitchenson Theatre Collection, London; The Raymond Mander & Joe Mitchenson Theatre Collection, London; Wide World Photos
144 French ed.: Librairie des Champs-Elysées (1947)
147 20th Century-Fox, courtesy of National Film Archive/Stills Library, London
148 Seven Arts Pictures; EMI Films Ltd., courtesy National Film Archive/Stills Library, London
150 Pocket Books (1965) 29 pr
152 Dell (1972)
156 British ed.: Penguin (1978); Pocket Books (1947) 21 pr/1974
158 Pocket Books (1959) 14 pr/1971; Pocket Books (1959) 20 pr/1974
159 Wide World Photos
162 The Raymond Mander & Joe Mitchenson Theatre Collection, London
163 S. Zaffarano/A. Allutto/D. Sarsfield
165 S. Zaffarano/A. Allutto/D. Sarsfield
167 Pocket Books (1947) 16 pr/1971
171 Dell (1968)
174 Dell 2 pr/1977; British ed.: Fontana
177 United Artists Records, Inc.
178 United Artists Corporation
179 United Artists Corporation; United Artists Corporation
183 Radio Times Hulton Picture Library, London

187 Pocket Books (1951) 8 pr/1975
189 Dell (1965); Dell (1977) 5 pr/1978
192 Pocket Books (1951) 5 pr/1970
194 Pocket Books/Cardinal Ed. (1952)
200 The Bettmann Archive
203 The Raymond Mander & Joe Mitchenson Theatre Collection, London; The Raymond Mander & Joe Mitchenson Theatre Collection, London
205 Pocket Books (1953) 3 pr/1967; Pocket Books (1953) 11 pr
209 Pocket Books (1955) 5 pr/1970; Pocket Books (1955) 10 pr/1976
211 Pocket Books (1954) 14 pr
214 The Raymond Mander & Joe Mitchenson Theatre Collection, London; Radio Times Hulton Picture Library, London
214-15 The Raymond Mander & Joe Mitchenson Theatre Collection, London
216 EMI Films Ltd; EMI Film Distributors Ltd.
217 Columbia Pictures Industries, Inc.; The Raymond Mander & Joe Mitchenson Theatre Collection, London
221 S. Zaffarano/A. Allutto/D. Sarsfield
224 Pocket Books (1956) 4 pr/1970
226 Pocket Books (1961) 8 pr
228 Spanish ed.: Editorial Molino (1958); Pocket Books (1958) 13 pr
232-33 Alexander Wilensky
237 Pocket Books (1960) 8 pr/1976
241 Pocket Books (1961) 5 pr/1970
243 British ed.: Fontana (1963) 5 pr/1978
245 Alexander Wilensky
249 Metro-Goldwyn-Mayer Inc.
250 Metro-Goldwyn-Mayer Inc.
251 Metro-Goldwyn-Mayer Inc.
253 Pocket Books (1963) 6 pr/1974; Pocket Books (1963) 4 pr/1970; British eds: Fontana (1964) 2 pr/1964, Fontana (1964) 6 pr/1969
255 Pocket Books (1964) 9 pr
260 Pocket Books (1965) 5 pr/1972
262-63 Tracy Garner
264 Spanish ed.: Editorial Molino (1965)
267 Pocket Books (1967) 6 pr/1973
270 Pocket Books (1968); Pocket Books (1968) 11 pr/1976

272 Pocket Books (1969) 2 pr/1969; Pocket Books (1969) 8 pr/1977
275 Wide World Photos
279 Radio Times Hulton Picture Library, London; The Mansell Collection, London; Radio Times Hulton Picture Library, London
280 The Bettmann Archive
282 Pocket Books (1969) 7 pr/1974
285 Spanish ed.: Editorial Molino (1970)
287 Pocket Books (1972)
289 Spanish ed.: Editorial Molino
291 S. Zaffarano/A. Allutto/D. Sarsfield
297 Alexander Wilensky
299 Pocket Books (1973)
301 Dell (1973) 4 pr/1975
303 Dodd, Mead (1973)
307 Bantam (1974)
313 Pocket Books (1976) 3 pr/1976
315 Bantam (1977) 5 pr/1977
316—17 Allied Film Distribution Corp.
318—20 CBS Inc.
322 Mobil-funded PBS *Mystery!*
327—28 Warner Brothers, Inc.

332 Miriam Goldstein Sommer and *The Connecticut Traveler;*
333 Theodora Litsios and the *Stamford* (CT) *Advocate*
335 Pocket Books; Berkley Books
338 Charter Books
339 Mobil-funded PBS *Mystery!*
341 *TV Guide;* CBS Inc.
345 Eddie Cope

Poster credits:
Witness for the Prosecution: United Artists Corp.
Murder Ahoy: Metro-Goldwyn-Mayer Inc.
Murder on the Orient Express: EMI Film Distributors
Death on the Nile: Paramount Pictures Corporation
Evil Under the Sun: Universal Studios
The Mirror Crack'd: EMI Films

AGATHA CHRISTIE TITLE CROSSWORD (*page 273*)

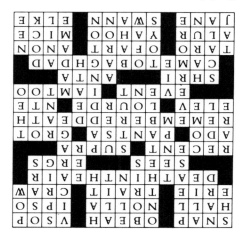

About the Contributors

DICK RILEY comes naturally to Agatha Christie. A playwright and novelist, he collaborated on the thriller *Black Sunday*, has written the mystery, *Rite of Expiation*, and served as editor of Ungar's *Recognitions* series, which focuses on writers of detective/suspense fiction and science fiction.

PAM MCALLISTER is a lecturer, writer, and the editor of *Reweaving the Web of Life: Feminism and Nonviolence*. She is on the staff of a rape crisis center in Brooklyn. Currently she is writing a new nonfiction book and has completed a collection of essays related to her lectures.

BRUCE CASSIDAY has written mysteries for radio, television, magazines, and books. He is a board member of the Mystery Writers of America, general editor of Ungar's *Recognitions: Mystery Writers* series, and anthologist of *Roots of Detection: The Art of Deduction before Sherlock Holmes*.

LIBBY BASSETT has been a New York City reporter and a foreign correspondent in Ethiopia and in Cairo, where her apartment overlooked the Nile. She now edits the World Environment Report, which covers international environmental issues.

GRANVILLE BURGESS is a playwright and director. His work has appeared on national television and his latest play is scheduled for Off-Broadway production in 1980.

MARCIA CLENDENEN is a psychotherapist who lives and practices in Staten Island, N.Y.

PHIL CLENDENEN reads serious fiction only when he is out of work, which is as often as possible.

ANN COHEN is a newspaperwoman in Detroit.

DALE G. COPPS is the author of *The World's Greatest Sherlock Holmes Quiz* and *The Sherlock Holmes Puzzle Book*.

JANICE CURRY is a free-lance writer and mystery fan.

JOAN DANIELS is an educational consultant and writer.

CATHERINE DELOUGHRY is a college student and novice free-lance writer.

RUTH FARMER is a writer and poet who lives in Brooklyn, N.Y., and is an avid mystery reader.

JEAN FIEDLER is a free-lance writer and editor who succumbed to the wiles of Agatha Christie at an early age.

MARK FISCHWEICHER is a lyric poet masquerading as a New York City cabdriver. He is currently learning to smoke a pipe.

PETER J. FITZPATRICK, in his brief career as a Los Angeles police officer, never investigated a murder. He is now a free-lance writer.

JOAN GERSTEL is a free-lance writer.

ANITA GREENFIELD is a fifty-year-old school teacher and the author of an unpublished memoir entitled *And Now Dimitri*.

BRIAN HAUGH is a New York freelancer.

EDWARD D. HOCH, a past president of the Mystery Writer of America, is the author of seven hundred short stories, mainly in the mystery field. His twenty-seven published books include the annual *Year's Best Mystery & Suspense Stories*.

RUSS KANE is a newspaper editor who is often mystified.

HELENE KENDLER is a poet who lives in New York City. Her work has been published in several small press magazines and she was the recipient in 1978-79 of a NY State Creative Artists Public Service (CAPS) grant for poetry.

JERRY KEUCHER is a church organist who is not normally mixed up in murder.

KADEY KIMPEL is an herb grower and nascent mystery fan.

PAUL KIMPEL is a set and costume designer for the stage.

RO KING is a psychotherapist in private practice in New York City. She also teaches at NYU.

GERALD M. KLINE is an actor who has read Miss Christie's works between engagements. He has also portrayed a number of cops — among them Sgt. Mel Jacoby on ABC's "All My Children."

EMMA LATHEN, a nom de plume of Mary Jane LATsis and Martha HENissart, is the author of some twenty mystery novels featuring banker-detective John Putnam Thatcher. *The New York Times* has called Lathen "Wall Street's Agatha Christie."

ELIZABETH LEESE lives in London, where she worked for many years for the National Film Archive. She is the author of *Costume Design in the Movies* and does free-lance research on costume, crime, and assorted activities.

CINDY LOOSE is a writer and a teacher.

PATRICIA MAIDA is a professor of English on the faculty of the University of the District of Columbia. A veteran mystery reader, she has been studying the successes of various detective fiction writers — including Agatha Christie.

ANITA McALLISTER is a feminist social worker employed at the Bedford Hills (NY) Prison for Women.

JIM MELE is a poet and journalist.

LISA MERRILL is a poet, actress, teacher, and feminist (in whatever order of preference the moon dictates). She is currently teaching speech and theater courses at New York University.

JOANNA MILTON has worked on the staffs of *Mademoiselle* and *Cosmopolitan* magazines and is currently completing her first novel. She is a free-lance writer living in New York City.

JACK MURPHY is a newspaperman in Cleveland, Ohio.

ALBERT NORTON is an actor, director, and long-time Agatha Christie fan, partial to locked-room problems and stories with a hint of the supernatural.

JAN OXENBERG is an independent filmmaker in New York City who was grateful for the chance to read Agatha Christie all day without feeling guilty.

GAILA PERKINS (COUGHLIN) is a teacher and free-lance writer, editor, educational consultant, and quiltmaker.

DEBORAH J. POPE is a graduate student in theater and a director for the Lincoln Center Performance Ensemble.

CYNTHIA A. READ is a dancer, craftswoman, paralegal, and omnivorous reader.

RICHARD REGIS is a newspaper reporter and free-lance writer based in New York City.

EDWIN A. ROLLINS is a criminal lawyer in New York City who defends people accused of crimes and loves it. He's also a murder mystery buff.

ANN ROMEO is an avid fan of all variations of the mystery novel and is currently a member of the staff of Foul Play Mystery Bookstore in New York City.

REGINA SACKMARY is a free-lance editor and reviewer, with a long-term fascination for the criminal mind.

NORMA SIEBENHELLER is a nature columnist and free-lance writer.

BETH SIMON is a fiction writer and teacher.

ROBERT SMITHER is a psychologist who specializes in refugee affairs.

JERRY SPEIR is a novelist and the author of *Ross MacDonald*, a book-length study of the detective-story writer.

NICK SPORNICK is a professor of English on the faculty on the University of the District of Columbia. A Shakespeare scholar as well as a detective-fiction reader, he has a wide range of literary interests.

MAUREEN STODDARD is a student at St. John's University who has been a mystery fan for one-third of her life.

JOHN STURMAN bought an Agatha Christie novel in 1973 when he needed something to read on the train from Bristol to London. It was the first of many. He is now an editor and free-lance writer in New York City.

JULIAN SYMONS is an English novelist, biographer, and critic. His novels have won awards from both the British Crime Writers' Association and the Mystery Writers of America. His *Mortal Consequences* (1972) is an acclaimed study of the detective story.

MICHAEL TENNENBAUM is a free-lance writer whose work has appeared in Isaac Asimov's *Science Fiction* Magazine, *People's Almanac II* and various film journals.

HELENE VON ROSENSTIEL, author of *The Needleworkers Dictionary* and *American Rugs and Carpets*, is by trade a restorer of antique costumes and textiles.

SUE ELLEN YORK is a radical feminist who is struggling for the three-hour work day and the time to complete her novel.

Title Index